The Early Ford V8

AS HENRY BUILT IT

A PRODUCTION FACTS BOOK 1932-38

Edward P. Francis and George DeAngelis

Ford V-8 50th Anniversary Commemorative Printing

Motor Cities Publishing Company
South Lyon, Michigan

Revised Edition

Printed August 1987

First Printing December 1982

Art Direction: George DeAngelis
Layout: Ronald R. Smith

Photographs courtesy of Ford Archives, Henry Ford Museum, Dearborn, Michigan, except those otherwise acknowledged.

Published by Motor Cities Publishing Company, 10405 Rushton Road, South Lyon, Michigan

Manufactured in the United States of America

Other Publication: *The Ford Model A—As Henry Built It.*

Library of Congress Cataloging in Publication Data

Francis, Edward P.
The early Ford V-8 as Henry built it.

"Ford V-8 50th anniversary commemorative printing."
Includes index.
1. Ford automobile. 2. Ford automobile--Restoration.
I. DeAngelis, George. II. Title.
TL215.F7F74 1983 629.2'222 82-22955
ISBN 0-911383-03-4

About the Authors

Edward Francis and George De Angelis began researching Ford cars as a team in 1962. Together they wrote a series of "Authentically Speaking" articles which have been published in various car club magazines. They were joined by Leslie R. Henry in 1971 and published their first book, *"The Ford Model "A" — As Henry Built It,* now in its third edition.

Edward P. Francis received his bachelor of science degree in Metallurgical Engineering at Case Institute of Technology; bachelor of science degree in Electrical Engineering from Lawrence Institute of Technology; and master of science degree in Engineering Mechanics from the University of Michigan.

He has worked at Ford Motor Company for the past 32 years and is currently Supervisor of the Material and Fastener Engineering Section, Chasis Engineering Office.

Ed Francis acquired and restored his first Model "A" in 1958 and has been researching Ford cars since then. He currently owns two Model A's and a 1932 Model B. He is a member of the Early Ford V-8 Club, Model "A" Restorers Club and Antique Automobile Club.

Francis resides in Birmingham, Michigan, with his wife.

George De Angelis recently retired after 39 years as an employee of Ford Motor Company. Starting as an apprentice, he became a journeyman tool and die maker in 1943. After serving two years in World War II, he returned to Ford and transferred to the Engineering Illustration Department, where he advanced to Section Supervisor of the Technical Illustration Section.

De Angelis' love for antique cars started in 1954, and while he favors Fords, his interests have broadened to include many other makes of cars and early engines. He has restored a Model T, Model A and a 1941 Ford V-8. As Editor of the *Model "A" News* magazine, a publication of the Model "A" Restorers Club, he has written many articles about the Model "A." He is also "Ford Facts" editor for *Antique Automobile* magazine and a member of the Model "T" Ford Club International, and the Early Engine Club.

De Angelis and his wife live in Green Oak Township, Livingston County, Michigan.

The authors, DeAngelis (left) and Francis (right) at the Ford Archives with archivist David Crippen.

ACKNOWLEDGEMENTS

In order to provide complete and authentic information about the Ford V-8 as it was built, the authors researched original sources in the engineering records at Ford Motor Company and the historical records at the Ford Archives and Research Library in Dearborn. The authors wish to gratefully acknowledge the valuable assistance rendered by the following researchers:

Henry Edmunds, former Director of Ford Archives, Henry Ford Museum

Douglas A. Bakken, Director of Archives and Research Library, Henry Ford Museum

David R. Crippen, Archivist, Ford Archives

Winthrop Sears, former Archivist, Ford Archives

Dolores Kearny, Ford Casting Division Manufacturing Development Engineer

Jake Jurgenson, former Supervisor, Ford Product Information Section

Herbert Alle, former Ford Body Engineer

Of particular value were conversations with old time fellow employees Warren Meridith, Thomas Stevenson, Henry Todd and Emil Zoerlein, all former engineers or supervisors at Ford Motor Company during the Ford V-8 production years. These friends answered many questions and explained, from their personal experience, the how and why of the V-8 production.

Also deserving mention are numerous books and periodicals which provided interesting information and inspired the need for further research. They are: The trilogy by Nevins and Hill, *Ford: The Times, The Man, and the Company*; *Ford: Expansion and Challenge 1915–33*; and *Ford: Decline and Rebirth*; *Henry Ford's Last Mechanical Triumph* by Michael Lamm; *Half-hour History of V-8 Engines* by Maruice Hendry; *Last Act: The V-8 Years of Henry Ford* by Beverly Rae Kimes; *Emil Zoerlein* by Lorin D. Sorensen; *Ford Trucks Since 1905* by James K. Wagner; *Ford Motor Company Foundry Operations* by Dolores Kearny; and *The V-8 Affair* by Ray Miller.

Special thanks are due to our wives who typed the manuscript and allowed us time to prepare this work, which is actually an extension of our antique automobile hobby.

The Authors

INTRODUCTION

Today, fifty years after the introduction of the Ford V-8, some are still in use. Most, however, are in the hands of collectors who seek to restore these cars to their original condition. Unfortunately, some go too far and over-restore, while others fail to go far enough and under-restore. This book will help those who wish to have their V-8 just as Henry Ford built it.

Complete and accurate information about the Ford V-8, as it was produced at the assembly plants, has been difficult to obtain up to now. Much of the available information was drawn from misconception and too literal interpretation of sales catalogs, advertisements, aftermarket service and parts books, and the fallible memories of erstwhile owners and repairers of the car. This book now brings together in one authoritative source all the production details, including numerous original photographs from the company's historical file.

It is the result of eight years of research into primary material such as original specifications, engineering drawings and releases, manufacturing directives, and historical records at Ford Motor Company and the Ford Archives. Because of the scope and complexity of these documents, they can only be interpreted by those who have a thorough knowledge of the Company's internal system for engineering and releasing of documents for production. In this the authors are well qualified.

Emphasis is placed on the general features and facts about the V-8 to aid in its restoration. There will undoubtedly be some exceptions to these generalizations. Since there were a number of assembly plants, occasional minute changes in production were dictated by a matter of expediency and so were never recorded. This occurred since the object of each assembly plant was to produce as many cars of acceptable quality as possible; not to produce every V-8 car exactly alike. Consequently, the sincere restorer will find it more rewarding to follow the general rules rather than to try to defend any rare exception on his car. It is usually better to restore a car to conform to the usual pattern which will be readily recognized and readily accepted.

Some of the information included here has been published in short articles in antique car club publications and has already been accepted as a guide by qualified field judges. Nevertheless, this book is a new manual for restoring all passenger cars and commercial vehicles with the passenger car chassis, 1932–1938. It is a what-to-do, not a how-to-do-it book. It is a guide for the correct and authentic way to utilize your own restoration skills, or to help you supervise the hired restorer.

The authors do not claim that all information about the production of the early Ford V-8 is included. As new information is uncovered, some mistakes may become evident and new interpretations may be made. Therefore, it is the intent of the authors to up-date this book as the need becomes apparent.

Contents

I—Design, Development and Introduction

In the fall of 1930, almost a year after the stockmarket crash, America was in the grip of The Great Depression. Unemployment was widespread, and as car sales declined, some automobile companies started to cut back on production. As the leader in the low-price market, Ford Motor Company was not affected to the point of losing money, as some automakers were. Even though sales were down, it appeared to be headed for a $40,000,000 profit for that year. Improvements for the 1931 Model A, due to be introduced in January, were off the drawing board and well into the tooling stage. Ford designers and engineers already were starting to make plans for the 1932 car.

The 1932 design, designated by engineering as Model 10, was to be a major face-lift of the 1931 Model A. It would have an improved four-cylinder engine, a new fuel system, a slightly longer wheelbase, and a heavier frame. But, in appearance, it resembled the Model A.

By September 1931, engineering drawings for the 1932 car were complete, and contracts for new tools and dies were placed with suppliers. Those parts which were carryover from the Model A were to retain the "A" prefix on the part number. But in October, it was decided that the new car would be called the Model B, necessitating the relabeling of all Model 10 drawings and the carryover Model A drawings to the "B" prefix number. When this task was completed, the new Model B was ready for production.

The last U.S. built Model A came off the Rouge assembly line on October 31, and as production came to a halt at the end of the day, production employees, except key personnel, were laid off. The next morning, retooling of the plant for the new car began.

On December 1, the Purchasing Department was instructed to start procuring parts at the rate of 1,000 cars per day, and the employment office started recalling some Rouge production employees. Within a week, the first Model B's were coming off the assembly line. And then, without warning, on December 7, Henry Ford brought everything to a halt and, after a conference with Edsel, announced that in addition to the four cylinder the company would design, develop and mass-produce a new V-8 engine for the 1932 car. He was convinced that by casting a one-piece V-8 block, his company could produce a V-8 engine economically enough to fit his customers' pocketbooks.

As the Model B was being designed, engineers close to Henry Ford sensed that he was not satisfied with its development. Even though the Model A practically eclipsed the Model T, to him it was only an interim car. The thought of a V-8 engine cast "en bloc" (one piece block) had been at the back of his mind for years. He had considered a six, but Chevrolet had gone from a four to a six in 1929, and if Ford went to a six, he would be a follower, not a leader.

While Henry Ford's precise reasons for going to a V-8 are unrecorded—aside from his desire to outdo the six-cylinder engines of Chevrolet and the newcomer Plymouth—it can be assumed there were other reasons behind his dramatic move. Cars were getting larger and therefore heavier in response to the demands of a more sophisticated buying public. A V-8 would easily supply the extra power needed for the bigger cars—and keep Ford in a leadership position.

Ford had been the industry leader since the early days of the Model T. In 1913, even though the company was producing one half the automobiles in the country, Ford and his engineers revolutionized the industry by installing the moving assembly line. The mass-production system made it possible to build the automobile in greater quantity and at a price affordable to the average person.

After the low production years of World War I and a brief recession in 1920–21, the company established a new one-year production record of 1,373,331 units in 1922. In 1923, with the Rouge plant going at full blast, output of the Model T soared to the fantastic mark of 2,120,898 units, as recorded in Ford's World Production Report. Ford took 57 percent of the U.S. market that year. Along with increased production, Ford had consistently reduced the prices of its cars. By 1923, the lowest-priced Roadster was selling for only $319. The highest-priced Sedan sold for $645, compared to $875 for its nearest competitor.

One of 2,120,898 Model "T's" produced in 1923.

By 1924, however, the mood of the buying public started to change. In keeping with the postwar boom, buyers were

With Henry Ford seated next to him and Charles Sorensen in the back, Edsel Ford drives the 15,000,000th Ford.

beginning to want more than economy and reliability. They wanted their cars to have more style, and as trips became longer, they wanted more speed, comfort, and driving convenience. As a result, Ford car sales began to decline. By 1925, they were down to 1,675,000, and Ford's share of the market had slipped to 47 percent. Other makes, more attuned to the changing market, were taking a bigger share of sales. Ford's downward trend continued through 1926 and into 1927. Then, on May 26, 1927, Henry Ford, finally admitting that the Model T had run its course, suspended production, even though he had no firm plans for a successor model.

Most automobile companies had research departments, engineering staffs, and styling departments of skilled personnel who worked on advance projects. Henry Ford preferred to go on his own instincts and would not permit such an operational arrangement. As the job of developing a new car was undertaken, he skillfully delegated various responsibilities to his associates. He gave his son Edsel a free hand in styling the body. Eugene Farkas had charge of chassis design at first, but was later assigned to develop such specific components as brakes and axles while Henry Ford chose to direct chassis development himself. Laurence Sheldrick developed the engine plus part of the chassis, and Frank Johnson the clutch and transmission. Joe Galamb designed and engineered the body and frame under Edsel's direction. Edsel insisted that the new body had to be much closer to the ground than the Model T.

Designers, engineers, draftsmen, toolmakers and suppliers worked on a "crash" schedule for five months, and by November 1, 1927, the task was completed. Changeover of such scope and urgency was unheard of and some observers called the rebirth of the Ford car one of the most striking industrial achievements of the 20th century. The retooling of the Rouge in 1927 was a feat unparalleled.

Since the car represented the rebirth of Ford Motor Company, (the Model T had been in production almost 19 years) Henry Ford decided to start anew with its alphabetical designation. He called the new car the Model A, the same designation used on Ford Motor Company's first car in 1903. Other models produced by Ford prior to Model T were Models A, B, C, F, K, N, R and S.

Although impressive, the changeover virtually shut down the company during the period of May to December, 1927—and Ford lost industry leadership. In 1927, Ford's production was only 518,400 units, and in 1928, only 788,000 units. Chevrolet, Ford's closest competitor, became the new leader for both years. But, by the start of 1929, Ford's assembly plants had again reached high production levels. By mid-February, production hit 7,500 units per day, and by June exceeded 9,000 units. When the year ended, 1,851,092 units had rolled off the assembly lines, the highest mark since 1925. This was 34 percent of the market, and Ford regained industry leadership, out-producing runnerup Chevrolet by 400,000 units.

The Model A was such a vast improvement over the Model T that many thought it would be *the* Ford car for many years, perhaps paralleling the 18-year span of the Model T. But, after four years of production and with the new Model B ready for introduction, Henry Ford dropped a new bombshell on the automotive world with the announcement of a low-price, mass-production V-8 engine.

But mass-producing a V-8 would be an enormous task. New parts had to be designed, machinery had to be replaced with machinery not yet designed, and new foundry processes had to be perfected. More important, there would be no Ford car production or factory sales during this development period, a repeat of the Model T to Model A changeover, which resulted in severe financial losses for the company.

Henry Ford no doubt considered all these factors. He also must have given serious thought to his company's sagging

The 20,000,000th Ford with Henry Ford at the wheel.

sales and the increased competition from Chevrolet and Plymouth. After regaining the Number One position in 1929, Ford increased its lead in 1930 by out-producing Chevrolet almost two to one. In 1931, however, the rising automobile production curve collided with The Great Depression and the automobile market plummeted. As the end of the year approached, it became apparent that Chevrolet would hang on to its 600,000-plus market, while Ford sales would dip to barely over 500,000 units. At the same time, Chrysler's Plymouth, introduced in 1929, was coming up as a strong third.

Henry Ford's decision to go to the V-8 seemed sudden, but actually he had assigned several experimental engineers to work on the project as early as 1928. C. J. Smith was the first engineer assigned to design a V-8 under Ford's direction. Several engines were built, but each had overheating problems. The next development was assigned to Arnold Soth who worked with a draftsman in a room at the south end of the Engineering Laboratory. He designed a 60-degree V-8 about the size of the Lincoln engine (299 CID), but it had poor oil circulation and it, too, ran hot.

Early in 1930, Carl Schultz and Ray Laird were the next to receive the assignment. Their design was a 90-degree, scaled-down version of the Lincoln engine which could be fitted to a Model A-sized body. Their work was carried out in secrecy at Edison's Fort Myers Laboratory in Greenfield Village. Several approaches had been tried when, in November, Henry Ford took a personal hand in the project by acting as his own chief engineer, telling the designers what he wanted.

The cramped Fort Myers Laboratory where the V-8 engine was designed and tested. (Photograph by Authors)

An early experimental V-8 engine. Note the unusual arrangement of the exhaust manifold, water inlet manifold, and the vacuum assisted clutch booster. None of these items were incorporated on the production engine.

The ignition system was especially troublesome. Accounts of the problems are recorded by some of the engineers in their "Reminiscences" on file at the Archives and Research Library, Edison Institute. "Mr. Ford," recalled Larry Scheldrick, "placed some controlling factors on the design of the ignition system. It had to be driven off the front of the camshaft. The coil must be a unit with the distributor. Again, the distributor body could not be rotated, which was the same limitation put on the Model A."

Emil Zoerlein, who worked on the prototype ignition system, stated: "Mr. Ford wanted high tension wires from the distributor to the spark plugs all molded in plastic, with just the ends of the spark plugs attached. As a matter of fact, he just wanted the terminals coming out of the side of the molded harness and then use spring clips. . . . A lot of time and energy and cost went into that. It was finally decided that it wouldn't work, and we used Bakelite tubes. We put in regular ignition wires, high tension wires, and thread them through these tubes."

Most of the engine design work was done against time. As soon as a part was sketched, a pattern was made and rushed to the Rouge Foundry for casting. Finally came the task of casting the one-piece V-8 block. Herman Reinholt, head of the pattern shop, made the pattern and had the block secretly cast at the Rouge Foundry. By February 1931, the engine was assembled and ready for its first test. Zoerlein related that it ran very rough at first and it would run in either direction. The cause, he said, "was a combination of carburetion, manifolding, and timing." With continued experimenting, the engine was made to run successfully. As a result, Henry Ford authorized construction of an experimental garage with test stand and two car stalls. The development was still being done in secrecy, but additional key personnel were assigned to the project. Charles Sorensen, Ford's foundry wizard, and Reinholt combined in solving some of the casting problems as additional engines were needed. "By mid-June," Zoerlein recalled, "we were ready to install V-8 engines in revamped Model A's for road testing."

By fall of 1931, Ford had not yet made up his mind about a new engine. He had had several groups of engineers experimenting with different engine designs, including a six-cylinder. Meanwhile, the production department was in the process of preparing to change the plants from Model A to B production. According to close associates, Ford was noticeably intense and unsure of being on the right track.

The problem confronting Henry Ford was not only designing a V-8, but mass producing one to fit a car in the

$550 price range. The history of the V-8 engine configuration can be traced back to 1900. However, these early designs ran very rough with balance and manifold porting being the major problems. It was not until 1923, when Cadillac engineers developed the counterbalanced 90-degree crankshaft, that the V-8 started challenging the smooth-running straight eight. The V-8 engines of the 1930 era featured the two- and three-piece bolted-together block. They were very expensive to produce and only available on luxury cars such as Cadillac, Mercer, and Ford's Lincoln. Starting in 1929, General Motors had cast a one-piece V-8 block—about 4,000 per year—for the Olds Viking and Oakland/Pontiac. Ford was thinking of 4,000 to 5,000 per day. He must have recognized that such volume production of a V-8 block would require another "breakthrough" from his foundry engineers.

In order to understand the magnitude of the problem, we should review the Rouge foundry practices of that period. Basically, the operation of the foundry consisted of forming a sand mold and cores to shape the part to be cast. The assembled mold was transported by conveyor to the metal pouring area, where the mold cavity was filled with molten iron. As soon as the molten metal had cooled and solidified enough to hold its given shape, the mold was opened and the still-hot casting removed and allowed to finish cooling. Next, sand and any projecting pieces of excess metal were removed from the casting surfaces before machining. This was basically the method used to produce such complex castings as cylinder blocks and heads, intake and exhaust manifolds, water pump bodies, flywheels, and flywheel housings. The operation sounds simple, but to accomplish it on a mass-production basis required employees of many skills and machinery capable of handling thousands of tons of metal and sand per day.

After the part was designed, the pattern-maker created the three-dimensional form that produced the desired cavity in a mold. The pattern, however, was not an exact reproduction of the part as it appeared in the design. The pattern had to allow for metal shrinkage, machine finish, and a draft allowance so the pattern could be removed from the mold. From the pattern, a sand mold was made. This was accomplished by ramming sand into a flask (a box containing neither top nor bottom) placed over the pattern fastened to a plate. The sand was packed so tightly that when the pattern was removed, an impression was left in the box of sand.

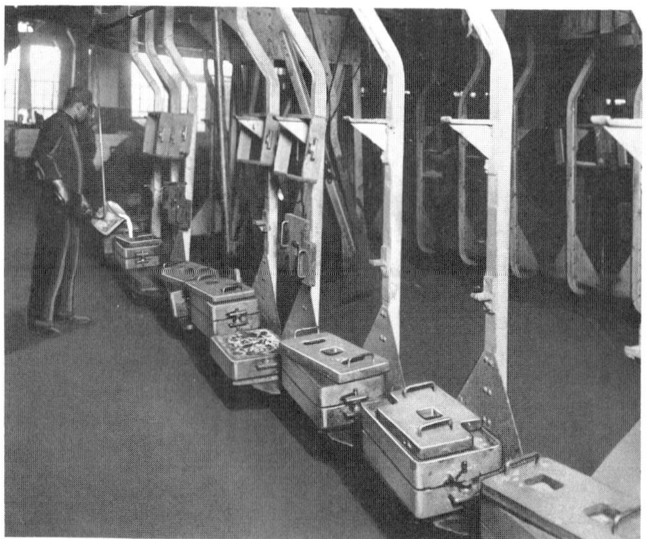

The pendulum mold carriers at the Highland Park Foundry. (Courtesy Ford Motor Company)

To reduce weight and machining time, castings were made to require the least amount of machining work. This was done by placing sand cores and inserts in the mold cavity, such as for the cylinders and water passages, to prevent molten metal from filling these spaces in the casting. Since the core and sand mold formed from the pattern were destroyed in the process of producing one single casting, tons of sand were used in every foundry operation. For example, a daily production schedule of 8,000 Model A blocks in 1929 required approximately 2,000 tons of sand that had to be transported and reprocessed every day.

Ford had long been a leader in foundry operations. In 1908, with the introduction of the Model T, Ford was the first to mass-produce a one-piece four-cylinder block. At the Ford Highland Park Foundry, one of the first important innovations was the "sand gallery." In prior practice, the journeymen molders and coremakers mixed their own sand and transported it, usually by wheelbarrow, to each work station. With the new process, sand was mixed in bulk by unskilled labor on the floor directly above the core moldmaking station and delivered to the molders through individual chutes located over each work station.

Another improvement was the pendulum mold carriers used to handle a large volume of cores and molds. This system consisted of a pendulum arm suspended on an electric-powered overhead endless chain that carried the assembled molds to the metal-pouring areas and then to the shake-out grating where the castings were separated from the sand mold.

The endless chain conveyer method was also installed at the core operation. Cores were placed on drying racks hanging from the conveyor which carried the cores through the oven at the rate required to properly bake them. Some historians believe that this endless conveyor method of transporting molds may have led to Ford's concept of the moving assembly line a few years later.

With the advent of the moving assembly line and improved production methods, the cost of the Model T was lowered significantly and the savings led to lower car prices. The demand for more cars in turn increased the need for manufacturing facilities. Henry Ford saw that the Highland Park Plant would soon be outmoded. He saw as elements of production the relationship of iron, coal and water power; rivers and railroads; power plants and assembly lines. As early as 1914, Ford had eyed land southeast of Dearborn along the Rouge River, which could accommodate the elements. By 1915, he had acquired some 2,000 acres of land, and in January 1917, preliminary blueprints of the Rouge facility were completed. They included blast furnaces and the Rouge Production Foundry.

Ford's objective was to efficiently integrate the flow of materials and operations. With the construction of the Rouge plant, raw material, such as iron ore, coal and limestone, were delivered by ships and unloaded into huge storage bins along the dock. Next to the bins were the blast furnaces and the coke ovens, then the cupolas (a cylindrical-type furnace used to melt "pig iron" and scrap metal for making castings) and the foundry building. Molten iron

The Rouge Production Foundry with the cupolas, blast furnaces, and unloading docks in the background.

was transported by rail cars from the blast furnace to the foundry which was then alloyed with metal from the foundry cupolas. Electrically activated pouring ladles suspended from a monorail coupled to the mold conveyer chain permitted pouring into the mold while moving, a sophisticated updating of the system that had proven so successful at Highland Park.

The foundry building was the largest in industry, consisting of 18 bays, each 66 feet wide, having an overall measurement of 595 feet by 1,188 feet, or about 16 acres of floor space. Three main functions were together under one roof—the melting operation with the 24 cupolas, the foundry, and the machine shop. In operation, it was identical to the Highland Park Foundry—but it was far more efficient, had a greater capacity, and contained the highest degree of mechanization for volume production than any other foundry in existence.

The first casting at the Rouge Production Foundry, as it was originally known, was poured on December 25, 1920 (no holiday time off then). The foundry's production reached 7,700 engine blocks per day by 1922. By 1924, production hit 10,055 blocks a day, an all-time high for a single facility. Henry Ford is credited for the development of the moving assembly line, but his automobile production records of the 1920's could not have been attained without the highly successful casting operation of the Rouge Foundry.

In 1927, the foundry was shut down for the Model A changeover, but by 1929, it had regained its production efficiency. By the end of 1931, it was due for another shutdown as it reached the brink of another mass-production first—the production casting of a one-piece V-8 block.

Production of a V-8 engine in a low price field seemed impossible, but Henry Ford had directed his engineers to do it. Charles Sorensen and Herman Reinholt, who had combined to produce the experimental V-8 block, now had the task of developing the method and machinery to produce it on a mass production basis.

To work out some of the casting problems, Sorensen set up a small pilot casting line long before any production schedule was announced. One of the major problems of casting the V-8 stemmed from Ford's insistence that the exhaust passages go through the water jacket of the cylinder block. This required thin-wall casting with close tolerances between cores. More cores were required than would have been needed if the exhaust passages were outside the block. The V-8 block thus had 43 cores inside the mold while the 4-cylinder block had only 11. There was another major problem. Since production of the four-cylinder engine was going to continue, none of its machinery and fixtures could be converted. New machines had to be designed and built for the V-8 set-up.

At the same time, chassis engineers were pressed to make production drawings for the new clutch, transmission and other parts of the V-8 drive line. As drawings were completed they were rushed to the tool room or to outside parts suppliers. Some parts such as the aluminum heads, pistons, and intake manifold were turned over to vendors for engineering and tooling development.

The body, which was ready for production as the Model B, would require some changes to accommodate the new V-8. Some of the components that went back to the drawing board were the floor pan, floor mats, and dash.

Ford had insisted on mounting the distributor on the cam shaft in front of the block and that the coil and distributor be combined in one unit. Emil Zoerlein recalled how that problem was solved: "We just took an existing Model A coil with an outside primary and inside secondary and designed a housing for it. We made a two-piece Bakelite housing for it and shoved the tall Model A coil up inside and sealed the base on and stuck it on top of the distributor.

Within three months, the designing, engineering and production tooling of the V-8 had been accomplished, an achievement that must be ranked as the greatest single advancement in the history of the V-8 engine.

Production of the V-8 began on March 14, 1932 at a scheduled rate of 200 units per day. On the second day the first day's castings went through the production machine shop. After the machining operation, not a single block was acceptable for assembly. William F. Pioch, head of production engineering, recounted, "When we went to the V-8 engine, it was a different type engine, and from our past experience we really went into high-production machinery, like for instance, boring the block. We bored all eight bores at one time. In fact, our machining time on the V-8 block wasn't much more than it was on the four-cylinder engine. We had a lot more machining, but it didn't take much more time in labor.

"This was the problem: The exhaust cores were loose cores, and the production men would just lay them in the mold, and the cores would shift on them. They would have to put them (cores) in there and judge proper placement with their eyes only. . . . the V-8 engine had the exhaust (passage) going through the water jacket of the cylinder block. These cores would shift and, of course, you would get scrap castings."

Sorensen, Pioch and some of the production engineers worked around the clock for the next few days, catching naps when they could. After many attempts the problem of the shifting cores was finally solved by the use of refractory paste. The cores were actually pasted in place so they could not shift, thus holding the thin wall tolerance

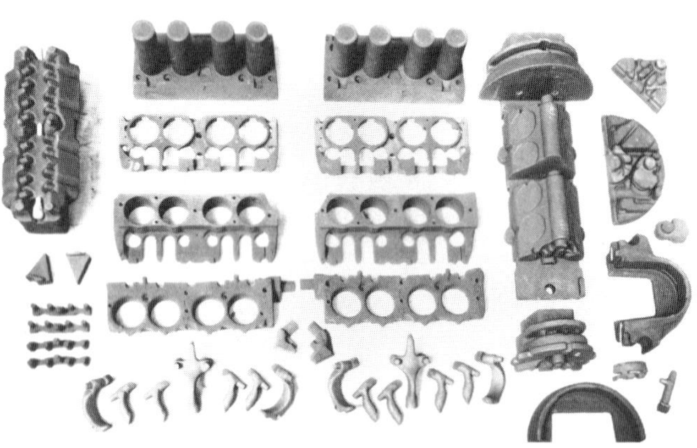

By August 1932, the number of cores for the V-8 block had been reduced from 43 to 40.

The block casting operation.

The Dearborn assembly line on April 21, 1932. The front car is a Model "B".

THE NEW FORD 8

THE NEW FORD EIGHT *De Luxe Tudor Sedan*

Eight-cylinder, 90-degree V-type, 65-horse-power Engine * Vibrationless Roomy, Beautiful Bodies * Low Center of Gravity * Silent Second Gear Synchronized Silent Gear Shift * Seventy-five Miles per Hour * Comfortable Riding Springs * Rapid Acceleration * Low Gasoline Consumption * Reliability

New self-adjusting Houdaille double-acting hydraulic shock absorbers with thermostatic control . . . New rear spring construction . . . Automatic spark control . . . Down-draft carburetor . . . Carburetor silencer . . . Bore, 3 1/16 inches. Stroke, 3 3/4 inches . . . Piston displacement, 221 cubic inches . . . 90-degree counterbalanced crankshaft . . . Large, effective fully enclosed four-wheel brakes . . . Distinctive steel-spoke wheels with large hub caps . . . Handsome V-type radiator . . . Graceful new roof line and slanting windshield of clear polished plate safety glass . . . Single-bar bumpers, chromium plated . . . Low, drop center frame . . . Mechanically operated pump drawing fuel from fourteen-gallon gasoline tank in rear . . . Choke on instrument panel . . . Individual inside sun visors . . . Cowl ventilation . . . Adjustable driver's seat . . . Choice of Mohair, Broadcloth or Bedford Cord upholstery in all de luxe closed types. Rich, enduring body colors.

THE NEW FORD 4-CYLINDER CAR

An improved Ford four-cylinder, 50-horsepower engine, operating with new smoothness, is available in fourteen beautiful body types at an unusually low cost.

FORD MOTOR COMPANY

One of the early Ford V-8 ads.

of the V-8 castings. Though the idea was not new, the use of refractory paste was the most important single factor leading to the successful casting of the V-8 block. However, the first shipment of 11 engines was not delivered to the Dearborn Assembly Plant until March 25. Next day 94 engines were assembled and the following day 90 were completed by noon. A Departmental Communication dated March 26 stated that 150 vehicles were built that day—90 V-8 passenger cars, 37 BB trucks and 23 B pickups. Because of the slow start-up, it was not until April 25 that enough V-8 engines could be produced to permit assembly plants at Sommerville, Chicago, Kansas City and Louisville to start production.

Public introduction of the new Ford V-8 took place on March 31. But fewer than a thousand cars had been built for distribution by that date—and the company had about 8,000 dealers. As a result, new cars were shipped only to select dealers located in major metropolitan areas. Other dealers had to be content with showing posters and photographs of the new models. On the same day film clips introducing the V-8 were shown, free of charge, at more than 6,000 theaters throughout the country.

Company news releases crowed over the V-8 achievement: "The new Ford V-8 represents a notable advance in motor car engineering. It is large, long, roomy, fast, powerful and alert. Its eight cylinder V-type engine develops 65 horsepower. The car is capable of 75 miles an hour.

"Long standing Ford engineering practices governing the relation of weight to safety, speed and economical operation are exemplified in the new V-8. The result of months of tests and research is that the V-8 actually weighs only about 100 pounds more than the Model A and the new four cylinder Ford weighs even less than its predecessor.

"To produce a car with an eight cylinder V-type engine without materially increasing the weight necessitated a most painstaking study of the design of every part of the car. Wherever possible in the new car, lighter, but equally serviceable and durable materials have been utilized without loss of strength."

Despite unemployment, business failures, and hunger in the cities, during this Depression period, an estimated 5.5 million people visited the Ford showrooms across the nation to see the 14 new body types. But even with its new V-8, could Ford Motor Company regain that third of the national automobile market it held in 1929 and once more lead the field in the sale of low-priced cars?

The Depression had brought on a drastic drop in sales—from four million in 1929 to barely two million in 1931. Furthermore, most of the automotive production had been placed in the hands of the Big Three—General Motors, Ford and Chrysler. While Ford pondered over the introduction of the V-8, Chevrolet, under the leadership of William Knudsen—was improving production, reducing cost and challenging Ford. When Ford introduced the new V-8, it could not match Chevrolet's prices which were $10 to $25 lower on various body styles. With the Depression at rock bottom, sales continued to decline and Ford's full production capabilities were never utilized. Ford sales for the eight months of 1932 were just over 258,000 while Chevrolet's sales barely reached 322,000 for the full 12 months.

In 1933 Ford went all-out with a completely restyled streamlined body and a new chassis designed for the V-8. Ford sales in 1933 improved, climbing to 334,000—but so did Chevrolet's. Its sales totaled more than 480,000, and Chevrolet continued to edge Ford on price.

It was not until 1935 that Ford was able to regain the industry leadership, outselling Chevrolet 942,000 to 793,000. But it was only for one year; Chevrolet regained the lead in 1936, and kept it until the mid 1950s.

II—Ford's Production Practices

During the high production Model A era, Ford Motor Company built automobiles at thirty five United States assembly plants. Of these, thirty-two were reopened for production of the 1932 models. However, by December of that year declining sales brought about by the depression reduced the number of operating assembly plants to twenty-one. After the shut down at the end of the 1932 production, only eight plants were retooled to produce the 1933 vehicles. These plants were: Dearborn, Michigan; Chester, Pennsylvania; Chicago, Illinois; Cincinnati, Ohio; Edgewater, New Jersey; Kansas City, Missouri; Norfolk, Virginia; and Richmond, California. In March the Louisville, Kentucky and Sommerville, Massachusetts plants were added, but at the same time the Cincinnati and Norfolk plants were closed.

For 1934, Norfolk was reopened along with plants in Buffalo, New York and Dallas, Texas. Five more plants were added for the production of 1935 models: Long Beach, California; St. Louis, Missouri; Cincinnati, Ohio; Memphis, Tennessee; and the Twin City Plant in St. Paul, Minnesota. In addition, the Atlanta Plant in Georgia was reopened in February 1937, making a total of seventeen plants producing 1937 and 1938 models.

The plants were divided into one of three categories—major, standard or minor assembly plants. A major assembly plant such as the Dearborn Assembly Plant in the Rouge Complex, in addition to the assembly line, was equipped with stamping and production machinery to enable it to produce completely finished cars from bare metal. These plants also produced stampings and "knock-down" assemblies (partly assembled bodies) to supply the standard and minor assembly plants.

A standard assembly plant such as the Louisville one did not have stamping machinery, but did have the capacity to assemble chassis and build completely finished bodies from supplied stampings or partly assembled knock-down assemblies. It also supplied knock-down and complete body assemblies to a few smaller minor assembly plants which had limited capacity.

In addition, Budd, Briggs and Murray produced parts, knock-down assemblies, and completely finished bodies for the Ford plants.

All engines and transmissions were produced at the

Fender installation at the Dearborn Assembly Plant.

Typical body assembly operation at major assembly plants.

Complete body assemblies were also produced by Budd, Murray and Briggs companies.

Rouge Complex for shipment to the assembly plants. These engine and transmission assemblies were shipped minus the generator and fan, spark plugs, carburetor, and gear shift lever which were installed on the engine dress-up line at the assembly plants.

The parts, tools, and assembly procedures used at these plants were determined by the home office in Dearborn. The procedure started with the Engineering Department. After a part was designed, tested and tooling was completed, the department issued a document known as an engineering release. This release identified the part by number, the models on which it was to be used, and the effective date. If the part replaced another part, the release also stated the disposition of stock on hand, such as "use up," "send to service," "rework," or "scrap." At model change, all parts which were to be carried over were re-released.

A copy of the release was sent to the purchasing, scheduling and production departments. These three departments, in turn, coordinated the actual production of each vehicle. Every operation at the assembly plants was specifically detailed in a continuous flow of "Instruction and Change" letters issued by the Production Department. These letters dictated the parts, tools and procedures to be used, including color combinations and interior trim schemes announced by the "General Assembly Letters" issued by the Sales Department.

In general, the system worked very well. The fact that cars built at different assembly plants looked exactly alike, was one of the wonders of mass production. However, because of the distance between plants and the time lag in transportation and communication, strict control by the home office was not always possible and occasional variances between vehicles of the same model did occur.

Some of the causes of the variances were inherent with the system. For example, in addition to the engine storage area at the Engine Assembly Plant at the Rouge, the company had engine storage areas at each of the assembly plants. But Ford's largest storage space was actually the railroad cars filled with engines enroute to the various assembly plants. Because the engines were not shipped in sequential numerical order, and since engines placed in storage areas were removed on a "first in—last out" sequence, it was possible for a car being built at a plant in California to have an engine two months older than a car being built on the same day at the Dearborn plants. Another example was when a part was changed and the old part was designated for use until supply was exhausted. One plant may have had only enough parts to last two weeks, while another might have had a two months supply.

Another reason for variances occurred because the plant manager, whose job it was to produce as many cars as possible of an acceptable quality, did not always make changes as directed by Dearborn. This is evident in letters on file in the Ford Archives which restate specific directions already issued in a previous communication.

Some deviations in body colors were permitted, but these were generally in conjunction with fleet sales. These deviations were covered in the General Assembly Letters and could vary from plant to plant. Fleet sales consisted of multiple orders of the same body style for commercial use. A variety of color combinations was possible, limited only by the colors in stock at the plant at the time of the order.

The dates published in this book showing effective changes in production were obtained from copies of the original engineering releases. As a guide to the restorer, any new part could not have been used on cars built before such dates, but the obsoleted part might have been used on some cars as long as two months after the change date.

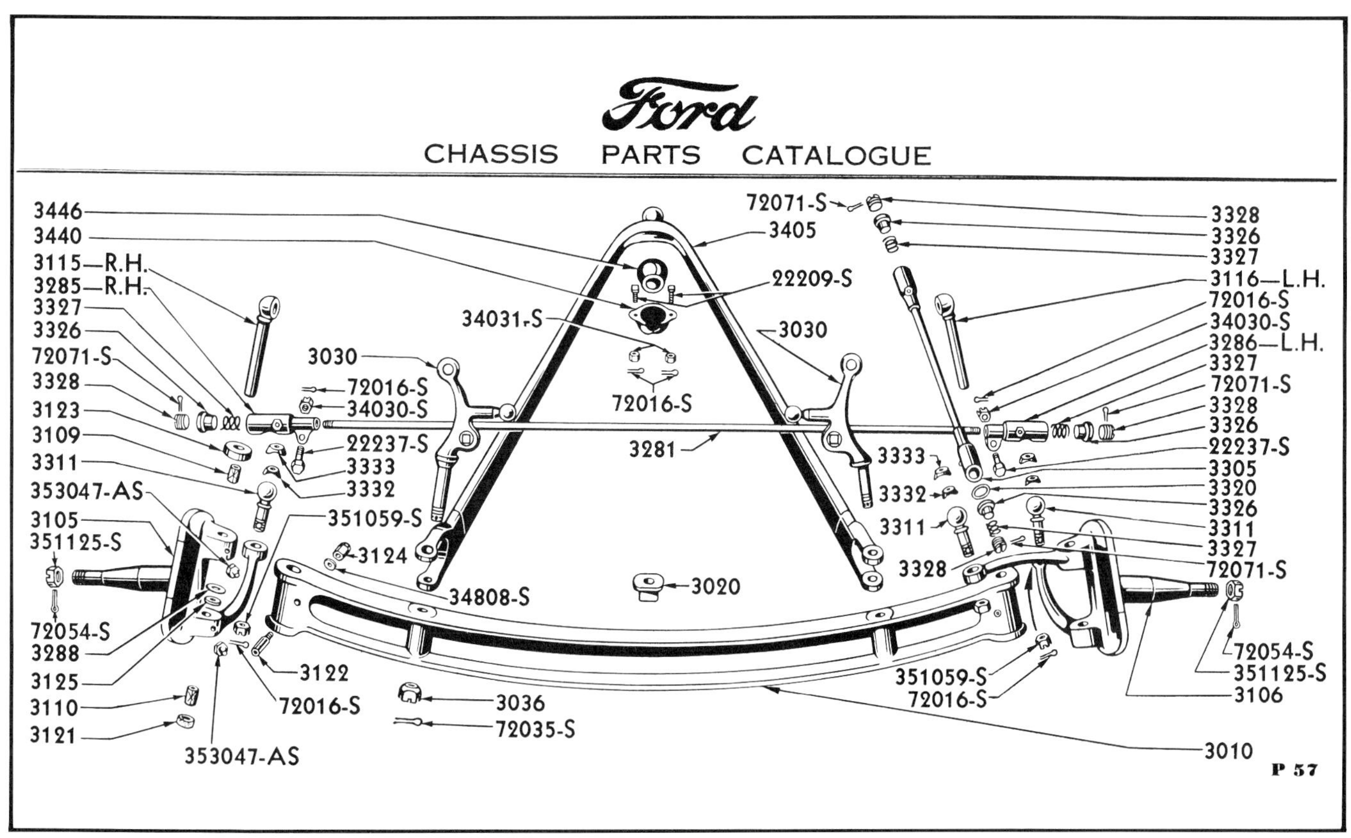

Example of basic part numbers for the front axle. 1933-34 illustration shown.

For identifying parts Ford used a basic numbering system, referred to within the company as the "UPC" number (Universal Parts Classification). In this system each part was given a basic part number within a block of numbers assigned to each major component of the vehicle. Consequently, all rear axle parts were numbered from 4000 to 4900, frame parts 5000 to 5150, engine parts 6000 to 6900, etc. The same part carried the identical basic number year after year. As an example, the front spring basic part number, which is 5310, identified the front spring for all years—whether it was for 1932, 1937, or 1940.

A prefix code letter or number was used to identify the model or model year—The B-5310 front spring was for 1932, the 40-5310 spring was for 1933–34, the 48-5310 spring was for 1935–36, etc. The first design of any part was identified by a letter "A" following the part number, the second design had a suffix letter "B," the next design a suffix "C," continuing through the alphabet each time the part was redesigned.

Standard parts, such as bolts, screws, nuts, washers, and cotter pins, which were in the 20,000 to 24,000 basic part numbers, did not always change with the parts they held. Also, their surface finish may have been different. In some usage the assembly plant had a choice between two finishes. The finish of these parts was designated by an "S" suffix code number following the part number. For example, the water pump to cylinder block bolt was part number 20408-S7. The S7 designates cadmium plate finish.

The standard parts numbers and "S" codes in the Ford parts list are indented and follow the part with which they are used, but the sizes of these parts are printed on a separate list, following the parts list. The restorer, however, should keep in mind that the parts list was an after market publication for service and some of the parts and standard parts listed may not be the same as the original parts.

In the automotive industry, the first day of full production on a new model is referred to as the "Job-one" date. In the 30's, that date at the Ford Motor Company generally occurred in October, November or December of the preceding year. Job-one for the 1932 cars was originally the first week in December 1931, but because of Henry Ford's decision to produce a V-8, production was stopped and not resumed until the last week in March 1932. Public introduction day was March 31, 1932. The other years are as follows:

Model Year	Job-one	Public Introduction
1933	First week, Jan. 1933	February 11, 1933
1934	Third week, Nov. 1933	December 9, 1933
1935	Third week, Nov. 1934	December 27, 1934
1936	Third week, Sept. 1935	October 19, 1935
1937	Third week, Oct. 1936	*November 6, 1936
1938	Third week, Oct. 1937	**October 27, 1937

*At the National Dealer Show and again at the New York Automobile Show on November 11, 1936. Introduction at Dealers was November 14, 1936.

**At both the New York Automobile Show and the Midwest Automobile Show in Detroit on November 3, 1937.

The models described in the following sections are all the passenger cars and all the commercial vehicles produced in 1932 through 1938. These commercial vehicles are those produced on the passenger car chassis such as the Station Wagon, Panel and Sedan Delivery, and Pickup Truck.

Introduction show of the 1935 models.

III—V-8 And Model B Engines, 1932–1938

The V-8 Engine

The new V-8 engine was the most notable change from the 1931 Model A to the 1932 Model 18. Edsel Ford was very fearful at the suddenness with which it was done—fearful of the lack of background, lack of experimentation and tests performed on it. He was fearful that it would have trouble, and it did. Some problems were described by Ford employees in their reminiscences.

Engineer Larry Sheldrick said, "We were using the public as our testing crew. The ignition system was a troublesome thing. We had coil breakdowns and the people in the field didn't know how to service this ignition."

Clem Davis, a Ford tool and die maker recalled, "They had trouble with motors using oil. They came out with it in too much of a hurry . . . we were in piston difficulty for quite a while. As soon as they would wear out a set of pistons, they would go back and the dealer would replace the pistons. We gave away millions of pistons."

Introduction of the new V-8 occurred on March 31, but it was April 21 before any cars were delivered to customers. By directives, the sales branches were told that cars after number 4250 could be sold. All cars through 4250 had to be re-worked and were then to be used as demonstrators.

Engines with number 1,929 or less were to have the front cover, valves, push rods, valve guides and camshaft replaced. Engines with numbers 1,930 to 4,250 were to have the front cover replaced before delivery to dealers.

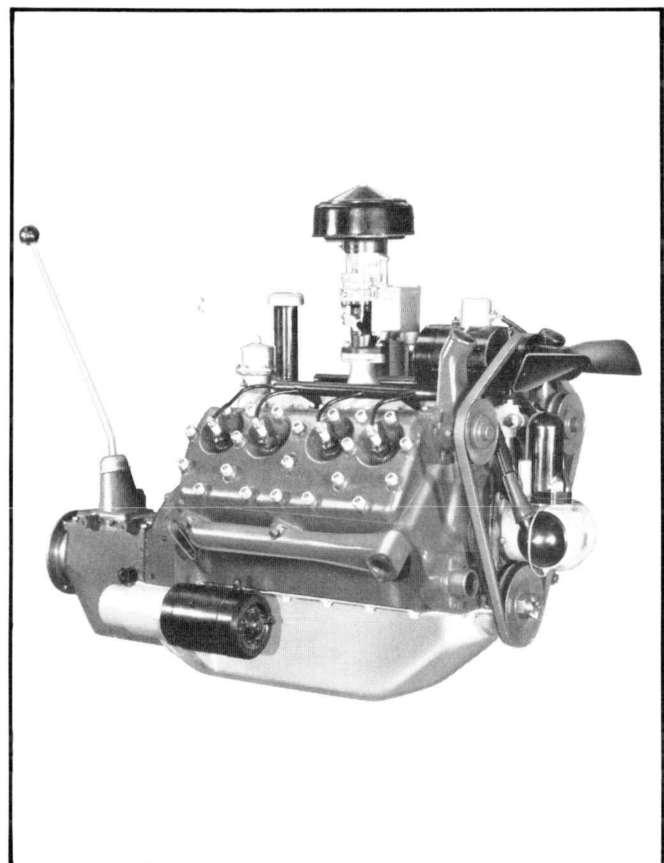

An early V-8 engine with the aluminum oil pan, two-blade fan, the high coil, cast iron heads, and Detroit Lubricator Company carburetor. (Courtesy Ford Motor Company.)

At its beginning in 1932, the V-8 had a very poor start. But with quick changes it improved, and by 1934 with the additions of the duplex Stromberg carburetor, revamped pistons, and a modified distributor, it became a powerful, speedy, desirable V-8 engine. An engine which in later years became the pattern for the entire automobile industry.

Engine Specifications

The 1932 through 1938 Ford V-8s were the L head design with the 90° crankshaft configuration. The 1932 engine developed 65 HP at 3400 RPM and had a standard compression pressure of 114 pounds at 1000 RPM. Displacement was 221 cubic inch with a bore and stroke of 3.062 inches by 3.75 inches. The cylinder heads were made of cast iron, producing a compression ratio of 5.5 to 1.

In 1933 the cylinder heads were changed to cast aluminum and the compression ratio was raised to 6.3 to 1. As a result, the power output was increased to 75 HP at 3800 RPM with a maximum torque of 147 foot pounds at 2350 RPM. Compression pressure was 138 pounds at 1800 RPM. The duplex carburetor was introduced on the 1934 engine which upped the horsepower to 90 at 3800 RPM. (From specification chart in Ford Service Bulletin.) Compression pressure was changed to 138 pounds at 1600 RPM. This combination was continued through 1934 and 1935.

The 1936 engine was slightly modified with changes in compression pressure, 140 pounds at 2500 RPM, and maximum pressure, 149 foot pounds at 2000 RPM.

Changes were made again for 1937. The cylinder heads were changed back to cast iron as well as aluminum reducing the rating to 85 HP at 3800 RPM, and the compression ratio to 6.12 to 1. Compression pressure was 135 pounds at 2500 RPM. For 1938 the compression pressure was increased to 141 pounds at 2400 RPM. Maximum torque was 150 foot-pounds at 200 RPM.

A long conveyor transported the machined castings from the foundry to the Motor Building.

Engine Color

The engine green which was used on the Model A was continued into the V-8 engine production and was used through 1941. This color was used on all cast iron parts (except some truck heads) produced at the Rouge Engine Foundry. It included all castings on the engine, flywheel housing, clutch housings, and transmission. These parts were painted Ford engine green after the part was machined, but before assembly.

Stamped parts on these assemblies were painted black and aluminum castings were unpainted.

The edges of the gaskets between these parts were unpainted.

Castings made by suppliers were used for service and were painted black.

Engine Numbering

All V-8 engines were produced at the Rouge Plant and shipped to the various assembly plants. Similar to the Model A process, each engine was assembled at the Rouge Plant Motor Building, moved by conveyor to an engine break-in line and placed on a break-in stand. Each engine was then connected to water and oil lines and coupled to a direct current shunt wound electric motor. The electric motor spun the engine for a short break-in period until the resistance of the electric motor fell below a set amperage. At the same time the operator checked for any water and oil leaks and listened for any sound which might suggest a problem. After the engine passed the break-in test, it received its engine number in sequential order. An engine which did not pass the test was sent to an adjoining shop for repair. After the repair was made, it then received an engine number. If an engine could not be repaired, it was scrapped.

Each engine number for the V-8 engines was preceded by a star, then the prefix "18" followed by a dash, the sequential number, starting with number one, and concluded with a star (*18-1*). The number was stamped on the transmission case between the two top bolts. The "18" prefix for V-8 engine numbers was used through 1942.

After the numbering operation, the engines went by conveyor to the Rouge Assembly line or to a crating area for shipping to other assembly plants. When the engines were dropped onto the chassis, they were no longer in sequential order.

The Motor Building engine assembly line.

Publicity photograph of the motor block testing room. In normal operation more employees would be at work and not every station would have a motor.

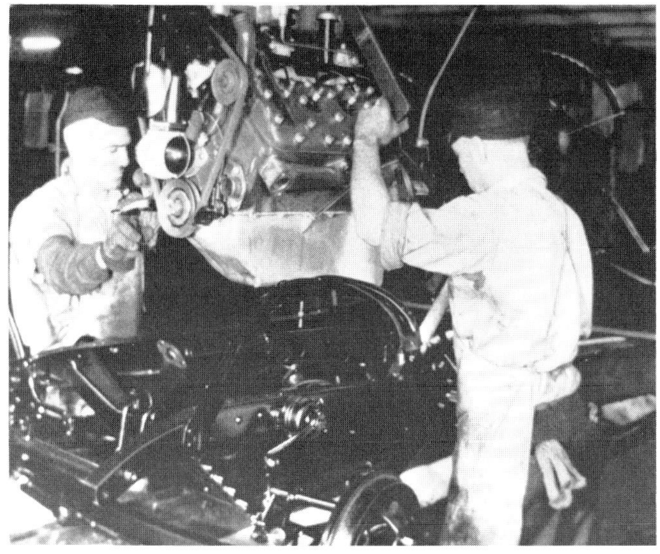

Engine installation at the assembly line.

At the assembly plants, when the engine was dropped on the chassis, the engine number was stamped on top of the left side rail of the frame, just in front of the dash body mounting bracket. The number could be seen when the hood was raised. In addition the engine number, less the "18" prefix number, was stamped at two more places on the frame. One was near the rear edge of the front door and the other was directly over the rear axle.

Assembly of V-8 engines for trucks was started in August, 1932. The number for truck engines had a "BB18" prefix (*BB18-340*). The engine numbers ran in sequence with the passenger car engines. At the assembly plant, the same engine number was stamped on the left truck frame rail just in front of the dash body mount, similar to the passenger car. The number was not stamped anyplace else on the truck frame.

The Cylinder Block

The one-piece cylinder block was the heart of the new V-8 engine. But because it was new, requiring new methods of manufacturing, it presented the most problems. An indication of the problems was reflected in a management report on March 25, eleven days after production was started. It stated, "Motor Building 7th hour report showed 18 blocks shipped to motor room, one block at welder, six blocks were scrapped, 27 blocks in the machine operation and 11 motors shipped to final assembly." This was at a time when production was scheduled for 200 engines per day.

Production of the V-8 block started off very slowly, but once the manufacturing problems were solved, very few changes were made. The standard cylinder bore tolerance was 3.0625 to 3.0635 inches. In June 1932, the hole for the fuel pump rod bushing was enlarged to improve operation. In November, 1932, the flange around the oil pump boss was increased to improve sealing with the new steel oil pan. At the same time, the drain cock hole was changed from a straight down position to a slight angle out. No other changes were made through the end of 1934 production. These blocks were identified with the "18" prefix part number (18-6010).

Fixture for machining the valve seats.

Starting with job one, 1935, the block was modified with minor casting changes so as to provide a positive crankcase ventilation system. This new block was given a "48" prefix for its part number (48-6010). In February 1935, the 1/4-inch pipe thread hole for the water drain was moved to provide additional clearance between the drain cock and the front cross member.

For 1936, two cylinder blocks were in use. The 1935 block with the cast babbit bearings was continued to the end of 1936 production. In addition, starting in September 1935, a new block with the new main bearing inserts was introduced (68-6010). The blocks with the bearing inserts were identified with the letters "LB" cast at the top of the left front face of the block.

The new 1936 block was redesigned for 1937. The water jacket was extended down on each side to improve cooling and provisions were made on the front of the block to match the new block mounted water pump. Block number was 78-6010. In 1938, the block was modified again. The main bearing sizes were increased and the head stud locations were changed to the 24 stud pattern (81-6010). However, due to the slow production of the new block, the 1937 block assembly was continued until June 1938.

Cylinder Front Cover

The cast iron front cover had very minor changes from 1932 through 1938. The original design which had four holes for mounting the distributor was used until May 1932. After May, three holes were used for mounting the distributor. One other change was made in March 1935. The top mounting hole and bolt were changed to provide a tighter fit and improve alignment for installation. Since the front cover held the distributor, the improved location of the cover in turn improved correct distributor location.

Engine Front Support

The front engine support (engine mounting bracket) for the V-8 consisted of two steel forging brackets, a right hand and left hand. When the V-8 was introduced, it used a different mounting system than the four cylinder Model B. In April 1932, the mounting system was revised by changing the front frame cross member and designing a new rubber insulator and support so that the four cylinder and the V-

8 used the same type of engine support insulator. Shipment of the new frames to the assembly plants began on April 27. The new modified design of the front engine support bracket was put in production in the first week in May. This bracket was used until March 1933.

In March 1933, the front engine support bracket was redesigned to incorporate the water inlet connection. These brackets, left hand and right hand, were made of malleable iron and were used through 1934.

For 1935 the casting was modified at the engine mounting pad area. The pad was raised, causing the engine to sit lower.

In 1936 the support bracket was changed for the passenger cars while the commercial vehicles continued to use the 1935 design.

Of the 85 HP engines for 1937, the engine support bracket was redesigned, incorporating the water pump and water inlet connection. This design was used through the end of 1938.

Cylinder Heads

The V-8 cylinder heads went through many changes from 1932 to 1938. These changes were brought about by changes in piston design, compression ratios, cooling system, mounting studs pattern, and casting materials. Most changes were made beginning with a new model year, some were made during the model year, and a few overlapped model years. The 1932 cylinder heads (18-6049 and 18-6050) were made of cast iron with a combustion chamber volume of 70 to 72cc for each cylinder. The spark plug hole was for a ⅞-18 thread spark plug, and a 21-stud hole pattern was used for mounting the head. A water pump was mounted on the upper front corner of each head. The part number was not cast on the top surface of the head.

A new aluminum head was released for the 1933 engines. The new head had the same 21-stud mounting pattern but its reduced combustion changer was 57 to 62cc, and the spark plug hole was tapped for an 18 mm spark plug. This head was identified as the A1 head. The part number 40-6049-A1, right hand, and 40-6050-A1, left hand, was cast on the top of the head. In August 1934 a "Ford" script raised lettering, .03 inches high, was also cast on the top surface. It was used with the flat head pistons on passenger and commercial cars to the end of 1935. It was also used as an option for passenger cars only until February, 1936.

In July 1935, an alternate low production (about 20%) head was also used. This head had a modified combustion chamber design, volume of 58 to 61cc. It was identified as the A2 head (40-6049-A2) and had the Ford script and the part number cast on the top surface of the head. It, too, was used with the flat head pistons. It was obsoleted in April 1936. A special aluminum head based on the 1933 design was released in August 1934 as special orders for high altitude areas. The combustion chamber volume was 39 to 41cc. This head was used with the flat head pistons until February 1936. Part number 40-6049-C or 40-6050-C and the Ford script was cast on the head.

Starting in April 1935, a new cast aluminum high compression head was used on an experimental basis with new domed steel pistons. The combustion chamber volume was 75 to 78cc. Engines with these experimental parts were limited for use on some trucks, commercial vehicles and fleet orders. Their performance was monitored for service. This head (and piston combination) became the main head for the 1936 production. It was used on passenger cars starting with job one and in April, management removed the "Experimental Manufacture" notation and it was designated for use on all passenger cars, commercial vehicles and trucks. In August 1936, it was modified slightly. Some internal webs were added around the water pump mounting flange and the previously blind mounting holes were drilled and tapped through. The head was identified with part number 68-6049A or 68-6050A and the Ford script cast on the head.

For 1937 production, the head was completely redesigned. The water pump was moved to mount on the block and the head was changed with the water outlet located at the center of the top edge of the head. The new head was interchangeable left and right and had the Ford script plus the part number 78-6050 cast on the head.

Two heads were produced, one made of cast aluminum and one made of cast iron. The aluminum head was available only on passenger cars produced in late 1936 and was terminated in December 1936. The cast iron head was used on passenger cars, commercial vehicles and trucks. It was continued in use with the "78" prefix block until mid-1938.

In 1938, with the introduction of the new 24-stud block a new 24-stud holes head was used. Spark plug hole was for a 14mm plug. The new head was produced in cast iron and aluminum, both with the same combustion chamber volume. With the 24-stud pattern the left and right head was no longer interchangeable. Both heads had the Ford script cast on their top surface. In addition, the cast iron left head had a cast number 81A-0 while the right head had 81A-9. The aluminum heads had the entire number cast on the surface, 81A-6049-B or 81A-6050-B.

A special equipment cast iron high compression head for high altitude areas and for engines using alcohol or natural gas fuels, was also available.

Compression ratios of the various heads were as follows: the "18" prefix head—5.5 to 1; the "40" prefix head—6.3 to 1; the "48" prefix head—6.3 to 1; the "68" prefix head—6.3 to 1; the "78" prefix head—6.1 to 1; and the "81A" prefix head—6.1 to 1.

If authenticity of restoration is not important, all of the 21-stud hole heads are interchangeable, however, heads used on flat piston engines cannot be used on engines with domed pistons.

Pistons

Four-cylinder engines and the V-8 used pistons that were the aluminum alloy type with a split skirt constant clearance design. The fit was .0005 to .0025 inch clearance.

The skirt of the piston tapered approximately .001 inch in its length. The larger diameter was at the bottom where it was supposed to contribute to the wiping action of the cylinder. Starting in June 1931, Ford had been using a "cam ground" piston (not round). The design was to compensate for the expansion of the piston at the piston pin boss area. When the piston warmed up, it assumed a round shape.

Since the piston skirt was neither straight nor round and with addition of the split, it was impossible to check the piston size with micrometers. However, piston sizes were held within one thousandth of an inch at manufacturing. Standard piston sizes were 3.061 and 3.062 inches.

The flat head aluminum pistons were made by three companies, The Aluminum Company of America, Bohn Aluminum and Aluminum Industries. The 1932 design had one saw cut slot on the thrust side and five holes in the oil ring groove. In 1933, it was changed to included two saw cut slots, one on each side, and the number of holes in the oil ring groove was increased to 12. This piston was used until April 1936.

In 1935, a steel-domed piston was put in limited use on an experimental basis. Starting in April 1936, the steel dome piston became the standard piston on all engines. Later, in July, about 25% of the pistons were cadmium plated. The steel piston was used through the end of 1938, but in November 1936, an aluminum-domed piston was introduced as an alternate. A steel strut around the wrist pin hole was added in 1937 for truck use and in 1938 the same piston was also used on passanger cars.

Camshaft

The camshaft for the new V-8 was the steel forging type. In June 1932, its lubrication was improved by the addition of a spiral cut oil groove at the front and center camshaft bearing area. The change became effective with engine number 18-33621 and was used until July 1937. Starting in October, 1934, a chilled cast iron camshaft was introduced and was used as an optional until July 1937. These shafts were superior in that they had a soft center and chilled hard outer surface.

In 1937, a new cast iron camshaft was designed to give better operation and economy at low speed. This was accomplished by decreasing by about 10% the amount of overlap between the opening and closing of the intake and exhaust valve. At first it was used on only 10% of production, but by July 1937, production was increased for use on all engines through 1938.

Crankshaft

Similar to the camshaft, the 1932 V-8 crankshaft was a steel forging. The main bearings were 1.999 inches in diameter by 1.839 inches wide for the front bearing, 1.734 inches wide for the center bearing and 2.254 inches wide for the rear bearing. The connecting rod bearing areas were 1.999 inches in diameter by 1.938 inches wide.

Beginning in December 1933, a cast iron crankshaft was also introduced. Both of these shafts were in use until the end of the 1936 production. In September 1935, a new crankshaft with main bearing inserts in the block was introduced on a limited basis. This new crank had a main bearing diameter of 2.399. Engines with the new bearing insert feature were identified with the letters "L B" cast on the left top front surface of the cylinder block. This shaft was used through 1937. In January 1938, the bearing areas were again increased: the main bearings were 2.499 inches in diameter by 1.719 inches wide at the front, 1.674 inches at the center bearing and 2.254 at the rear bearing. Rod bearings remained at 1.999 diameter, but were reduced to 1.752 inches wide.

Connecting Rods

The connecting rods were steel forgings with the I-beam cross section design. The bearing consisted of a full floating bushing, babbit coated on the inside and outside surface, and was an exclusive Ford feature. Each rod and rod cap was machined as a set and after all the rods and caps were assembled in the engine, they were stamped with a number one through eight to eliminate mixing the parts at any future disassembly. Two rods were connected to each crankpin with .010 clearance between rods.

Flywheel

Along with the new clutch, the flywheel assembly for the 1932 V-8 was also completely new. The ring gear was the tight shrink fit design. Starting with the 1935 models, a groove was provided into which the ring gear contracted. The small ridge on the outer lip of the flywheel was .030 to .040 inches high. With this design, a lesser shrink pressure was needed to provide a good grip.

Valve Chamber Cover (Intake Manifold)

The valve chamber cover mounted on top of the engine and covered the openings between the two banks of cylinders. It was also integral with the intake manifold and provided mounting places for the carburetor, generator and fuel pump. The 1932 cover was made of aluminum, and had a one-hole and air-fuel intake passage which supplied all eight cylinders. In April, a boss and ¾ pipe plug was added to permit adjustment of the oil relief valve. For 1933 models, the cover was modified at the generator mounting area from a post bracket to a flange bracket. However, production was slow and some 1932 covers were used on 1933 cars.

In November 1933, a new cast aluminum valve cover with an over and under dual air passage design was introduced in conjunction with the new Stromberg duplex (two throat) carburetor. Since engine production for the 1934 models was already started, assembly plants were instructed to remove the old covers from the 1934 passenger model engines and replace them with the new cover. The old covers were to be accumulated for use on trucks. In March 1934, a cast iron dual passage cover was released for use on trucks and the old 1932 cover was phased out.

Early in 1935, the valve cover was further improved to provide smoother air flow for better breathing. This design was continued through 1936. Minor improvements were made for 1937 and were carried through to the end of 1938.

Similar inprovements were made on the cast iron covers which were used on commercial vehicles and trucks.

Oil Pump

The oil pump for the V-8 was the gear type similar to the Model "A" and "B." It was located in the left rear corner of the oil pan. In May 1932, the oil pump cover was changed by adding an inlet pipe which picked up oil from a sump. This change coincided with the addition of an oil sump in the pan. The change was needed to reduce oil surge. In September 1932, the oil pickup tube was made bell-shaped at the connection to the oil pump cover to reduce any possibility of sediment build-up at that point. This pump was used through the end of 1934 models. A minor change was made to the pickup tube for the 1935 cars and the early 1936.

In January 1936, the oil pump was completely redesigned. The new pump featured a four-inch diameter screen assembly, thereby eliminating the pickup tube. The pump

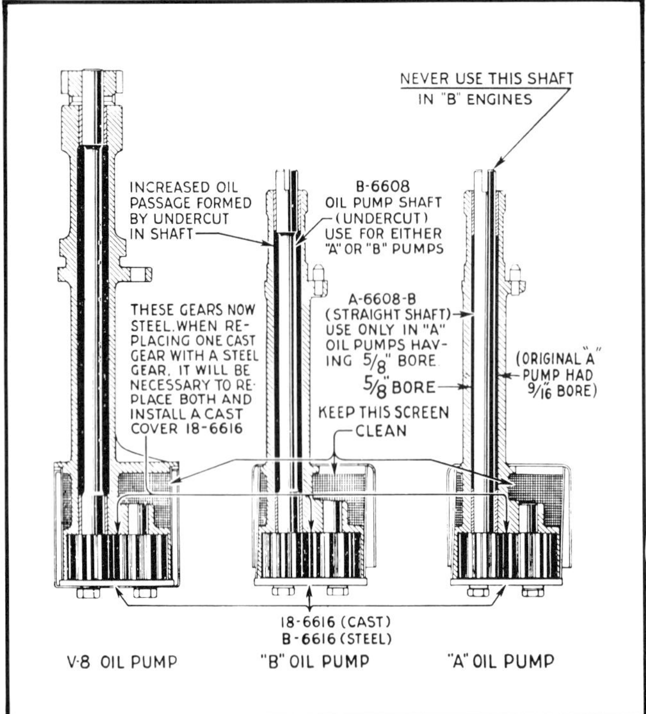

Comparison of the Models A, B and V-8 oil pumps.

remained unchanged through the end of 1938.

Oil Pan

The first oil pan for the V-8 engine was an aluminum casting because the dies for stamping the steel pan were not as yet completed. Extending beyond the rear of the block, the oil pan assembly also formed the lower half of the flywheel housing. The steel pan became available in May 1932, beginning with engine number 18-15164. A new feature of the steel pan was the addition of the oil level indicator (dip stick) located on the left side. On previous engines, the oil level indicator was located on the block at the rear right corner. Between 1932 and 1935, five different oil level indicators were used with the various pan designs. See drawing for details. Also, with the new pan, the oil sump location was changed to the center of the pan to coincide with the change of the oil pump pickup tube.

In July, 1932, a minor change was made. The oil outlet hole at the bottom of the flywheel housing area of the pan was moved rearward and on the back face to reduce any possibility of picking up dirt on deep rutted dirt roads. The change was effective with engine number 18-78500.

Another minor change was made in July 1934. The thickness of oil drain boss was increased to provide more threads, thereby reducing the possibility of stripping the threads.

Starting with the 1935 models, the oil pan was completely redesigned and its oil capacity was increased. Later in April, the oil pan tray was eliminated and, in August, clearance between the oil pan and the drag link was increased.

Two minor changes were made in 1936. In January, the drain plug location was changed from the side to the bottom of the oil pan and the oil sump was eliminated. This pan was used through the end of 1938.

The steel oil pan was painted black and the aluminum pan was left unpainted.

Oil Level Indicator (Dip Stick)

Between 1932 and 1935 five different oil level indicators were used for checking oil in the V-8 engines (see drawing). The oil level indicators were made of unfinished half round steel rod. An "F" and "L" were stamped on the flat side of the indicator. In September 1933, the marking was changed to Danger, Fill and Full. The 1935 indicator

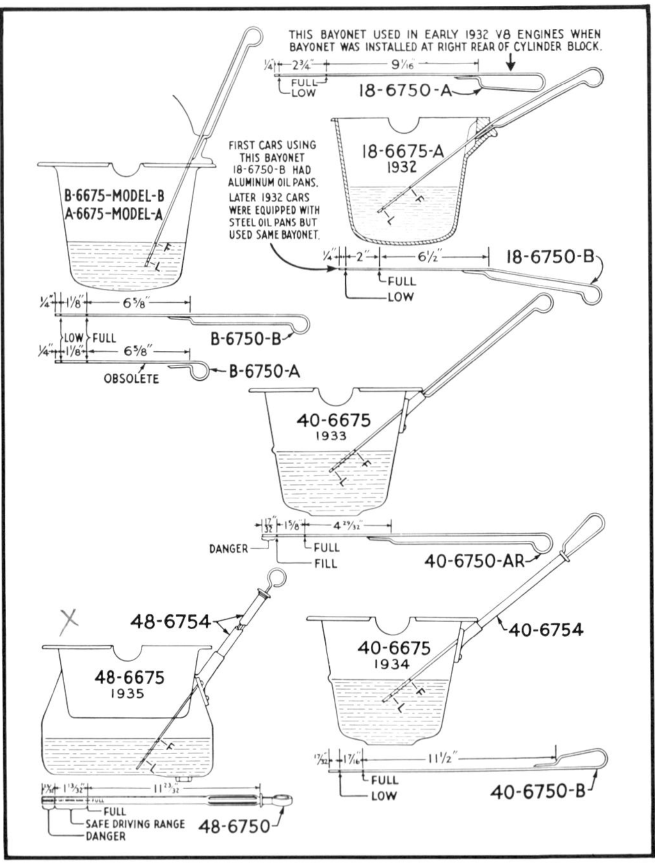

Drawing for identifying the various oil level gauges.

was made of flat steel stock and was split and spread near the top to form the retaining section. A washer and gasket above the pierced area formed a cap for the indicator tube. Lettering at the lower end was Danger, Safe Driving Range, and Full. The indicator was used through 1938.

Oil Filler Cap

The oil filler cap for the V-8 was similar to that used on the four-cylinder engine. There were two makes, one made of terne plate and the other of sheet steel. The terne plate caps were unfinished while the sheet steel caps were painted black. The 1932 design was used through 1934 model production.

A new air scoop design cap was adopted for the 1935 cars. It was made by AC and consisted of a scoop and filter element. The filter element was a coiled piece of 16 mesh galvanized wire cloth 106 inches long. The new cap was part of the positive crank case ventilation system and was painted black. In February, an oil dip treatment was added to the filter element to improve air cleaning. In April, a blue decalcomania with white lettering was added to the top of the cap. It read: Wash in gasoline and re-oil filter element every 2000 miles or oftener under severe conditions. In March, 1935, an alternate design round cap with an oil dipped copper crimp filter was released for use in dust prone areas.

For a short time, December 1935 to February 1936, a third alternate was introduced for use in warm climate areas only. It was a flat round cap with a wire screen filter element.

The AC scoop cap was obsoleted in December 1936, and the round cap was the only one used through 1938 production.

Water Pump

Engine cooling on the V-8 was based on Ford's old thermosyphon action theory and the water pumps were used only to accelerate the flow of water. Two pumps were used, one at the top front of each cylinder head. The 1932 pumps were designed as left and right assemblies. The difference was the location of a left or right grease fitting boss in the neck of the housing. In October 1932, a grease fitting boss and hole was located on each side of the pump body so that there no longer was a left-hand and right-hand pump. One hole would receive a grease fitting and the other hole would receive a plug. This pump assembly was first released for service and later adopted for production.

Starting with 1933 production, an alternate design was introduced featuring oil lubrication rather than grease. A small reservoir was cast in the neck of the pump housing and lubrication was done with an oil can. The bearing was made of cindered bronze and there was no water seal packing. The pump was first used at the Rouge Assembly Plant on an experimental basis at the rate of 25 per day. By January 1935, its usage had reached 1000 cars per day.

With the beginning of 1935 production, a boss and hole was added to the water outlet part of the casting. The hole was for the new heat indicator connection. As a result, the left-hand and right-hand pumps were no longer interchangeable. The change was made on both the grease lubricated and the oil lubricated pumps. Both of these pumps were used through 1936 production with only minor impeller design improvement being made in July 1935, and again in May 1936.

The biggest change on water pumps occurred on 1937 cars. The pumps were completely redesigned and the location was changed from the head to the block. With the new design, the pump was forcing the water through the block and head rather than pulling the water up as in the thermo-syphon design. The new pump castings also incorporated the front engine support brackets. This design was used through the end of 1938.

The same pumps were used for passenger cars, commercial and truck engines. In 1935, a double sheave pulley was released for special orders where a larger generator or a larger extra cooling capacity fan was desired.

Thermostat

A brass thermostat designed and produced by the Dole Company was adapted for use on the V-8 engine starting in December 1933. The unit was installed in the radiator inlet hose with the heat sensitive coil spring toward the engine. The thermostat was used only on vehicles scheduled to be sold above the Mason-Dixon line.

Starting with the 1937 production, the thermostat was redesigned so as to fit in the water outlet casting of the cylinder head. In February 1937, the company also started to use a thermostat produced by the Detroit Lubricator Company. Both thermostats were used through 1938.

Fan Assembly

The first fan used on the V-8 was the two-bladed type, same as the Model B which was a carryover from the Model A. The hub, however, was redesigned so it could mount on the generator pulley. In April 1932, the overall hub length was increased from $3^{15}/_{16}$ to $4^{5}/_{16}$ to provide more clearance between the fan and the distributor.

The first V-8 design fan was released in May 1932. It was a four blade type, $15\frac{1}{2}$ inches in diameter. The pulley diameter was slightly larger than the two-blade fan, thereby reducing its speed, but providing more air and a quieter operation. In February 1933, with the use of the new shorter distributor, the hub length was shortened to $1^{29}/_{32}$. In addition, the leading edge of the fan blades were slanted back. This fan was used on passenger cars through 1934, 1935 and 1936. For the 1937 and 1938 cars, the fan diameter was increased to $15\frac{3}{4}$ inches.

Commercial vehicles used the passenger car fan through 1934. For 1935 models, the overall hub length was increased to $2\frac{1}{2}$ inches. Starting with the 1936 models, a new 17-inch diameter fan was used on commercial vehicles. This fan was used through 1938.

A special equipment six-blade fan was released in July 1933 and continued through 1938 for use on all engines where conditions demanded increased cooling.

All fan blade assemblies were painted black.

Fuel Pump

The fuel pump for the V-8 was located at the top back portion of the valve corner. It was produced by A.C. It was

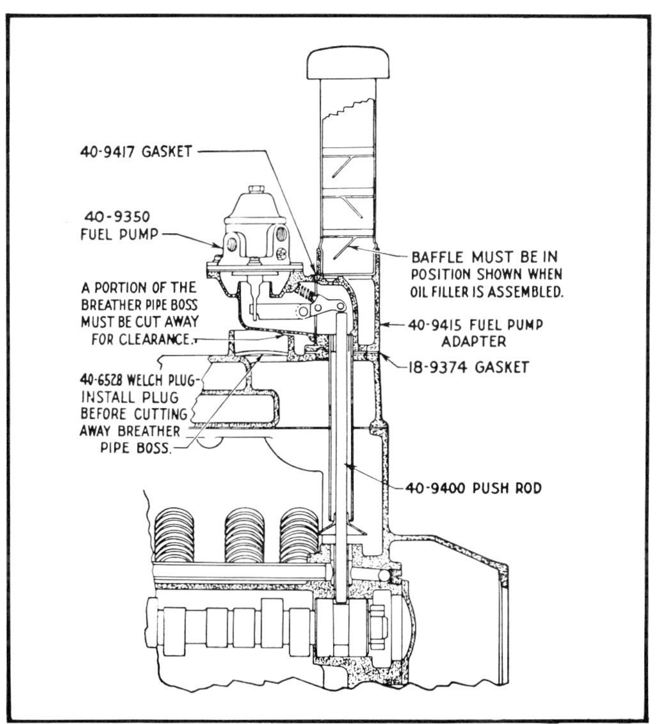

Service Bulletin drawing showing the rocker arm type fuel pump installed on an early engine.

a diaphragm and sleeve type operated by a push rod, which followed an eccentric on the camshaft. In May 1932, the sleeve diameter was reduced so as to minimize any sticking. At the same time, the cadmium plating on the sleeve was eliminated.

An alternate rocker arm type fuel pump, also made by A.C., was released in August 1932. This fuel pump had condensation problems. In December, two $\frac{3}{4}$ inch holes were added to the base to relieve condensation and possible freeze-up. Then in May 1933, a clip was introduced to cover the holes to prevent dust and dirt from getting in the pump body during the summer. Instructions were to remove the clip during the winter to prevent condensation and possible freezing. Both fuel pumps were used on 1932 and 1933 cars.

In September 1933, a new offset rocker arm type fuel pump was released, but the old pumps were not phased out until November. The new pump was the side mounted type and had an adaptor to fit on the manifold boss. At the same time, the breather oil filler pipe was relocated behind the fuel pump at the rear of the intake manifold. In February 1934, the rocker arm lubrication was improved with the addition of a smaller brass oiler which directed oil to the rocker arm and the oil filler pipe baffles were modified to reduce any possibility of moisture dripping on the rocker arm. This pump assembly was used on all V-8 engines through 1934, 1935 and to June of 1936.

A larger capacity A.C. fuel pump was used in June 1936, and through 1938.

Exhaust Manifold

The exhaust manifolds were made of cast iron and had no other finish. The left hand and right hand were symmetrically opposite and very few changes were made through 1938. The 1932 right-hand manifold was used through 1936, but the left-hand manifold was changed for the 1933 models. After that, it too was used through 1936. Both manifolds were redesigned for the 1937 and 1938 models.

Carburetor

The first carburetor for the V-8 was a single throat down draft type which had been specifically designed for the V-8. Its $1\frac{1}{4}$ inch throat could provide sufficient air to meet the engine's need at its highest speed. The carburetors were produced by Detroit Lubricator Company and Ford. The units produced by Detroit Lubricator Company had the words "MFD by Detroit Lubricator" on the upper part. Those produced by Ford had a script "F."

The 1932 carburetor was used through 1933, with minor changes. One such change was the addition of a control on the left side of the butterfly valve which was connected to the dash throttle knob. The change was started on a limited basis in December 1932, and full production in January 1933.

In October 1933 a "Bracke" design carburetor, produced by Holley was released for very limited use (200 per assembly plant).

A new dual down draft (dual throat) carburetor produced by Stromberg was released in November 1933, for use on 1934 models. This change was made in conjunction with the new dual intake manifold (valve cover). Due to the slow changeover, it was used on passenger cars only and ex-

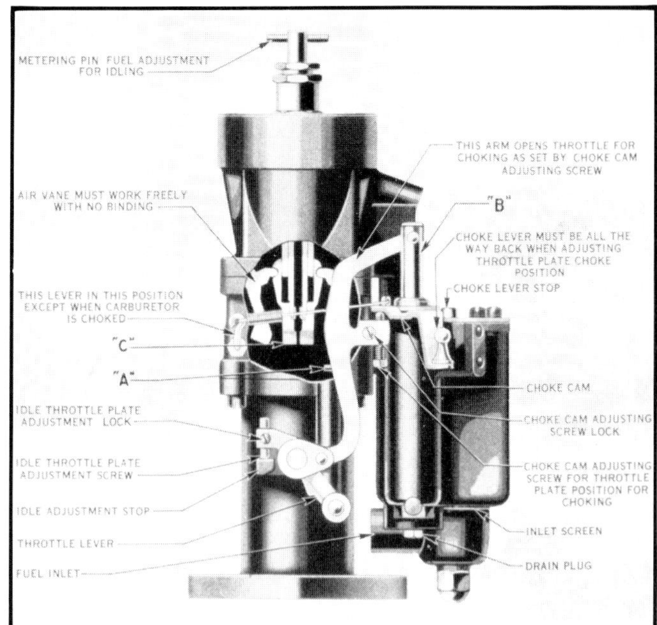

The 1932 Detroit Lubricator Company carburetor.

panded to commercial vehicles and trucks by February 1934. Several improvements were made to the carburetor in August. A bushing was added to the throttle body which protruded from the body so that the hand lever was mounted on it instead of on the shaft. This change reduced the possibility of the throttle lever binding on the throttle shaft. In addition, the orifice size of the fuel needle valve and seat assembly was reduced from .113 to .098 inches to minimize flooding. The change was identified by having the number ".098" stamped on the fuel needle valve seat assembly. This carburetor was a carryover for the early 1935 cars.

In January 1935, a revision was made to improve idling. The upper body gasket and lower body were changed to move the idle air vent closer to the fuel supply hole. This carburetor model was identified with the number "48" stamped on the upper and lower body flanges. The plants were instructed to use up all 1934 carburetors before installing any 1935 units. The new carburetor was also released for service use on 1934 cars, but parts from the 1935 carburetor could not be interchanged with the earlier 1934 assemblies.

A minor change was made to the accelerator linkage and the power jet assembly for the beginning of 1936 production. However, in January 1936, a new carburetor was released. It was designed for fuel economy and was started in use late in 1935 on 20% of production of trucks and commercial vehicles. By December, production was increased to fifty percent and by January 1936, it was released for use on all vehicles.

The main features of the new carburetor were: a smaller venturi, $\frac{31}{32}$ instead of $1\frac{1}{32}$; recalibrated jets; the addition of a plunger and spring on the upper body to hold the air shutter plate secure in the open position; and a throttle lever with a two-position connection, one marked "S" and the other "W." The "S" connection was for summer driving and the "W" for winter. For identification purpose, a number "97" was cast on the side of the carburetor body. This carburetor was used through 1938.

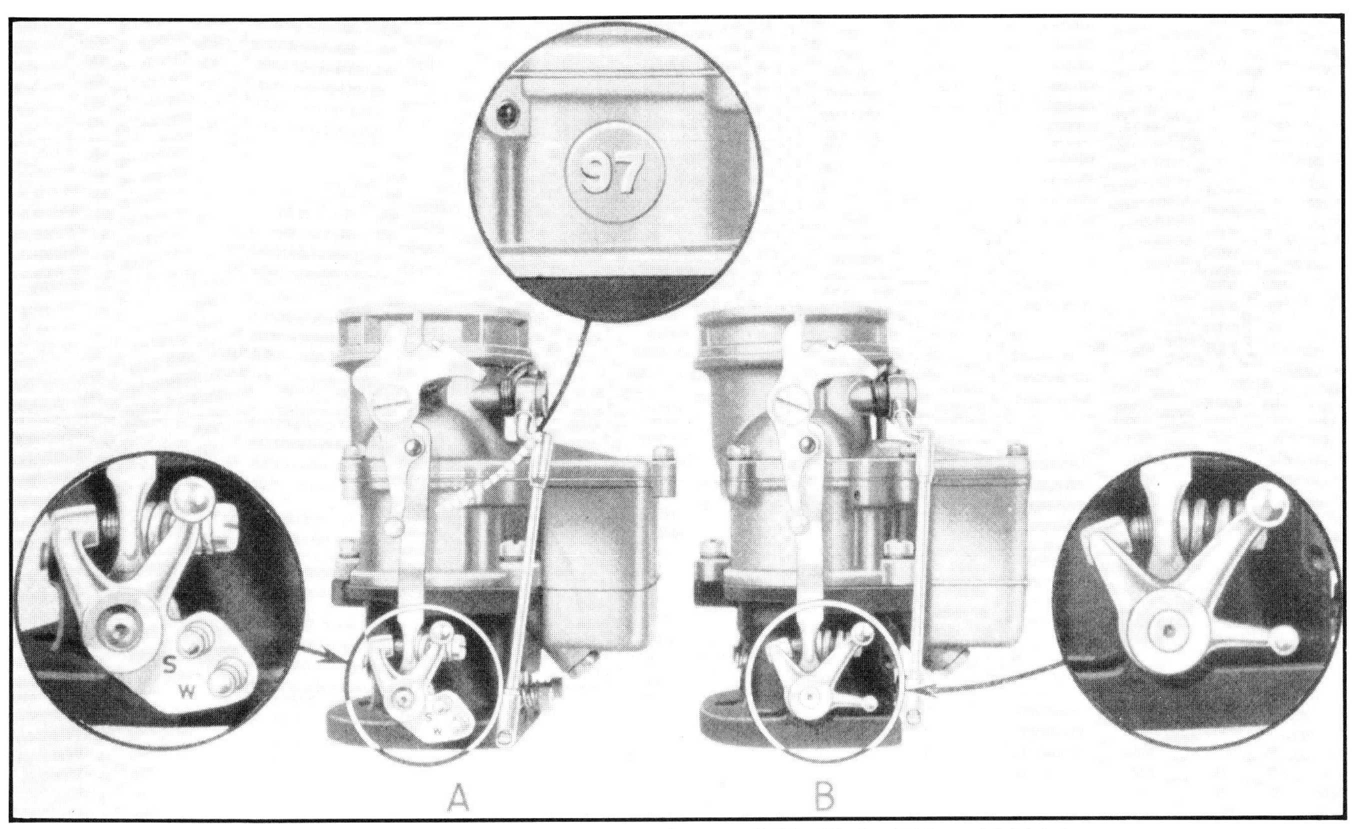

Comparison of the improved 1936 carburetor (left) with the 1935 model (right).

In May 1936, a special order Stomberg carburetor with a smaller venturi, 13⁄16, was also released. It was intended for use on Sedan Deliveries where stop and go driving was encountered, and was available on special order through 1938.

Beginning in April 1937, and continuing through 1938, an alternate carburetor made by Chandler-Grove Co. of Detroit, was used on a limited production, 25% of production at the Rouge Plant only.

High altitude versions of the various carburetors were available through dealer service starting in August 1933. The Detroit Lubricator carburetor was marked on the bottom side of the float bowl cover. Stromberg carburetors had a reduced size main metering jet. The size was stamped on the edge of the upper housing flange. Starting with 1935, there were four different sizes available; Normal to 5,000 ft., 5,000 to 10,000 ft., 10,000 to 15,000 ft., and over 15,000 ft.

Air Cleaner—Silencers

The air cleaner and silencer was standard equipment on the V-8 engines. There were three makes used on the early 1932-33 V-8s. Two were made to fit the Detroit Lubricator carburetor and the third was made to fit the Bracke design carburetor. These air cleaners were manufactured by Burgess and Holley.

The Burgess air cleaner for the Detroit-Lubricator carburetor was 7½ inches in diameter by four inches high. The Holley design had the same diameter, but was ⅝ inches higher. In May 1932, Holley added a 16-mesh galvanized wire screen and a decal which stated, "Clean screen in gasoline every 4,000 miles." As a cost saver the screen was eliminated at the end of December 1932.

Holley also produced the air cleaner to fit the Bracke design carburetor. It was 7½ inches in diameter by five inches high. Its decal had the Ford name in script and it stated,"Remove cleaner element—wash in gasoline—respray with oil every 4,000 miles—oftener on dusty roads—Holly Carb. Co." All of these air cleaners were painted with black enamel.

An oil bath air cleaner was also available on special order for use only on the Detroit-Lubricator carburetor. It was produced by United and mounted on the right-hand cylinder head. It was painted black with gold decal and black letters stating,"Caution, clean and refill with engine oil each time crankcase is drained. Remove filter occasionally and wash in gasoline."

A new air cleaner produced by A.C. was released for use on all V-8 engines with the Stromberg dual manifold carburetor 1934 through 1936. It was seven inches in diameter by six inches high with eight air inlet openings within 240° of its circumference and the word "front" stamped on it. The lower portion of the unit featured a tuning chamber and it used a copper crimp filter element. The outside was painted with black lacquer and the decal read, "Filter must be kept oiled—wash in gasoline at least every 1,000 Mi.—oftener under dusty conditions—reoil with engine oil—drain well before assy.—Warning, do not wash or oil felt."

An oil bath type air cleaner was also available on special order for use with the Stromberg carburetor. It was similar to the 1932–33 style, but it was produced by Donaldson. It had a large three pint oil capacity and was available on all V-8 engines through January 1935, when it was designated for use on truck engines only.

In January 1935, two new hat type oil bath air cleaners

were introduced for special order on all engines. One, produced by United, was 9¾ inches in diameter by six inches high, and the other, produced by Donaldson, was 10 inches in diameter by six inches high. Both were painted with black enamel. They were available on special order through 1938.

Two new designs were used on 1937–38 engines as standard equipment. One was produced by A.C. and the other by Burgess. Both were the same size, $6^{15}/_{16}$ diameter by six inches high. The copper crimp element was mounted on top with a shield which had the word "Front" stamped on it. Both were painted with either black enamel or lacquer.

The 60 H.P. V-8 Engine

For those desiring "Four-cylinder economy combined with eight-cylinder smoothness," Ford introduced an optional power plant in 1937, a scaled-down version of the 85 H.P. V-8 engine. First introduced on the European market, the new engine had a 2.6 inches bore by 3.2 inches stroke, a displacement of 136 cubic inches, developed 60 H.P. and could provide an economy option of 25 MPG when installed in a standard body style. It was enthusiastically received with sales of slightly over 300,000 in 1937. Performance-wise, however, it could not compete with the older four-cylinder Model "B," developing 94 foot pounds

The 60HP V-8 Engine.

of torque at 2500 RPM, compared to 127 foot pounds at 2800 RPM for the "B." Owners soon discovered that the small V-8 was underpowered for the weight of the car and sales began to decline. Because of continued poor sales, the small V-8 power option was discontinued with the end of 1940 production.

Even though the small V-8 was a scaled down version of the 85 HP V-8, it had some unique design features. The cylinder heads were interchangeable, the front cover was a one-piece design, incorporating the water pumps and the engine mounts, and the oil pump was incorporated with the front main bearing cap and was gear driven off the crankshaft gear. Production methods and engine color were similar to the larger V-8.

Engine production was started in 1936. With the exception of development engines, all 1936 engines were shipped overseas. Domestic engines were identified with the prefix 54 for passenger cars and BB54 for trucks. Engine numbers for 1937 started with 54-6602. There were few changes made on the small V-8 during its four year production.

Engine Block

The engine block had one minor change. After engine number 15466, the block was lengthened slightly at the rear main bearing to accommodate a new, longer crankshaft.

Front Cover and Water Pumps

There were two designs of the front cover, A1 and A2. The difference was in the machining of the water pump hole. On the A1 design, the hole was tapered while on the A2 it was straight. The pump body for each of these covers matched the hole. In both designs, the water pump was held in place with a large nut which threaded into the front cover. In June 1937, the pump body was redesigned making the nut an integral part of the pump body. The A1 design was discontinued after July 1937, while the A2 design was used through 1940.

Cylinder Head

Interchangeable left and right cylinder heads were made of cast aluminum with a 17 stud hole pattern. Combustion chamber volume was 41 to 43 cc and the compression ratio was 6.6 to 1.

Crankshaft

One change was made on the crankshaft. After engine number 15466, the rear main bearing was moved rearward 0.22 inches.

Valve Cover (Intake Manifold)

There were two valve covers used on the 60 HP V-8, one for mounting an electric fuel pump and the other for mounting a mechanical fuel pump. The electric fuel pump was only used through 1937, while the mechanical fuel pump was used on 1937 and 1938 engines. Both covers were made of aluminum.

Oil Pump

The oil pump assembly for the 60 HP V-8 was a unique design in that the pump housing also served as the front crankshaft bearing. The assembly consisted of a screen and cover, an oil pickup tube, a gear type pump, driveshaft and a drive gear which was driven by the crankshaft gear. A minor change was made in March 1937. The pickup tube, screen and cover were made larger.

Oil Pan

The oil pan was a steel stamping, and similar to the large V-8, the back portion included the lower half of the flywheel housing. In March 1937, the oil pump area was redesigned to insure positive oil pickup when the engine was operating on a steep incline. After engine number 15466, the pan was lengthened to match the longer crankshaft and block. The oil level indicator was the same as that used on the 1934 V-8 engine.

Oil Filler Pipe and Cap

Located at the back of the block, just behind the valve cover, the oil filler pipe slanted forward away from the firewall. The cap had a copper filter element. Both pieces were painted black.

Fan Assembly

The small V-8 used the same 15¾ inch diameter fan that was used on the large 1937 passenger car V-8. The commercial cars used a radiator shroud for added cooling. In March 1937, the fan hub length was increased to four inches and the shroud on the commercial vehicles was eliminated.

Exhaust Manifold

Similiar to the heads, the left and right exhaust manifolds were designed to be interchangeable.

Carburetor

The small V-8 used the Stromberg small venturi, 13/16, carburetor which had been available on special order for the 1936 large V-8 engine. It was used through 1938.

Air Cleaner-Silencers

Two air cleaners were used for the small V-8, one produced by AC and the other by Burgess. From the outside both units looked alike, but the tunning chambers were different.

The Model B Engine

The 1932-34 four-cylinder engine was basically an improved Model A engine. Some of the major changes were the addition of a fuel pump and redesigned cylinder head,

A preproduction 1932 four cylinder engine.

oil pan, crankshaft, camshaft and water pump. Ford stopped producing the four-cylinder engine in March 1934, 26 years after its introduction in 1908.

Engine Specifications

Having a bore of 3.875 inches by 4.25 inches stroke, a displacement of 200.5 cubic inches and a compression ratio of 4.6 to one, the new four-cylinder engine was rated at 50 HP at 2800 RPM with a compression pressure of 90 pounds at 1500 RPM. Maximum torque produced was 127 pounds at 2800 RPM.

Engine Numbering

Similar to the Model A process, each engine was produced and assembled at the Rouge Plant. After assembly, each engine was moved to an engine break-in line where it was spun by an electric motor for a short break-in period. At the same time, it was checked for any oil or water leaks. Engines which passed the test were stamped with an engine number in sequential order. If an engine did not pass the test, it was sent to an adjoining shop for repair. After the engine was repaired, it was stamped with an engine number, and those engines which could not be repaired were scrapped.

Engine numbers were stamped on the flywheel housing directly over the starter motor instead of on the side of the block as was done on the Model A. Similar to the Model A and the V-8, all engine numbers were preceded by a star and terminated by a star. The engine numbers continued from the Model A numbers starting with 5,000,000. Engine numbers prior to 5,062,387 had a prefix of AB for passenger cars (*AB-5062386*) and ABB for trucks. Starting with engine number 5,062,387 the prefix was changed to B for passenger cars (*B-5062387*) and BB for trucks.

At the assembly plant, when the engine was dropped on the chassis, the engine number was also stamped on the top rail of the frame at the same locations as described for the V-8 engine.

Engine Color

The Ford engine green used on the Model A was continued in use on the Model B engine. It was used on all cast iron parts on the engine, flywheel housing, clutch housing, and transmission. The paint was applied after the parts were machined, but before assembly. Stamped steel parts were painted black and aluminum parts were left unpainted.

The Cylinder Block

The Model B block was a modified Model A block. Major changes were the addition of a boss on the side of the block for mounting the fuel pump, larger main bearings, and an improved lubrication system, which eliminated the exterior oil return tube.

Cylinder Front Cover

With the exception of a change in the location of the timing pin hole, the front cover for the Model B was a carry-over from the Model "A." The new location was 9½° higher.

Cylinder Head

An improved combustion chamber, providing a compression ratio of 4.6 to one, and an improved water outlet were the new features of the cylinder head for the Model B. For identification, it had a letter "C" cast on the top surface of the head. There was no Ford script cast on the head.

Crankshaft

The crankshaft was made from a steel forging similar to the Model A, but had larger main bearing areas and connecting rod bearing areas. Main bearings were 1.997 to 1.999 inches in diameter and the cranks were 1.872 to 1.874 inches in diameter. In November 1932, a new balanced crank with counter weights was put in production.

This was a running change and was not made at model changeover. The Model B engine identification was not changed.

Camshaft

This was similar to the Model A, except the Model "B" had a new cam profile to improve intake and exhaust.

Valve Chamber Cover

The valve chamber cover was modified, eliminating the oil return outlet. The cover was made of cast iron or cast magnesium.

Oil Pan

A stamped steel lower flywheel housing was added to the oil pan; otherwise it was identical to the Model A. It was painted black. The oil level indicator was a carry-over from Model A.

Oil Filler Pipe and Cap

The oil filler pipe and cap were a direct carry-over from the Model "A," but in May, 1932, both were redesigned. To improve ventilation, the pipe was increased in size and it had more baffles to reduce oil from splashing out. The new cap included a screen. The oil pipe was painted black, but the cap had two finishes: those made of plain steel were painted black and those made of terne plated steel were unfinished.

Water Pump and Fan

The water pump was a new design with a larger impeller and the housing included the water outlet connection. The fan, which mounted on the end of the water pump shaft, was the same two blade design as the Model "A" and two types were used. The Ford design was made of two pieces, sandwiched together and welded. On the Holly design, each blade was made from one piece which wrapped around the hub and extended part way up the opposite blade.

In May 1933, the two blade fan was discontinued and replaced with a 15½-inch diameter four bladed fan similar to the V-8 fan. All fan assemblies were painted black while the water pump castings were painted engine color.

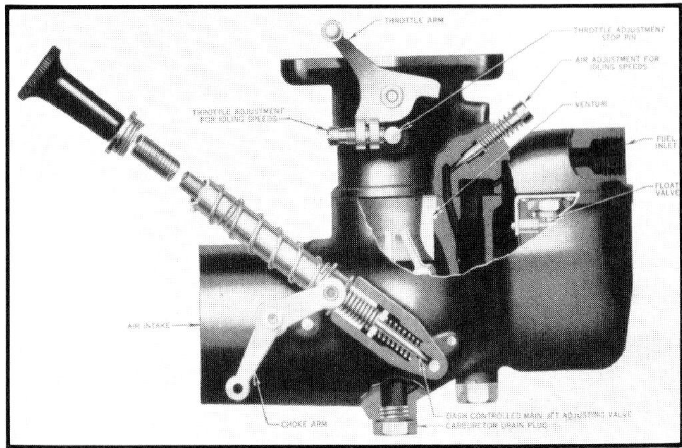

The four cylinder carburetor.

Carburetor and Air Cleaner-Silencer

The Model B carburetor was an improved and revised Zenith carburetor. The carburetor throat was made larger and the float chamber was changed.

The air cleaner and silencer were standard equipment on the passenger car engine. The assembly was made of a steel stamping with a silencer chamber and a thin filter screen. It was painted black with an oval decal stating, "Clean screen in gasoline every 4000 miles." This unit was used to the end of the four cylinder production.

In August 1932, the passenger car air cleaner was also released for use on commercial vehicles.

An oil bath air cleaner was released in June 1932. It was 6½ inches in diameter by 9¼ inches high and was mounted on the fire wall. A formed pipe and a rubber hose connected the air cleaner to the carburetor. The assembly was produced by United Specialties, and was painted black with a decal stating, "Caution, clean and refill with engine oil each time crankcase is drained." This air cleaner was released as special equipment for commercial vehicles in June 1932, and for passenger cars in September 1932.

1932-1938 V-8 ENGINE NUMBERS (Prefix 18)

Compiled by authors from original production log book

Month	First No.	Last No.
1932		
March	1	1,195
April	1,196	8,066
May	8,067	31,411
June	31,412	79,186
July	79,187	139,501
August	139,502	163,301
September	163,302	185,001
October	185,002	202,192
November	202,193	208,789
December	208,790	212,238
1933		
January	212,239	224,451
February	224,452	237,502
March	237,503	249,729
April	249,730	280,947
May	280,948	319,801
June	319,802	361,501
July	361,502	408,901
August	408,902	459,701
September	459,702	502,101
October	502,102	527,478
November	527,479	537,353
December	537,354	561,592
1934		
January	561,593	629,379
February	629,380	697,187
March	697,188	771,780
April	771,781	849,791
May	849,792	944,776
June	944,777	1,030,758

Month	First No.	Last No.
July	1,030,759	1,095,201
August	1,095,202	1,159,278
September	1,159,279	1,218,942
October	1,218,943	1,238,293
November	1,238,294	1,268,647
December	1,268,648	1,352,202
1935		
January	1,352,203	1,453,345
February	1,453,346	1,572,687
March	1,572,688	1,707,190
April	1,707,191	1,850,565
May	1,850,566	1,969,876
June	1,969,877	2,066,818
July	2,066,819	2,142,481
August	2,142,482	2,201,636
September	2,201,637	2,265,324
October	2,265,325	2,349,456
November	2,349,457	2,427,431
December	2,427,432	2,503,757
1936		
January	2,503,758	2,617,512
February	2,617,513	2,699,301
March	2,699,302	2,809,915
April	2,809,916	2,918,966
May	2,918,967	3,015,651
June	3,015,652	3,101,880
July	3,101,881	3,209,943

Month	First No.	Last No.
August	3,209,944	3,281,836
September	3,281,837	3,339,698
October	3,339,699	3,385,902
November	3,385,903	3,445,808
December	3,445,809	3,216,674
1937		
January	3,216,675	3,610,119
February	3,610,120	3,699,375
March	3,699,376	3,801,576
April	3,801,577	3,904,846
May	3,904,847	3,992,051
June	3,992,052	4,082,325
July	4,082,326	4,119,401
August	4,119,402	4,179,648
September	4,179,649	4,246,719
October	4,246,720	4,320,521
November	4,320,522	4,388,053
December	4,388,054	4,438,368
1938		
January	4,438,369	4,450,249
February	4,450,250	4,471,551
March	4,471,552	4,499,135
April	4,499,136	4,499,834
May	4,499,835	4,557,128
June	4,557,129	4,587,197
July	4,587,198	4,625,616
August	4,625,617	4,650,603

Artist's section drawing of an early V-8 engine. (Courtesy Ford Motor Company)

60 H.P. V-8 ENGINE NUMBERS (Prefix 54)

Compiled by authors from original production log book

Month	First No.	Last No.
1935 (For Overseas Use)		
July	1	20
August	21	584
September	585	890
October	891	2,099
November	2,100	2,475
December	2,476	3,250
1936		
January	3,251	5,218
February	5,219	6,253
March	6,254	6,601
(For U.S. Use)		
June	6,602*	7,879
July	7,880	15,467
August	15,468	17,801
September	17,807	29,298
October	29,299	47,764
November	47,765	67,205
December	67,206	89,920
1937		
January	89,921	116,033
February	116,034	145,996
March	145,997	185,705
April	187,706	219,457
May	229,458	260,782
June	260,783	299,759
July	299,760	320,341
August	320,342	351,663
September	351,664	385,923
October	385,924	422,514
November	422,515	456,028
December	456,029	468,894
1938		
January	468,895	469,014

*Engine production for domestic use was started in June, but car assembly was not started until October.

FOUR CYLINDER ENGINE NUMBERS (Prefix B)

Compiled by authors from original production log book

Month	First No.	Last No.
1931		
November 29th	5,000,000	5,000,015
December	5,000,016	5,001,863
1932		
January	5,001,864	5,013,187
February	5,013,188	5,032,500
March	5,032,501	5,049,492
April	5,049,493	5,064,906
May	5,064,907	5,087,732
June	5,087,733	5,132,621
July	5,132,622	5,144,010
August	5,144,011	5,146,668
September	5,146,669	5,157,918
October	5,157,919	5,165,401
November	5,165,402	5,175,635
December	5,175,636	5,179,579
1933		
January	5,179,580	5,187,129
February	5,187,130	5,192,755
March	5,192,756	5,203,772
April	5,203,773	5,208,842
May	5,208,843	5,216,030
June	5,216,031	5,227,763
July	5,227,764	5,234,547
August	5,234,548	5,241,341
September	5,241,342	5,245,552
October	5,245,553	5,248,333
November	5,248,334	5,249,669
December	5,249,670	5,263,534
1934		
January	5,263,535	5,267,507
February	5,267,508	5,275,064
March	5,275,065	5,277,589
April	5,277,590	5,285,357
May	5,285,358	5,287,403
June	5,287,404	5,288,942
July	5,288,943	5,290,174
August	5,290,175	5,292,536

Comparison of 85HP V-8 engine and 60HP V-8 engine.

IV—The Chassis, 1932–1938

The 1932 chassis that was designed during 1931 for the Model B was substantially a major face-lift of the Model A chassis. When Ford announced he would produce a V-8 engine, changes were made to accommodate both the V-8 and four cylinder engines and their respective drive lines. A new V-8 type chassis was developed for the 1933 cars which then became the basic V-8 passenger car chassis through 1938. Chassis with the four cylinder engine were identified as Model B and those with the V-8 engine as Model 18.

Frame

The frame is the foundation of the automobile. On it is mounted the body, power plant, drive line and all the com-

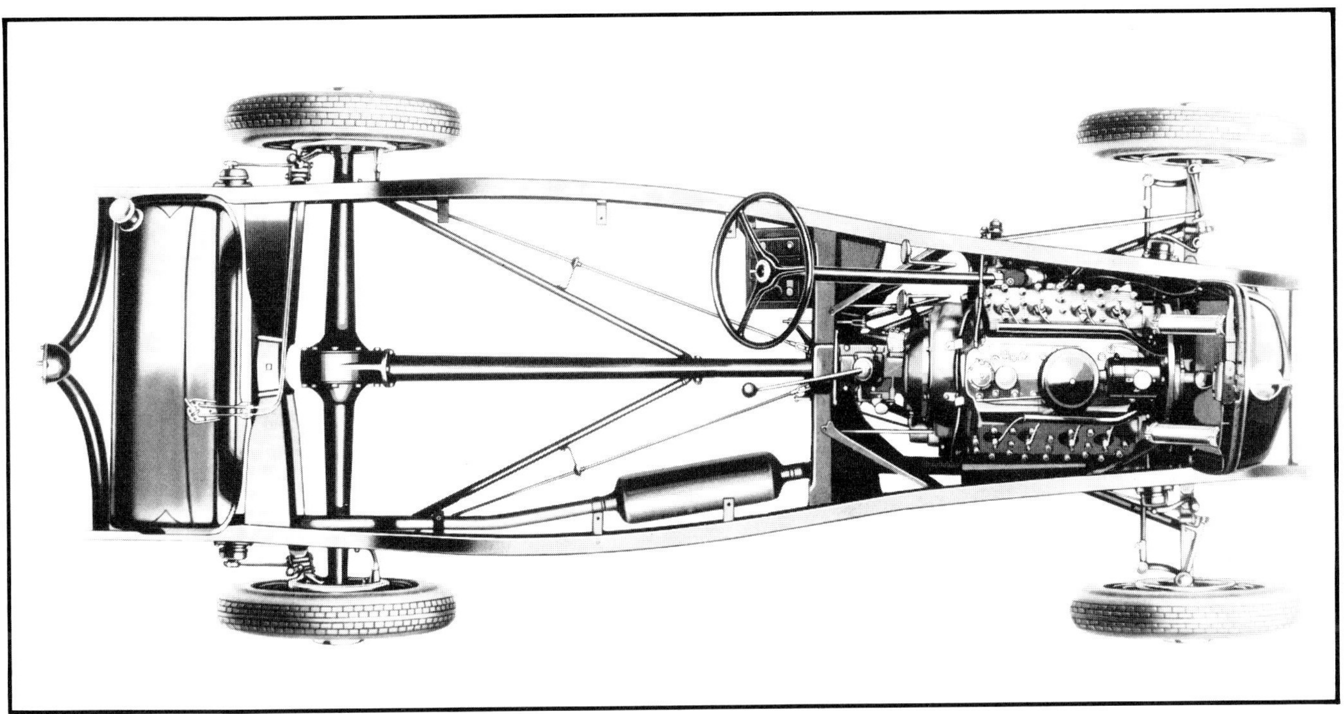

The 1932 chassis showing the ladder type frame similar to the Model "A".

This 1935 chassis was typical of the V-8 chassis, 1933 through 1938.

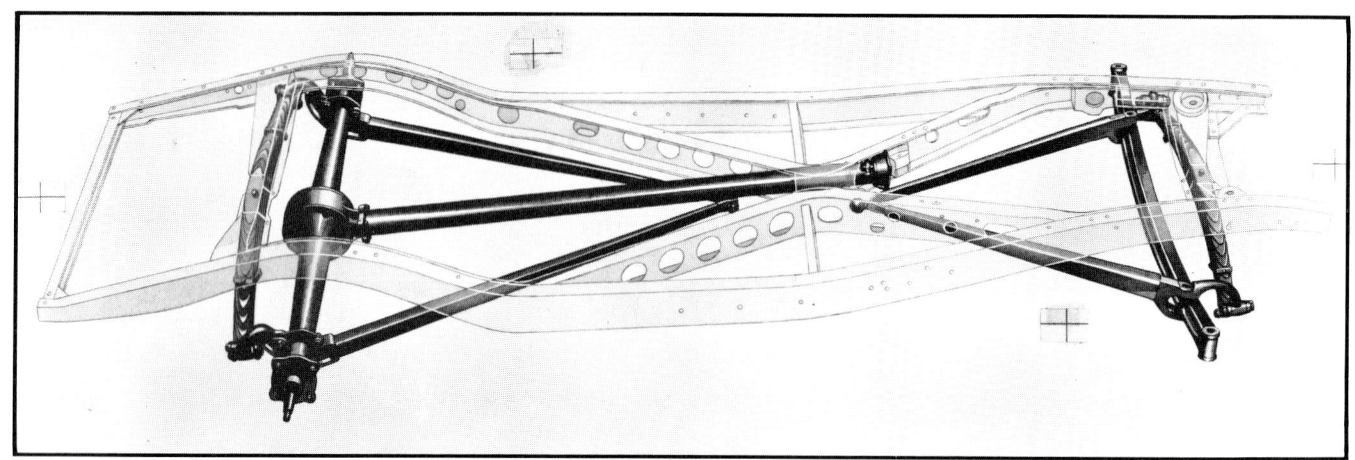

A retouched photograph illustrating the 1935 overhanging spring mounts. This arrangement gave the body a longer spring base than the wheel base and permitted lowering the springs.

ponents necessary to safely operate and stop the automobile.

The 1932 passenger and commercial frame was the ladder type consisting of two side rails connected by three crossmembers. After the first 600 units were produced, a brace was added to the front of the center crossmember, connecting diagonally to each side rail. This addition was also made to the 600 frames which had been produced previously. Frames manufactured before May 1932, had one of two types of front crossmembers, one for mounting the four cylinder engine and the other for mounting the V-8 engine. After May, the engine mounts and the crossmember were redesigned so that the same crossmember was used for accepting either engine.

During May, a reinforcement was added to the inside of the side rails at the rear crossmember area. This addition also reduced the length of the rear crossmember. A similar improvement was made by dealers to cars in the field when they were brought in for service. The spare wheel carrier was not part of the frame assembly, but it did add rigidity to the rear of the frame. On those models which had no spare wheel carrier, a special bar was installed in its place. When the engine was mounted on the frame at the assembly plants, the engine number was stamped on top of the left side rail as described in the engine section.

The rear engine support was a rubber ring molded to a metal bracket which mounted between the universal joint bearing retainer and the frame crossmember. The rubber specification was 40 durometer, 2500 PSI minimum tensile and 600% minimum elongation. In July 1932, it was changed to an all rubber part, but in January 1933, it was changed back to the rubber ring molded to a metal bracket. This unit was used through 1934.

For 1933 vehicles, a new frame with the "X" type center crossmember was introduced. This type of construction combined torsional strength with beam rigidity. Two frames were produced, one drilled for mounting passenger bodies and another drilled for mounting the commercial bodies. In March 1933, the front engine mount was modified to accommodate a new engine mount design. Also, in September 1933, a reinforcement was added to the front crossmember on commercial frames only.

The 1933 frame was a carryover for the 1934 vehicles until August when the front crossmember metal thickness was increased from 0.156 to 0.187 inch, thereby eliminating the necessity for the reinforcement on commercial frames.

Because of the mid-ship ride concept (moving the rear seat in front of the rear axle), the 1935 frame was completely new. The change placed the engine and transmission further forward. As a result, the "X" member was lengthened, while a reinforcement plate was added across the intersection of the "X." The rear end of the frame rails, which were previously open and connected with the spare wheel carrier, was connected with a new frame crossmember. There was also a minor difference between the passenger car frame and the commercial frame, in that the passenger car frame had two additional brackets on the side rail at the rear connection of the "X" member. The rear engine support was similar to 1934, but the metal bracket was changed to fit the new "X" member.

The next change occurred in April 1936, when the "X" crossmember was redesigned and made shorter.

Models for 1937 had five variations of the frame. Two frames were classified as "light" and the other three were classified as "heavy." One of the light frames was used on passenger cars with the new 60 H.P. V-8 engine, while the other light frame appeared on Tudor, Fordor and Coupe style bodies using the 85 H.P. V-8 engines. Of the heavy frames, one was used on all other passenger cars with the

Assembly line at the Dearborn Assembly plant. Note the canvas guard over the frame side rail to keep it from being scratched.

85 H.P. V-8 engine, the second was used on all commercial vehicles with the 60 H.P. V-8 engine, and the third on all commercial vehicles with the 85 H.P. V-8 engine. In September 1937, the holes for mounting the shock absorbers were changed from round to square. All of these frame combinations were used through the end of the 1938 production.

The rear engine support was also redesigned for 1937. The engine support bracket became part of the frame crossmember and utilized an insulator on each side similar to the front engine support. All frames, 1932 through 1938, were painted black.

Wheels, Hub Caps, and Tires

The 1932 wheel was the steel spoke type with 32 spokes, a 3.25-inch wide rim by 18-inch diameter and a 5¼-inch diameter mounting bolt circle. The standard tire size was 5.25 × 18, black. Wheels on the standard models and commercial vehicles were painted black. On deluxe models they were painted black or to match or complement the stripe color. The same steel spoke wheel design, with changes only in the rim diameter, was used on all passenger cars and commercial vehicles through 1935. For each of these years, the wheels were painted black on the standard and commercial vehicles, but painted to match or complement the stripe color on the deluxe vehicles.

The 1932 size wheel and tire was available as special equipment through 1935 to provide greater road clearance if desired.

In April 1934, a chrome-plated wheel was released on special order at extra cost. By July 1934, the use of the deluxe wheel color was extended to include the Sedan delivery.

Wheel size for 1933 and 1934 was reduced to 17 inches. The tire size was 5.50 × 17, four ply with black side wall. In 1935, the rim diameter was reduced to 16 inches and the rim width was increased to 3½ inches. Tire size was 600 × 16, four-ply black side wall.

A six-ply tire while standard on the Station Wagon, was also available on special order for other models, 1933 through 1935.

In 1932, the spare tire was not installed at the factory, but installed by the dealer at extra cost. As a result, the spare tire was not always the same make as the other four tires. Beginning in July 1933, however, spare tires were installed at the assembly plants on all passenger cars.

White wall tires for 1932 cars were available only from the dealer as an accessory. However, beginning with the 1933 cars, white wall tires became available as a factory installation for the first time.

Beginning with March 1934, an attempt was made at wheel balancing at the assembly plant. After the tube and tire were assembled on the wheel, the unit was checked for balance. The operator then hand-stamped a letter "L" on the tire casing near the outer wheel rim, indicating the lightest point of the assembly. This mark was matched to the heavy point on the drum when the wheel was mounted to the chassis.

The hub caps for the 1932–35 wheels were all the same size, 6¾-inch diameter. They were made of rustless steel, spherical shaped with the Ford or V-8 symbol in the center. Two hub caps were used, one for chassis with the four cylinder engine (Model B) and the other for chassis with the V-8 engine (Model 18).

On the 1932 four cylinder chassis, the hub cap had the oval with the Ford script trade mark stamped in the center. The outer rim of the oval and the Ford name were painted Corporate blue (also called Harding blue). Three circles formed by a slight step were around the oval. This cap was used through the end of the 1933 production. For the 1934 models, the hub cap was simplified by reducing the number of rings to one. This cap was used until the end of the four cylinder production.

The 1932 hub cap for the V-8 chassis was similar to the four cylinder but had an embossed V-8 symbol in the center within a 2¾-inch flat area which was painted Corporate

The 1932 steel spoke wheel with the rustless steel V-8 hub cap.

The 1934 wheel and hub cap. The depressed V-8 symbol was painted Corporate blue.

blue. For the 1933 chassis, the V-8 symbol was restyled and made larger, while the center circle background was reduced to 2¾ inches, so that it was smaller than the V-8 symbol.

Five hub caps were installed on each vehicle, including one for the spare wheel. Starting in July 1933, the spare tire cover and locking cap were installed at the factory as standard equipment, and the fifth hub cap was no longer provided.

Hub caps for the 1934 V-8 chassis were identical to the four cylinder, except that the center was stamped with a new style V-8 symbol and the center circle was eliminated. The depressed part of the symbol was painted Corporate blue. For 1935, the V-8 symbol was redesigned larger and again enclosed within a circle. However, the Corporate blue color was only within the inside of the number eight.

With the end of the 1935 model, Ford departed from the steel spoke wheel and adopted the stamped metal spider wheel. In addition, the wheel mounting bolt circle was increased to 10¼-inch diameter. The wheel rim diameter for 1936 remained the same at 16 inches, but the width was increased to four inches. The standard tire was 600 × 16, four ply, with black side wall. White walls were available at extra cost. As a sales incentive at model introduction, 50% of the first 1000 deluxe passenger cars were equipped with white wall tires at the factory.

Wheel color for the standard and commercial vehicles was black. Deluxe models had wheels painted to match the body color.

A chrome-plated wheel was available as special equipment until April 1936, when it was obsoleted by the introduction of a full stainless steel wheel cover which covered the wheel spider.

An 18-inch wheel with a 3.62-inch width rim was also released in January 1936 for customers who desired additional road clearance. This wheel was available through 1938.

In July 1936, as a cost saving measure, the tire size on all standard model passenger cars was changed to 5.50 × 16, 4 ply, with black side wall. White wall tires of this size were not available.

The 1936 wheel was used through 1938 on all chassis with the 85 HP engine.

With the introduction of the new 60 HP V-8 engine, a new wheel size was put in production. Chassis with this engine were equipped with a 16-inch diameter wheel with a 3.50-inch wide rim. Standard tires for this chassis were 600 × 16, four ply, with black side walls. The wheel with the 3.50-inch width rim was used until June 1938, when it was replaced with the 85 HP chassis wheel.

Beginning in March 1937, tire sizes for the 85 HP chassis were changed to 600 × 16, six ply, for all passenger cars and commercial vehicles, except Station Wagons which used a 6.50 × 16, six ply tire.

In August 1937, tire specifications were revised for both chassis. The 85 HP chassis was equipped with four ply tires, but the Station Wagon used 600 × 16, six ply tires. The 60 HP chassis was equipped with 550 × 16 four ply tires. White wall tires were not available in the 550 × 16 size.

A 15-inch wheel with 5.5-inch wide rim was released in 1937 for use with the new super balloon tires.

Hub caps for the 1936–38 cars were made from two parts, an inner ring which snapped on the wheel spider and an outer center cap that fastened to the inner ring. The ring was a sheet steel stamping painted the body color. The rustless steel center cap was approximately 7⅝ inches in diameter.

For 1936, a new modernized V-8 symbol was stamped in the center within a 5¾-inch diameter circle. The V-8 symbol was painted the body color. On the 1937 center cap, the V-8 symbol was embossed and the surface within the circle was painted the body color. Two hub caps were used for the 1938 cars, one for the standard and the other for the deluxe cars. On the standard models the center cap was again changed. The circle was eliminated and the V-8 symbol was restyled to a seven-inch size. It was stamped on the surface of the cap and painted the body color. The deluxe center cap was different, however, in that it was larger with a 10-inch diameter.

An accessory cap was also available for the 1936–38 wheel. Beginning with the 1936 models, the ring portion of the cap was available as chrome plated rather than body color. However, this part was obsoleted in April 1936 when a full spider rustless steel hub cap was released. Introduction of this new accessory also terminated production of the chrome-plated wheel which had been available since 1934. The full spider cap was produced through 1938.

Spare Tire Covers and Locks

There was a variety of spare tire covers produced during the 1932 to 1936 period, and all but one were the metal type. Their style was similar, but the size changed from year to year in order to fit the changing wheel and tire sizes. Since the spare tire was not installed at the factory until July 1933, the tire covers were an accessory item. After that date, the metal tire cover became standard equipment for 1933 and 1934 passenger cars.

With the introduction of the cars in 1932, there were four tire covers available. The simplest one was made of black fabric with a rustless steel moulding trim. On its side wall, it had the Ford script and oval trade mark. The inside of

Front end of a 1936 standard model. Ford abandoned the 1935 steel spoke wheels and adopted stamped metal spider type wheels.

the oval was Corporate blue, while the Ford script and the double line around the oval were silver. This fabric cover was phased out in July 1933. The other three covers were made of metal and painted black. One cover had two pieces of rustless steel mouldings, one on the outer circumference and the other at the inner edge. This cover was obsoleted in May 1932. Of the other two covers, one had the outer ring made of rustless steel while the other had a chrome plated outer ring. Both of these were obsoleted in April 1932. A new steel cover was introduced in May 1932. It was all black with a rustless steel moulding in the center of the side wall area. However, starting in December 1933, it was painted the body color. This style of cover was used until the end of 1935 production, changing only in size.

Spare tire lock bands and locking caps were also available during the 1932 to 1936 period. The first locking band for 1932 was a simple design consisting of a black steel strap and a nickel-plated lock with a rustless steel bezel. This was obsoleted in May 1932 and replaced with a similar steel strap plus the addition of a spare wheel locking hub cap. Two locking hub caps were produced, one for the V-8 and the other for the four-cylinder chassis. The locking caps for both chassis were made of rustless steel and were designed to match the wheel hub caps. The four cylinder chassis locking cap was used until January 1934. However, the V-8 chassis locking cap was used only through the end of 1932 production.

For the 1933 V-8 chassis, the spare wheel locking cap was changed to match the 1933 hub caps.

By 1934, both the four cylinder and the V-8 chassis used the same type of locking cap. In the center of the cap there was a large oval plate which concealed the lock. The Ford script, painted Corporate blue was stamped on the plate. This cap was used to the end of 1935 production.

The locking band was also available with or without the spare wheel cover. The metal strap was made of case hardened steel, painted black.

Starting with the 1935 models, the Company implemented a new policy for spare tire covers. The tire cover, locking cap, and locking band were special equipment and available at extra cost. However, these items were part of a basic accessory group including front and rear bumpers and a set of four bumper guards. They were installed at the factory on all cars at extra cost to the customer.

This 1934 spare tire cover and lock band was typical through 1936.

Two locking caps were used in 1935, one for passenger cars and one for commercials with the side mounted spare. The difference was in the location of the slot for the locking band. On the passenger cars it was on center below the Ford script, but on the commercial cap the slot was 40° off center.

With the introduction of the new disc wheels for 1936, a new metal tire cover was used. It was a deep dished full face cover with a hinged rustless steel cap concealing the lock assembly. The cap was stamped with the Ford script and oval and a three-inch diameter circle, all painted Corporate blue. A rustless steel moulding ring was located at the center of the side wall area.

In July 1936, a new shallow dished full face cover was introduced with a rustless steel moulding, 10¼ inches in diameter, which gave the center a hub cap effect. The center had a rustless steel oval Ford script cover concealing the tire lock. This cover was designated for use on the standard passenger cars only.

A larger version of the deluxe cover was also available for the Sedan Delivery and Station Wagon. After 1936, the tire cover was only used on commercial vehicles with side mounted spare tires.

The Brake System

The 1932 through 1938 passenger cars and commercial vehicles were equipped with the Ford mechanical brake system. From 1932 through 1936 rods were used to activate all four wheels, but cables were used during 1937 and 1938. The emergency brake lever also activated the brakes at all four wheels.

The front and rear hub and drum assemblies were basically the same for 1932, '33, and '34 models. The drum was made of malleable cast iron and the hub was made of an alloy cast iron. In March 1934, a notch was added to the outside flange of the front drum designating the heaviest point of the drum assembly. When the wheel and tire were installed at the assembly line, the letter "L" marked on the tire to designate the lightest point, was lined up with the notch on the drum (see wheel and tire description). This was the first attempt at balancing the front wheels at the factory.

For 1935 production, new hub and drum assemblies were designed. Two types were used on the rear. One was a two-piece malleable iron casting, while the other was a one-piece hub and drum steel casting. The front hub and drum was a one-piece casting made of either malleable iron or cast steel. These drums had openings between the mounting bolt holes to reduce weight and provide cooling.

The hub and drum for 1936 were similar to the 1935 style, but were modified to fit the larger mounting bolt circle of the new disc wheel. The front units had two variations. The first was a one-piece casting made of malleable iron, and the other was a two-piece design with a solid cast steel hub and gray iron cast drum. There were five variations for the rear wheels, two of which were obsoleted in the first month of production. The two designs used most were a one-piece cast steel, and a two-piece with a cast

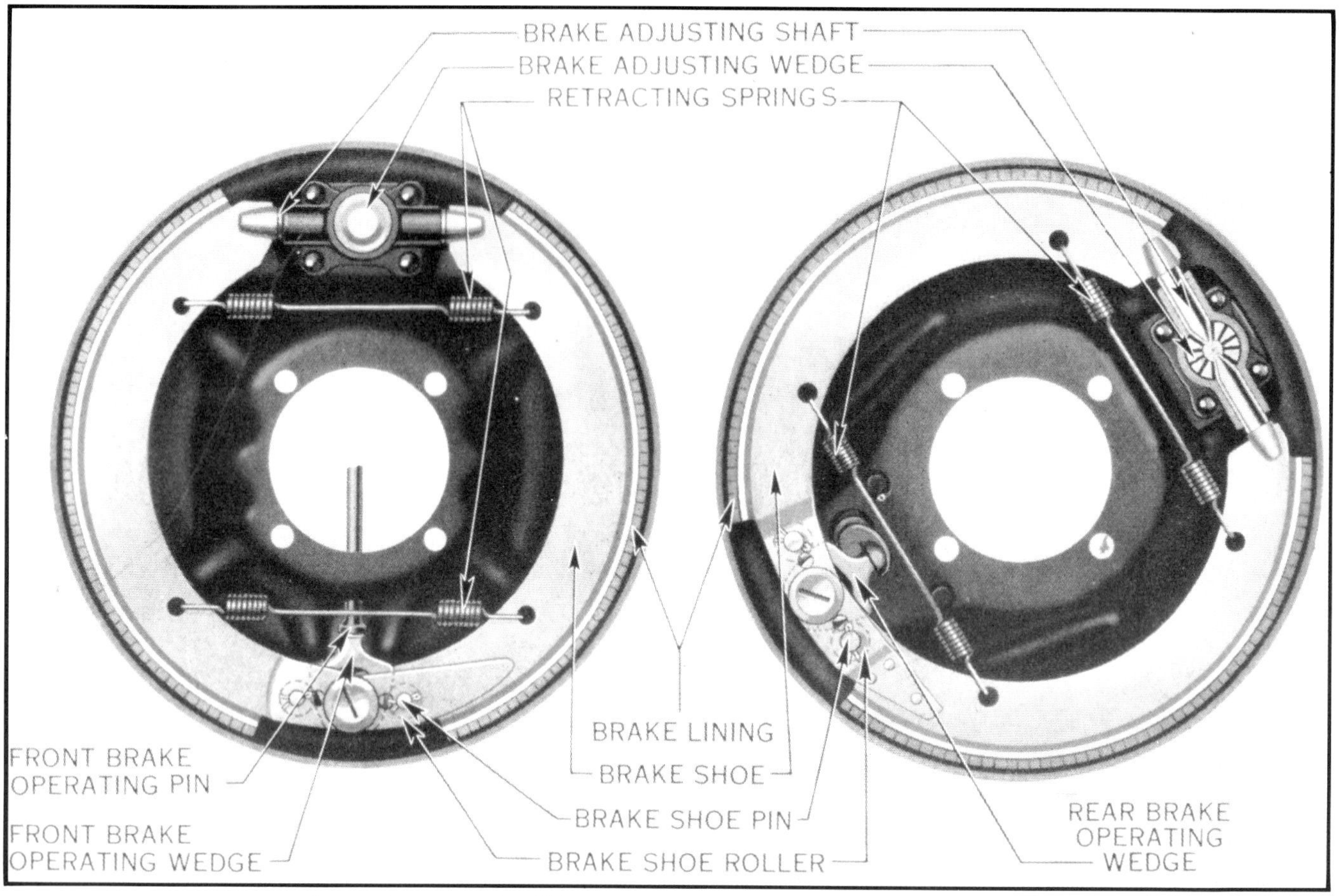

Service illustration identifying the various components of the 1934 brakes.

steel hub and a cast gray iron drum. These drums had a pressed steel bearing sleeve and used a new $2\frac{13}{16}$-inch diameter roller bearing. The former design drums with the $3\frac{3}{16}$-inch diameter bearing were phased out. The fifth design, which had an integral bearing race (no sleeve), was used on a limited basis starting in June 1936.

In February, the backing plate and drums were modified by adding a lip to the outer edge of the backing plate which matched a groove cut on the edge of the drum. This development provided a better dust and water seal for the brake shoes. A careful phasing out of old stock had to be implemented at the assembly plants to assure that the new drums were not used with the old style backing plates which, of course, would cause interference.

Balancing weights were added to the two-piece drum starting in June 1937. At the same time the one-piece drum was obsoleted.

The 1937 drums were a carryover into 1938 along with an additional option of drums with forged hubs. Rear hubs with and without the pressed steel bearing sleeve were used with the $2\frac{13}{16}$-inch diameter bearing.

The brake assembly, backing plate, shoe and lining, springs, etc., changed along the same pattern as the hub and drum assembly. It was the single action internal expansion type.

The 1932 design was used through the 1934 production. Two types of lining used, a woven asbestos with zinc wire and a hard rubber compound with brass wire. However, they were not mixed. The same type was used on all four wheels of any vehicle. In May 1932, the backing plate

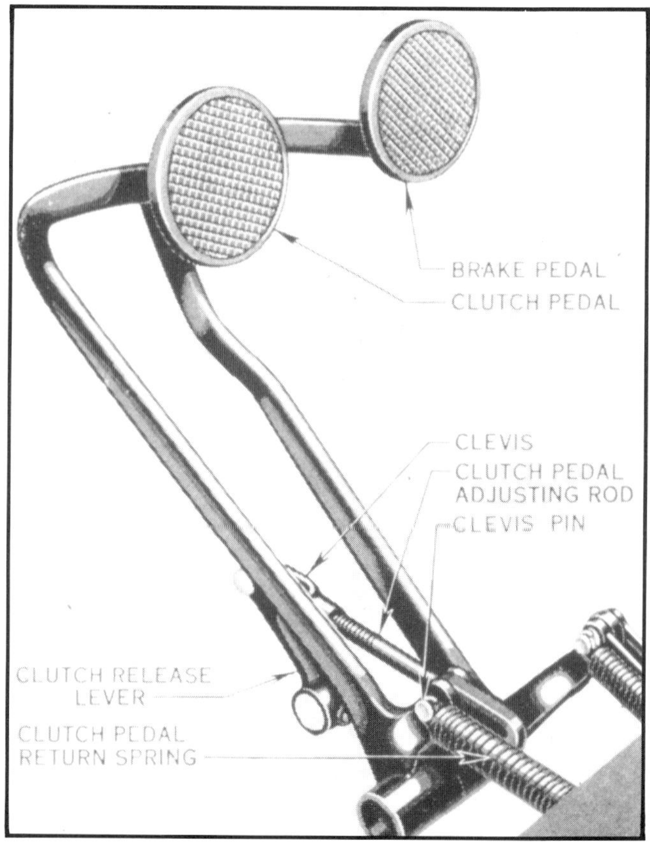

The 1932 brake and clutch pedal assembly.

thickness was increased. As old stock was phased out, the new thicker backing plates were used on the V-8 chassis, whereas the old plates were used on the Model B chassis.

Brakes for the 1935 models were made stronger and the braking area was increased. The linings were ¼-inch wider and thicker. This change was used through the 1936 production.

Additional improvements were made in the brakes for 1937. Ford adopted the self-energizing design and used steel cables instead of rods to actuate the brakes. In addition, two types of lining were used on each wheel. A woven asbestos with brass wire was used on the primary shoe, while a woven asbestos with zinc wire was used on the secondary shoe. In May 1937, a phenolic asbestos molded lining was released as optional on both primary and secondary shoes. No other changes were made for 1938, other than the instruction that the molded lining should be used with the cast steel drums, while a molded primary and woven secondary was to be used with the cast iron drums.

The brake pedals for all models 1932 through 1938 were made of forged steel and painted black. The first design did not provide a lubrication fitting. This was corrected in April 1932, with instructions to drill and tap all original parts on hand. In May 1932, the pedal was redesigned by lowering the pedal pad location ⅜-inch in order to standardize the Model B and V-8 chassis parts. Minor changes were also made in May 1933 in pad mounting, while the metal thickness was increased in August 1933. There were no further changes through the end of the 1934 production.

For 1935, the pedal was slightly modified in size and shape. This was used until August 1936, when the length of the pedal pad shank was increased 1¼ inches, moving the pedal closer to the driver.

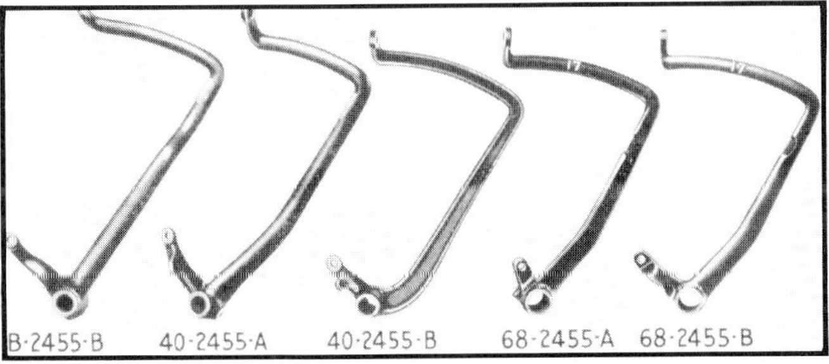

Brake pedals identification drawing, 1932 through 1937. The 1935 pedal 48-2455-A is not shown.

The 1937–38 pedal was a new design with a slight change in shape and mounting shank.

The brake and clutch pedal pads were identical for all vehicles from 1932 through 1938. The initial design was a two-piece unit consisting of a round plate with a mounting stud in the center. A rubber pad three inches in diameter with a ⅝-inch diameter pyramid pattern in the center was molded to the two pieces. In May 1933, the pedal was changed to a one-piece metal stamping with the same rubber moulding.

The hand brake lever for 1932 through 1934 was a carryover of the Model A lever. It was a straight piece with satin chrome finish on the shaft and bright chrome finish on the hand grip area.

Starting with the 1935 production, the hand grip area was bent forward and the plating was changed from chrome to nickel, with satin finish on the shaft and bright nickel on the hand grip areas. By November 1935, the finish on the shaft was changed to Benton gray paint, and in December, the nickel plating was totally obsoleted as the entire lever was painted Benton gray. Beginning in June 1936, and continuing to the end of 1936 production, there were three methods of finishing the lever. For the standard models: Tudor, Tudor Touring, Fordor, Fordor Touring, five window Coupe, Sedan Delivery, and Panel Delivery, the lever was painted black. For the deluxe models: Tudor, Tudor Touring, Roadster, three window Coupe, Fordor, Fordor Touring, Fordor Convertible, Phaeton, Cabriolet, five window Coupe, and Station Wagon, the lever was painted brown to match the grained interior trim. All other commercial vehicles continued to use the Benton gray painted lever.

With the introduction of the 1937 models, the hand brake lever was changed from a floor mounting to dash mounting. The new short lever was mounted under the dash on the left side of the vehicle. A cable transferred the action from the handle to the brake cross shaft. On standard passenger cars and commercial vehicles, the lever was painted black. But on the deluxe passenger cars, it became Rustic brown. For 1938, the lever color was changed to Zephyr beige for all passenger cars, while the commercial vehicles retained the black.

Front Axle

The front axle group consists of the axle, spindles, and the spindle connecting rod assembly. The 1932 axle was similar to the Model A, but had a much deeper arch in the center. The same style axle was used through 1938 with minor modifications in 1935 and 1937.

The 1932 spindle was used through 1934, except for a minor change in August 1934, reducing the lubrication fitting hole size. After 1934, the spindles were modified each year and, consequently, are not interchangeable.

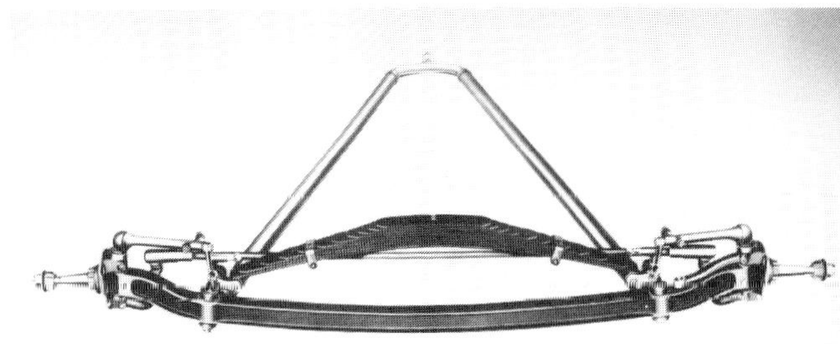

Service illustration of the 1932-34 front axle assembly.

The spindle connecting rod assembly (tie rod), which was a carryover from the Model A, was used through 1934. It consisted of a rod with adjustable sockets at each end. These sockets were attached to a ball at the end of each spindle arm. The design was changed in 1935 when the ends of the connecting rod were fitted with a ball stud and socket assembly. The studs were attached to a hole in the spindle arm. This new combination was used through 1938.

In March 1937, optional Thompson Products connecting rod ends were introduced. These units provided both lower steering effort and less wear. By February 1938, the Ford design rod ends were phased out as the Thompson Products units were used on all passenger car chassis.

The steering drag link for 1932 through 1934 was iden-

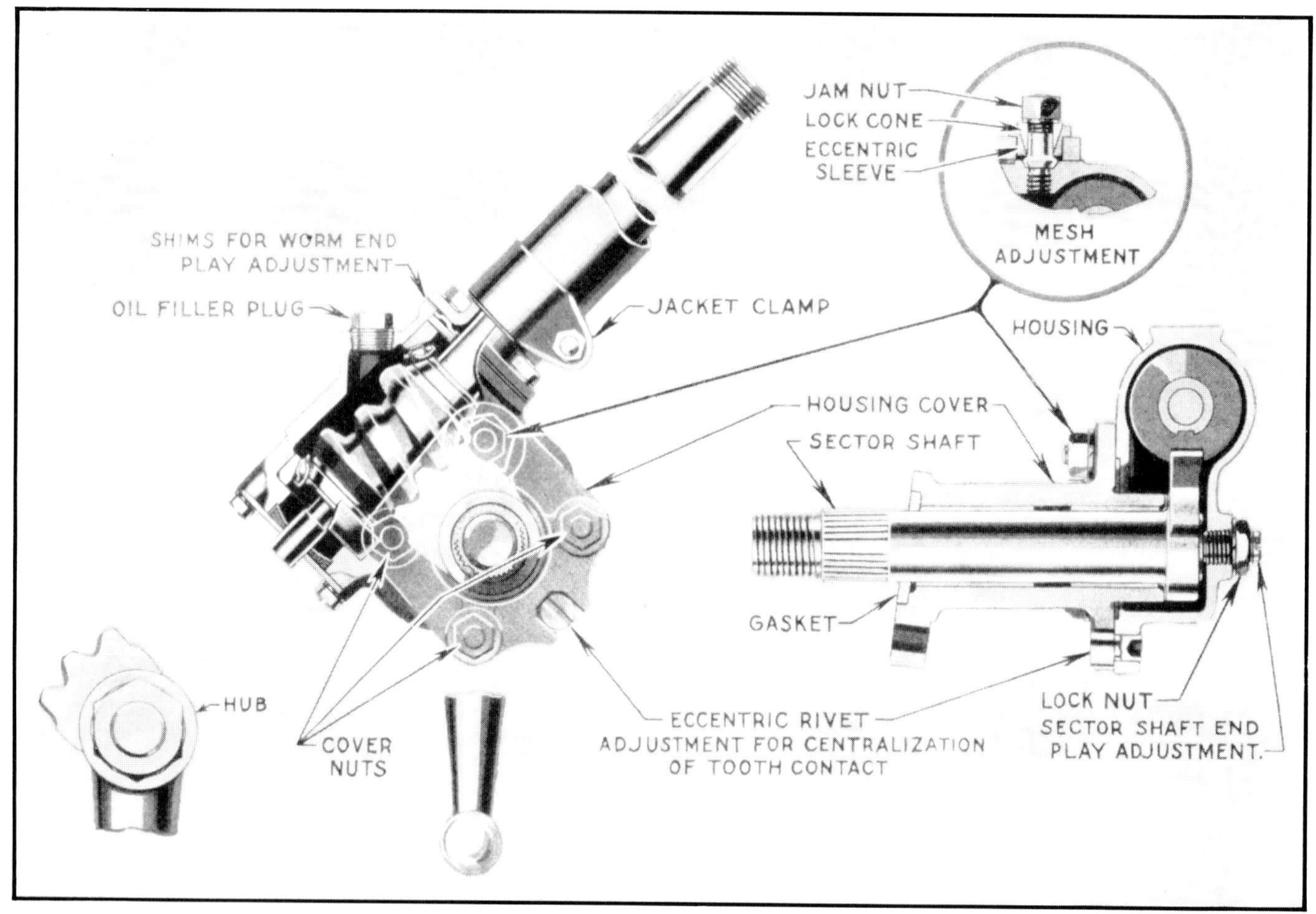

Cut-away illustration showing the various components of the 1932 steering gear.

tical to the Model A, except for length difference. The big change was made in 1935 when the steering gear assembly was changed from a horizontal shaft design to the vertical shaft with a transverse steering linkage.

Steering Gear and Column

Two steering gear assemblies were used with the beginning of 1932 production, one for passenger cars and the other for commercial vehicles. Both were the worm and sector type with a 15 to 1 gear ratio, but each had a different mounting angle. In July 1932, the mounting holes on the frame were elongated to allow the passenger car steering gear to be used on the commercial vehicles. Consequently, the commerical unit was obsoleted.

A new steering gear was designed for the 1933 cars and commercials. The gear ratio was reduced to 13 to 1 and a new sealing method was used at the lower end of the gear housing. The cork seal previously used was replaced by a metal plate which had a tube that extended up through the center of the steering shaft to a point above the lubricant. The lower ratio resulted in stiffer steering effort, so the gear ratio was changed back to 15 to 1 in August 1933. The new worm and sector, however, were interchangeable with the previous design. These new parts were stamped with the number "15" for identification. In addition, there was a difference in the column lock between the passenger and commercial steering gear assembly.

The steering gear used on the 1935 models was completely new. It mounted so that the sector shaft was vertical rather than horizontal. Prior to 1935, all steering gear and column assemblies were painted black. Starting with 1935 production, these assemblies were painted black on the standard model passenger cars and commercials and a taupe color on the deluxe passenger cars. In March 1935, to reduce the amount of play, a minor change of two degrees was made in the location of the splines of the steering worm in relation to the steering shaft. This was deemed necessary to reduce road shock transmitted through the steering gear. To identify these units, either a chisel mark was made on the end of the sector shaft or a slotted nut and cotter pin was used to hold the arm.

The steering ratio was increased to 17 to 1 for 1936, and needle bearings were used on the sector shaft to provide almost frictionless movement. On the standard models and commercials the columns were painted black, while on deluxe models, the columns became Benton gray. In June 1936, the Benton gray was changed to brown to match the new wood grain instrument panel.

For 1937 models, the ratio was increased to 18.2 to 1 and the sector shaft needle bearings were changed to bushings. Column color for the deluxe model was changed to Rustic brown. On 1938 models, the column size was increased and the color for deluxe cars became Zephyr beige.

A new theft-proof locking system was developed for the 1932 cars. The ignition switch and steering lock were combined into the steering column bracket. To operate the system, the switch at the top of the bracket was pushed to the off position. This opened the ignition circuit and shut off

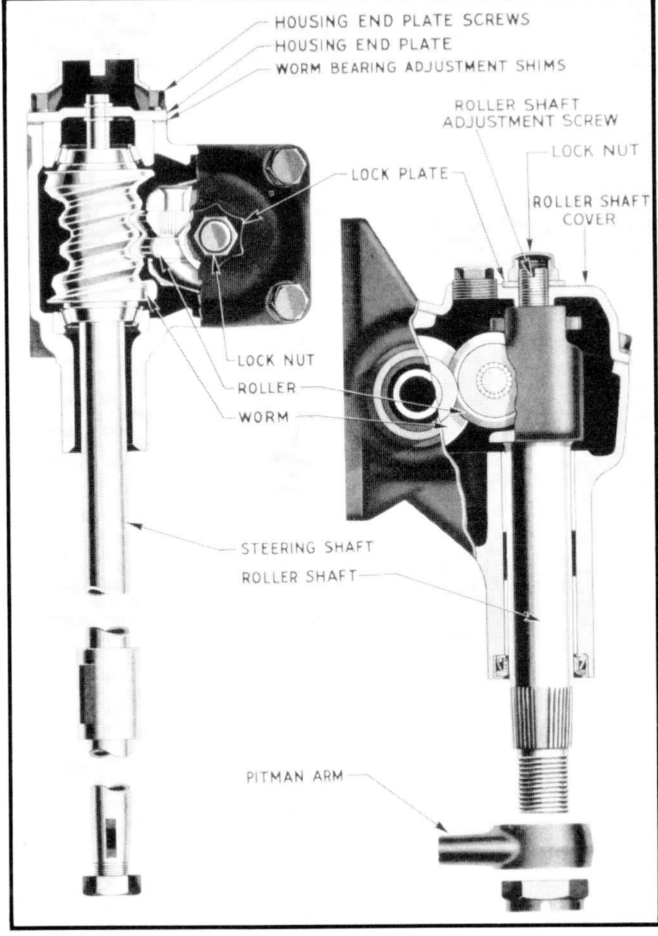

The worm and roller steering gear used in 1937.

the engine. The key was then turned in a counterclockwise direction compressing a spring behind the lock bolt. This action forced the bolt toward the steering column to engage a slot in a sleeve on the steering shaft. The steering shaft could be locked with the front wheels in a straight ahead position or turned full right or left. If the steering shaft were not in any of these positions, the compressed spring behind the bolt would force it to engage automatically when the steering wheel was turned. "Twist off screws" were used for clamping the locking unit to the steering column.

The lock switch was located between the steering column and the dash, with the lock cylinder on the right side. Its on-off plate was made of a nickel-silver alloy with a bright edge and the letters ON and OFF in bright finish against a black enamel background. The round, flat lock switch level was a bright nickel-plated zinc die casting. In June 1932, the lever's shape was changed to oval.

For 1933 and 1934, the steering column bracket and lock assembly was designed into an "L" shape with the lock unit on the right side of the column. The lever operated from front to rear instead of side to side, and the on-off plate was changed to fasten along side of the lever. The off position was forward, while on was to the back.

In May 1933, as an improved theft protection measure, a "twist off head" screw was used to fasten one side of the steering lock unit to the belt rail finish panel.

On the 1935 through 1937 models, the lock remained the same. However, the shape of the lock control plate was changed to oval with the lever in the center and the off position forward. The plate was made of aluminum with brightly polished borders and letters on a black gloss background. In January 1935, the lock plunger hole was elongated to reduce the chance of the key sticking in the lock. Starting with the 1937 production, the off-on position was changed. The off was back and the on was forward.

The steering column bracket and lock assembly was redesigned for 1938. The lock and ignition switch were again placed between the steering column and the dash similar to the location in 1932. The lock switch lever was "L" shaped on the passenger cars, but the same as the 1932 on commercial vehicles and trucks. The on-off letters on the switch plate read vertically rather than horizontally.

The steering column bracket and lock housing was painted to match the steering column color on all years.

Steering Wheel

The steering wheel for 1932 was 17 inches in diameter and had three spokes. It was made of hard black rubber molded over a steel core. The rubber was polished and buffed. There were two constructions of the rim, although both looked the same. One had a solid steel core and the other had a steel tube core. The light switch and horn button were located in the hub of the wheel. The light switch had one ear toward the driver for turning the lights on or off. It was made of zinc die cast and was bright chrome plated. A black hard rubber horn button was in the center within a bezel made of chrome-plated brass or cold rolled steel.

For 1933 and 1934 passenger cars and commercial units, the steering wheel was restyled in the center hub and spokes area. The light switch ring and horn button were larger and made of black plastic. There were two ears on the light switch ring for easier operation.

In 1935, the steering wheel was finished in two colors, black for the standard passenger cars and commercial units and taupe on the deluxe models. The light switch and horn button were finished to match the steering wheel. Also, the V-8 symbol was added to the horn button.

A 1934 steering wheel.

The 1935-36 steering wheel.

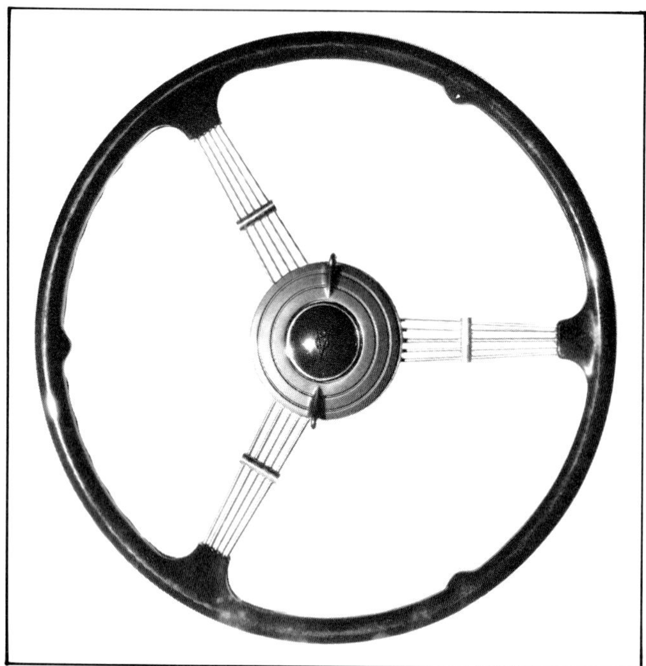

The 1936 deluxe steering wheel.

The 1935 steering wheel was continued into 1936 with black for the standard models and commercials, but the deluxe wheel color was changed to Benton Gray. However, in June 1936, the Benton Gray deluxe wheel was phased out as a new deluxe wheel was released. The new design (referred to as the "banjo wheel") was first introduced as an accessory. It was 17 inches in diameter with three spokes. Each spoke was made up of five $\frac{9}{64}$-inch diameter rustless steel rods supported by a $\frac{3}{8}$-inch diameter rustless steel bar. The spokes were molded to a reinforced hard rubber wheel and a zinc die cast hub. Both the hub and the wheel were painted Rustic brown to harmonize with the new wood grain interior trim on the deluxe passenger cars.

The light switch and horn button for the 1936 wheel was a carryover of the 1935 design, with colors to match the wheel. On the new deluxe (banjo type) wheel, the light switch was a flat zinc die cast ring with two equally spaced steps. The horn button was dome-shaped with a new stylized V-8 symbol.

With the beginning of 1937 production cars, three steering wheels were used. Two wheels, made of reinforced hard rubber, were a carry-over of the 1936 design. The one painted black was used on standard cars and commercials, while the Rustic brown one was used on the deluxe cars. The banjo style wheel, designated as special equipment, was available on deluxe cars at added cost. However, by February 1937, the banjo style wheel again became standard equipment on the deluxe cars. The light switch and horn button on the 1937 banjo style wheel was modified, however. The light switch ring became dome-shaped and the ears were rounded at the tips. The horn button was also dome-shaped with a new stylized V-8 symbol.

For 1938, the factory wheel color was changed to Zephyr beige for the standard cars and black for commercial vehicles. The banjo style deluxe wheel was restyled at the hub and the banjo type spokes were fanned out at the hub. The light switch ring and the horn button were also slightly restyled.

Rear Axle and Drive Shaft Assembly

Ford vehicles were equipped with a $\frac{3}{4}$ floating rear axle and torque tube drive system. In this arrangement, the vehicle load and road shock is placed on the axle housing, with the axle shaft used only to transmit torque to the wheels. The driving thrust is transmitted directly to the frame cross member by the torque tube and radius rods. With the torque tube system, there is no rear axle twist resulting from sudden braking or fast acceleration. And, since the torque tube pivots at the same point on the frame as the brake cross shaft, the function of the brake rods is not affected by rear axle movement or the size of load placed on the vehicle.

Two axles were released with the initial introduction of the 1932 passenger cars and commercial vehicles. One, with a 3.78 to one gear ratio (34 teeth ring and 9 teeth pinion) was used on the four cylinder Model B chassis. The other, a 4.33 to one gear ratio (39 teeth on the ring and 9 teeth on the pinion) was used on the V-8 Model 18 chassis.

In May 1932, a third axle was introduced. It had a 4.11 to one gear ratio with 37 teeth on the ring and 9 teeth on the pinion. This new axle was designated for use on all B chassis with closed passenger bodies. The original 3.78 to one ratio axle continued in use on B chassis with open bodies and commercials until stock was exhausted.

An improved axle design with 4.11 to one ratio was introduced in September 1932 for use on both the Model B and V-8 chassis. The new axle featured the straddle pinion mounting with bearings in front and back of the drive pinion. This axle design was continued into the 1933 production. However, due to a new design of the V-8 transmision, the V-8 chassis had a longer torque tube by about $1\frac{3}{4}$ inches. In April 1933, the inside diameter of the torque tube flange end was increased slightly to provide more clearance for the cage of the pinion bearing. In October 1933, the location of the lubrication fitting on the torque tube was moved to improve accessibility.

For 1935, the axle shaft and the housing were redesigned. In June the housing bell and flange wall thickness were increased, and ribs were added to the inside of the differential housing.

Early in 1936, an optional rear axle housing with a smaller $2^{13}/_{16}$-inch diameter wheel bearing was used.

For the various gear ratios and number of gear teeth available each year, see the Axle Ratio Chart.

Rear Axle Ring and Pinion Chart

Year and Model	Ratio	Ring Gear No.	Pinion Gear No.
1932, 4 Cyl. Pass.	3.78 to 1	B-4210-A (34)	B-4610-A (9)
4 Cyl. Com.	4.11 to 1	B-4210-B (37)	B-4610-B (9)
8 Cyl. Pass.	4.33 to 1	18-4210-A (39)	18-4610-A (9)
8 Cyl. Com.	4.11 to 1	18-4210-B (37)	18-4610-B (9)
1933, Pass. & Com.	4.11 to 1	18-4210-B (37)	18-4610-B (9)
	4.33 to 1	40-4210-A (39)	40-4610-A (9)
1934, Pass. & Com.	4.11 to 1	18-4210-B (37)	18-4210-B (9)
	4.33 to 1	40-4210-A (39)	40-4210-A (9)
	3.54 to 1	40-4210-B (39)	40-4210-B (11)
1935, Pass. & Com.	4.11 to 1	18-4210-B (37)	48-4610-A (9)
	3.54 to 1	40-4210-B (39)	48-4610-B (11)
	4.33 to 1	40-4210-A (39)	50-4610 (9)
1936, Pass & Com.	4.11 to 1	18-4210-B (37)	48-4610-A (9)
	3.54 to 1	40-4210-B (39)	48-4610-B (11)
	4.33 to 1	40-4210-A (39)	50-4610 (9)
	3.78 to 1	68-4210-A (34)	* 68-4610-A (9)
	3.78 to 1	68-4210-A (34)	** 68-4610-B (9)
1937, All 60 HP	4.44 to 1	74-4210-A (40)	74-4610-A (9)
All 85 HP	3.78 to 1	68-4210-A (34)	68-4610-A (9)
	4.11 to 1	18-4210-B (37)	48-4610-D (9)
	3.54 to 1	40-4210-B (39)	48-4610-E (9)
1938, All 60 HP	4.44 to 1	74-4210-A (40)	74-4610-A (9)
	4.11 to 1	18-4210-B (37)	48-4610-D (9)
All 85 HP	3.78 to 1	68-4210-A (34)	68-4610-A (9)
	4.11 to 1	18-4210-B (37)	48-4610-D (9)
	3.54 to 1	40-4210-B (39)	48-4610-E (9)
	4.44 to 1	74-4210-A (40)	74-4610-A (9)

* Used with solid drive shaft.
** Used with tubular drive shaft.

Transmission and Clutch

The Ford chassis parts list shows that the transmission, clutch and clutch housings were interchangeable in years 1932–34, 1935–36 and 1937–38. However, to be authentic, we must note some minor differences from year to year. Although some changes were made at model change over, others were running changes made during the year. Significant improvements over 1931 were the addition of the syncronized shifting feature and the change to helical gears.

Excluding the trucks, there were two transmission and clutch assemblies used in 1932; one for the four cylinder chassis and the other for the V-8 chassis. The internal parts were the same in both transmissions, but the clutch and transmission housings were different.

In May 1932, the location of the clutch release bearing grease cup on the V-8 chassis was moved from the left side to the top of the transmission case to improve accessibility for greasing. In addition, a larger hole was added to the number one floor board permitting greasing of the clutch release bearing on both the four cylinder and the V-8 chassis. Also, in May, the gear shift lever housing (transmission cover) was changed to improve the sealing around the gear shift lever. The distinguishing feature of the new housing was the full length extension of the rib opposite the emergency lever mounting bases. In balancing out stock, the old housings were reworked by adding a metal baffle on the lower face of the cover.

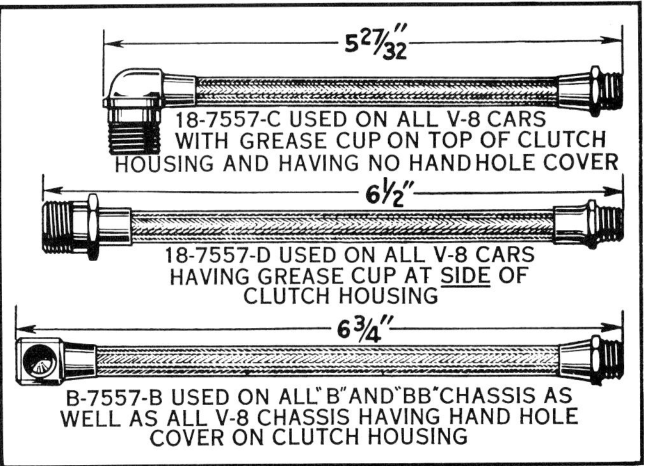

Three different types of grease connections used to grease the clutch release bearing.

Another improvement for the clutch release bearing lubrication occurred in July. An inner spiral woven brass lining was added to the manufacturing of the rubber connection hose leading to the bearing. The change was necessary because the walls of the rubber hose would swell, thus closing off the hose opening. As a result, there were three parts after that date; B-7557-B for the four cylinder chassis, 18-7557-C for V-8 chassis with the grease cup at the top of the transmission case, and 18-7557-D for service on V-8 chassis with the grease cup at the right side of the transmission case. Later, in August, an inspection plate, similar to one on the four cylinder chassis, was added to the transmission case, permitting the four cylinder grease cup and hose to be used on the V-8 transmission.

Also in August, the clutch retracting spring was shortened $3/_{16}$ inches to reduce the pedal pressure.

The gear shift lever had a slight bend toward the back similar to the Model A. The same lever, with a chrome plated satin finish, was used for both chassis. The knob was a glossy black phenolic ball with a horizontal $1/_4$-inch band around its circumference. In March 1932, the lever was offset two inches to the left so as to allow shifting into "high" when the passenger seat was folded down. This change was made on passenger cars only. The old stock was used up on vehicles without a folding passenger seat. Later, in July, the amount of bend to the rear was increased to provide greater clearance between the ball and the choke button when the lever was in second gear position.

The clutch pedal was the same on all passenger cars and commercial vehicles. It was forged steel and painted black. The pedal pad matched the brake pedal pad described in the brake section. The only change for the 1933 production was on the transmission cover and gear shift lever. The lever was no longer offset, but was bent back from center $10^{1}/_{2}$ inches for passenger cars and $9^{5}/_{8}$ inches for commercials. In January 1933, the $9\frac{5}{8}$ inches dimension was changed to $6\frac{1}{4}$ inches.

For 1934, the V-8 clutch disc was released for use on all four cylinder and V-8 chassis for passenger cars and four cylinder commercials. The heavier truck disc was used with the V-8 commercial chassis. Two more changes occurred in July 1934. The counter shaft gears were increased in width, and the oil groove in the intermediate gear was changed to improve lubrication. A new greaseless clutch release bearing was introduced at the Rouge Plant in August 1934. The old bearing and its lubricating cup and hose were phased out with the end of the 1934 model production.

An all new improved transmission and clutch assembly was released for the beginning of 1935 model production. In appearance, however, it looked similar to the 1934 units. The most distinguishing feature was the new contour of the gear shift lever. It was bent back and then up, forming a reverse "S." In January, this "S" shape was slightly modified to provide more clearance between the gear shift knob and the instrument panel. This new lever would also fit the 1932 through 1934 passenger cars and was available for service.

The gear shift knob was also new. It was oval shaped and painted black on the standard cars and commercial vehicles and Taupe on the deluxe cars. However, the oval knob was obsoleted in January and the round knob, in similar colors, was put back into production. The 1935 transmission was a carry-over into the beginning of the 1936 models until November 1935, when the gear teeth design was changed from a round profile to a chamfered tooth profile. The gear shift lever was slightly modified to a flatter "S" shape, and instead of being plated it was painted Benton gray. By May 1936, the color was changed to black for the standard models and commercials and brown for the deluxe models. The gear shift knob started as the round ball painted Benton gray, but, on passenger cars it was soon changed to oval design, painted black on standard models and brown on the deluxe models.

Beginning in December 1936, low and reverse gears which had been the spur gear type were changed to a helical gears design on a limited basis. As production increased, helical gears were installed on all transmissions.

The gear shift knob for 1937 was re-styled to include a raised V-8 on its top surface.

The only change in 1938 was the color of the gear shift knob. It was painted Zephyr beige on deluxe models.

A slightly smaller transmission with a higher gear ratio was used for the 60 HP chassis.

In addition, two special order transmissions were available. The first, released in April 1936, had a lower first and second gear ratio for use in exceptionally hilly areas. A second, released in May 1938, was a four speed unit for use on 60 HP commercial vehicle chassis.

Muffler and Tail Pipe

Muffler and tail pipe assemblies for the four cylinder and V-8 chassis were practically identical. The only difference was in the inlet pipe. On early production, the outlet pipe slid into the muffler outlet nipple, but in May the joint was reversed and the outlet pipe slid over the muffler outlet nipple. The muffler size was 6 × 23 inches.

For the 1933–34 models the muffler length was reduced to 18 inches. This change consequently increased the length of the outlet pipe.

Dimensions of the 1935–38 muffler remained the same but the interior baffles were changed. The 60 HP V-8 chassis used the same muffler from introduction to February 1937, when a smaller 15-inch long muffler was introduced.

Springs

All 1932–38 chassis were equipped with the Ford transverse spring suspension system. However, an improvement over the Model A, was the mounting of the rear spring in back of the rear axle. This arrangement gave the body a longer spring base than the wheel base. It also permitted lowering the ends of the spring mounting. In 1935, the front spring was also moved in front of the front axle.

The early models had a weaker front spring than later models. The spring had 12 leaves and a free height of $6\frac{1}{4}$ inches. The change, made in February 1932, increased the free height to $6\frac{7}{16}$ inches, with instructions to use the earlier springs on the Model B chassis.

Specific springs were used with each of the various body styles, and in addition, there were a variety of options for different loads and road conditions. Refer to the spring chart for the number of leaves and free spring height for each model. Up to the end of 1933 production, the ends of the springs were tapered. Starting with the 1934 models, the spring leaves were shortened about one inch and the ends were made square. The change was made to provide a softer spring and improve riding quality. However, this design was used only on 1934 models since new springs with tapered oval ends were introduced for the 1935 ve-

Front Spring Chart 1932-1938

S = Start of Production **EMP = End of Model Production**

Year and Chassis Number	Leaves	Part No.	Date Used
1932			
B (Early)	12	B-5310-A	
B & 18 Chassis	12	B-5310-B	to EMP
1933 & 34			
40 & 46	12	40-5310-A	S to Jan 1934
40 & 46	12	40-5310-C	Jan 1934 to EMP
40 Taxicab	12	40-5310-B	S to Jun 1934
40 Taxicab	12	40-5310-D	S to Jun 1934
40 Chicago Police	12	40-5310-E	
1935 & 36			
48, 50, 67, & 68	12	48-5310-A	S to July 1936
50 and 67 (SE Area)	12	48-5310-B	S to July 1936
48, 50, 67, & 68	12	48-5310-C*	S to July 1936
68 and 67	12	68 5310 A	Mar 1936 to EMP
67 (SE Area)	13	68-5310-B	Mar 1936 to EMP
68 and 67	13	68-5310-C*	Mar 1936 to EMP
1937 & 38			
74 and 73	11	74-5310-A	S to Feb 1937
74 and 82	10	74-5310-B	S to Feb 1937
78 and 77	12	78-5310-A	S to Feb 1937
78 and 77	13	78-5310-B*	S to Feb 1937
78, 77, 73, 81A, 81C, & 82C	11	78-5310-C*	Feb 1937 to EMP
78, 77, 73, 81A, 81C, & 82C	12	78-5310-D*	Feb 1937 to EMP
78, 77, 73, 81C, & 82C	13	78-5310-E	July 1937 to EMP

**Indicates usage for rough roads*

hicles. Beginning in April 1936, grooves were added on the surface of the spring leaves to permit lubrication by means of a lubrication fitting. The ungrooved springs were phased out by July 1936.

Spring shackels, at introduction, had a rubber bushing. In May 1933, the bushing was changed to a lubricant impregnated fabric with a metal sleeve. To further reduce friction, starting in July 1935, the shackel studs were made with a shoulder.

All springs and shackels were painted chassis black.

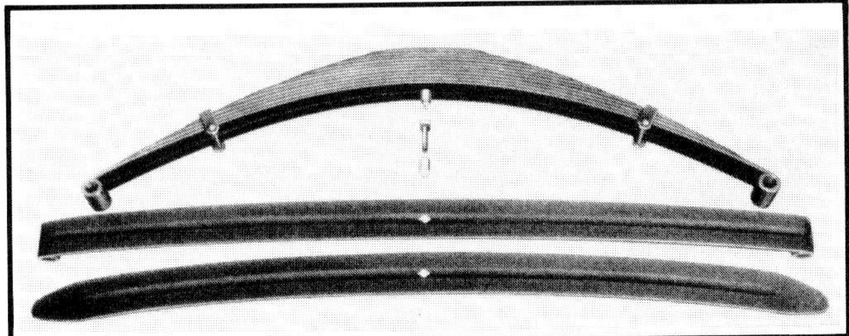

Detail of the grooved leaves and lubrication fitting.

Rear Spring Chart 1932-1936

S = Start of Production **EMP = End of Model Production**

Year and Model	Leaves	Part No.	Date Used
1932			
Tudor, Victoria, Conv. Sedan	10	B-5560-A	S to EMP
Phaeton, Coupe, Spt. Coupe,	9	B-5560-B	S to EMP
Cabriolet, Coupe (3W)	9	B-5560-B	S to EMP
Roadster	9	B-5560-C	S to EMP
Fordor	11	B-5560-D	S to EMP
Commercial Chassis	13	B-5560-E	S to EMP
1933-34			
Victoria	11	40-5560-A	S to Jan 1934
Victoria	11	40-5560-F	Jan 1934 to May 1934
Roadster	9	40-5560-C	S to Apr 1933
Roadster	10	40-5560-B	Apr 1933 to Jan 1934
Coupes, Phaeton, Cabriolet	10	40-5560-B	S to Jan 1934
Fordor, Tudor Panel & Sedan Deliv.	12	40-5560-D	S to Dec 1933
Fordor, Tudor	11	40-5560-J	Jan 1934 to May 1934
Victoria	11	40-5560-J	May 1934 to EMP
Fordor, Tudor	11	40-5560-F	May 1934 to EMP
Coupes, Phaeton, Roadster, Cabriolet	10	40-5560-G	Jan 1934 to EMP
Sedan and Panel Delivery	12	40-5560-H	Jan 1934 to EMP
Taxicab	12	40-5560-E	S to June 1934
Taxicab	12	40-5560-L	June 1934 to EMP
46 Commercial Chassis	13	B-5560-E	S to May 1934
46 Commercial Chassis	13	40-5560-K	June 1934 to EMP
1935-36			
Roadster, Coupes, Cabriolet	10	48-5560-A	S to July 1936
Roadster, Coupes, Cabriolet	10	68-5560-A	Mar 1936 to EMP
Tudor, Fordor, Phaeton, Conv. Sedan	11	48-5560-B	S to July 1936
Tudor, Fordor, Phaeton, Conv. Sedan	11	68-5560-B	Mar 1936 to EMP
Tudor TS, Fordor TS	12	48-5560-C	S to July 1936
Sedan Delivery, Panel Delivery	12	48-5560-C	S to July 1936
Tudor TS, Fordor TS	12	68-5560-C	Mar 1936 to EMP
Sedan Delivery, Panel Delivery	12	68-5560-C	Mar 1936 to EMP
Station Wagon, Commercial Chassis	13	48-5560-D	S to July 1936
Station Wagon, Commercial Chassis	13	68-5560-D	Mar 1936 to EMP
Taxicab	13	48-5560-E	S to July 1936
Taxicab	13	68-5560-E	Mar 1936 to EMP

**The 68-5560 springs went into production in March 1936 for use on 20% of production and increased to 100% of production by July 1936.*

Rear Spring Chart 1937

S = Start of Production **EMP = End of Model Production**

Year and Model	Leaves	Part No.	Date Used
1937			
78 Club Cabriolet	10	78-5560-A	S to EMP
78 Roadster, 78 Cabriolet,	10	78-5560-A	S to Feb 1937
74-78 5W Coupe	10	78-5560-A	S to Feb 1937
78 Roadster, 78 Cabriolet	9	78-5560-G	Feb 1937 to EMP
74-78 5W Coupe	9	78-5560-G	Feb 1937 to EMP
78 Tudor	11	78-5560-B	S to Dec 1936
78 Tudor	10	78-5560-A	Dec 1936 to Aug 1937
78 Tudor	9	78-5560-G	Aug 1937 to EMP
78 Tudor TS, 74 Tudor TS	12	78-5560-C	S to Dec 1936
78 Tudor TS, 74 Tudor TS	10	78-5560-A	Dec 1936 to Feb 1937
78 Tudor TS	11	78-5560-B	Feb 1937 to EMP
74 Tudor TS	11	78-5560-B	Feb 1937 to Aug 1937
74 Tudor TS	10	78-5560-A	Aug 1937 to EMP
78 Club Coupe, 78 Phaeton	11	78-5560-B	S to Dec 1936
78 Club Coupe, 78 Phaeton	10	78-5560-A	Dec 1936 to EMP
78 Convertible Sedan, 78 Fordor	11	78-5560-B	S to Feb 1937
78 Convertible Sedan, 78 Fordor	10	78-5560-A	Feb 1937 to EMP
74 Fordor	11	78-5560-B	S to Feb 1937
74 Fordor	10	78-5560-A	Feb 1937 to Aug 1937
74 Fordor	9	78-5560-G	Aug 1937 to EMP
78 Fordor TS, 74 Fordor TS	12	78-5560-C	S to Dec 1936
78 Fordor TS	11	78-5560-B	Dec 1936 to EMP
74 Fordor TS	11	78-5560-B	Dec 1936 to Aug 1937
74 Fordor TS	9	78-5560-G	Aug 1937 to EMP
74-78 Sed. and Pan. Delivery	12	78-5560-C	S to EMP
74-78 Sed. Del. (SE) Sta. Wagon and Commercial Chassis	14	78-5560-D	S to EMP
74-78 Taxicab	13	78-5560-E	S to EMP
74-78 South East Rough Roads	15	78-5560-F	S to EMP

Rear Spring Chart 1938

S = Start of Production **EMP = End of Model Production**

Year and Model	Leaves	Part No.	Date Used
1938			
81A Tudor, 81A Fordor	10	78-5560-A	S to EMP
	11	78-5560-B*	
	9	78-5560-G*	
82A Tudor, 82A Fordor, 81A, 82A Club Coupe, 81A, 82A Conv. Sedan, 81A, 82A Phaeton, 81A, 82A Conv. Club Coupe	10	78-5560-A	S to EMP
81A Conv. Coupe, 81A, 82A 5W Coupe	9	78-5560-G	S to EMP
81A, 82A Sed. and Pan. Delivery	12	78-5560-C	S to EMP
81A, 82A Sed. Delivery (SE), Sta. Wagon, Commercial Chassis	14	78-5560-D	S to EMP
81A, 82A Taxicab	13	78-5560-E	S to EMP
81A, 82A South East Rough Roads	15	78-5560-F	S to EMP

**Optional at customer request.*

Radiators and Radiator Caps

Four variations of radiators were used on the Model B and V-8 chassis. Ford produced its own radiator at the Dearborn Plant and the Green Island plant. In addition, radiators were supplied by McCord, Modine and Long manufacturing companies. The radiators made by each of these manufacturers had different shapes and tube arrangements. Refer to the sketches for specific details.

Radiators for the Model B chassis were made by Ford, McCord, Modine and Long, but all looked alike. The core was $2\frac{3}{32}$ inches thick and had three rows of oval tubes, 34 tubes per row and 132 fins. The radiators for the 1932 V-8 chassis were at first made only by Ford, but starting with June, they were also made by McCord and Long. All had a $2\frac{3}{4}$ inch thick core, but tube arrangements differed with each company. A special equipment radiator made by McCord became available in August for use in high altitude or hot climate areas. Refer to drawing for tube patterns and sizes.

Starting with 1933 models, Modine was added to the list of suppliers. Later in August 1933, Long was retooled for producing radiators for trucks only.

Prior to July 1933, commercial chassis did not use a splash shield between the radiator and grille. However, the passenger car shield was released in July for use on commercial vehicles.

To reduce loss of water due to surging, the radiator overflow pipe was re-routed outside the top of the radiator in February 1935.

Starting in June 1935, the smaller capacity Ford radiator was designated for use in those plants producing cars for sale in the milder climate upper half of the country. The Modine and McCord radiators were designated for use in plants supplying vehicles for the warm lower half of the United States. However, overheating must have continued to be a problem because the dealers were directed to widen hood louvers, install extra cooling capacity radiators, install six blade fans, or, in extreme conditions, remove the engine pans. At the same time a special equipment extra cooling radiator with a four inch thick core produced by Long, was released.

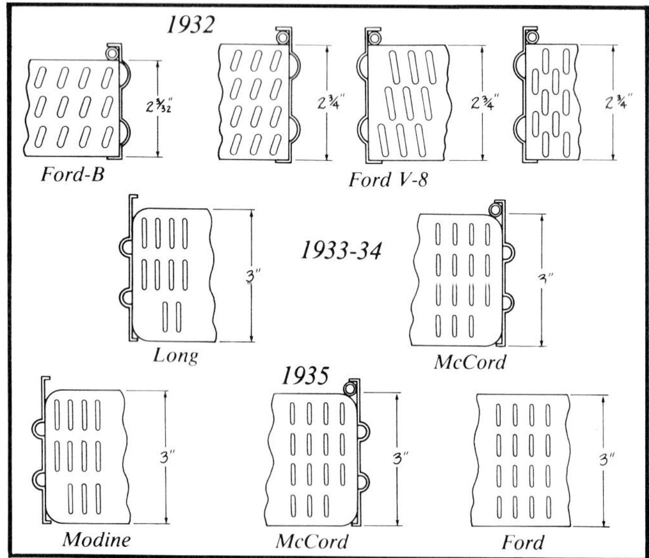

Sketch showing sizes and tube arrangement on the various radiator cores, (author's sketch).

Radiator Core Sizes

Year and Model		Part No.	Size
1932	All 4 Cyl.	B-8005-A	$23\frac{3}{16}$ x 17
	All 8 Cyl.	18-8005-A	$23\frac{3}{16}$ x 17
1933-34	All 4 Cyl.	46-8005-A	$22\frac{3}{4}$ x 17
	All 8 Cyl.	40-8005-A	$22\frac{3}{4}$ x 17
1935	Passenger	48-8005-A	$22\frac{1}{2}$ x 17
	Commercial	50-8005-A	$22\frac{1}{2}$ x $19\frac{3}{4}$
1936	Passenger	68-8005-A	23 x 17
	Commercial	67-8005-A	$22\frac{1}{2}$ x $19\frac{3}{4}$
1937	85 HP Pass.	78-8005-A	23 x 17
	60 HP Pass.	74-8005-A	$21\frac{3}{4}$ x $15\frac{3}{4}$
	85 HP Com.	77-8005-A	$22\frac{1}{2}$ x $19\frac{3}{4}$
	60 HP Com.	73-8005-A	$22\frac{1}{2}$ x $19\frac{3}{4}$
1938	85 HP Pass.	81A-8005-A	23 x 17
	60 HP Pass.	82A-8005-A	$21\frac{3}{4}$ x $15\frac{3}{4}$
	85 HP Com.	81C-8005-A	$22\frac{1}{2}$ x $19\frac{3}{4}$
	60 HP Com.	82C-8005-A	$22\frac{1}{2}$ x $19\frac{3}{4}$

The radiator caps on the 1932–34 passenger cars and commercials served two functions: a cap for the radiator as well as an ornament for the radiator shell. After 1934 the radiator cap on the passenger cars was located under the hood, no longer serving as an ornament. On the commercial vehicles, however, the cap continued to serve as cap and radiator shell ornament until the end of 1936.

The 1932 passenger car cap was $3\frac{7}{16}$ inches in diameter with a $\frac{3}{8}$ high fin which tapered to the front, blending in with the name plate ornamentation on the shell. It was made of zinc, finished in bright chrome plate. This same cap was also used on the Station Wagon and the deluxe Panel Delivery. All the other commercial vehicles used a larger $3\frac{1}{2}$-inch diameter cap made of rustless steel. In July 1932, in order to insure proper installation of the cap on passenger cars, one lug was made larger and the slot in the radiator filler neck flange was increased to match.

For the 1933 cars, the cap was elongated giving the hood ornamentation more of a streamlined effect. However, when the hood was opened there was a slight interference. The problem was not corrected until June 1933, when the hood opening around the cap was enlarged. The cap and radiator shell were restyled in October 1933, resulting in the cap being one-half inch higher and creating an illusion of a larger hood ornament. This style was retained on all passenger cars, Station Wagons and Sedan Delivery until the end of 1934 production.

The commercial vehicles cap for 1933 was round with a knurled edge, similar to that on the 1932 passenger cars. Starting with the 1934 production this cap was restyled to look like the 1933 passenger car cap.

In 1935 the radiator shell and hood was restyled with a pronounced V-8 hood ornament and the radiator cap was placed under the hood. The cap was square with round corners and a wire handle on top. All steel parts were zinc or cadmium plated. The cap was used through the 1936 model year.

The 1937–38 cap was round, $2\frac{13}{16}$ inches in diameter, with two one-half inch lugs opposite each other. It had a baffle dome on the under side which was intended to reduce surging of the coolant. All steel parts were zinc or cadmium plated.

The 1935 commercial cap was simliar to 1934. But after 1935 the commercial vehicles had their own style of cap.

Radiator Shell, Grill and Hood

Radiator shells, grills, hoods, fenders and running boards for Ford cars were Chassis Engineering responsibility but were designed by Styling as part of the overall body. The radiator shell became progressively smaller, finally being eliminated by 1936. The commercial grill and shell was generally one year behind in styling treatment, so the shell was not eliminated until the end of 1937. These items will be discussed in detail in the body section as part of the body styling changes.

Bumpers

In 1932 the bumpers were listed as special equipment at extra cost. However, bumpers were installed on each car at the factory. This was the Company's method for establishing a lower basic price. In 1933 the bumpers became standard equipment, but in 1935, they were made part of a basic accessory group including the spare tire cover. They were installed at the factory on all cars, but at extra cost to the customer.

The 1932 bumper was a single bar with a corrugated surface and curled ends. A plug, simulating a carriage bolt head, was inserted on top of the curl. The same bumper, chrome plated, was used on both passenger cars and commercial vehicles. The back surface of the bumper, though chrome plated, was unpolished.

Bumpers for 1933 passenger cars were made of spring steel with a slight curve from top to bottom and with a small horizontal groove in the center. The surface was chrome plated, with black paint in the groove. Originally the two round head mounting bolts were spaced 28 inches apart, but in January, the mounting bolts were changed to oval head and, in conjunction with redesigned mounting arms, the spacing was changed to 22 inches. Beginning in April, the top to bottom curvature was made flatter on the front bumper only.

At the beginning of production, all commercial vehicles, including the Station Wagon and Sedan Delivery, were equipped with the same shape bumpers as passenger cars. However, they were finished with black enamel rather than chrome. Starting in February, the bumpers for the Station Wagon and Sedan Delivery were changed to chrome plated, the same as passenger cars. In March, the commercial bumper was changed to a straight design with two grooves. For the standard commercials, the bumpers were painted black, while on the Deluxe Panel Delivery they were chrome plated with the two grooves painted black. In April, the wrap-around end of the front bumper was reduced and the bumper arm was shortened.

Starting with the 1934 production, the bumpers were changed by increasing the bolt spacing dimension to 26 inches and adding bumper guards at the mounting bolts. The bumper guards were chrome plated with black paint in a vertical groove. A unique rear bumper used on the Victoria had a curved shape $11\frac{1}{2}$ inches in depth. The commercial bumpers were the same as 1933, but with only one groove.

Bumpers for 1935 cars were a carry over of 1934, but had two grooves in the center, painted black. The two grooves also cut across the restyled bumper guards. In addition, the rear bumper was slightly modified to match the front bumper on all models except the Sedan Delivery which had a unique bumper. Four outside vendors supplied the bumper guards, but their parts were all interchangeable. The commercial bumpers had the same double groove design, but the bumpers had less arch from side to side.

The 1936 bumpers were similiar to 1935 except for the wrap-around ends which were restyled with a sharper taper. In addition, the mounting bolts without the bumper guards were changed from round head to square head on the front and oval head on the rear.

On 1937 cars the bumpers were all new, featuring a beveled edge slightly below center and round ends. The rear bar was the same shape as the front, but $1\frac{1}{4}$ inches longer. The bumper guards were also new that year. The 60 HP chassis bumper was similiar to the larger chassis but was made of thinner stock.

A new bumper bar was designed for 1938 with the bevel edge slightly above center. This bumper was used on the front and rear of the deluxe models, while the standard models, Station Wagon and commercials used the new bumper in the front with the 1937 bumper in the rear.

Shock Absorbers

The V-8 shock absorbers were the Houdaille type similar to the Model A, but with the addition of an automatic thermostatic control to adjust the resistance to the changing seasons. Clockwise rotation shocks were used on the right front and rear, and counterclockwise rotation shocks were used on the left front and rear.

Shocks for the early four cylinder chassis were similar to the V-8, but had the manual adjustment. These were obsoleted in April 1932 when they were replaced by the V-8 shocks. Unused stock was designated for use on commercial models.

In May 1932, an improved shock absorber was released for use on the rear only for Fordor cars. The new shock had a resistance of 1350 to 1620 inch pounds. In September, a third shock absorber with a resistance of 1665 to 1935 ip was used on the front and rear of Coupe bodies and on the rear only of the Tudor, Victoria, Convertible Sedan, Pickup, Panel, and Station Wagon. For identification purposes, the three different shocks were stamped with a letter on the cover next to the manufacturer's trademark, and the cap nut was painted with a color. Shocks with a resistance of 1350 to 1620 ip were stamped with the letter "A" and painted light blue; shocks with a resistance of 2430 to 2700 ip were stamped with "B" and painted yellow; and shocks with 1665 to 1935 ip resistance were stamped with "C" and painted light green.

The shock absorber link for 1932 ws a two-piece design made of steel forgings. The two halves were sandwiched together over two rubber bushings. The production links were riveted together while the service links were held together by nuts and bolts.

For 1933 passenger cars and commercials, the shocks' resistance numbers were modified but the identification code was retained. Shocks with resistance of 1350 to 1620 ip and the light blue color were used on the front of Roadsters, Cabriolets, Tudors, Fordors, Victorias, Pickups, Panels and Station Wagons. Shocks with resistance of 2600 to 2900 ip and the yellow code were used on the rear of Tudors, Fordors, Pickups, Panels and Station Wagon models. Shocks with resistance of 1900 to 2100 ip and the light green code were used on the front and rear of Coupes, and the rear of Roadsters, Phaetons and Cabriolets.

The shock absorbers were redesigned for 1934 so that the front shocks mounted on the outside of the frame, while the rear shocks mounted on the inside of the frame. Functionally they featured the adjustable valve and a fixed orifice, but in January they were changed to include an automatic thermostat. The shock arms and links were also changed in January so that the openings on the link for the shock arm ball and axle ball were on the same side.

The automatic thermostat type shock absorber adjustment must have had some problems because in August 1934, production was changed back to the adjustable valve and orifice type shock absorber.

The 1934 shock absorbers were a carry-over for the 1935 cars, but with new shock arms and links. The ball ends were eliminated from the shock arms and were made part of the shock link. In addition a forging and stamping type link was used.

For 1936, the rear shock absorber body was redesigned to mount on the upper frame flange. The front shocks were similar to the 1935 design but had a fixed orifice with no manual adjustment. However, by May the adjustable type was back in use. Factory settings were 1300 to 1500 ip resistance on the front and 2300 to 2600 ip resistance on the rear.

Minor body changes were made to the front shocks for 1937, but functionally they were unchanged. Also, the front shock link dimension between the ball ends was increased from three inches to four inches. The rear shocks and links were a direct carry-over.

Castings for the 1938 shock absorbers were different in appearance, although functionally, they were the same as those used in 1937.

Engine Pans (Splash Pans)

The engine pans, right and left, were located between the engine and the frame. Painted black on all models, the shape of these pans was unique to model years, and in some cases unique to the model. A simplified sketch has been provided to help identify the various designs.

Fuel Tank and Cap

The 1932 passenger cars were equipped with the fuel tank located at the rear of the car body, a major change from the cowel mounted Model A tank. All models of the four cylinder and the eight cylinder passenger cars used the same 14 gallon capacity tank, painted with black enamel. The same tank, with a different filler pipe, was also used on the Station Wagon and the Sedan Delivery.

The commercial Panel and the truck Panel had a 10 gallon tank under the driver's seat. Brackets welded on the tank permitted mounting of the seat. This provided a passageway instead of the passenger seat if desired. A larger 17 gallon tank, also mounted under the seat, was also available as special equipment, and as standard equipment on all other commercial vehicles and trucks.

The 14 gallon passenger car tank, rear mounted and with a longer filler neck, was also available on special order for the commercial Pickup and commercial Panel.

For the 1933 passenger cars, the 14 gallon tank was slightly modified and was no longer exposed. The fuel level

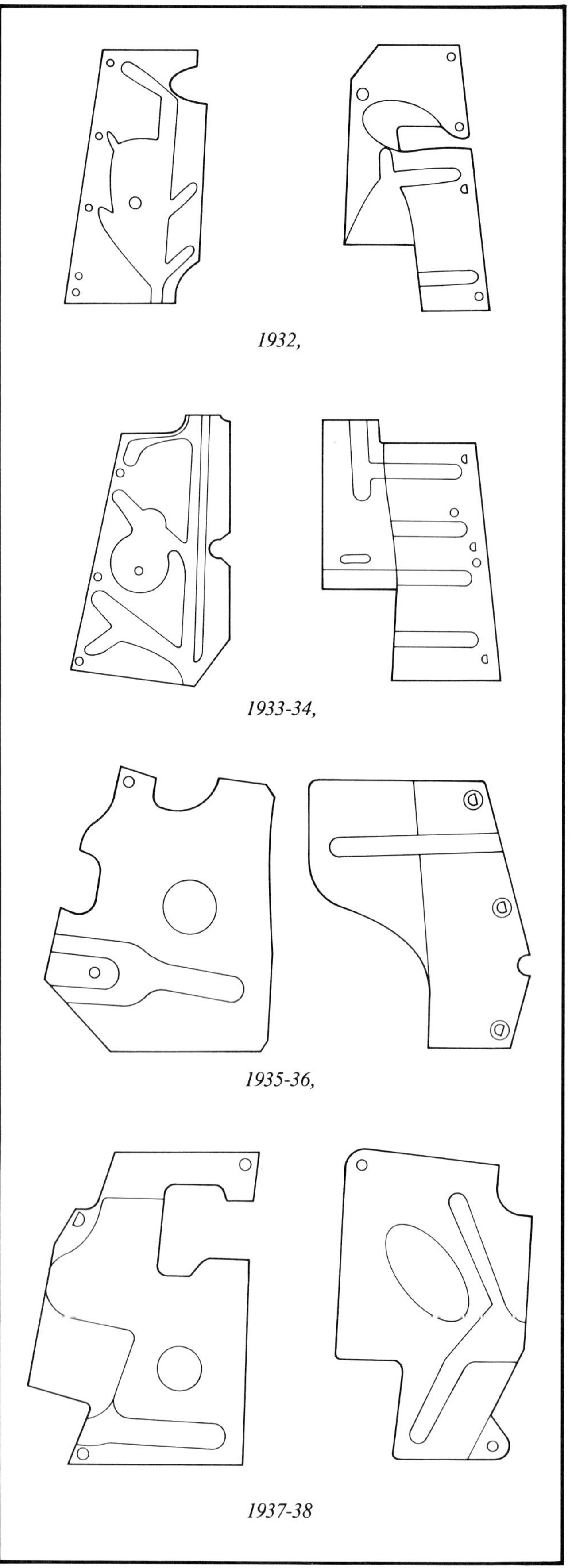

This author's sketch is provided to help identify the various engine pans.

sending unit was moved from the right side to the left, and the filler pipe was moved to the left rear corner. The 14 gallon tank with minor changes became the standard tank for all passenger cars, Station Wagons and Sedan Delivery through 1938.

In 1935 the fuel level sending unit opening was made larger and in 1937 the filler neck was changed. Also in 1937 and again in 1938 the sheet metal contour was modified to match the designs of the new bodies.

All commercial vehicles, starting in 1933 and continuing through 1934, were equipped with a 14 gallon commercial tank mounted in the rear. There were two filler pipes used, a short and a long. The short was used on the Pickup truck and, later, also on the 1934 Victoria. All other commercials used the longer filler pipe. The same tank with a changed top was used in 1935. Additional sheet metal changes were made for 1936 and 1937. Then, in 1938 the commercial vehicles were equipped with the passenger car tank then in use.

Two fuel tank caps were produced in 1932, one by Easy On and the other by Stant. Both had a knurl around the edge (14 pitch). The top of the passenger car cap was made of rustless steel and the other components of the cap were made of sheet steel finished in zinc or cadmium plate. All components of the commercial cap were made of sheet steel cadmium plated. The Easy On cap was obsoleted in September 1932 but the Stant cap was used through 1938.

Tools

All passenger cars, commercial vehicles and trucks, 1932 through 1938 were equipped with a tool bag and an assortment of additional tools. Two tool bags were used alternately. One 11½ by 7⅝ inches had its flap on the side with two snaps, the other 13½ by 6⅞ inches had a flap on the end with one snap. The bags were made of either pebble grain rubber base artificial leather or other artificial leathers and whipcord when available. The tool bag contained two open end wrenches, a screw driver, pliers, monkey wrench, spark plug wrench and lubricating gun, all carry-over from the Model A.

Of the two open end wrenches, one was sized 7/16 and ½ inch and the other was sized 9/16 and ⅝ inches. Both were painted black and had no Ford identification. The Ford script and "USA" in raised letters were added in June 1934. These wrenches were used through 1938.

The screw driver, with a plain steel blade and a black painted wood handle, had no changes made through 1938.

Similar to the open end wrenches, the black painted monkey wrench had no markings until June 1934 when the Ford script and USA in raised letters were added.

The original design pliers with a 7/16 inch wide by one inch deep jaws were finished either in black paint or cadmium plate until May 1937 when the finish was specified black only. Also, at that time an optional pair of pliers was released with ¼ inch wide by 1¼ inch deep jaws.

The spark plug and cylinder head nut wrench with 11/16 and 1 9/16 hex open ends was also a carry-over, but it was only installed in vehicles with engines equipped with 3X or C4 spark plugs. In December 1932, the part number B-17017 in raised letters was added to its shank. Beginning with the use of the new 18mm spark plugs on the V-8 engine, a new wrench was released with open end sizes 11/16 and 1 1/16 inches. The raised part number 40-17017 was cast on its shank for identity. Similar to the other wrenches after June 1934, the Ford script and USA was added next to the part number. This wrench was used on all vehicles with 85 HP engines through 1937 production. On 1938 models, when a smaller spark plug was introduced for the 85 HP V-8, a new wrench was released with open end sizes of 11/16 and 13/16 inch. The part number 81A-17017 and Ford USA was cast on its shank. The wrench for the 60 HP V-8 engine was also size 11/16 and 13/16 inch, but its part number, cast on the shank, was 52-17017. All spark plug wrenches were painted black.

The Alemite Model A lubricating gun (grease gun) with 1½ by 4 inch barrel, was used until August 1934 when it was made slightly larger. In March 1936, a new spring loaded plunger type gun produced by Lincoln Engineering Company was introduced for use at all plants except the Rouge assembly plant where it was used alternately with the Alemite gun. The Alemite gun was redesigned in February 1937, thereafter being used alternately with the Lincoln Engineering gun at all plants. Starting in January 1938, the lubricating gun was no longer provided as standard equipment, but was available as special equipment at extra cost. All guns were finished with either zinc or cadmium plating.

Other tools provided with each vehicle were a jack and jack handle, tire pump, tire iron, and hand starting crank.

Two jacks were released with the beginning of 1932 production. They were the enclosed screw type, 8⅜ inches high in the down position. One was made by Auto Specialty and the other by Noblitt Sparks. A new Auto Specialty double screw type jack which collapsed to 6 inches was introduced in January 1934 as an alternate, and by 1935, the Noblitt Sparks jack was also converted to the double screw type. In addition, a Noblitt Sparks jack which collapsed to 5⅝ inches was released for use on commercial vehicles only. This commercial jack was used through 1937.

Starting with the 1936 passenger car production a screw type bumper jack made by Auto Specialties was used at the Rouge assembly on limited basis, and by March 1936, a ratchet type jack produced by Ryerson Haynes was also used on a limited basis. By 1937, usage of the bumper jack was increased and the axle jack and the bumper jack were used on a 50–50 basis. Suppliers of the 1937 bumper jacks were: Ryerson Haynes, ratchet type; Bingham Stamping, ratchet type and screw type model 131.

The axle type jacks were discontinued at the end of 1937 and only bumper jacks were used. In addition to the three in use in 1937, a new pinch cam type produced by Auto Specialty, was introduced for 1938. In May 1938, an additional pinch cam type jack by Ryerson Haynes was introduced and all of the ratchet jacks were obsoleted.

Commercial vehicles which had been equipped with the Noblitt Sparks jack, were equipped with a new axle type jack by Auto Specialties during 1938.

All 1932 through 1934 vehicles were equipped with the same type of jack handle. It was made of round steel stock 41 inches long and was designed to fold in the center. In March 1933, the overall length was reduced to 37 inches so that it could fit in a new tool box used on passenger cars with a rumble seat. The 1935 through 1937 vehicles equipped with an axle jack had a jack handle 51 inches long which folded at two places, reducing its length to 17¾ inches for storage purposes.

Vehicles with the bumper jack were equipped with a flat stock combination jack handle, tire iron, and hub cap remover.

The 1938 commercial vehicles with the axle jack had a 49 inch jack handle which folded in the center.

The tire pump was standard equipment on all vehicles until June 1936, when it became special equipment at extra cost. Two tire pump designs were used until April 1935. One was produced by Michigan Steel Tube and the other by Noblitt Sparks. Slightly shorter pumps made by the same companies, were released in April 1935 for use only in Roadsters, Coupes and Cabriolets. In August, the Michigan Steel Tube pump was replaced with a new design by Moon.

The tire iron was a carry-over from the Model A, with a slight modification. A square hole for adjusting the brakes was added to one end. It was used until the end of 1935 production when a small flange was added to the end with the hole. The 1937 and 1938 cars were equipped with a combination tire iron, jack handle and hub cap remover.

The starting crank and wheel nut wrench had many changes from 1932 to August 1936, when it was changed from standard equipment to special equipment at customer option. The first Model B design was a modified version of the Model A crank. However, because of the limited space between the new grill and the bumper it was deleted from passenger car usage in March 1932, and the remaining stock was used on trucks. A new design, featuring an extension which allowed the crank to be forward of the bumper, was released as a replacement. The extension was supplied in two lengths, one for the V-8 and the other for the four cylinder chassis. The crank handle and the extension attached by means of a tapered joint. In May, an optional design was released with a square joint.

In April 1933, the tapered joint crank was obsoleted with only the square drive style being used until August 1936. The extension piece, however, was changed in length for each new model year to compensate for the variable distance between the engine and the bumper. Starting in August a new wheel nut wrench was released and the crank-extension combination was available as special equipment only. All starting cranks and wheelnut wrenches and their extensions were painted black.

Convertible Sedans, in 1935 and 1936, were equipped with an additional special tool and instruction booklet for fastening and unfastening the convertible top locking mechanism. The tool was a ½ inch open end wrench, 4¾ inches long with its handle curved in a 1¾ inch radius. Starting with the 1937 production, this tool was also released for the Roadster, Convertible Sedan, Phaeton, Cabriolet and Club Cabriolet.

Because of the limited space in cars with rumble seats, a deck side tool box was placed in the rumble seat compartment of the Cabriolet, starting the last week of April 1933. In May, this was expanded to include the Roadster and Coupes. The tool box also became available as a special equipment item in June 1934, for use in Cabriolets, Roadsters and Coupes which did not have a rumble seat.

V—Electrical System, 1932–1938

The electrical items covered in this section are the generator, cutout, starter, distributor, coil, condenser, spark plugs, horn wiring harness and electrical accessories. Headlights, cowl lamps and rear lamps are also part of the electrical system, but, because their variations were the result of body design changes, they are described in the body section.

Generator Assembly

Six generators were used on the 1932 cars. The two standard production generators were augmented by four special equipment ones. The front cover of the V-8 generator had a round post for mounting it to the front of the intake manifold. It had a welded steel housing and was the three brush type with the adjustable third brush for regulating the output. Output was set at the factory at 12 amperes and 6.7 volts. A code number was stamped on the rear end plate of the generator designating the month and year it was manufactured. The month was represented by a number: one for January, two for February, etc., but a letter designated the year: "L" for 1931 and "M" for 1932.

Production of the 1932 generators was started late in 1931. These units had an oiling cup on the end plate. On 1932 units, an oiless bearing was introduced in order to eliminate the oil cup. The 1931 generators which had been installed on early production V-8 engines were to be replaced with 1932 units by the dealers before the cars were sold. However, it is not certain that this was done on all early cars.

A new two-leg front end mounting plate was introduced with 1933 models, eliminating the round mounting post. A corresponding change was made on the manifold. However, due to a slow production changeover, some early 1933 cars had the 1932 generator mounting system. Later, in July 1933, seven ventilating holes were added to the rear plate.

In January 1934, the terminal post for the cutout was changed to a wire which fastened to the cutout. By Feb ruary 1934, vent holes were added to the front plate and cooling vanes were added to the back face of the generator-fan pulley. In addition, the third brush factory setting was increased to 19 amperes and seven volts. As a fan noise reduction effort, in July the pulley diameter was increased from four to 4$^{5}/_{16}$ inches on all passenger car and commercial engines. The 1934 generator was used as standard equipment on all passenger car and commercial V-8 engines through 1935 production and was used on a limited basis through 1937.

Starting with 1936 car production, a new Ford developed generator with a cast iron housing and a 4.2-inch pulley was released as an option. By February 1936, the new generator was used on 90% of the passenger cars, while the 1934 design was used on the remainder of the passenger cars and commercials. The same generator with a 3.4-inch pulley was available for Taxicabs and Police cars. Commercial vehicles for the years 1936 and 1937 used the 1934 or 1936 generator with a 5.18-inch pulley.

A two brush generator and voltage regulator were introduced in May 1937 on a partial production basis. During this period it was possible to have a car equipped with either the new two brush generator, the 1936 cast iron type generator, or the 1934 welded steel housing type generator. This option continued through the end of 1937 and early production of the 1938 vehicles. As production of the two brush generator reached full capacity, the earlier three brush generator was phased out. This occured in early 1938 (no specific date) with directions to use up old stock first.

The 60 HP V-8 used the same option generators, but with a 3.4-inch pulley rather than the 4.2-inch pulley used with the large V-8.

In addition to the standard generators, a variety of special equipment generators were available. The exterior appearance of these generators was identical to the standard generator, but they were built either for a higher output or had a different diameter pulley.

One special equipment generator with 150 watts output at speeds of 18 to 50 MPH became available in May 1933, and was used through February 1936. Another special equipment generator was made by Bosch. It had a four inch pulley and maximum output at 12 MPH. It was available on all vehicles from 1935 to the end of 1938. For 1937 passenger cars and commercials, three additional three-brush special equipment generators were available: one with high output which started at 11 MPH and reached maximum output at 30 MPH; another started at 9 MPH and reached maximum at 28 MPH; and the third, for vehicles with extra electrical equipment, started at 6 MPH. Similar high output generators were available with the two brush type.

The generator used on the four cylinder Model B engine was a carryover from the Model A. Produced by Auto-lite, it was a three brush type, factory set at 12 amperes and 6.25 volts. It was used to the end of the four cylinder production in 1934.

Two special equipment generators were also available for the Model B. One was used for low speed driving vehicles such as Police cruising cars, Delivery truck, etc. The other had a maximum output of 24 amperes.

Voltage Regulators and Cutout

The most common regulator was the round can-like cutout which had been used on the Model A. The cover was made of sheet steel finished either with cadmium plate or terne plate. The Ford script trade mark was stamped on the center of the top surface. It had a simple function, to open a set of points, thus keeping the battery from discharging when the engine was stopped, and to close those points when the generator was charging. The regulator was used on all engines, including radio equipped cars, through January 1934. After that date, it was used as an alternate until early 1938.

In July 1934, minor improvements were made and, for identification purposes, a letter "A" was stamped on the cover just below the Ford script and alongside the armature terminal. It was used on all cars except those with radios. Further refinements were made in April 1936, and the Letter "B" was stamped in place of the "A."

A special equipment cutout for use on high output generators became available starting in April 1932 for four cylinder engines, and in October 1932 for V-8 engines. It

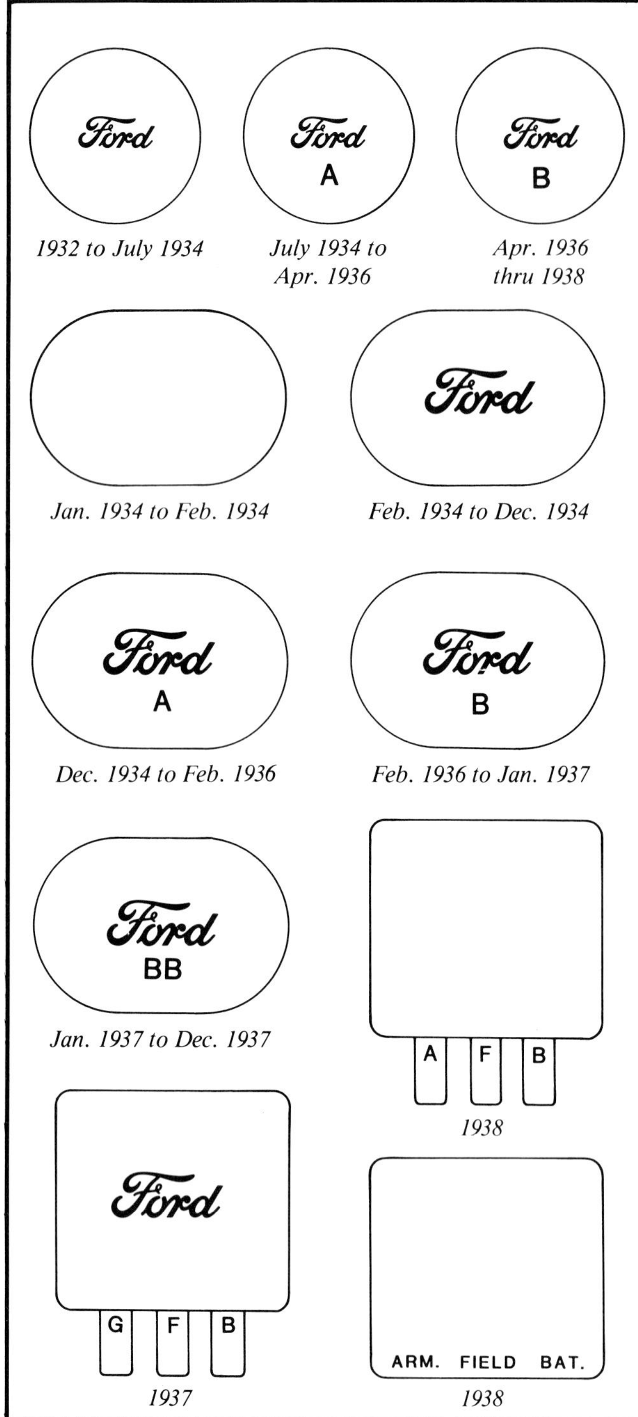

Drawings for identification of voltage regulators (Drawings by Authors.)

was used until March 1936. The letters "BUS" were stamped on the cover under the Ford script.

A new two-step cutout regulator was introduced in January 1934. It was oblong shape, almost twice as large as the round type (see chart). In addition to the cutout, it featured a relay which reduced the charging rate of the generator at 8½ volts. Used primarily on vehicles with radios, there was no trademark stamping on the cover of the units produced in January and February 1934. From February to December, however, the Ford script was added on its cover.

In December 1934, the opening and closing rate was improved and the regulator was scheduled for use on the 1935 models on a limited basis. To distinguish it from the 1934 units, the letter "A" was stamped on the cover just under the Ford script. When this regulator was upgraded in February 1936, the letter "B" replaced the "A." It was still used only on a limited basis as an alternate to the round style cutout of 1932. A further improvement as designated by the letters "BB" on the cover was released for use on all three brush generators from January to December 1937, at which time it was obsoleted. The 1932 type cutout was used on some early 1938 models which had the three brush generator.

For the two brush generator RBM supplied a regulator which mounted on the firewall. The cover was 2.7 × 2.48 inches with the Ford script stamped on the cover and the letters "G," "F" and "B" stamped on the terminals. The cover was zinc plated. Beginning with the 1938 models, the Ford script was eliminated and the terminals' stampings were changed to "A," "F" and "B." In March 1938, Ford also started producing a voltage regulator. On it, the terminals' identification "Arm, Field and Bat" were stamped on the top surface of the cover.

Battery

Ford used the positive ground electrical system. The battery was located below the floor on all cars from 1932 through 1936. But on 1937 and 1938 cars it was located on the firewall. All standard batteries had the oval and Ford script trademark cast on one side.

The 1932 battery was $9\frac{1}{8}$ inches long by $7\frac{1}{16}$ inches wide and $8\frac{11}{16}$ inches high. In addition to the Ford script cast on the side, the script was also on the top of each filler cap. When the battery was placed in the car, the positive post was at the back right corner. The same battery was used on both the four cylinder and V-8 chasis. In September, a metal shield was added to the front of the battery support to protect the battery from flying stones.

For 1933 cars the battery size was changed to $10\frac{1}{2}$ inches long by $7\frac{1}{4}$ inches wide and $7\frac{11}{16}$ inches high. Starting in June, the Ford script and oval on the side were painted gold.

The battery size was changed again for 1934. The new size for all passenger cars and commercials was $10\frac{1}{2}$ inches long by $7\frac{1}{4}$ inches wide and 8 inches high. The battery support had to be lowered $\frac{3}{8}$ inches to accommodate the 8 inch height. This battery was used through 1936.

The 1936 battery was carried over into 1937 with a minor modification. The filler caps were redesigned to include an adapter for adding water through the cap. Also, in December 1936, the vent hole in the filler caps was increased from $\frac{1}{16}$ to $\frac{3}{32}$ inches. For 1938 models, the filler caps were changed from the vent hole type to the bellows type.

A heavy duty special equipment battery made by Willard and Exide was made available starting in July 1933. It had no markings on the side but featured a pair of handles, one at each end, for easy removal.

A service battery with the Ford script and oval painted red was also available at dealers from February 1934 to the end of 1936. For 1937, the Ford script and oval on the service battery was painted green.

Starter and Starter Switch

Four starter motors and two starter drives were used from 1932 through 1938. Two starters were used on the four cylinder, one on the standard V-8 and the fourth on the 60 HP small V-8. All were equipped with a Bendix starter drive assembly. However, the 60 HP unit had a slightly longer shaft and was not interchangeable with the one used on the standard V-8.

The 1932 V-8 starter was a two field coil design with two-bolt end plates. The two bolts also served as mounting bolts. This design was used through 1938.

The four cylinder starter was the three field coil type with the three bolt mounting end plate similar to the one used on the Model A. With the new starter switch introduced in 1932 the terminal was changed from the flat block type to a screw and nut. For 1933 engines, a modified V-8 starter motor was used with a three bolt end plate for mounting to the four cylinder flywheel housing.

The starter motor for the 60 HP V-8 engine was similar to the larger V-8 starter, but was $\frac{27}{32}$-inch longer.

On early production of the four cylinder engine, the starter switch was mounted on the starter motor. Starting in May, however, the V-8 switch was adapted for mounting on the steering column at the floor. As a result, an additional piece of cable was required between the starter switch and the terminal on the starter motor. This system was used until the end of the four cylinder production.

The eight cylinder switch for 1932 was a foot operated one mounted on the steering column just below the floor, with only the button protruding through the floor and carpet. This arrangement was used through 1936 with minor changes on the mounting bracket to fit the differences in passenger and commercial bodies. In May 1934, the switch's outer body insulator was redesigned to minimize any possibility of the cable grounding.

In 1937, the starting system was changed to the dash mounted push button type with a relay mounted on the fender apron. This new system was used on all 1937 and 1938 vehicles.

Light Switch and Wiring Assembly

The V-8 light switch was located at the bottom of the steering column, and was the same switch introduced on the Model A. It was used on all chassis until June 1932. At that time the switch housing was modified to provide more clearance between it and the engine splash pan. This switch was used through 1937 when it was again modified. Even though the switch itself saw little change, the wiring was different from year to year, from standard models to deluxe models, and from passenger car to truck. Each passenger car and commercial had the additional variation of cowl lights or no cowl lights, one horn or two, and one or two tail lamps.

In January 1935, an asbestos tubing, $3\frac{1}{2}$ inches long was added around the wire where it came out of the switch. This tubing protected the wire from the heat emitted by the exhaust pipe.

For 1937 vehicles a special equipment wiring harness

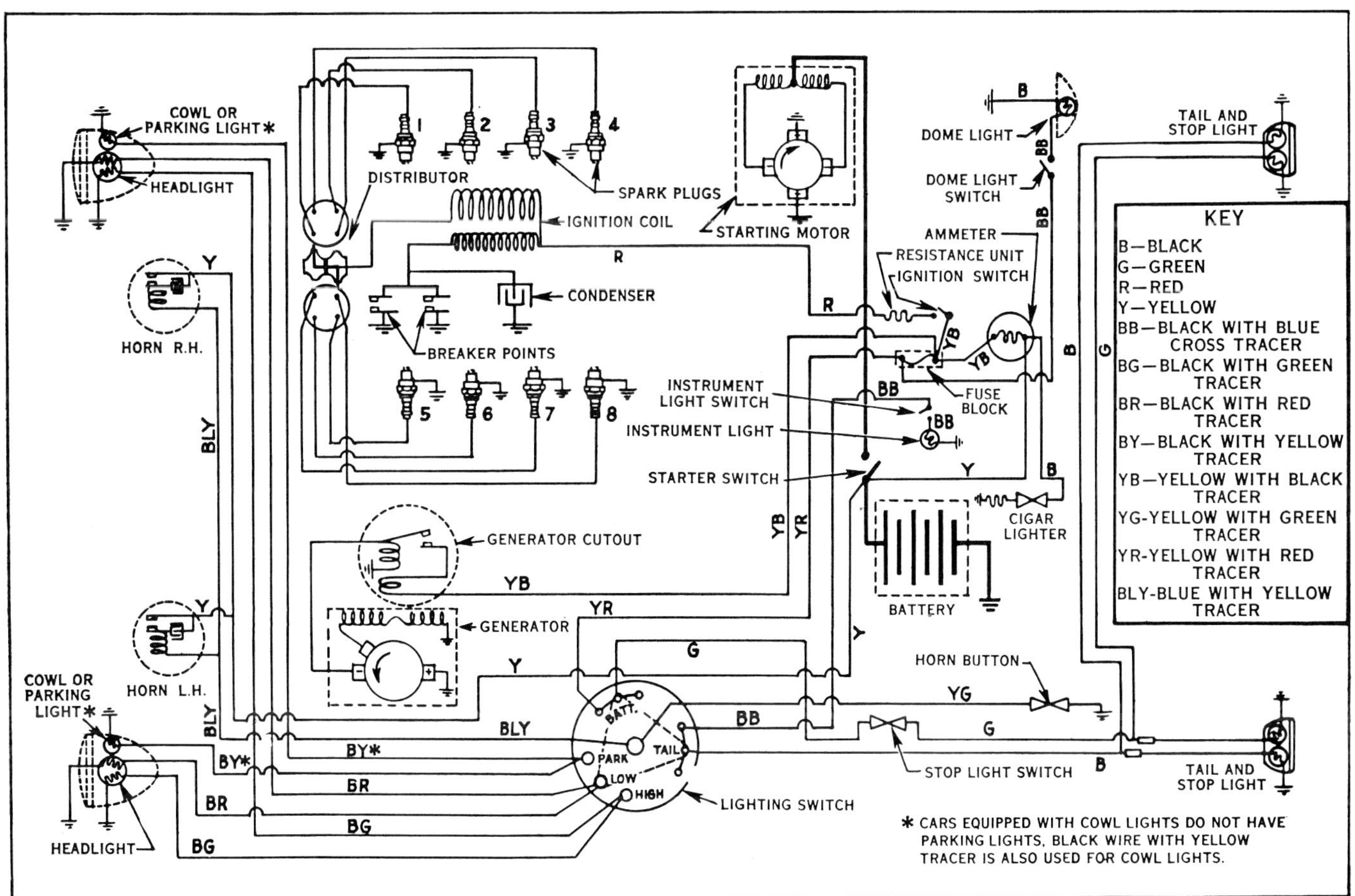

1933 — 8 cylinder wiring diagram.

with a foot operated dimmer switch became available.

The early 1932 four cylinder wiring assembly was obsoleted in May 1932 when the fuse block was added.

Distributor, Coil, and Condenser

The V-8 distributor was located at the front of the engine and was driven by the end of the cam shaft. The original design consisted of a two-piece bakelite housing with the Model A coil core and condenser sealed inside. Since the condenser was held in a recess, it therefore, required no mounting clamp. A significant improvement over the Model A, the distributor contained a centrifugal governor and vacuum system which provided an automatic spark control. The distributor was originally mounted to the front cover with four bolts, but after 4,250 cars had been built, the mounting method was changed to three bolts. Dealers were directed to install the new distributor and front cover on the early cars as stock became available.

In August 1932, the centrifugal governor was improved and the distributor caps and covers were modified. This design was identified by the addition of graduation marks on the manual spark adjustment screw plate.

A new Ford designed two-piece short coil held together with a metal band was released in May 1932 as a low production option. In November, a modified version without the metal band, went into full production for use on all V-8 engines. The Ford script was cast on its top for identification. This unit was used through 1936.

A low production optional short coil with a belt around its perimeter was used as an option for a short period from

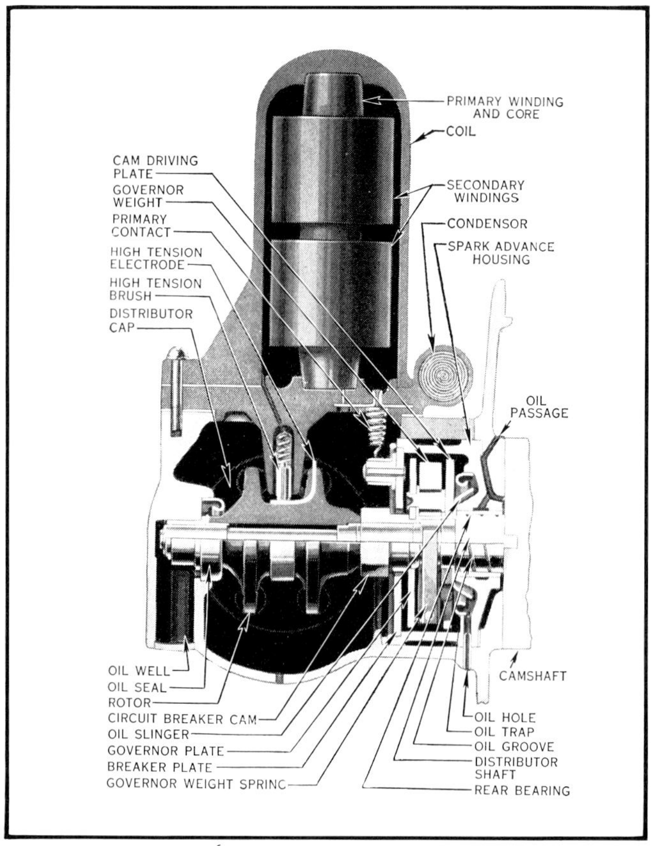

Section drawing of the V-8 distributor.

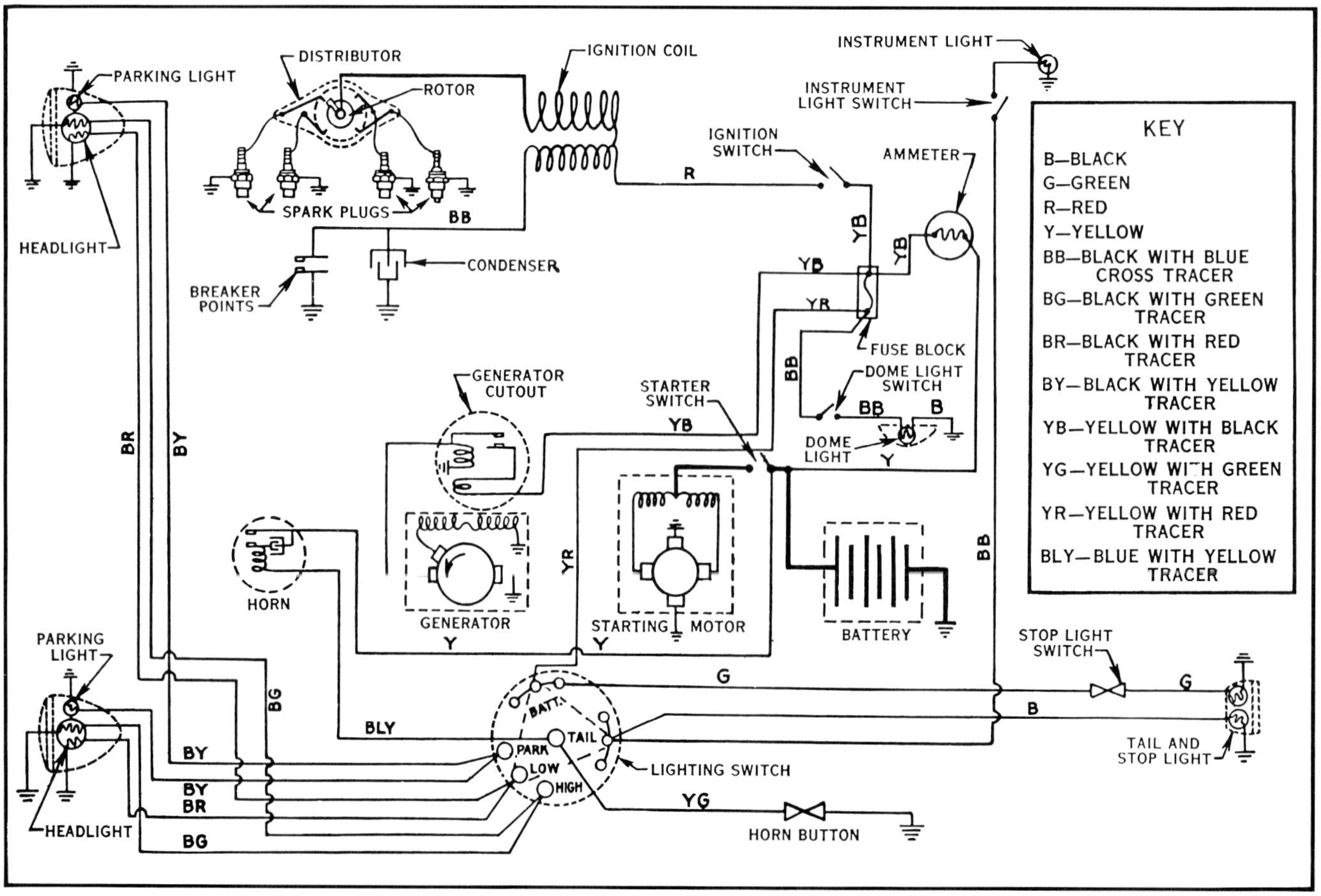

KEY
B—BLACK
G—GREEN
R—RED
Y—YELLOW
BB—BLACK WITH BLUE CROSS TRACER
BG—BLACK WITH GREEN TRACER
BR—BLACK WITH RED TRACER
BY—BLACK WITH YELLOW TRACER
YB—YELLOW WITH BLACK TRACER
YG—YELLOW WITH GREEN TRACER
YR—YELLOW WITH RED TRACER
BLY—BLUE WITH YELLOW TRACER

1933 — 4 cylinder wiring diagram.

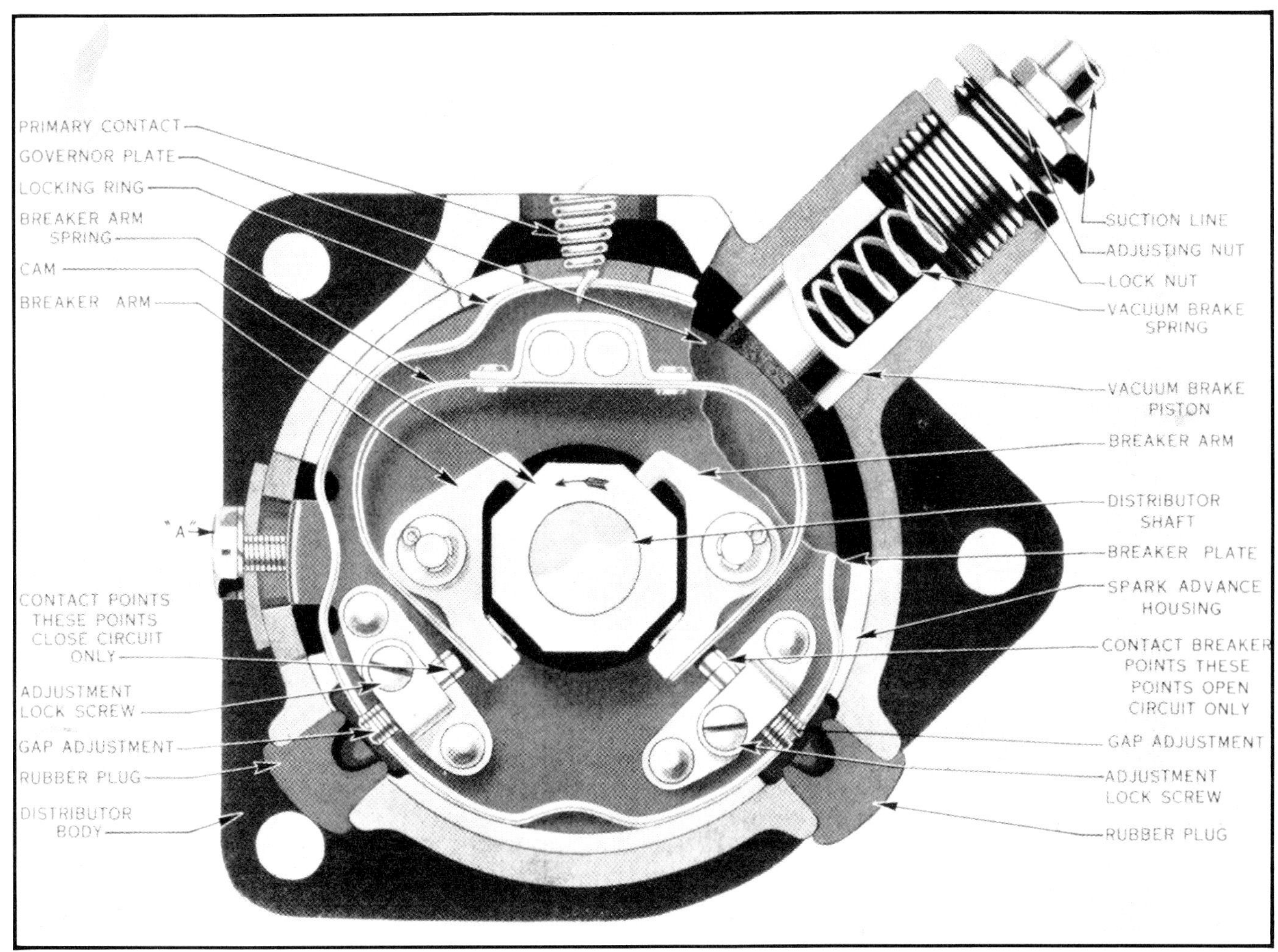

Section drawing of the V-8 distributor circuit breaker.

Spark Plug Chart

Engine and Effective Dates	Type	Thread
4 Cyl. Job-1, 1932 to October 1932	3X	7/8 x 18
8 Cyl. Job-1, 1932 to October 1932	C4X	7/8 x 18
4 Cyl. October 1932 to March 1934	C4	7/8 x 18
8 Cyl. October 1932 to December 1932	C4	7/8 x 18
8 Cyl. December 1932 to January 1936	C7	18mm
8 Cyl. August 1933 to May 1935	18*	18mm
8 Cyl. November 1933 to November 1937	7	18mm
8 Cyl. December 1934 to January 1935	6 Com*	18mm
8 Cyl. May 1935 to November 1937	6 Com*	18mm
8 Cyl. 85 HP, November 1937 thru 1938	H10	14mm
8 Cyl. 60 HP, Job-1, 1937 thru 1938	H10	14mm
8 Cyl. 85 HP, November 1937 thru 1938	JC10.64A*	14mm
8 Cyl. 60 HP, November 1937 thru 1938	JC10.64A*	14mm

*Heavy duty, customer option for Special Delivery, police cars, taxi cabs, etc.

June 1933 to July 1935.

Beginning with the 1933 passenger and commercial models, a new distributor body was released with an improved centrifugal governor. A number "40" was stamped on the end of the distributor shaft to distinguish these units from the 1932 assemblies. In May 1933, a hole was added to the shaft bushing in line with the hole in the distributor base to improve lubrication. In addition, a flat spot was cut on the shaft to allow crankcase fumes into the distributor, thus minimizing the possibility of corrosion forming on the distributor shaft. A special calcium soap grease, rather than vaseline, was recommended for greasing the distributor cam.

With the introduction of the duplex carburetor in December 1933, the centrifugal governor weights were made heavier. For these units, the "40" stamped on the end of the shaft was changed to "40-B." At the same time, service distributors to replace the "40" units were stamped "40-A." The 40-B distributor was used through 1936.

Starting with the 1936 production, a new distributor body with a short Ford script flat top coil was introduced on an experimental basis. By June 1936, it was being used on 40% of production, identified with the number "68" stamped on the end of the distributor shaft. For 1937 it was modified by the addition of a taller coil. The coil housing had the Ford script on top, but the condenser was mounted externally. This was used through 1938.

The condensers for these distributors were identical, but the mounting tail bracket differed with the various designs. The original condenser was rated at .30 to .34 microfarads. In May 1932, it changed to .28 to .30 and in October 1934 the rating became .33 to .36 microfarads. Starting in July 1936, the Ford script and a code number identifying the manufacturer was added—number one for Mallory, two for

Sprague, and three for Bosch. All condensers were cadmium plated except for the one used during May to October 1932, which was painted black.

The four cylinder engine distributor was identical to the Model A, except that it included the centrifugal governor for automatic spark advance. The externally mounted condenser had a long 3¼-inch connection wire. Exterior finish was black enamel or cadmium plated. The coil, which was a carry-over from the Model A, was mounted on the fire wall.

Stop Light Switch

The stop light switch was mounted on the frame below the floor and was actuated by the movement of the brake pedal. The original design for 1932 was produced by Douglas. In July 1932, however, a Ford designed switch became optional. Starting with the 1933 models this Ford switch was the only one used. A mounting bracket change was made for 1933 production and again for 1935 production. The stop light switch was cadmium plated.

Horn

The 1932 horn was a modified version of the Sparton motor driven Model A horn. The back cover was flat on each side to permit the horn to mount low in the V formed between the radiator shell and fender. In June, a new vibrator type horn was introduced and the old motor driven one was phased out. The new horn was slightly shorter with a domed back cover. Because of its operating characteristic, it required a new insulated spring steel mounting bracket. Both old and new horns were painted with black enamel.

For the all new 1933 passenger cars the horn was completely restyled. The domed vibrator assembly sat on top of the horn and the projector had a 90° bend. Also, for the first time, there were both a standard and a deluxe horn. For the standard model cars, including the Station Wagon and Sedan Delivery, one horn painted all black was mounted on the left side. However, the standard wiring harness had extra connections for installing a second horn on the right side at extra cost, if desired. The deluxe model cars were equipped with two horns. On these the domed cover was chromeplated and the projector was black with its bell chrome plated. This deluxe horn had a different vibrating system and its parts were not interchangeable with the standard horn. The 1933 horns were used through 1934.

Both the 1933 and 1934 commercial vehicles and trucks used the 1932 style horn. Starting in June 1934, the Station Wagon and Sedan Delivery were also equipped with the dual deluxe horns. However, the Sedan Delivery was changed back to the single standard horn in July.

The 1933 and 1934 style horn with minor design changes was used on the 1935 passenger cars. The commercial vehicles and trucks, except the Station Wagon and deluxe commercials, were updated with the all black standard 1933–34 horn. A standard style horn produced by Schwarze

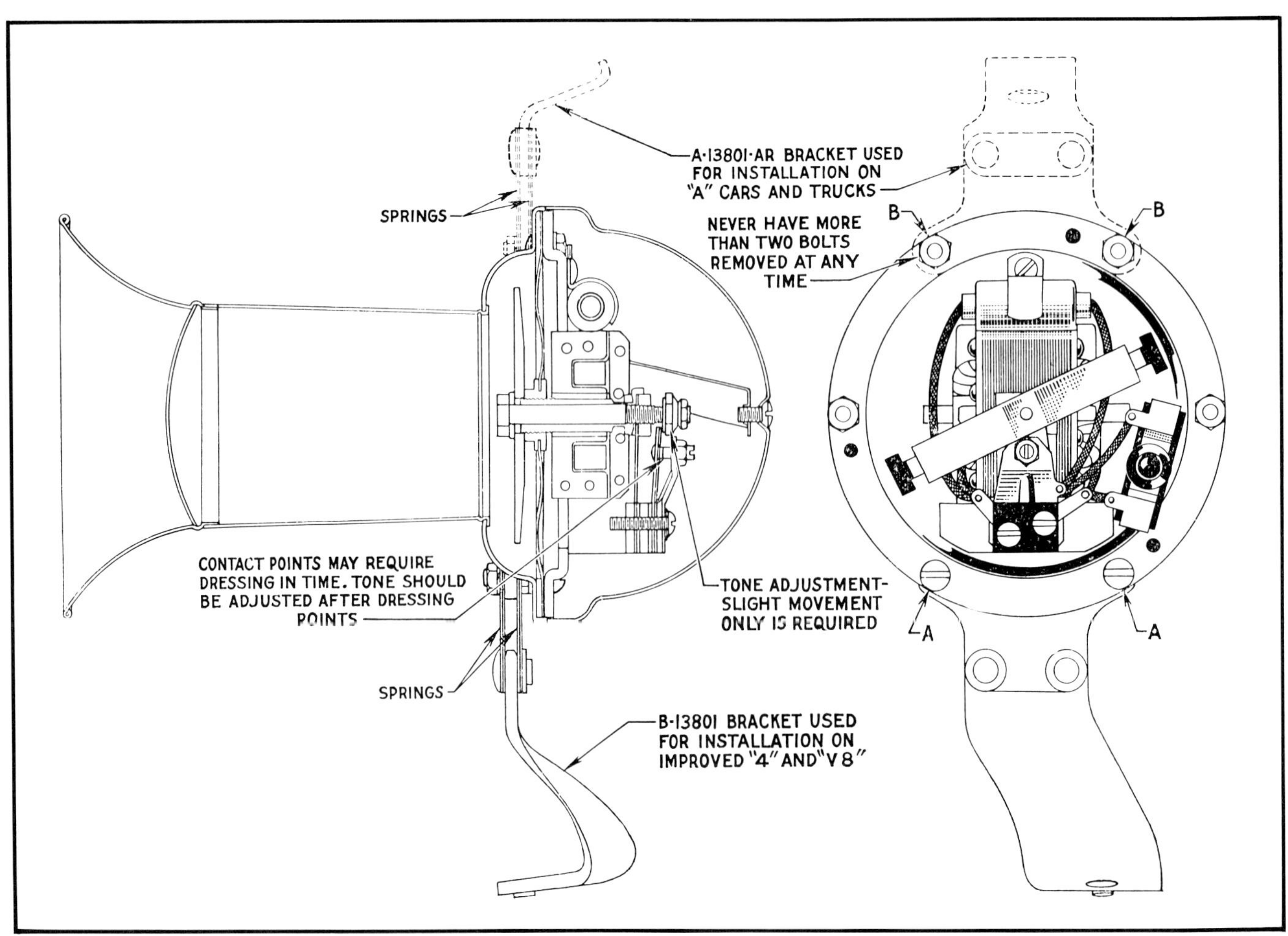

Section drawing of the vibrator horn.

became available in April 1935. Its appearance was identical to the Sparton horn.

Starting with the 1936 passenger cars, the horn was mounted behind the fender apron, with only a small grilled opening to indicate its location. Both Sparton and Schwarze produced these horns. One Schwarze horn was used on the standard passenger and commercial cars and two Sparton horns were used on the deluxe passenger cars. Both horns were painted black.

In 1937, the horn was mounted in the engine compartment. The standard passenger cars and commercials had a single vibrator type horn produced by Sparks-Withington, while the deluxe passenger cars had a set of dual horns produced by Sparton.

New air-electric horns, produced by Sparks-Withington, were introduced on the 1938 deluxe passenger cars. A pair of horns were used, one having a low pitch and the other a high pitch. The standard passenger cars were equipped with two vibrator Sparton horns mounted side by side. The commercial vehicles carried a single vibrator type horn produced by Sparks-Withington.

Radio, Glove Box Clock and Road Lamp

During the period of 1932 to 1938 three electrical items were available as factory installation. They were the radio, glove box clock and road lamp.

In 1932, an Engineering approved radio was offered for the first time on Ford cars. Produced by Grigsby-Grunow Company, it consisted of two metal containers, one for the motor generator "B" supply and the other for the chassis, speaker, and steering column mounted dial head. The metal boxes were inserted into and below the rear floor pan, and cables ran from the dial to the metal boxes. The radio, available as special equipment, was installed at the assembly plant. A slightly different style radio was also available for Police fleet vehicles.

The antenna for the 1932 cars was mounted to the running board. For 1933 cars, the antenna was still mounted to the running board on all models except the Tudor, Fordor and Victoria which had a roof mounted antenna.

In September 1933, a new six tube superheterodyne radio, which used a vibrator instead of a motor generator, was released as special equipment. It mounted behind the glove box door. To compensate for the lost glove box space a set of matching cowl cardboards was included. The right hand cowel cardboard contained a storage pocket. In November a spare wheel antenna was released for cars which did not use the roof mounted antenna.

A Zenith made radio became available in March 1934, while one manufactured by Philco was optional in May. The dial and controls of the Philco radio were installed in the ash tray opening on the dash of deluxe models and in the same relative location on the standard models. The radio chassis and speaker housing was hung under the dash, over the steering column. This unit, with its styled controls on the dash, was referred to as the Ford Center Control Radio and replaced all previous types.

Early in 1935, a header bar speaker was installed between the sun visors on closed cars. However, starting with the 1936 cars a smaller speaker was used whereby the header bar speaker was concealed behind the head lining. As a sales promotion, the first 1000 deluxe cars built at each assembly plant was equipped with a radio. In April, Zenith became a secondary supplier.

A new trend was established with the introduction of the 1938 cars. The dial, radio controls, and speaker grill were incorporated as part of the overall instrument panel design.

Before 1935, the electric clock was an accessory and only available at the dealers. Starting with the 1935 cars, however, the electric clock became standard equipment on some models and special equipment on others. The 1935 clock was mounted on the glove box door and its finish matched the speedometer. It was standard equipment on the Convertible Fordor but special equipment on all other car models. Because the glove box door was very shallow on the Roadster and Phaeton, a different bracket was used to mount the clock on those models.

The bezel around the face of the clock was finished bright chrome in 1935 but changed to satin chrome in 1936. In June 1936, when a new instrument panel was introduced, the clock was changed to match.

In addition to the electric clock, a stem wound one was introduced on 1937 cars. Starting in March electric clocks were installed at the factory on all deluxe models. In May, requirements were changed to install electric clocks in all deluxe models except Deluxe Tudor, Deluxe Tudor Touring, Deluxe Coupe and Club Coupe, which were equipped with the stem wound clock. Both clocks were available as special equipment on standard models. In July, factory installation of all clocks was discontinued and the item became available only at the dealers as an accessory.

In 1938, both the electric and the stem wound clocks were available, but, very few were installed at the factory as special equipment. Most clocks were installed at the dealers as an accessory.

The road lamp became available as a special equipment item in 1937. It mounted on the bumper support bar and was available on all passenger cars, commercials and trucks. It was finished in bright chrome plate.

Instrument Panel and Instruments

The instruments on the 1932 and 1933 vehicles were mounted to an instrument panel which in turn mounted to the dash panel. However, starting with the 1934 models, the instrument panel was eliminated and the instruments were individually mounted on the dash panel.

Oval shaped, the instrument panel on the 1932 V-8 had a chrome plated finish with an "engine turn" pattern. An identical instrument panel, painted black was used on the Model B, commercial vehicles, and trucks at introduction, but by April, the color of the instrument panel on the Model B passenger cars was changed to Thorn Brown. However, a month later, the V-8 chrome plated instrument panel was adopted for all vehicles. The panel consisted of a speedometer, ammeter, fuel gauge, throttle control, choke control and dash light switch.

Three manufacturers supplied the speedometers and speedometer cable assembly. They were Stewart Warner, Delco Appliance and Waltham. The speedometer bezel was finished in bright chrome plate with the inside surface between the lens and the dial, painted flat white. The dial face was black with white numbers 0 to 80. The odometer barrel was white with black numbers except the one tenth numbers which were red. In May 1932, the speedometer numbers on the V-8 passenger cars were changed to 0 to 90.

Late 1932 instrument panel. Also note the mounting of the sun visor, rearview mirror, and the stitching on the door panel.

The ammeter dial, located on the left side, was finished similar to the speedometer with the scale 0–10–20 and the words ampers, discharge, and charge in white on a black background.

Similar in size and finish, the Ford hydrostatic type fuel gauge was on the right side of the instrument panel. Its gage consisted of a vertical glass tube filled with a red fluid. The figures 0, ¼, ½, and F were on each side of the tube. A light window on the left side of the dial was covered with a frosted celluloid tinted light blue.

Also on the instrument panel were the throttle control, choke control, and dash light switch knobs which were all identically made of Thorn Brown phenolic. The faces of the knobs were Thorn Brown with white lettering within a white circle. The outer edge of the knobs had a knurled pattern. The mounting bushing was chrome plated. On the V-8 models, the throttle control was on the left, the dash light switch on the right, and the choke control on the lower center edge. On the B models and commercial vehicles, the throttle control was also on the left, but the choke control was on the right, and the dash light was not provided prior to June except for special order. Thereafter, the light became standard, similar to the V-8.

On the 1933 vehicles, the instrument panel shape was restyled and shifted from the center of the dash panel to a position above the steering column. Similar to the 1932 style, it was made of chrome plated steel with the engine turn pattern, but it contained only the speedometer, ammeter and fuel gauge. The other controls were then individually mounted to the dash panel. In October 1933 when the engine turn pattern was dropped, the instrument panel was painted one of three colors. On standard passenger cars and Sedan Deliveries it was maroon, on deluxe passenger cars it was painted a walnut wood grain pattern, but on the Station Wagon the panel became Winterleaf Brown.

The speedometer was still produced by the same three manufacturers, but the dial face finish was changed to butler finish chrome with the brush marks running vertically. The Ford oval trade mark, numbers, graduations and pointer were finished in black. The numbers went from 0 to 90. Starting in April 1933, the speedometer installed on standard vehicles had a 100 mile trip odometer while those installed on the deluxe vehicles had a 1000 mile trip odometer.

The ammeter and fuel gauges were oval shaped in a vertical position. The dial faces, made of sheet brass with a brushed silver finish, had black lettering to match the speedometer. The scale on the fuel gauge was changed to 0, ½ and F. In May 1933, the two post terminal on the back of the ammeter was changed to a "U" shaped terminal. Introduction was on a limited basis at the Rouge line, but by October it was used on all vehicles.

Early 1933 dash and instrument panel with the new glove box door, ash tray and window regulator handle. The rearview mirror was a carry over from 1932. The visors are covered with headlining material and trimmed with artificial leather.

Mid 1934 dash panel including the radio and heater installation, typical of that period. Other features include the tunnel mat and the relocated door handle and lock latch.

The throttle and choke controls, located in the center of the dash, were separated by the ash tray. The throttle was on the left and choke on the right, with knobs identical to 1932. However, the material was changed to a mixed maroon and Thorn Brown phenolic.

The instrument panel light switch, changed to the toggle type, was located under the instrument panel on the left side.

On the 1934 dash panel, the major change was the elimination of the instrument panel. The shape of this instrument panel was stamped into the dash panel and the carryover 1933 instruments were mounted directly to it. The change actually started with job one in November 1933, but due to production problems, some 1934 models were equipped with the 1933 style instrument panel. In May 1934, the maximum calibration on the ammeter dial was increased from 20 to 30; in July, the same change was made on the commercial vehicles.

With the introduction of the two barrel carburetor in 1934, the throttle and choke controls were redesigned. The length of the new knob was reduced ¼ inch, the flat shape of the head was changed to spherical, and the knurl pattern around the head and the white circle around the lettering were eliminated. In addition, the metal bezel was replaced by a rubber grommet which came in three colors: maroon for the standard models, mahogany for the deluxe, and black for commercial vehicles and trucks.

An all new dash and instrument panel was designed for 1935. The speedometer was the same size as 1934 but it had a new silver face with a vertical brush pattern and a gray inner ring. Its speed scale and numbers were also gray, except the five mile marks, which were Salvia red. The needle was white with its tip and counterbalance also finished in Salvia Red. In addition, the maximum calibration was increased from 90 to 100 MPH. Similar to 1934, the deluxe vehicles had a speedometer with a 1000 miles trip odometer, while all other vehicles had the 100 miles trip odometer.

The face of the fuel gauge and the ammeter were finished to match the speedometer, but their shape was changed from oval to round. The fuel gauge was still the hydrostatic type with the word "fuel" on the right side and a scale "E, ½, F" on the left. For the first time, a combination fuel and oil pressure gauge became available as special equipment. The ammeter unit was used only on the standard Tudor, Fordor, Coupe, Sedan Delivery, commercial vehicles, and trucks. The other body styles used a new combination ammeter and temperature gauge. In August the single ammeter was discontinued and all vehicles were equipped with the combination ammeter-temperature gauge instruments.

The passenger car choke and throttle knobs were made slightly shorter, though the head was made larger. Maroon phenolic knobs with white letters and a maroon rubber grommet were installed on standard vehicles, but light taupe plastic knobs with vermillion letters and a taupe rubber grommet were installed on the deluxe. Commercial vehicles and trucks used the carryover 1934 style knobs made of maroon phenolic.

The instrument light switch on the passenger cars changed from the toggle type to the push-pull type mounted on the dash. It was made of the same material and was finished to match the choke and throttle knobs. However, the commercial vehicles and trucks continued to use the 1934 toggle switch.

Instruments for 1936 vehicles were mostly a carryover of the 1935 instruments with some minor modifications. The bezel finish was changed to bright chrome plate and the Ford trade mark oval was added to the dial face of the speedometer. A more notable change was made on the fuel gauge when the old hydrostatic type gave way to a new electric fuel gauge. As in 1935, the standard cars were still equipped with a fuel gauge only, while the deluxe models were produced with the combination fuel and oil pressure gauges. However, the combination fuel and oil pressure gauges were available on all other vehicles as special equipment.

In May 1936, with the introduction of the new wood grain finish on the dash panel the finish on the faces of the instruments was changed to harmonizing shades of brown mahogany.

The choke, throttle and instrument light switch knobs for the standard cars were changed to Benton Gray plastic with white letters and Benton Gray grommets. On the deluxe cars, the knobs were light gray with black letters and also a Benton Gray grommet. In May with the introduction of the wood grained finish on the dash, the knobs were changed to Benton Gray plastic with white letters for all passenger cars. As a match, the grommets were changed to a neutral brown rubber. The choke and throttle knobs on the commercial dash were dark taupe with white letters, but by January 1936 they were changed to Benton Gray with white letters, similar to the standard passenger cars. The instrument lamp switch on the commercials was the toggle type, a carryover from 1935.

For 1937, the dash panel was restyled and the ammeter, temperature gauge, fuel gauge and oil pressure gauge were clustered in one unit to match the size of the speedometer face. The backgrounds of the dials were finished in brushed silver plate while the calibrations, letters, and pointers were dark taupe. This cluster of gauges became standard equipment for all 1937 vehicles.

The speedometer dial was about the same size as the 1936 unit, but the scale, pointer and numbers were restyled. The face of the dial was finished in brushed silver plate and dark taupe to match the gauges.

The choke, throttle, and dash light knobs were all made of taupe plastic and had a corrugated outer edge. The letters were black and the dash grommets were Rustic Brown rubber. On commercial vehicles and trucks, the 1936 Benton Gray knobs with white letters and the toggle type instru-

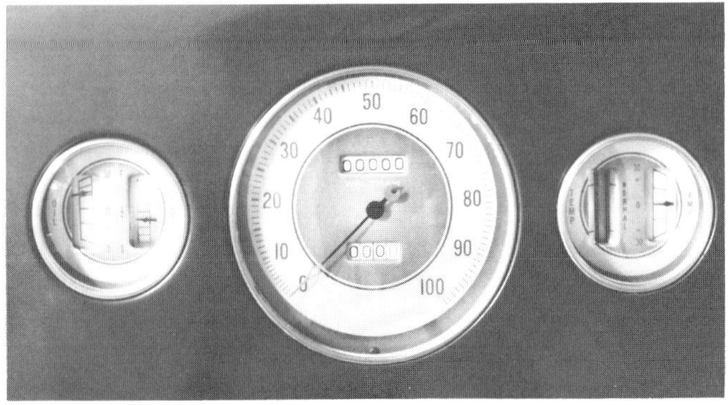

Typical 1935-36 instrument cluster.

The early 1935 front compartment showing dash and seat back.

An early 1936 dash panel showing the restyled center trim panel, glove box handle and windshield regulator handle.

The 1937 style dash panel and the banjo type steering wheel which was standard on deluxe models. Note that a special opening was provided for the radio installation.

The 1938 dash panel and modified banjo type steering wheel. For the first time, the dash provided space for a complete radio installation including speaker. The oval shaped mirror was introduced in 1937. The clock was a factory installed accessory.

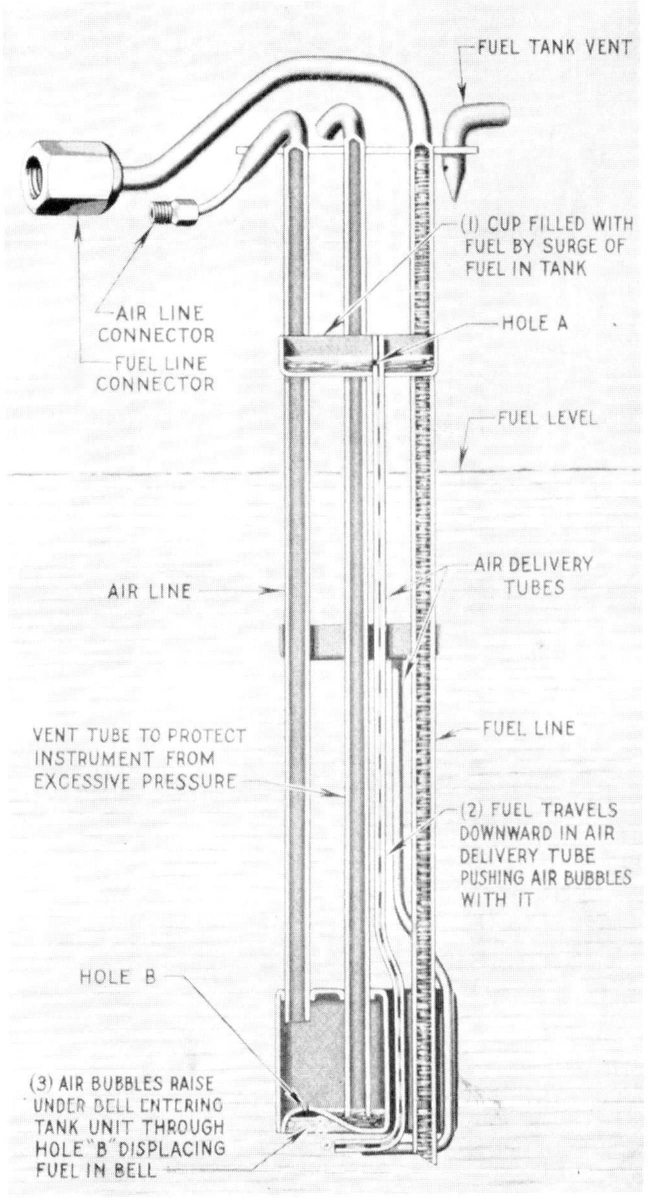

Cross section of fuel gauge tank unit.

ment light switch were used through the years 1937 and 1938.

Instruments for 1938 were a carryover of the 1937 style except for the finish. Standard passenger car gauges were finished with vertically brushed silver, while letters, calibration marks, and pointers were brown. On deluxe passenger cars the dials were finished in a rich low sheen brass with black letters, calibration marks, and pointers. Commercial vehicles and trucks were equipped with the same

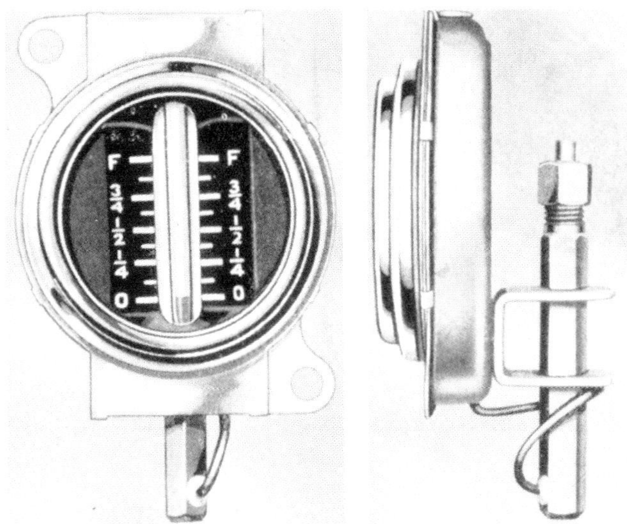

Fuel gauge head unit.

gauges and finish as 1937.

The speedometer face for 1938 had restyled numbers and pointer but the background finish was similar to the instruments.

A new trend was established with the 1938 dash panel. The radio grill and controls were moved to the dash board, and the choke and throttle controls were included as part of the overall design. The knobs were made smaller but longer, and were set in a depression on the dash. They were made of Zephyr Beige plastic, and instead of the words "choke" and "throttle," only the black letters "C" and "T" were on the face.

Fuel Gauge Tank Sending Unit

The Ford hydrostatic type fuel system used from 1932 through 1935, consisted of three units—the head, tank unit, and air lines which connected the two. The heart of the system was the sending unit in the tank. In operation, as the tank was filled, the gasoline trapped air in the air chamber of the sending unit as well as in the air lines connecting to the head unit on the instrument panel. The pressure of the rising gasoline, communicated through the air tubes and air lines to the head unit, was recorded by the rise of a red liquid in a thermometer-like glass tube.

Two different sending unit assemblies were used, one for passenger cars and another for commercial vehicles. The system was modified for 1935 vehicles and those units are not interchangeable with the earlier design.

Starting with the 1936 models, an electrical sending unit actuated by a cork float was used. In December 1936, the length of the float arm was increased by 3/8 of an inch. This system was used through 1938.

VI—Body Construction and Finish

Body building for passenger cars was a natural evolution from carriage bodies. When carriage builders were commissioned to supply bodies for automobiles, the art had already become both highly skilled and competitive. During the early period forming of surface sheet metal on a volume basis was introduced, but parts were fabricated merely by bending and without drawing of metal. The hood, fenders, cowel panels and body skins, however, had very little shape and offered little if any contribution to body structure. The load carrying members—sills, door frames, tonneau frames, and floor boards—were generally wood.

Around 1912, the art of drawing sheet metal became feasible and presses with great capacities were developed. At the same time, the art of die making was advancing—and the metallurgy of sheet metal had developed enough to provide steel with deep drawing characteristics. The manner in which the steel was used over the wood marked the beginning of Body Engineering and the transition from hand made carriages to the machine made automobiles.

In the 20s, as demand for enclosed automobile bodies increased, and the ability to draw, arc, and spot weld sheet metal progressed, more and larger structural steel parts were utilized. As part of the transition from wood to steel, the high volume body types had steel for their structural parts while low volume bodies still used wood.

When Ford changed from the Model T to the Model A, its high volume Tudor body closely approached the all steel automobile body. Later, in August 1931, Ford introduced the first all-steel body shell. Even though it was a commercial pickup truck, it was the industry's first all-steel body. Development and production of the 1932 bodies was an extention of the process used on the Model A—more steel and less wood. Ford's exterior body finishing operation in 1932, a process developed at the new Rouge Assembly Plant when Ford changed from Model T to the Model A in 1927, was regarded as one of the best in the industry.

The first production step was the assembly of the bare metal body shell, known as the "body-in-white." This included putting into place all exterior metal panels, sills, pillars, braces, doors and deck lids, with the exclusion of interior and exterior trim, hardware, locks, latches and regulators. A body shell so constructed then moved from the body-in-white line to the paint line.

Here, prior to painting, the sheet metal was treated with

Typical 1914 body assembly operation. (Courtesy: Herbert Alle.)

a metal cleaning solution containing a phosphoric acid base to remove all surface oil and contaminants. Next was a water rinse followed by a drying with the conveyor running through a tunnel-like oven for five minutes.

After drying, the sheet metal required putty glazing. In this step, pyroxylin glaze was knifed on manually as a filler for any low spots, dings or scratches. The putty glaze was feathered out to the surface of the original metal, thus creating a smooth base for the painting operation.

The next step was that of spraying on a primer. The spray booth was actually a tunnel with an operator stationed at each side. The car bodies on a conveyor moved through the spray booth or tunnel.

The primer material used was of the red oxide type. The first coat of the two coat process was sprayed on horizontally over the entire surface of the body, while the second coat was sprayed vertically.

Body assembly fixture for the five window Coupe.

Prime bake was next. Here the wet bodies ran along the conveyor through a prime bake oven. All ovens received their heat from steam pipes and operated at temperatures between 190–220 degree Fahrenheit. The speed at which the body moved through this oven was regulated so that the primer was subjected to the same temperature range for about one hour—sufficient time for it to set to a hard surface.

From the oven, the conveyor moved across what was known as a "wet sand" deck. This was simply an area with drains to carry away the water with which the sandpaper was used. A manual operation was performed here with the water used to reduce the cutting action of the sandpaper, thus providing a smoother surface. At the same time, the water flushed off the abrasive and waste materials.

The first color spray followed the sanding operation. This again was a spray booth operation with a conveyor line running through another tunnel-type booth where a spray operator was stationed on each side. As in the primer application, color spraying was also a two-coat operation—one horizontal and one vertical. The body finish was pyroxylin lacquer, reportedly the finest and most enduring finish of that time. The main body color also covered the entire inside of the fire wall. Any wood braces and frames had a gray-black wood preservative applied earlier, so no special effort was made to paint them with the body color.

The body subsequently moved out of the spray booth and was allowed to air dry for five minutes. Then, it moved through a second spray booth where two more coats of color, one horizontal and one vertical, were applied.

From this station the bodies were carried through a primary color bake oven where the units remained for twenty minutes. Next came the masking operation for two-tone models. Any second tone or moulding trim color was applied over the base body color.

A third coat of paint, air dried for five minutes; a fourth coat followed by a second twenty-minute color bake completed the paint application. Now the body was ready for the final wet sanding operation, accomplished as before.

The final step in body finishing was that of polish. A special lacquer polishing compound was applied over the body by polishers who worked the entire painted surface with polishing wheels covered with lambs wool. This method produced the luster of which the pyroxylin or lac-

Body soldering operation.

Primed bodies going through the bake oven.

Typical painting operation.

The application of the stripe added the final touch to the body finish.

quer was capable. The polishing compound itself had some solvent action but no abrasive effect. It brought out an even texture and removed minute scratches that might have resulted from the wet sanding operation.

After polishing, the completely painted body, except for stripe, was then ready for the interior trim line. The stripe was added after the body was placed on the chassis.

The body finishing method described here was used until April 1933, when Ford started the change over from pyroxylin lacquer to baked enamel. Ford had been experimenting with baked enamel on commercial bodies at the Chicago and Edgewater assembly plants before converting the entire Chicago plant in April. Following the Chicago conversion, other assembly plants changed to the baked enamel finish at the rate of one plant per week. Chester was converted the first week in May followed by Edgewater, Somerville, Kansas City, Richmond and Louisville.

The new baked enamel provided a more durable finish, but the real advantage was the reduction in painting time by five to seven hours per body.

Passenger Car Miscellaneous Data

	1932	1933	1934	1935	1936	1937	1938
Wheel Base (in inches)	106	112	112	112	112	112	112
Tread Front	55.0	55.2	55.2	55.47	55.47	55.47	55.47
Tread Rear	56.28	56.68	56.68	58.25	58.25	58.25	58.25
Overall Length	165.5	175.9	175.9	182.75	182.75	179.5	183.75
Spring Base	113.54	119.54	119.54	123.13	123.13	123.13	123.13
Width	67.4	67.4	67.4	69.5	69.5	69.7	69.7
Weight (in pounds)							
Std. Fordor (8 cyl.)	2512	2675	2675	2849	2845	2761	2800
Std. Fordor (4 cyl.)	2432	2595	2995	–	–	–	–
Std. Fordor (60 HP)	–	–	–	–	–	2543	2579
Pickup Truck (8 cyl.)	2496	2514	2514	2714	2714	2705	2705
Pickup Truck (4 cyl.)	2416	2434	2595	–	–	–	–
Pickup Truck (60 HP)	–	–	–	–	–	2508	2508

Model Identification Numbers

Body Types	1932	1933-34	1935	1936	1937	1938
Passenger Cars, 8 Cyl.	18	40	48	68	78	81A
Passenger Cars, 4 Cyl.	B	40	–	–	–	–
Passenger Cars, 60 HP	–	–	–	–	74	82A
Commercials, 8 Cyl.	B	46	50	67	77	81C
Commercials, 4 Cyl.	B	46	–	–	–	–
Commercials, 60 HP	–	–	–	–	73	82C

Body Types Identification Numbers

Body Types	1932	1933	1934	1935	1936	1937	1938
Tudor Sedan Std.	B-55	700	700	700	700	700-A	700-C
Tudor Sedan Dlx.	B-55	700	700	700	700	700-B	700-B
Tudor Touring Sed. Std.	–	–	–	–	700	700-C	–
Tudor Touring Sed. Dlx.	–	–	–	700	700	700-D	–
Roadster Std.	B-40	710	–	–	–	–	–
Roadster Dlx.	B-40	710	710	710	710	710	–
Coupe (3W) Std.	–	720	–	–	–	–	–
Coupe (3W) Dlx.	B-520	720	720	720	720	–	–
Club Coupe	–	–	–	–	–	720	–
Club Coupe Dlx.	–	–	–	–	–	–	720
Sport Coupe	B-50	–	–	–	–	–	–
Fordor Sedan Std.	B-160	730	730	730	730	730-A	730-C
Fordor Sedan Dlx.	B-160	730	730	730	730	730-B	730-B
Fordor Touring Sed. Std.	–	–	–	–	730	730-C	–
Fordor Touring Sed. Dlx.	–	–	–	730	730	730-D	–
Victoria	B-190	740	740	–	–	–	–
Convertible Sedan	B-400	–	–	740	740	740	740
Phaeton Std.	B-35	750	–	–	–	–	–
Phaeton Dlx.	B-35	750	750	750	750	750	750
Cabriolet	B-68	760	760	760	760	760-A	–
Club Cabriolet	–	–	–	–	760	760-B	–
Dlx. Convertible Coupe	–	–	–	–	–	–	760-A
Dlx. Conv. Club Coupe	–	–	–	–	–	–	760-B
Coupe (5W) Std.	B-45	770	770	770	770	770-A	770-A
Coupe (5W) Dlx.	–	770	770	770	770	770-B	770-B
Std. Coupe (5W) Pickup	–	–	–	–	–	–	770-C
Sedan Delivery	B-410	850	850	780	780	–	–
Sedan Delivery Std.	–	–	–	–	–	780	780-A
Sedan Delivery Dlx.	–	–	–	–	–	780	780-B
Station Wagon	B-150	860	860	790	790	790	790
Open Cab	B-76	800	800	–	–	–	–
Closed Cab	B-82	810	810	810	810	–	810
Closed Cab Std.	–	–	–	–	–	810	–
Closed Cab Dlx.	–	–	–	–	–	810	–
Panel Delivery	–	–	–	–	–	–	820
Panel Delivery Std.	B-79	820	820	820	820	820	–
Panel Delivery Dlx.	B-79	820	820	820	820	820	–

VII—The 1932 Models

The design of the 1932 Ford was predominately a major face lift of the 1931 Model A. However, with its longer lower body and a longer hood featuring a V type radiator grille, it portrayed a beautiful well proportioned automobile. In its advertisements the company stated: "The compactness of the V-8 engine which requires no more space than the four cylinder type permits the use of roomy bodies for passenger comfort. The deep seats are low, and as the center of gravity is also low, you ride with a new sense of ease and security."

Production of the 1932 bodies was started at the Rouge Plant on December 1, 1931, but less than a week later, Henry Ford stopped everything with his announcement of plans to produce a V-8 engine. When production resumed in March 1932, body changes had to be made to the floor pan and dash to accommodate the new V-8 engine.

When the 1932 models were initially released, the color break followed the pattern used on the Model A, with a different color for upper body, lower body and belt. The five color combinations were Washington Blue Medium with black, Old Chester Gray with Tunis Gray, Brewster Green Light with Brewster Green Medium, Ford Medium Maroon with black, and all black. The reveals were painted lower body color similar to the Model A. Wheels were black except on the deluxe models which could have Tacoma Cream, Apple Green or Aurora Red, depending on body color. In addition to the standard combinations, other color choices were possible through special orders and fleet sales. These special order combinations, however, were limited to the colors in stock at the assembly plants.

While the V-8 engine was being developed, the Sales Department, which at this time was responsible for selection of exterior body colors, decided to change the body colors. As a result, on April 15, 1932, the original color combinations were replaced by eight new ones. These new combinations eliminated the upper and lower pattern, but still used a different color for the belt molding. Bodies already produced with the original color combinations continued to be used. The number of bodies produced by that date was not recorded, but it can be assumed to be a large number since production of the bodies in March was at full pace even though the foundry was having problems in casting the V-8 block.

By April 21, 1932, the only cars distributed were those produced at the Rouge Assembly Plant. On that date the Branch distributors were directed that all cars produced after number 4250 could be sold, but cars produced before that number were to be reworked and used only as dealer demonstrators. It is a good guess that those early cars were eventually sold—if not as new vehicles, certainly as used demonstrator models.

The 14 body styles that were announced included the Standard and Deluxe Phaeton, Standard and Deluxe Roadster, Standard and Deluxe Tudor, Standard and Deluxe Fordor, Standard Coupe, Sport Coupe, Cabriolet, Victoria and Convertible Sedan. The Deluxe Coupe was on the original list, but before production began, it was replaced with a new design, the three window coupe. Although the Sport Coupe started as a deluxe model, it was changed to a standard model in mid-April.

1932 PASSENGER CARS EXTERIOR COLORS

Start of Production to April 1932

Lower Body, Reveals (1) and Radiator Shell	Upper Body (1) and Mouldings	Stripe Color	Wheels Color (2)
Washington Blue Med.	Black	Tacoma Cream	Tacoma Cream
Old Chester Gray	Tunis Gray	Tacoma Cream	Tacoma Cream
Brewster Green Lt.	Brewster Green Med.	Silver Gray	Apple Green
Black	Black	Gold	Apple Green
Ford Medium Maroon	Black	Gold	Aurora Red

(1) Does not apply to Phaetons and Roadsters.

(2) These colors plus black were for deluxe models. Standard models had black wheels, but color wheels were available on special order.

1932 PASSENGER CARS EXTERIOR COLORS

April 1932 to end of 1932 production

Body and Radiator Shell	Moldings (1)	Stripe Color	Wheels Color (2)
Washington Blue Med.	Black	Tacoma Cream	Tacoma Cream
Old Chester Gray	Tunis Gray	Tacoma Cream	Tacoma Cream
Tunis Gray	Old Chester Gray	Tacoma Cream	Tacoma Cream
Winterleaf Brown Lt. (3)	Winterleaf Brown Dk.	Tacoma Cream	Tacoma Cream
Emperor Brown Lt. (3)	Emperor Brown Dk.	Tacoma Cream	Tacoma Cream
Brewster Green Med.	Brewster Green Lt.	Silver Gray	Apple Green
Black	Black	Gold	Apple Green
Ford Medium Maroon	Black	Gold	Aurora Red
Lower Body, Reveals and Radiator Shell	**Upper Body and Moldings**	**Stripe Color**	**Wheels Color**
Brewster Green Lt.	Brewster Green Med.	Silver Gray	Apple Green

(1) Includes drip molding on closed cars.

(2) These colors plus black were for deluxe models. Standard models had black wheels, but color wheels were available on special order.

(3) Winterleaf Brown Lt. was replaced by Emperor Brown Lt. in June 1932.

Hood, Radiator Shell, and Fenders

There were two variations of the hood used on 1932 vehicles. The hood used on all passenger cars, Station Wagon and Deluxe Panel Delivery, had a rustless steel hinge top. A second hood with a painted hinge top was installed on all other commercials and trucks. The hood with the painted hinge top, obsoleted in August 1932, was replaced with the rustless steel hinge top hood. Another change, made in September, increased the number of vent louvers on the side of the hood from 20 to 25.

The early hood catch handle was the "L" design with the handle portion chrome plated, while the barrel area was painted black. This hood catch was replaced early in production with a "T" shaped handle. A chrome plated handle with a black barrel was used on all passenger cars, Station Wagon and Deluxe Panel Delivery, but a painted handle appeared on all other vehicles.

Two radiator shells and grills were used on 1932 vehicles, one for passenger cars and the other for commercials. The passenger car shell was painted body color while the grill became Sea Gull Gray. On commercial vehicles the shell was also painted body color, but the grill was black until July 1932. After that, it was either painted black on the dark colored vehicles or body color on light colored ones.

The Ford oval name plate, combined with a chromed strip mounted on the top front edge of the shell, provided the semblance of a hood ornament. The oval, with chrome plated Ford script letters against a Harding Blue porcelain enamel background, was $2\frac{3}{16}$ by $1\frac{1}{16}$ inches. It was either a zinc die casting or a steel stamping.

The 1932 fenders were basically a facelift of the Model A style. The front fenders were the same on all body styles including passenger cars, commercial vehicles and trucks. Spare wheel welled front fenders were available for both left and right sides. The right hand welled fender was standard equipment on commercial vehicles but special equipment on all passenger cars except the Deluxe Coupe. A fender mounted spare tire could not be used on the Deluxe Coupe because it interfered with the opening of the door. The left hand welled fender was special equipment on both passenger and commercial vehicles. Trucks had a unique welled fender which was not interchangeable with passenger or commercial vehicles.

Two rear fender designs were used for the passenger cars: one appeared on the Roadster, Coupe (5w), Cabriolet, Sports Coupe, and Deluxe Coupe; and the second was for the Phaeton, Tudor, Fordor and Victoria. This second fender with one less mounting hole was also used on the convertible sedan. Commercial vehicles also had two types of rear fenders: one for use on Panel Delivery and Station Wagon and the other for Pickup trucks.

In July 1932, a reenforcement bracket was added to the front fender at the running board mounting area. All fenders were painted black at this time.

The running board was a rubber covered steel stamping. It bolted to the frame side rail and no splash shield was used between the running board and the body. The same running board was used on passenger cars and commercial vehicles.

Lights

Headlights for the 1932 vehicles were a modified version of the Model A "Twolights," and were produced in three designs. A two-bulb assembly was used on standard passenger cars, a one-bulb assembly appeared in conjunction with cowl lights for deluxe cars, and a two-bulb assembly was on standard commercial vehicles and trucks. The head lights for passenger cars were made of rustless steel with the Ford script oval and the words "Twolight Headlamp" stamped on the top surface. The case of the commercial head lights was of plain steel painted black, while its lens door was rustless steel. All lamps were equipped with 21-21 CP light bulbs, but 32-21 CP and 32-32 CP bulbs were also available as special equipment. The lens was the fixed focus type made of crystal glass with a $1\frac{1}{4}$-inch crown.

The 1932 style lights, grill, hood and bumper.

The headlights were mounted on a support tie rod in front of the grill. This support rod was painted black, but on passenger cars the part between the lights was covered with a rustless steel sleeve.

Two-bulb headlights were used on the standard Phaeton, Roadster, Coupe, Sport Coupe, Tudor and Fordor. The single-bulb headlights and cowl lamps combination was standard equipment on the Deluxe Phaeton, Deluxe Roadster, Deluxe Tudor, Cabriolet, Deluxe Fordor, Victoria, Convertible Sedan, Deluxe Coupe, Deluxe Delivery and Deluxe Panel Delivery. The Station Wagon used the two-bulb headlights until July 1932 when a change was made to the one-bulb lights and cowl lamps.

Cowl lamps were identical to the headlights in shape. The passenger car assemblies were made of rustless steel with a chrome plated mounting bracket. While they were standard equipment on the deluxe passenger and commercial vehicles, they became extra equipment on standard cars. A black enameled steel cowl lamp and bracket with a rustless steel lens door was also available as extra equipment for commercial vehicles and trucks.

The rear lamps were the tea cup design similar to those on the Model A. Three different lamp assemblies were produced. A rustless steel unit with the white glass license plate lens light on top was used on the left side of all passenger cars and deluxe commercials. A similar assembly with a black enamel body was used on standard commercials, but a rustless steel assembly without the license plate lens was available as special equipment on the right side of the passenger cars. The black commercial lamp was installed with the license plate lamp pointing down.

Two different lens were used in the rear lamps. One was a plain lens for use on vehicles shipped to most states. The second, a reflex design, was installed on vehicles shipped to states which had specific laws governing rear lamps, such as Colorado, Kansas, New Hampshire and Utah. The plain lens was made of high transmission ruby colored glass with a bull's eye in the lower part of the lens. The surface behind the bull's eye was stippled while the rest of the surface was covered with $\frac{1}{8}$-inch diameter hemispherical prisms. The reflex design had two bull's eyes, upper and lower. The inside surface of the eyes was stippled while the rest of the lens surface was covered with $\frac{3}{16}$-inch wide cubical reflecting prisms. The word "Duolamp" was cast on the front surface of the lens.

The passenger car rear lamp bracket was a steel stamping finished with black enamel. Carried over from the Model A was a malleable iron cast bracket painted black to be used on the Pickup, Station Wagon and trucks. However, a unique design bracket was used on the Panel Delivery.

Door Handles

The open cars, Phaeton, Roadster and the commercial open cab, were equipped with outside door handles similar to those used on the Model A open cars. The shape of the handle was semi-rectangular, four inches long by $\frac{7}{8}$ inches wide at the center. A depressed area in the center of the handle added style. Two alternate handles were used. One was a stamped design made of either rustless steel or chrome plated brass. The other was an aluminum die cast design, also chrome plated.

All other passenger car bodies had a flat "S" style door handle made of rustless steel. The handle used on the Cabriolet and Deluxe Coupe however, had a slightly longer shank and a different escutcheon plate. Bodies with either a rumble seat or a trunk deck lid had an "L" shaped handle, three inches long, stamped from rustless steel.

Door handles for the Station Wagon were a scroll design, a direct carry-over from the Model A. These handles were either chrome plated or made of rustless steel.

Commercial vehicles such as the closed cab body and the Panel Delivery were equipped with a carry-over handle from the Model AA trucks. It was made of rustless steel.

Three styles of interior door handles were used on all closed and convertible cars. They were identified as long point (B-46210-A), short point (B-46250-B) and round nose (B-46250-C). Each was die cast and nickel plated. The long point handle was used until early April when it was replaced by the short point handle. However, the latter was only used until late April when it in turn was replaced by the round nose handle. In May, the long point handles still in stock were designated to be used up on the Deluxe Coupe. This continued until August when they were finally replaced with the round handle.

The inside door handle used on the Station Wagon (B-151250-A) was a carry-over from the Model A. This nickel plated handle was also used for the rear door of the B and BB Panel Deliveries.

Inside handles for the Phaeton, Roadster and commercial cabs were a new design and were an integral part of the door opening mechanism. They were finished with butler nickel plate.

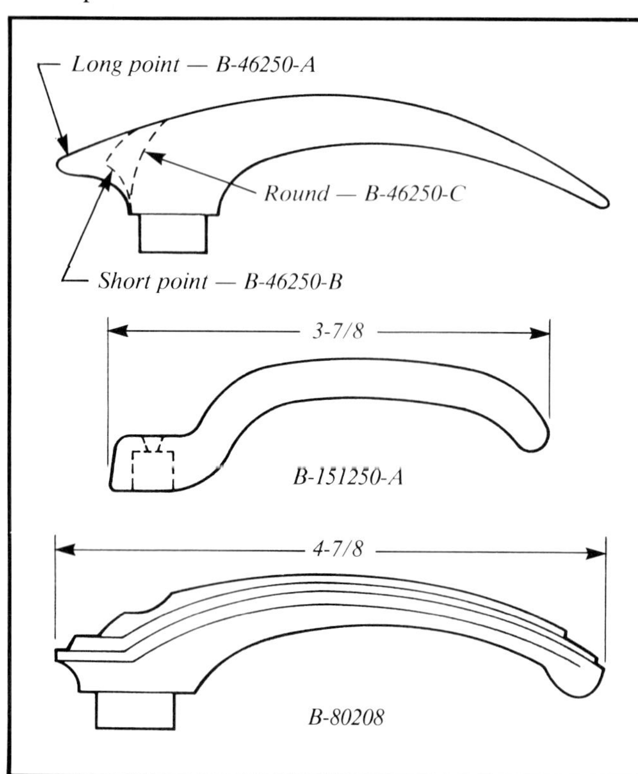

Sketch of 1932 door handles (drawings by authors).

Closed cab commercial vehicles and Panel Deliveries used a carry-over AA Panel Delivery handle with a butler nickel plated finish. The handle had a hole added to permit fastening it to the new opening mechanism.

The window regulator handles followed the same design patterns as the door handles—long point, short point and round nose. Their change dates were the same as the door handles to insure a matching set of handles on each body. However, the window regulator handles had knobs which were designated for specific body styles. The different makes were die cast bright nickel plate for use on standard models, plastic mixed brown and tan for deluxe models, and mixed red plastic for use on the Deluxe Coupe only. The Sport Coupe started as a deluxe model but was changed to a standard model in mid-April. The handle portions of the regulator handles were all zinc die casting finished with bright nickel plating.

Miscellaneous Interior Plating

The cowl vent lever on passenger bodies was chrome plated butler finish. On commercial and truck bodies it was painted with black enamel.

The gear shift lever and hand brake lever for passenger and commercial bodies were also chrome plated butler finish, except the hand grip area of the brake handle which was bright chrome plated.

Chrome butler finish was also used on the front seat adjusting handle and the driver's seat adjusting arm on the Tudor, Victoria and Convertible Sedan.

Interior Visor

All closed car bodies were equipped with two interior visors, one on the passenger's side and the other on the

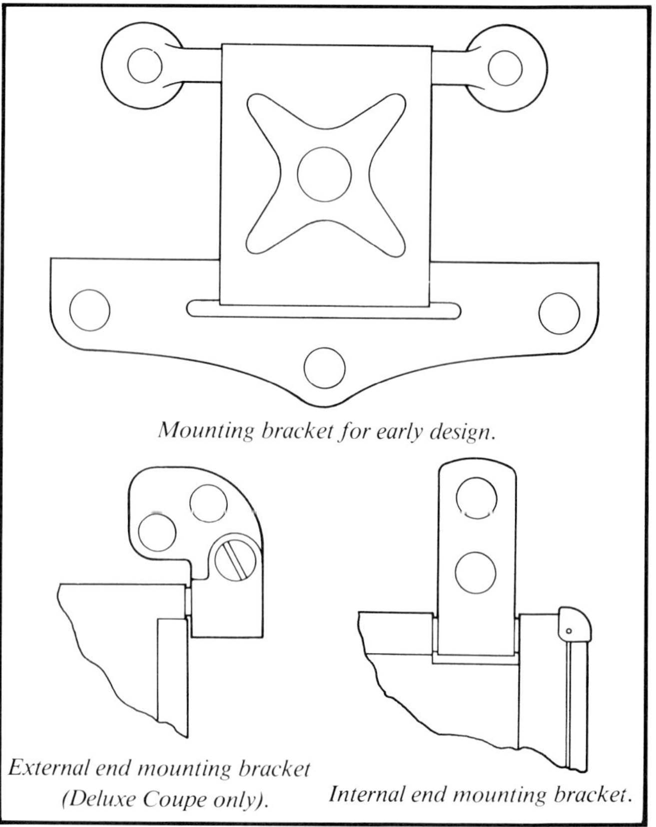

Mounting bracket for early design.

External end mounting bracket (Deluxe Coupe only).

Internal end mounting bracket.

Sun visor brackets.

driver's side. Three different designs were used from the beginning to the end of 1932 production.

The first design (B-47360-A) was the center mounted style and folded up against the headlining. Its dimensions were 14¾ inches long by 5½ inches wide. These visors were covered with Spanish Brown Colonial Grain embossed cardboard. The mounting bracket was painted with a natural brown lacquer to blend with the headlining materials. This style was used on the standard Coupe, Sport Coupe, standard and Deluxe Tudor, standard and Deluxe Fordor and Victoria.

In mid-May, a new slightly larger design with an internal end mounting bracket was introduced on all bodies except the Sport Coupe, which continued to use the original design until the end of its 1932 production. Dimensions of the new visor were 15 inches by 5¾ inches. The mounting brackets, bright nickel plated stampings, were fastened on the top edge, approximately ⅝-inch from the edge. The visor itself was made of a wire frame covered with pressed cardboard which in turn was covered with headlining material. These cloth covered visors had a Russet Brown Fine Colonial Grain artificial leather binding around the edge. A leather trim visor, to match the leather trim scheme, had a Copra Drab Fine Colonial Grain artificial leather binding. In September, a corner finish plate was added to the visor.

The Deluxe Coupe was introduced with its own unique visor. This, too, was made of pressed cardboard over a wire frame covered with head lining material, but it had two external pins and mounting brackets at the top edge of the visor. The brackets, made of bright nickel plated die castings, had a screw which was used for adjusting the clamping force on the visor. With this type of mounting, the visor folded against the windshield header instead of the headlining. In mid-June this design was phased out to be replaced with the same visor being used on the other body styles.

Floor Mats and Carpets

Two designs of front floor coverings were used in early production, one for the Model B chassis and the other for the Model 18 chassis. This arrangement was continued until June 1932 when the starter switch was placed in the same location for both chassis. In addition, some body styles had rubber floor mats while others used carpet. Refer to the interior trim charts for proper usage of floor mats for each body style.

The tan rubber floor mat had a pebble grain outer border and a simulated rope design rib inner border. The main part of the mat had a pyramid pattern to simulate a carpet weave.

The brown carpet floor mat had either an artificial leather binding or a brown cloth binding to match the interior trim. A brown pebble grain artificial leather binding or brown cloth binding appeared on floor mats in the deluxe bodies with the cloth trim schemes; a Russet Brown Fine Colonial Grain artificial leather binding came with the russet brown leather trim scheme; while a Copra Drab Fine Colonial Grain artificial leather binding was used with the Copra Drab leather trim scheme. However, on the Standard Tudor and Fordor bodies a brown cloth binding complemented the Thorn Brown mohair trim scheme; a medium brown cloth binding came with the brown stripe trim; and a light brown cloth binding was used with the brown diagonal dash and brown small check trim schemes.

All front floor carpets had a tan rubber heel pad made of the same pyramid pattern that was on the rubber floor mats.

Due to a surplus of brown carpet material, the rumble seat floors of early production Coupes and Roadsters were covered with the brown carpet floor mat rather than the tan rubber floor mat as originally scheduled. This plan continued through May 1932.

On the Station Wagon the front floor mat was tan rubber but the rear mat was tan rubber with a rib pattern running the length of the mat. The ribs were $\frac{1}{16}$-inch wide at the top and were spaced five per inch.

Body Changes

In April, the driver's seat mounting location on the Tudor, Convertible Sedan and Victoria was moved 2⅛ inches to the rear to provide more leg room in the front compartment. The same month, the walnut grain pattern on the front belt finish panel on some models was changed to a walnut burl grain pattern, while on other models it was changed to a walnut crotch grain pattern (see trim charts).

It was discovered in May that the inner edge of the back window frame on Sedans came in contact with the back panel causing a squeak. This condition, caused by an accumulation of tolerances in manufacturing, was corrected on later parts by trimming. Squeaks were also suspected at the front and rear corner joints of the roof frame assembly. Assembly plants were instructed to add additional screws to the corner blocks in these areas. The rear corner blocks were also reduced by ¼ inch so they could not touch the side rail. These corrections were made on all Sedans produced after May 19, 1932.

In October, two reinforcing brackets were added to the Coupe, Sport Coupe and Cabriolet bodies to correct suspected structural weakness. One bracket was added at the lower corner of the deck door opening to strengthen the weld joint of the rear quarter panel to the back panel, and the other at the joint of the cowl to pillar. This cowl to pillar joint reinforcement was also added to all other bodies.

Phaeton (B-35) Standard and Deluxe

The Phaeton was available in two models, Standard and Deluxe. The standard model was equipped with windshield wings, two-tone Black Brown Fine Colonial Grain artificial leather trim, black rubber top and tan rubber floor mats. In April 1932, the windshield wings were no longer standard but were available on special order at extra cost. By May the black rubber top material was replaced with rubber innerlined black and white cloth. The back light frame was painted glossy black enamel on the outside and satin finish black enamel on the inside. The dust hood (or boot) was only available as special equipment.

The Deluxe Phaeton was equipped with cowl lights, windshield wings, Copra Drab Fine Colonial Grain genuine leather trim, rubber innerlined drab cloth top, drab dust hood, and tan rubber floor mats. The front belt finish panel was coated with a walnut grain finish until April; thereafter it was coated with a walnut burl grain finish. As a cost saving, the windlace cover was changed from genuine leather to artificial leather in June. The back light frame was bright chrome on the outside and painted Golden Beryl

The Deluxe Phaeton. The windshield frame and stantions were chrome plated. The standard model had no cowl lights and the wheels were black.

The Deluxe Phaeton with top and windshield down.

satin finish on the inside.

Striping on both Phaeton models was identical. Two stripes were on the belt molding and one stripe was on the lower body molding, all $\frac{1}{16}$ inch wide. The belt molding stripes began at the front edge of the hood and went completely around the body. The upper stripe was one-quarter inch from the top edge of the molding, while the lower stripe was one-quarter inch above the bottom edge of the molding. The lower body molding stripe also began at the front edge of the hood and circled the body. It was one-quarter inch below the top edge of the molding until it went past the rear fender, and then it was one-half inch below the top edge of the molding around the back of the body.

1932 STANDARD PHAETON INTERIOR TRIM SCHEMES

Black Brown Trim Scheme
Doors and cowl panels: Two-tone Black Brown Fine Colonial Grain Cardboard.
Seats, seat sides, quarter and windlace: Two-tone Black Brown Fine Colonial Grain Artificial Leather.
Front and rear floors: Tan Rubber.
Front belt rail finish panel: Gray with Rustless Steel Molding.
Top: Black Short Grain Rubber Coated Fabric until May 1932, then changed to Black and White Interlined Fabric.
Dust hood: Drab Rubber Coated Fabric until May 1932, then changed to Black and White Top Material.
Hardware: Escutcheons-Brown Enamel; Handles-Nickel Plated Butler.

1932 DELUXE PHAETON INTERIOR TRIM SCHEMES

Copra Drab Trim Scheme
Seats, doors, and lock pillars: Copra Drab Fine Colonial Grain Leather.
Cowl panels: Copra Drab Fine Colonial Grain Artificial Leather.
Front and rear floor: Tan Rubber.
Seat bottom carpet: Brown Tapestry Carpet.
Front belt rail finish panel: Walnut Grain with Rustless Steel Molding until April 1932, then changed to Walnut Burl Grain.
Windlace: Copra Drab Fine Colonial Grain Genuine Leather until June 1932, then changed to Artificial Leather.
Top and dust hood: Drab Rubber Interlined Fabric.
Hardware: Nickel Plated Butler.

Roadster (B-40) Standard and Deluxe

The standard Roadster was equipped with windshield wings, two-tone Black Brown Fine Colonial Grain artificial leather trim, black rubber top material and tan rubber floor mat. After April 1932, the windshield wings were no longer supplied as a standard item, but could be ordered as special equipment. In May the black rubber top material was changed to rubber innerlined black and white cloth. The rumble seat and the dust hood (boot) were not standard items, but were available as a customer option at extra cost. The trim material for the rumble seat was two-tone Black Brown Fine Colonial Grain artificial leather. A tan rubber mat was originally released as a floor mat, but due to surplus stock, brown carpet mats were actually used on early production. The back light frame was painted with gloss black enamel outside and satin black enamel on the inside.

Equipment on the deluxe Roadster included cowl lights, windshield wings, Copra Drab Fine Colonial Grain genuine leather trim, drab rubber innerlined fabric top, dust hood, tan rubber mats, and a rumble seat trimmed with Copra Drab Fine Colonial Grain artificial leather. Similar to the Phaeton, in May the front belt rail panel finish was changed from walnut grain to walnut burl grain. In June, the door windlace cover material was changed from genuine leather to artificial leather.

Both the standard and deluxe models were striped identically. Stripes $1/16$ inch wide were on the belt molding, lower body molding and rear deck moldings—all $1/4$ inch from the molding edge. Two stripes formed a point on the belt molding at the front edge of the hood. The top stripe followed the belt molding around the back of the top, while the lower stripe followed the belt molding to the rear quarter, then down to the back corner of the body where it reversed to the lower body molding, over the rear fender and on the lower body molding to the radiator shell. Another stripe connected the belt molding, rear quarter molding and the deck lid molding. A final stripe was on the moldings around the deck lid.

The 1932 Deluxe Roadster. The rumble seat was not a regular production, but was available on special order.

A Deluxe Roadster with rumble seat and dust hood.

1932 STANDARD ROADSTER INTERIOR TRIM SCHEMES

Black Brown Trim Scheme

Doors and cowl panels: Two-tone Black Brown Fine Colonial Grain Cardboard.

Seats, seat sides, package tray, seat back rail and windlace: Two-tone Black Brown Fine Colonial Grain Artificial Leather.

Front floor: Tan Rubber.

Front belt rail finish panel: Gray with Rustless Steel Molding.

Rumble seat: Deck seat – Two-tone Black Brown Fine Colonial Grain Artificial Leather; Deck sides – Two-tone Black Brown Fine Colonial Grain Cardboard; Deck floor – Tan Rubber.

Top: Black Short Grain Rubber Coated Fabric until May 1932, then changed to Black and White Interlined Fabric.

Dust hood: Drab Rubber Coated Fabric until May 1932, then changed to Black and White Top Material.

Hardware: Escutcheons-Brown Enamel; Handles-Nickel Plated Butler.

1932 DELUXE ROADSTER INTERIOR TRIM SCHEMES

Copra Drab Trim Scheme

Seats, seat sides and door panels: Copra Drab Fine Colonial Grain Leather.

Cowl panel, seat back frame and package tray: Copra Drab Fine Colonial Grain Artificial Leather.

Front floor: Tan Rubber.

Front belt rail finish panel: Walnut Grain with Rustless Steel Molding until April 1932, then changed to Walnut Burl Grain.

Rumble seat: Deck seat – Copra Drab Fine Colonial Grain Artificial Leather; Deck sides – Copra Drab Fine Colonial Grain Cardboard; Deck floor – Tan Rubber.

Top and dust hood: Drab Rubber Interlined Fabric.

Hardware: Nickel Plated Butler Finish.

Coupe, Five Window (B-45) Standard

The five window coupe body was produced by Ford, Murray and Briggs. It was equipped with a dome light, sun visors, rear window curtain, rear window regulator, either Thorn Brown mohair or mixed brown cloth trim schemes, and a tan rubber mat. In June, the original mixed brown trim, Brown Diagonal Dash was replaced with a small brown check material with the same shade of brown. It in turn, was replaced in July with a darker brown stripe material. Also in June, the windshield header body cloth was changed to the less expensive head lining cloth. This change was coordinated with the change of the sun visor's cover material.

A genuine Copra Drab Fine Colonial Grain leather trim scheme was also available as special equipment on this five window coupe. In August, a less expensive but identical artificial leather trim was added to the special equipment list.

Another item available on special order was the rumble seat which came in two trim schemes. For the cloth trimmed bodies, the seat was trimmed in two-tone Black Brown Fine Colonial Grain artificial leather, but in the leather trim bodies the seat was trimmed in Copra Drab Fine Colonial Grain artificial leather. The rumble seat floor was covered with brown carpet on early models but with a tan rubber mat thereafter.

Compared to the Roadster, the coupe body had an additional cowl molding just in front of the windshield, therefore, its striping pattern was different. Two stripes formed a point at the front edge of the belt molding. The top stripe followed the top edge of the molding and crossed over the top of the cowl. The lower stripe followed the lower edge of the belt molding to the rear corner of the body where it reversed and followed the lower body molding to the radiator shell. Another stripe was on the cowl molding, $5/32$ inch from the molding's rear edge. It went to the corner of the windshield pillar, then followed the upper edge of the belt molding, $3/8$ inch from the top edge of the molding,

A preproduction five window Coupe on a Model "B" chassis. Cowl lights were not included on regular production.

and across the top of the back deck. The rear deck striping was similar to that of the Roadster with stripes on the rear quarter molding and on the molding around the deck lid opening. All of these stripes were $\frac{1}{4}$ inch from the edge of the molding.

1932 STANDARD COUPE (5W) INTERIOR TRIM SCHEMES

Brown Mohair Trim Scheme
Seats and seat sides: Thorn Brown Mohair.
Doors, quarters, back, roof sides, package tray, seat wind break: Thorn Brown Mohair.
Headlining: Brown Napped Cotton.
Windshield header: Thorn Brown Mohair until June 1932. After June: changed to Brown Napped Cotton.
Cowl panels: Two-tone Dark Brown Dash Grain Cardboard.
Windlace: Dark Brown Worsted Cloth.
Window curtain: Brown Window Curtain Cloth Oxford Weave with Tab.
Window cord: Brown Braided.

Brown Diagonal Dash Trim Schemes (dropped June 1932)
Seats and seat sides: Brown Diagonal Dash.
Doors, quarters, back, roof sides, package tray, seat wind break: Plain Light Brown Cloth.
Headlining: Light Brown Napped Cotton.
Windshield header: Plain Light Brown Cloth until June 1932. After June: changed to Light Brown Napped Cotton.
Cowl panels: Two-tone Light Brown Dash Grain Cardboard.
Windlace: Light Brown Worsted Cloth.
Window curtain: Light Brown Window Curtain Cloth Oxford Weave with Tab.
Window cord: Light Brown Braided.

Brown Check Trim Scheme
Seat and seat sides: Brown Small Check.
Doors, quarters, back, roof sides, package tray, seat wind break: Plain Light Brown Cloth.
Headlining: Light Brown Napped Cotton.
Windshield header: Plain Light Brown Cloth until June 1932. After June: changed to Light Brown Napped Cotton.
Cowl panels: Two-tone Light Brown Dash Grain Cardboard.
Windlace: Light Brown Worsted Cloth.
Window curtain: Light Brown Window Curtain Cloth Oxford Weave with Tab.
Window cord: Light Brown Braided.

Brown Stripe Trim Scheme
Seats and seat sides: Brown Stripe.
Doors, quarters, back, roof sides, package tray, seat wind break: Plain Brown Cloth.
Headlining: Brown Napped Cotton.
Windshield header: Plain Brown Cloth until June 1932. After June: changed to Brown Napped Cotton.
Cowl panels: Two-tone Dark Brown Dash Grain Cardboard.
Windlace: Dark Brown Worsted Cloth.
Window curtain: Brown Window Curtain Cloth Oxford Weave with Tab.
Window cord: Brown Braided.

Genuine Leather Trim Scheme (special equipment)
Seats and seat sides: Copra Drab Fine Colonial Grain Leather.
Artificial Leather Trim Scheme (special equipment August 1932)
Seat and seat sides: Copra Drab Fine Colonial Grain Artificial Leather.
On both schemes – doors, quarters, back, roof sides, windshield header, package tray, seat wind break, headlining, cowl cardboards, windlace: Copra Drab Fine Colonial Grain Artificial Leather.
Window curtain: Brown Curtain Cloth Oxford Weave with Tab.
Window cord: Brown Braided.

Items which were identical for each trim scheme
Front floor and side sills: All schemes – Tan Rubber.
Finish moldings: All schemes – Painted Gray Enamel or Pyroxylin.
Front belt rail finish panel molding: All schemes – Rustless Steel.
Body hardware: All schemes – Bright Nickel Plate.
Rumble seat trim for cloth trim schemes: Seat – Two-tone Black Brown Fine Colonial Grain Artificial Leather; Deck side – Two-tone Black Brown Fine Colonial Grain Cardboard; Front seat back carpet – Brown Carpet; Floor mat – Tan Rubber.
Rumble seat trim for leather trim schemes: Seat – Copra Drab Fine Colonial Grain Artificial Leather; Deck sides – Copra Drab Fine Colonial Grain Cardboard; Front seat back carpet – Brown Carpet; Floor mat – Tan Rubber.
Sun visor: Spanish Brown Colonial Grain Cardboard until June 1932, then changed to headlining material.

The 1932 Sport Coupe was produced as a standard model. This body style was discontinued after 1932 production.

Sport Coupe (B-50)

The sporty looking Sport Coupe with its soft top and decorative landau bar, did not have deluxe features such as cowl lights and chrome windshield frame, but it did have a rumble seat. Standard equipment included mixed brown cloth trim, light brown Landau Grain artificial leather top, sun visors, and a rumble seat trimmed with two-tone Black Brown Fine Colonial Grain artificial leather. The early floor mats were brown carpet but then changed to the tan rubber mat.

Similar to the Standard Coupe, the interior trim scheme of the Sport Coupe was changed twice during the year. In June the original trim, Brown Diagonal Dash, was replaced with a similar shade of brown check material, which in turn was replaced in July with a darker brown stripe material.

Striping on the Sport Coupe was identical to the Standard Coupe.

The Sport Coupe body style was terminated after the 1932 production.

1932 SPORT COUPE INTERIOR TRIM SCHEMES

Brown Diagonal Dash Trim Scheme (dropped June 1932)
Seat and seat sides: Brown Diagonal Dash.
Brown Check Trim Scheme (available only in June and July)
Seat and seat sides: Brown Check.
Brown Stripe Trim Scheme (available after July)
Seat and seat sides: Brown Stripe.
The following items were identical on each trim scheme.
Doors, quarter, seat wind break: Plain Brown Cloth.
Roof bow, roof side rail, upper quarter, quarter lock pillar, package tray, top deck headlining, roof side, back: Gray Brown Mock Twist Sport Headlining Cloth.
Cowl panels: Two-tone Light Brown Dash Grain Cardboard.
Windlace: Light Brown Worsted Cloth.
Front floor and side sill: Tan Rubber.
Top: Light Brown Landau Grain Artificial Leather.
Finish moldings: Painted Gray Enamel or Pyroxylin.
Body hardware: Bright Nickel Plated.
Back light frame: Outside – Bright Chrome; Inside – Gray Enamel.
Rumble seat trim: Seat – Two-tone Black Brown Fine Colonial Grain Artificial Leather; Deck sides – Matching Cardboard; Front seat back carpet – Brown Carpet; Floor mat – Tan Rubber.

Tudor (B-55) Standard and Deluxe

The Tudor sedans were the backbone of the 1932 production, outselling all other body styles. They were available in two body styles, standard and deluxe. The standard model came with dome light, sun visor, rear window curtain, and a choice of two trim schemes, brown mixed cloth or Thorn Brown mohair. The brown mixed cloth, in turn, had three patterns and two shades of brown. From job one to June the Brown Diagonal Dash was used, during June it was Brown Check, but from July to the end of production it was Brown Stripe. During June leftover Model A window curtains with tassels were installed on Tudor bodies trimmed with Thorn Brown mohair.

In addition to the items on the standard model, the deluxe Tudor was equipped with cowl lamps, rear seat arm rests, assist loops, and ash trays. The deluxe trim schemes consisted of rose beige mohair, brown Bedford cord, tan pinstripe and Copra Drab Fine Colonial Grain genuine leather. In July, the leather trim was changed from regular production to special equipment at extra cost.

The hood and cowl stripe on the Tudor was the same as the coupe. The lower belt molding stripe started at the hood and followed the lower edge of the belt molding around the back of the body. The upper stripe on the belt molding, which came across the cowl molding, went under both windows and up the rear window molding to the drip molding, then back down to the belt and around the back of the body. The 1/16 inch stripe was 5/32 inch in front of the windshield, 3/8 inch below the top edge of the belt molding and 1/4 inch from the edge on the rear window molding. There was no stripe on the lower body molding.

Interior of a Deluxe Tudor, typical closed body front compartment.

1932 STANDARD TUDOR SEDAN INTERIOR TRIM SCHEMES

Thorn Brown Trim Scheme
Seats, doors, rear quarter, lock pillar, back, sides, roof rail sides: Thorn Brown Mohair.
Headlining: Spanish Brown Colonial Grain Cardboard until June 1932, then Brown Napped Cotton.
Cowl panel and seat bottom: Two-tone Dark Brown Dash Grain Cardboard.
Windlace: Dark Brown Worsted Cloth.
Window cord: Brown Braided.
Window curtain: Brown Window Curtain Cloth Oxford Weave with tab.

Brown Diagonal Dash Trim Scheme (used until June 1932)
Seats: Brown Diagonal Dash.
Doors, rear quarter, lock pillar, back, sides, roof rail sides: Plain Light Brown Cloth.
Headlining: Light Brown Napped Cotton.
Cowl panel and seat bottom: Two-tone Light Brown Dash Grain Cardboard.
Windlace: Light Brown Worsted Cloth.
Window cord: Light Brown Braided.
Window curtain: Light Brown Window Curtain Cloth Oxford Weave with tab.

Brown Check Trim Scheme (used June and July 1932)
Seats: Brown Small Check.
Doors, rear quarter, lock pillar, back, sides, roof rail sides: Plain Light Brown Cloth.
Headlining: Light Brown Napped Cotton.
Cowl panel and seat bottom: Two-tone Light Brown Dash Grain Cardboard.
Windlace: Light Brown Worsted Cloth.
Window cord: Light Brown Braided.
Windshield header material was changed to headlining material after June 1932.
Window curtain: Brown Window Curtain Cloth Oxford Weave with tab.

Brown Stripe Trim Scheme
Seats: Brown Stripe. (Used July 1932, to end of production.)
Doors, rear quarters, lock pillar, back, sides, roof rail sides: Plain Brown Cloth.
Headlining: Brown Napped Cotton.
Cowl panel and seat bottom: Two-tone Dark Brown Dash Grain Cardboard.
Windlace: Dark Brown Worsted Cloth.
Window cord: Light Brown Braided.
Window curtain: Brown Window Curtain Cloth Oxford Weave with tab.

Artificial Leather Trim Scheme (special order after August 1932)
Seats, door, rear quarters, lock pillar, back, sides, roof rail sides, windshield header, headlining, visors, and windlace: Copra Drab Fine Colonial Grain Artificial Leather.

Items which were identical on each trim scheme
Front floor on all schemes: Tan Rubber.
Rear floor on all schemes: Brown Carpet.
Finish moldings: Painted Gray Enamel or Pyroxylin.
Front belt rail finish panel molding: Rustless Steel.
Windshield header: Same as door panel until June 1932, then changed to headlining material.
Sun visors: Spanish Brown Colonial Grain Cardboard until June 1932, then changed to headlining cloth.

1932 DELUXE TUDOR SEDAN INTERIOR TRIM SCHEMES

Rose Beige Trim Scheme
Seats, doors, rear quarters, lock pillars, back, sides, roof rail sides, arm rests: Rose Beige Mohair.
Headlining: Brown Napped Cotton.
Cowl panels and seat bottom: Two-tone Light Brown Dash Grain Cardboard.
Windlace: Tan Worsted.
Assist loop: Tan Herringbone Pattern.
Window curtain: Brown Curtain Material with Tassel.
Window cord: Brown Twisted.
Sun visors: Spanish Brown Colonial Grain Cardboard until June, then changed to Brown Napped Cotton.

Brown Trim Scheme
Seats and arm rests: Brown Bedford Cord.
Doors, rear quarters, lock pillars, back, sides, roof rail sides: Plain Brown Broad Cloth.
Headlining: Light Brown Napped Cotton.
Cowl panels and seat bottom: Two-tone Dark Brown Dash Grain Cardboard.
Windlace: Brown Worsted.
Assist loop: Brown Herringbone Pattern.
Window curtain: Brown Curtain Material with Tassel.
Window cord: Brown Twisted.
Sun visors: Spanish Brown Colonial Grain Cardboard until June, then changed to Light Brown Napped Cotton.

Tan Trim Scheme
Seats, doors, rear quarters, lock pillars, back, sides, roof rail sides, arm rests: Tan Pinstripe.
Headlining: Tan Napped Cotton.
Cowl panels and seat bottom: Two-tone Light Brown Dash Grain Cardboard.
Windlace: Tan Worsted.
Assist loop: Tan Herringbone Pattern.
Window curtain: Tan Curtain Material with Tassel.
Window cord: Brown Twisted.
Sun visors: Spanish Brown Colonial Grain Cardboard until June, then changed to Tan Napped Cotton.

Genuine Leather Trim Scheme (changed to special equipment in July)
Seats, doors, quarter, back, sides, roof rail sides, windshield header, windlace, arm rests: Copra Drab Fine Colonial Grain Leather.
Headlining and assist loop: Copra Drab Fine Colonial Grain Artificial Leather.
Cowl panels and seat bottom: Copra Drab Fine Colonial Grain Cardboard.
Window curtain: Brown Window Curtain Cloth Oxford Weave with Tab.
Window cord: Brown Braided.
Sun visors: Spanish Brown Colonial Grain Cardboard until June, then changed to Copra Drab Fine Colonial Grain Artificial Leather.

Items which were identical on each trim scheme
Floors, rear seat heel board and door bottom: Brown Carpet.
Windshield header: Same as door panels until June, then changed to headlining material.
Finish moldings: Walnut Grain until April, then changed to Walnut Crotch Grain.
Front belt rail finish panel molding: Rustless Steel.
Front carpet heel pad: Rubber.
Body hardware: Bright Nickel Plate.

The V-8 Deluxe Tudor Sedan. With the exception of the V-8 emblem and the hub caps, the Model "B" was identical in appearance.

Cabriolet (B-68)

The Cabriolet's convertible top gave the car the sporty open car look, while its roll-up windows provided the advantage of a closed car. It came equipped with the deluxe features—cowl lamps, ash trays, top dust hood, rumble seat, and a choice of two trim schemes. One of these trim schemes was genuine Russet Brown Fine Colonial Grain leather, while the other was brown Bedford Cord. After April, the front belt finish rail was finished in walnut crotch grain, but the interior finish moldings were walnut burl grain. Both the inside and outside back light frames were finished in bright chrome plate.

The striping on the Cabriolet was the same as the Coupe except that the Cabriolet body did not have moldings around the rumble seat lid.

The Cabriolet, with chrome plated windshield and window frames, was produced only in the deluxe style.

With its top down, the Cabriolet provided the sporty open car style of a Roadster.

1932 CABRIOLET INTERIOR TRIM SCHEMES

Brown Cloth Trim Scheme
Seat, seat sides and seat belows: Brown Bedford Cord.
Doors, quarter lock pillar, quarter wind break, and package tray: Plain Brown Cloth.
Cowl panels: Two-tone Brown Dash Grain Cardboard.
Windlace: Light Brown Worsted.

Brown Leather Trim Scheme
Seat, seat sides and seat belows: Russet Brown Fine Colonial Grain Leather.
Doors, cowl panels, quarter lock pillar, quarter wind break, and package tray: Russet Brown Fine Colonial Grain Artificial Leather.
Windlace: Russet Brown Fine Colonial Grain Artificial Leather.

Items which were identical on both trim schemes.
Roof bows, door header, windshield header, upper quarter lock pillar, back belt rail: Drab Cloth.
Front floor, side sill and door bottom panel: Brown Carpet.
Top and dust hood: Drab Rubberized Fabric.
Finish moldings: Walnut Grain until April, then changed to Walnut Crotch Grain.
Front belt rail finish panel: Walnut Crotch Grain until April, then changed to Walnut Burl Grain.
Rumble seat: Seat – Russet Brown Fine Colonial Grain Artificial Leather; Deck sides – matching cardboard; Front seat back carpet – Brown Carpet; Floor mat – Tan Rubber.
Back light frame: Bright Chrome inside and outside.
Body hardware: Bright Nickel Plated.

Fordor (B-160) Standard and Deluxe

The Fordor was the top of the passenger car line, although its sales were only one-third of the Tudor. Ford ads stated, "The bodies are roomy and richly finished. Seats are of new style and designed for utmost comfort."

Fordor Sedan rear compartment.

An early Deluxe Fordor Sedan showing the two-tone color combination of that period.

Rear quarter view of the Deluxe Fordor Sedan showing the accessory spare tire cover.

Standard items on the standard Fordor were dome light, sun visor, rear window curtain and two interior trim schemes, Thorn Brown mohair or brown mixed cloth. The front compartment floor mat was made of tan rubber while the back was brown carpet. Similar to the Tudor, the brown mixed cloth came in three patterns. Early production to June, Brown Diagonal Dash was used; during June, Small Check was used; and from July to the end of model production, the Brown Stripe was used. Also in June, the surplus Model A window curtains with tassel were installed on bodies trimmed with the Thorn Brown mohair.

The deluxe Fordor features were: cowl lamps, robe rail, ash trays, dome light, sun visors, rear window curtain, rear seat arm rests and assist loops. The four trim schemes offered were Rose Beige mohair, Brown Bedford Cord, Tan Pinstripe and Copra Drab Fine Colonial Grain genuine leather. However, in July the leather trim was dropped as regular production, being made available as special equipment at extra cost. The floor mats in the deluxe body were brown carpet in both front and back.

Striping on the Fordor bodies was identical to the Tudor.

1932 STANDARD FORDOR SEDAN INTERIOR TRIM SCHEMES

Thorn Brown Trim Scheme
Seats and seat sides, doors, quarters, lock pillars and hinge pillars, back, roof rail sides: Thorn Brown Mohair.
Headlining: Brown Napped Cotton.
Cowl panels: Two-tone Dark Brown Dash Grain Cardboard.
Windlace: Dark Brown Worsted.
Window curtain: Brown Window Curtain Cloth Oxford Weave with Tab.
Window cord: Brown Braided.

Brown Diagonal Dash Trim Scheme (used until June 1932)
Seats and seat sides: Brown Diagonal Dash.
Doors, quarters, lock pillars and hinge pillars, back, roof rail sides: Plain Light Brown Cloth.
Headlining: Light Brown Napped Cotton.
Cowl panels: Two-tone Light Brown Dash Grain Cardboard.
Windlace: Light Brown Worsted.
Window curtain: Light Brown Window Curtain Cloth Oxford Weave with Tab.
Window cord: Light Brown Braided.

Brown Check Trim Scheme (used during June and July)
Seats and seat sides: Brown Small Check.
Doors, quarters, lock pillars and hinge pillars, back roof rail sides: Plain Light Brown Cloth.
Headlining: Light Brown Napped Cotton.
Cowl panels: Two-tone Light Brown Dash Grain Cardboard.
Windlace: Light Brown Worsted.
Window curtain: Light Brown Window Curtain Cloth Oxford Weave with Tab.
Window cord: Light Brown Braided.

Brown Stripe Trim Scheme (July to end of production)
Seats and seat sides: Brown Stripe.
Doors, quarters, lock pillars and hinge pillars, back, roof rail sides: Plain Brown Cloth.
Headlining: Brown Napped Cotton.
Cowl panel: Two-tone Dark Brown Dash Grain Cardboard.
Windlace: Dark Brown Worsted.
Window curtain: Brown Window Curtain Cloth Oxford Weave with Tab.
Window cord: Brown Braided.

Artificial Leather Trim Scheme (became available August 1932)
Seats and seat sides, doors, quarters, lock and hinge pillars, back, roof rail sides, headlining, and windlace: Copra Drab Fine Colonial Grain Artificial Leather.
Cowl panel: Copra Drab Fine Colonial Grain Cardboard.
Window curtain: Brown Window Curtain Cloth Oxford Weave with Tab.
Window cord: Brown Braided.

Items which were identical on each trim scheme.
Front floor and rear side sills: Tan Rubber.
Rear floor: Brown Carpet.
Windshield header: Same as door panels until June 1932, then changed to headlining material.
Sun visors: Spanish Brown Colonial Grain Cardboard until June, then changed to headlining material.
Finish moldings: Painted Gray Enamel or Pyroxylin.
Front belt rail finish panel molding: Rustless Steel.

1932 DELUXE FORDOR SEDAN INTERIOR TRIM SCHEMES

Rose Beige Trim Scheme
Seats and seat sides, doors, quarters, lock and hinge pillars, back, roof rail sides, arm rests: Rose Beige Mohair.
Headlining: Brown Napped Cotton.
Cowl panels: Two-tone Light Brown Dash Grain Cardboard.
Windlace: Tan Worsted.
Assist loop: Tan Herringbone Pattern.
Window curtain: Brown Curtain Material with Tassel.
Window cord: Brown Twisted.

Brown Trim Scheme
Seats and seat sides, arm rests: Brown Bedford Cord.
Doors, quarters, lock and hinge pillars, back, roof rail sides: Plain Brown Broadcloth.
Headlining: Light Brown Napped Cotton.
Cowl panels: Two-tone Dark Brown Dash Grain Cardboard.
Windlace: Brown Worsted.
Assist loop: Brown Herringbone Pattern.
Window curtain: Brown Curtain Material with Tassel.
Window cord: Brown Twisted.

Tan Trim Scheme
Seats and seat sides, doors, quarters, lock and hinge pillars, back, roof rail sides, arm rests: Tan Pinstripe.
Headlining: Tan Napped Cotton.
Cowl panels: Two-tone Light Brown Dash Grain Cardboard.
Windlace: Tan Worsted.
Assist loop: Tan Herringbone Pattern.
Window curtain: Tan Curtain Material with Tassel.
Window cord: Brown Twisted.

Genuine Leather Trim Scheme (changed to special equipment in July)
Seats and seat sides, arm rests, windlace: Copra Drab Fine Colonial Grain Leather.
Doors, quarters, lock and hinge pillars, back, roof rail sides, headlining, assist loop: Copra Drab Fine Colonial Grain Artificial Leather.
Cowl panels: Copra Drab Fine Colonial Grain Cardboard.
Window curtain: Brown Window Curtain Cloth Oxford Weave with Tab.

Items which were identical on each trim scheme.
Front floor: Brown Tapestry Carpet with Tan Rubber Heel Pad.
Rear floor, rear side sills, rear heel board and bottom of doors: Brown Tapestry Carpet.
Windshield header: Same as door panel until June 1932, then changed to headlining material.
Sun visors: Spanish Brown Colonial Grain Cardboard until June, then changed to headlining material.
Finish molding: Walnut Grain until April, then changed to Walnut Crotch Grain.
Front belt rail finish panel: Walnut Crotch Grain until April, then changed to Burl Grain.
Front belt rail finish panel molding: Rustless Steel.
Body hardware: Bright Nickel Plate.

This close-up shows the cowl light location and the stripe treatment on the cowl molding.

The 1932 Victoria, available only in the deluxe trim.

Victoria (B-190)

The Victoria, with its continental looking bustle back was one of Edsel Ford's favorite body styles. It had all the deluxe features of the deluxe Fordor except the robe rail, plus the luggage compartment behind the rear seat. Choice of upholstery consisted of Rose Beige mohair, Brown Bedford Cord or Tan Pinstripe.

Striping on the Victoria was the same as on the Tudor.

1932 VICTORIA INTERIOR TRIM SCHEMES

Rose Beige Trim Scheme

Seats, doors, quarters, back, lock pillar, roof rail sides, arm rests: Rose Beige Mohair.
Headlining: Brown Napped Cotton.
Cowl panels and seat bottom: Two-tone Light Brown Dash Grain Cardboard.
Windlace: Tan Worsted.
Assist loop: Tan Herringbone Pattern.
Window curtain: Brown Curtain Material with Tassel.
Window cord: Brown Twisted.

Brown Trim Scheme

Seats and arm rests: Brown Bedford Cord.
Doors, quarters, back, lock pillar, roof rail sides: Plain Brown Broadcloth.
Headlining: Light Brown Napped Cotton.
Cowl panels and seat bottom: Two-tone Dark Brown Dash Grain Cardboard.
Windlace: Light Brown Worsted.
Assist loop: Brown Herringbone Pattern.
Window curtain: Brown Curtain Material with Tassel.
Window cord: Brown Twisted.

Tan Trim Scheme

Seats, doors, quarters, back, lock pillar, roof rail sides, arm rests: Tan Pinstripe.
Headlining: Tan Napped Cotton.
Cowl panels and seat bottom: Two-tone Light Brown Dash Grain Cardboard.
Assist loop: Tan Herringbone Pattern.
Windlace: Tan Worsted.
Window curtain: Tan Curtain Material with Tassel.
Window cord: Brown Twisted.

Items which were identical for each trim scheme

Windshield header: Same as door panels until June 1932, then changed to headlining material.
Front floor: Brown Carpet with Tan Rubber heel pad.
Rear floor and bottom of doors: Brown Carpet.
Sun visors: Spanish Brown Colonial Grain Cardboard until June 1932, then changed to headlining material.
Finish moldings: Walnut Grain until April, then changed to Walnut Crotch Grain.
Body hardware: Bright Nickel Plated.

Convertible Sedan with top up. Note the fabric tire cover. 1932 was the last year for this body style.

Convertible Sedan with top down and dust hood in place. Windshield frame was chrome plated.

Convertible Sedan (B-400)

The convertible Sedan with its unusual fixed side windows styling and folding top is very popular among today's collectors, but was not too popular in 1932. As a result of poor sales, this body configuration was discontinued after 1932 production. It had a rubber interlined drab cloth top, chrome plated windshield, and all the other deluxe features. The interior was finished in either Brown Bedford Cord or Russet Brown Fine Colonial Grain genuine leather. The back light frame was chrome plated on the outside and finished in black walnut plate grain on the inside.

1932 CONVERTIBLE SEDAN INTERIOR TRIM SCHEMES

Brown Cloth Trim Scheme

Seats and arm rests: Brown Bedford Cord.
Doors, quarters and back belt rail: Plain Brown Broadcloth.
Cowl panels and seat bottoms: Two-tone Light Brown Dash Grain Cardboard.
Windlace: Light Brown Worsted.
Bottom of doors: Brown Carpet.

Brown Leather Trim Scheme

Seats and arm rests: Russet Brown Fine Colonial Grain Leather.
Doors, quarters, back belt rail, cowl panels, and windlace: Russet Brown Fine Colonial Grain Artificial Leather.
Seat bottom: Russet Brown Fine Colonial Grain Cardboard.

Items which were identical on each trim scheme

Front roof rail and bows: Drab Cloth.
Floor mat: Brown Carpet with Tan Rubber heel pad.
Top: Drab Rubberized Fabric.
Finish moldings: Walnut Grain until April, then changed to Walnut Crotch Grain.
Front belt rail finish panel molding: Rustless Steel.
Back light frame: Outside-Bright Chrome Plated; Inside-Black Walnut Grain.
Front belt rail finish panel: Walnut Crotch Grain until April, then changed to Walnut Burl.
Body hardware: Bright Nickel Plated.

The new Deluxe three window Coupe with the front opening doors, a feature which carried over into the 1933-34 models. This body style was available only with the deluxe features.

The Deluxe three-window Coupe, the only closed model with a chromed windshield frame.

Coupe, Three Window (B-520) Deluxe

The all new deluxe three window Coupe was not introduced until April 1932. It was the only model with the front opening "suicide doors." That feature made the optional fender mounted spare tire unavailable since it would interfere with the door swing.

The deluxe features included cowl lights, dome light, arm rest on doors, sun visor, rear window curtain, rear window regulator, dash compartment (glove box), ash tray, cigar lighter and chromed windshield frame. There was a choice of these four interior trim schemes: Rose Beige mohair, Brown Bedford Cord, Tan Pinstripe and Copra Drab Fine Colonial Grain genuine leather. In July the genuine leather trim was made special equipment.

A rumble seat was not a standard item on this Coupe, but was available on special order. On bodies trimmed with cloth upholstering the rumble seat was finished in Russet Brown Fine Colonial Grain artificial leather. Those bodies upholstered with leather received a rumble seat trimmed with Copra Drab Fine Colonial Grain artificial leather.

The striping of the three window Coupe was unique. The two belt molding stripes followed the belt molding to the rear corner of the body, then one reversed and followed the lower body molding over the fender and under the doors, while the other went across the back of the body.

1932 DELUXE COUPE INTERIOR TRIM SCHEMES

Rose Beige Trim Scheme

Seats, seat back bellows and frame, seat sides, doors, arm rests, hinge pillar, back, roof rail sides: Rose Beige Mohair.
Headlining, sun visors, windshield header: Brown Napped Cotton.
Cowl panels: Two-tone Light Brown Dash Grain Cardboard.
Windlace: Tan Worsted.
Door pull cord: Russet Brown Fine Colonial Grain Leather.

Brown Trim Scheme

Seats, seat back bellows and frame, seat inner side, arm rest upper piece: Brown Bedford Cord.
Doors, arm rest lower piece, hinge pillar, back, roof rail side, seat outer side: Plain Brown Broadcloth.
Headlining, sun visors, windshield header: Light Brown Napped Cotton.
Cowl panels: Two-tone Light Brown Dash Grain Cardboard.
Windlace: Brown Worsted.
Door pull cord: Russet Brown Fine Colonial Grain Leather.

Tan Trim Scheme

Seats, seat back bellows and frame, seat sides, doors, arm rests, hinge pillar, back, roof rail sides: Tan Pinstripe.
Headlining, sun visors, windshield header: Tan Napped Cotton.
Cowl panels: Two-tone Light Brown Dash Grain Cardboard.
Windlace: Tan Worsted.
Door pull cord: Russet Brown Fine Colonial Grain Leather.

Genuine Leather Trim Scheme (changed to Special Equipment in July 1932)

Seats, seat back bellows and frame, seat inner sides, arm rest upper piece, door pull cord: Copra Drab Fine Colonial Grain Leather.
Doors, arm rest lower piece, hinge pillar, back, roof rail side, seat outer side, headlining, sun visors, windshield header, windlace: Copra Drab Fine Colonial Grain Artificial Leather.
Cowl panels: Copra Drab Fine Colonial Grain Cardboard.

Items which are identical on each trim scheme

Floor mat and front side sill: Brown Tapestry Carpet.
Front floor mat heel pad: Tan Rubber.
Window curtain: Brown Curtain Material with Tassel.
Window cord: Brown Twisted.
Package tray: Body side wall cloth until May 1932, then changed to headlining material.
Finish moldings: Walnut Grain until June 1932, then changed to Plain Mahogany Grain.
Door window finish strip lower: Walnut Burl Grain.
Front belt rail finish panel: Plain Mahogany Grain with Burl Grain on center and right embossments.
Rumble seat on cloth trim bodies: seat - Russet Brown Fine Colonial Grain Artificial Leather; deck sides - Matching Cardboard; floor mat - Brown Tapestry Carpet.
Rumble seat on leather trim body: seat - Copra Drab Fine Colonial Grain Artificial Leather; deck sides - Matching Cardboard; floor - Brown Tapestry Carpet.
Body hardware: Bright Nickel Plated.

Commercial Vehicles

Commercial vehicles were those built on a passenger car chassis but, with the exception of the Station Wagon, were not primarily used for carrying passengers. They were available as a plain chassis (no cab on body), with an open or closed cab, and with or without a pickup box. The other commercial models were the Station Wagon, Standard and Deluxe Panel Delivery, and Sedan Delivery.

Chassis items such as hood, fenders, radiator shell and grille, lights, frame, wheels, axles and drive train were identical to those in the passenger car. The only exception was the finish of some items such as the grille, radiator shell, headlight, etc. These differences are described in the chassis section.

Five exterior colors were available for commercial vehicles. On early production, the body and belt were painted the same color, but after May the belt could have been painted a color for the additional cost of $2.50 per body. No additional charge, however, was made on fleet orders of five bodies or more.

Due to the slow production of the V-8, the early commercial vehicles were available only with the four cylinder engine. The V-8 became available after May at extra cost, but most buyers preferred the four cylinder.

1932 COMMERCIAL VEHICLES EXTERIOR COLORS
Except Station Wagon

Body, Moldings, and Radiator Shell	Radiator Grill (1)	Wheels Color (2)
Mountain Brown	Mountain Brown	Tacoma Cream
Vermillion	Deep Black	Aurora Red
Blue Rock Green	Blue Rock Green	Apple Green
Golden Orange	Deep Black	Tacoma Cream
White (3)	White	Tacoma Cream

(1) Grills were painted black until July 1932, except on the Deluxe Panel Delivery which had Sea Gull Gray.
(2) All wheels were black until June 1932 – after June, black or color on special order.
(3) For Deluxe Pickup only – on other models by special order.

Open Cab (B-76), Closed Cab (B-82) and Pickup Box (B-78)

Prior to May, only the closed cab was produced. It came equipped with a two-tone Black Brown Fine Colonial Grain artificial leather interior trim on the seat and windlace, black masonite door panels, and cardboard cowl panels. The finish moldings were painted black and the floor mat was tan rubber. The remainder of the cab was painted body color.

The Open Cab was introduced in May with interior trim similar to the Closed Cab. Its top and side curtains were made of black Short Long Grain rubber coated fabric.

Striping was not provided, but was available on special order. Two stripes on the body molding were similar to the passenger cars. They went around the body 5/16 inch from the upper and lower edges of the molding.

The box was painted body color and was not striped.

Midyear production closed cab Pickup. The stripe was available on special order.

Regular production open cab Pickup Truck. Most commercial vehicles were produced on a Model "B" chassis.

1932 OPEN AND CLOSED CAB TRUCK INTERIOR TRIM SCHEMES

Black Brown Trim Scheme

Seat, windlace and back belt rail on open cab: Two-tone Black Brown Fine Colonial Grain Artificial Leather.
Cowl and seat sides on open cab: Two-tone Black Brown Fine Colonial Grain Cardboard.
Doors: Black Painted Masonite.
Floor: Tan Rubber.
Finish moldings: Black Enamel or Pyroxylin.
Top and curtains (Open Cab): Black Short Long Grain Rubber Coated Fabric.
Front belt rail finish panel molding: Rustless Steel.
Body hardware: Nickel Plated Butler Finish.

Panel Delivery (B-79) Standard and Deluxe

A completely restyled Panel Delivery body was introduced in May 1932. It featured all steel construction, a sloping windshield similar to the passenger car, and a generous 72.5 by 48.5 interior.

The standard model came equipped with outside rear view mirror, right front fender mounted spare wheel, dome light, and an interior trim of two-tone Black Brown Fine Colonial Grain artificial leather.

In addition to the above items, the deluxe Panel Delivery had cowl lights, passenger car grille, radiator shell, rustless

Early production Panel Delivery. The spare tire was not installed at the factory, but supplied by the dealer at added cost. As a result, the spare tire did not always match the other four.

steel tail and head lights, and trim panels on the front doors and head lining.

The cargo floor in both models was made of hard maple boards with metal skid strips. On the Masonite covered sides, a metal panel extended from the floor to the top of the wheel housing. The exterior was painted Commercial Drab until July when options of Pembroke Gray, Arabian Sand Light, Dawn Gray Light, Chickle Drab and Buff Light were released to stimulate customer appeal.

On the deluxe model, a chrome plated rear view mirror and windshield wiper arm and blades were released in July to improve appearance.

1932 STANDARD PANEL DELIVERY INTERIOR TRIM SCHEME

Black Brown Trim Scheme

Seats and windlace: Two-tone Black Brown Fine Colonial Grain Artificial Leather.
Cowl panels, seat bottom, seat back, roof rail: Two-tone Black Brown Fine Colonial Grain Cardboard.
Doors and inside of top: Painted (No trim material).
Front floor mat: Tan Rubber.
Finish moldings: Painted Black Enamel or Pyroxylin.
Front belt rail finish panel molding: Rustless Steel.
Hardware: Nickel Plated, Butler Finish.

1932 DELUXE PANEL DELIVERY INTERIOR TRIM SCHEME

Black Brown Trim Scheme

Seats and windlace: Two-tone Black Brown Fine Colonial Grain Artificial Leather.
Doors, cowl panels, seat bottom, seat back, roof rail: Two-tone Black Brown Fine Colonial Grain Cardboard.
Headlining: Two-tone Black Brown Fine Colonial Grain Artificial Leather.
Front floor mat: Tan Rubber.
Finish moldings: Painted Black Enamel or Pyroxylin.
Front belt rail finish panel molding: Rustless Steel.
Hardware: Nickel Plated, Butler Finish.

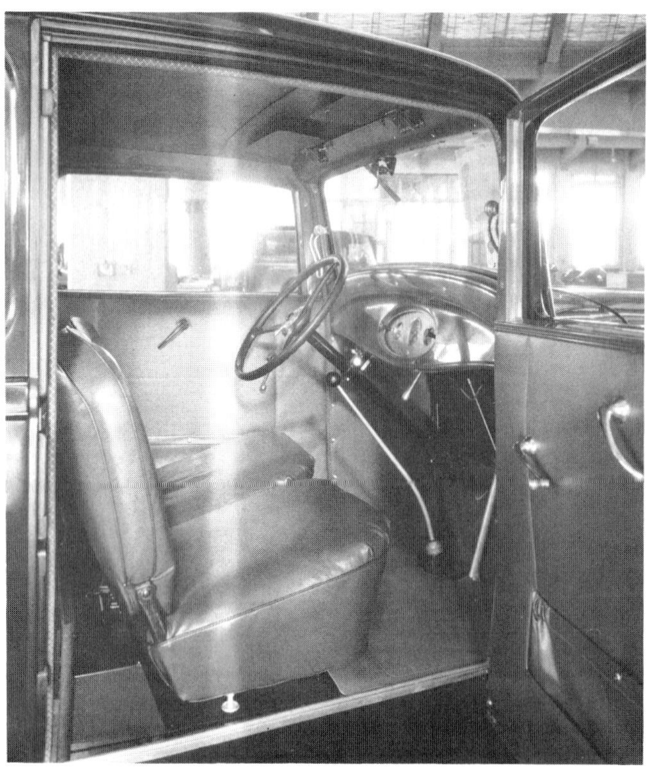

Front compartment of the Sedan Delivery. Note the passenger car instrument panel.

Sedan Delivery (B-410)

The Sedan Delivery introduced in September was the last body style to go into production. It was basically a Tudor body with the elimination of the rear quarter windows. It was equipped with a passenger seat, cowl lamps, a Tudor rear view mirror, passenger car cowl, grille, headlights, tail lamp, and because of the rear compartment door, standard right hand fender spare wheel carrier. The interior trim consisted of Copra Drab Fine Colonial Grain artificial leather. Striping was identical to the Tudor Sedan.

1932 SEDAN DELIVERY INTERIOR TRIM SCHEMES

Leather Trim Scheme

Seats, doors, headlining, windlace, sun visor: Copra Drab Fine Colonial Grain Artificial Leather.
Cowl panels and seat bottom: Copra Drab Fine Colonial Grain Cardboard.
Roof rail sides, rear doors: Brown Painted Masonite.
Floor mat: Tan Rubber.
Finish moldings: Painted Gray Enamel or Pyroxylin.
Front belt rail finish panel molding: Rustless Steel.
Body hardware: Bright Nickel Plated.

Rear compartment of the Sedan Delivery showing the floor treatment and side panels.

The Sedan Delivery was the last 1932 model introduced. Only 400 units were produced.

Station Wagon (G-150)

The 1932 Station Wagon, produced by Baker-Raulang was a new body, slightly larger than its Model A predecessor. Though in the commercial class, it was available only with the passenger car appointments. Standard equipment included outside rear view mirror, right front fender mounted spare wheel, side curtains in channel slides, and birch plywood panels with solid maple wood trim finished with spar varnish. For passengers, it had two bucket seats in the front and two full seats in the back. The interior trim material was two-tone Black Brown Fine Colonial Grain artificial leather with tan rubber innerlined fabric curtains. The floor mat was made of tan rubber.

The inside door handles (B-151250-A) were a carryover from the Model A. They were either stamped steel or aluminum die casting, both bright nickel plated. This handle was also used on the rear door of the B and BB Panel Delivery.

Three exterior colors were used on the sheel metal part of the Station Wagon (hood and cowl). Manila Brown was used from job-one to May 1932, Winter Leaf Brown Light from May to July, and Emperor Brown light from July to the end of production.

Starting in July, a tool compartment was provided under the number seven floor board. Cowl lamps which were special equipment originally, became standard equipment in August 1932.

Rear compartment of the 1932 Station Wagon. Many features were direct carry over from the Model "A".

The 1932 Station Wagon.

1932 STATION WAGON INTERIOR TRIM SCHEME

Black Brown Trim Scheme

Seats: Two-tone Black Brown Fine Colonial Grain Artificial Leather.
Cowl panels: Two-tone Black Brown Fine Colonial Grain Cardboard.
Door locks: Brown Pyroxylin Paint.
Tail gate chain cover: Black Short Long Grain Artificial Leather.
Curtains: Tan Fabric.
Floor mats: Tan Rubber.
Curtain: Tan Fabric.
Finish moldings: Black until May 1932, then changed to Winter Leaf Brown.
Body hardware: Nickel Plated, Butler Finish.

Domestic Production of 1932 Models

Model		V-8	4 Cyl	Total
Phaeton (B 35)	Standard	600	612	1,212
	Deluxe	978	300	1,278
Roadster (B 40)	Standard	568	984	1,552
	Deluxe	7,318	3,727	11,045
Coupe (B 45)	Five Window	31,112	20,682	51,794
Sport Coupe (B 50)		2,169	742	2,911
Tudor (B 55)	Standard	62,697	37,122	99,019
	Deluxe	20,200	4,082	24,282
Cabriolet (B 68)		6,062	429	6,091
Station Wagon (B 150)		331	1,052	1,383
Fordor (B 160)	Standard	9,984	4,224	14,208
	Deluxe	20,471	2,684	23,155
Victoria (B 190)		8,054	526	8,580
Convertible Sedan (B 400)		884	42	926
Deluxe Coupe (B 520)		21,178	970	22,148
B Pan. Delivery (B 79)	Standard	46	3,457	3,503
	Deluxe	69	2,550	2,619
Sedan Delivery (B 410)		58	342	400

1932 WINDSHIELD WIPER DATA

B = Black Paint   C = Chrome Plated   K = Cadmium Plated

Car Models	Wiper Number	Mounting Method	Finish	Wiper Arm Length	Wiper Arm Finish	Wiper Blade Length	Wiper Blade Finish
Standard Phaeton, Roadster	B-17508-D	Two screws	B	*6 7/64 •6	B B	7½ (1) 8 (2)	C B
Deluxe Phaeton, Roadster	B-17508-E	Two screws	C	*6 7/64 •6	C C	7½ (1) 8 (2)	C C
Standard Tudor, Fordor, Coupe (5W)	B-17508-A	Two screws and threaded shaft	K	*8¼ •8¼	B B	8¼ (1) 8	B B
Deluxe Tudor, Fordor	B-17508-A	Two screws and threaded shaft	K	*8¼ •8¼	C C	8¼ (1) 8 (2)	C C
Cabriolet	B-17508-G	Threaded shaft sleeve	C	*6⅛ •6	C C	6½ (1) 8 (2)	C C
Sport Coupe	B-17508-C	Threaded shaft	B	*6⅛ •6	C C	7½ (1) 8 (2)	C C
Convertible Sedan	B-17508-B	Threaded shaft	C	*6⅛ •6	C C	7½ (1) 8 (2)	C C
Deluxe Coupe (3W)	B-17508-A (1) B-17508-M (2)	Two screws and threaded shaft	K K	*8¼ •8¼	C C	7½ (1) 8 (2)	C C
Victoria				*8¼ •8¼	C C	8¼ (1) 8 (2)	C C
Station Wagon	B-17508-K (3) B-17508-L (4)	Two screws and threaded shaft	B	*9½ •9½	B C	8¼ (1) 8 (2)	B C
Closed Cab	B-17508-F	Two screws	B	*9½ •9½	B B	8¼ (1) 8 (2)	B B
Open Cab	B-17508-H	Two screws	B	*6¾ •6¾	B B	8¼ (1) 8 (2)	B B
Standard Panel Delivery	B-17508-J	Two screws and threaded shaft	B	*9½ •9½	B C	8½ (1) 8 (2)	B B
Deluxe Panel Delivery	B-17508-J	Two screws and threaded shaft	B	*9½ •9½	B C	8¼ (1) 8 (2)	B C

*Spring and rod design – Discontinued June 1932
•Spring, rod and clip design – Adapted June 1932
(1) Discontinued June 1932
(2) Adapted June 1932
(3) Discontinued May 1932
(4) Adapted May 1932

VIII — The 1933-34 Models

An early 1933 Deluxe Tudor Sedan, the base design model for all 1933-34 passenger cars. The standard model was identical, but did not have the cowl lights nor the dual horns and tail lamps as regular production equipment. The windshield frame was chrome plated on all deluxe cars but painted body color on standard cars.

As soon as the 1932 passenger cars were off the drawing boards and in production, Ford engineers started designing the 1933 models. The Great Depression had reached its lowest ebb in 1932, but the recovery seemed ever so slow. In an effort to stimulate sagging sales and with an eye to its fiftieth anniversary in 1933, the company developed an all new series of automobiles. With an improved V-8 engine, new "X" type frame, a six inch longer wheel base, and new streamlined body, the 1933 model was regarded as Ford's first car specifically designed for the V-8 power train. Other new features included a sloping heart shaped grille, fender mounted headlamps, skirted fenders, longer body and the rear hinged doors which were introduced on the 1932 three window Coupe.

With the introduction of the 1933 models, the company departed from its past system of identifying new models with a new prefix. While the 1933 models were designated as "Model 40," the engine numbers, which also served as the vehicle serial numbers, continued to carry the "18" prefix for the V-8 and "B" for the four cylinder. In addition, the various body styles were assigned a new series of identification numbers. As a result, it is sometimes difficult for collectors to determine which engine was used with a particular model. The situation was further confused by the differences in the body styles of the passenger cars and commercials. Some commercial vehicles had the passenger car grille, hood, and fenders while others retained the 1932 style grille, hood and fenders.

Because of a strike at the Briggs plant as well as the usual problems associated with a new car, the 1933 models were not introduced until February 1933. Within the first 4,000 units, six major manufacturing changes were made to correct some early design deficiencies. They were: 1) a reinforcement was added to the lock pillar before the dies were changed to strengthen that area; 2) to reduce breakage at the joint of the toe board to the cowl side, gas welding the joint was replaced by spot welding; 3) a reinforcement was added to the dash to toe board joint to reduce splitting; 4) reinforcement flanges, mistakenly omitted at the body assembly, were added to the cowl front end; 5) the distance between the steering wheel and the belt rail finish panel was increased one-half inch by redesigning the panel; and 6) the front fender apron to body bolt was eliminated to permit free movement at that joint. After these early changes were made, the 1933 bodies remained virtually unchanged through 1934.

A "deck side tool box" was released in April 1933 for installation in the rumble seat compartment of the Cabriolet. Starting in May it was also installed in all Coupes and Roadsters with rumble seats.

Contrary to the belief of most collectors, the straight grille and corresponding two handle hood usually associated with the 1934 style passenger cars was actually a late 1933 running change. That change began in September 1933, whereas production of the 1934 models was not started until November 1933. The grille and hood were modified simultaneously. Engineering releases affecting these parts were issued September 13 to 21 marked "Effective at once," accompanied by instructions to coordinate the change of all parts at the same time.

The company regarded the 1934 models as an "improved line of '40' passenger cars." The introduction announcement was issued October 19, 1933 by J. Crawford of the Sales Department. It stated: *"Mr. Edsel Ford has set December 9th as the date on which dealers should have sufficient passenger cars on hand for the initial showing of the improved models. By this date the dealers should have in their possession 10,000 passenger cars of the improved type.*

In order to make this possible, shipments of cars should commence from assembly branches (plants) on November 27, which would allow two weeks production to build up the above dealers' stock.

Therefore, to meet the above requirement, the assembly branches would commence operation on approximately November 20, which would allow them five days to fill up their system and be ready to commence shipment on the 27th.

The Rouge plant and body builders program should be arranged to meet the above requirements."

In addition to the grille and hood, other improvement features on the chassis were hub caps and spare wheel lock, carburetor, valve chamber cover, water thermostat, distributor, choke and throttle controls, and colored fenders on some models. For the first time bumper guards became available on special order from the factory. Improvements to the bodies included a ventilation system, cove trimmed roof, new passenger and driver's seat on Tudors, improved seats on all other closed bodies, new door finish strips, and deluxe type visors that were adjustable to the side as well as to the front. An insect screen was added to the cowl vent late in February.

The change to the 1934 models was very subtle with most improvements taking place between November 1933 and January 1934. Even though balancing out of old stock was carefully planned, the change over to new parts was not made on the same day at every plant. As a result, cars built during this period had both 1933 and 1934 items, while a body style built at one plant did not always match one built at another plant.

The window ventilation system, a 1934 feature.

One of the 1934 features, the side window ventilation system, was considered in 1933 but was not introduced until 1934. Patent rights for the system were held by W. D. Crowell of St. Louis, Missouri. Negotiations between Ford, its body builders and the inventor began in May 1933, but were not concluded until fall of that year. The mechanical function of the system permitted the window glass to move two inches backward without affecting the up and down movement. The small opening produced a ventilating vacuum effect when the car was in motion.

Body colors for 1933, three of which were carried over from the previous year, were somewhat limited. In addition to the Brewster Green Medium, Old Chester Gray, and black, the new colors were Emperor Brown Medium, Duncan Blue, and Coach Maroon. However, Brewster Green Medium and Emperor Brown Medium were eliminated in May 1933. Black was the standard wheel color on all models, but because of an overstock of Apple Green, this color was available as an alternate wheel color on early production.

A new series of color combinations was released for the 1934 cars, including three colors which were available on special order only. It should be kept in mind, however, that the company would create other combinations on fleet orders of five vehicles or more. One such order was for the Corn Products Refining Company consisting of standard Coupes, Tudors, and Sedan Deliveries. The bodies were painted Karo Blue with a white stripe, while the fenders and wheels were painted Japan Black.

1933 PASSENGER CARS EXTERIOR COLORS

Body	Stripe	Wheels (1)
Old Chester Gray	Tacoma Cream	Tacoma Cream
Black	Vermillion	Aurora Red
Duncan Blue	Silver Gray	Tacoma Cream
Brewster Green Medium (2)	Silver Gray	Tacoma Cream
Emperor Brown Medium (2)	Tacoma Cream	Tacoma Cream
Coach Maroon	Vermillion	Aurora Red
	Colors used for export vehicles	
Brewster Green Light	Silver Gray	Tacoma Cream
Winterleaf Brown Light	Tacoma Cream	Tacoma Cream

(1) Wheels on standard models were black or color by special order. On deluxe models wheels were option black or color as shown. Apple Green was also a color option.

(2) These colors were discontinued in May 1933.

Front and rear fenders, fender aprons, front fender spacer, tail lamp bracket, and tire cover were painted black. In August dealers were supplied with all the body color paints for painting the fenders if customers desired.

1933 COMMERCIAL VEHICLES EXTERIOR COLORS

(Excluding Station Wagon)

Body	Stripe	Wheels (1)
Black	Catawba Green	Black
Vermillion Red	Silver Gray	Black
Mountain Brown	Gold or Tacoma	Black
Golden Orange	Cream Optional	Black
Blue Rock Green		Black

(1) Passenger colors were available by special order.

Other body color combinations were available by special order or for fleet orders.

Fenders and related parts were painted black.

1933 STATION WAGON EXTERIOR COLORS

Cowl Sheet Metal	Body Wood	Wheels
Mountain Brown	Clear Spar Varnish	Black

Fenders and related parts were painted black.

1934 STANDARD PASSENGER CARS EXTERIOR COLORS

Body	Stripe	Fenders (1)
Medium Luster Black	Tacoma Cream	Black
Dearborn Blue	Tacoma Cream	Black
Cordova Gray	Tacoma Cream (4)	Cardova Gray
Vineyard Green (2)	Silver Gray	Vineyard Green
Vineyard Green (2)	Tacoma Cream	Vineyard Green
Coach Maroon (3)	English Coach Vermillion	Black or Coach Maroon

(1) Included fenders, front fender apron and spacer, tail lamp bracket and tire cover.
(2) Released for west coast and Florida only, but became available as special order after January 1934.
(3) Released for special order in January 1934.
(4) Changed to English Coach Vermillion in April 1934.

Wheels were normally black but deluxe colors were available on special order.

1934 DELUXE PASSENGER CARS EXTERIOR COLORS

Available on all models

Body	Stripe	Wheels
Medium Luster Black	Tacoma Cream	Tacoma Cream
Dearborn Blue	Tacoma Cream	Tacoma Cream
Cordova Gray	Tacoma Cream (1)	Cardova Gray or Tacoma Cream
Available only on Fordor, Cabriolet, Victoria and (3W) Coupe		
Coach Maroon	English Coach Vermillion	Aurora Red
Available only on Tudor, Cabriolet, Victoria, Roadster, Phaeton and (5W) Coupe		
Vineyard Green	Silver Gray or Tacoma Cream	Vineyard Green or Tacoma Cream
Available for export only		
Winterleaf Brown Light	Tacoma Cream	Tacoma Cream

(1) Changed to English Coach Vermillion or Aurora Red in April 1934.

1934 COMMERCIAL EXTERIOR COLORS

(Except Station Wagon which was same as 1933)

Body Colors: Vermillion Red and Black for entire year. Mountain Brown, Golden Orange, Blue Rock Green until February 1934, then replaced by Dearborn Blue, Vineyard Green, Cordova Gray, Coach Maroon and Winterleaf Brown Light. Other combinations were also available for fleet orders.

Stripe: The following were optional – Catawba Green, Silver Gray, Gold, or Tacoma Cream.

Wheels and fenders: Black.

Hood Radiator Shell and Fenders

In comparison with the 1932 design, the grille and radiator shell of the new 1933 passenger cars were combined and moved forward creating a longer hood. The headlight bar was omitted and the stylish front fenders were extended across the bottom of the grille, eliminating the splash shield. The oval name plate was reduced slightly to $1^{15}/_{16}$ inches wide and the V-8 ornament was attached to the grille, just below the name plate. Along with the grille and hood change in September, the name plate and radiator cap were combined to form the semblance of a radiator ornament. At the same time the V-8 radiator emblem was restyled to include a Harding Blue triangular shield.

The front end styling of the new 1933 passenger cars.

The early 1933 fenders did not have fender skirts. This feature was added to both the front and rear fenders in February 1933. Old stock of the earlier design were designated for use on Sedan Delivery and Station Wagon. After the old stock was used up, these two body styles were equipped with the same fenders as the passenger cars. All through 1933, the fenders, fender aprons, front fender spacer, tail lamp bracket and tire cover were painted black, but starting with the 1934 models these items were painted body color on all but a few standard models. Welled fenders were standard on the right side on the Station Wagon, Sedan Delivery and Panel Delivery. They were also available as special equipment for other models, but because of their high profile they were not very popular.

Two distinguishing features of the 1933 passenger car hood were the single hood locking handle and the curved venting louvers. In September 1933, the locking handle was replaced with two hood locking handles and the curved louvers were made straight. A further change, simplifying the handles, was made effective with Job-one 1934.

Lights

The 1933 headlights were three inches longer than the 1932 design. They were produced in two styles: a two bulb assembly for the standard passenger cars and a one bulb assembly used in conjunction with the cowl lights on the deluxe cars. Both were equipped with 32-32 CP light bulbs. The door and case were made of either chrome plated brass or rustless steel. For 1934, the headlight case was redesigned one inch shorter. The Ford oval trade mark and "Twolite Headlamp" was stamped on the case during both years.

The 1933–34 cowl lamps were similar in shape to the headlights but were $^{7}/_{16}$ inches smaller than the 1932 lamps. The door and case were made of rustless steel while the mounting bracket was chrome plated. Cowl lamps were standard equipment on deluxe vehicles and available as special equipment on standard vehicles and commercials.

The rear lamp body, lens door, lens, and lamp bracket were all redesigned for 1933. The new lamp used one dual filament light bulb and the lamp bracket mounted on the fender. The left side rear lamp was standard equipment on all passenger cars, while the right side lamp was standard equipment on deluxe cars but special equipment on the standard models. The left side lamp body had a license plate white lens on the top with the letters "Duolamp-B" stamped between the lens door and the white lens. The right side lamp had neither the white lens opening nor the "Duolamp-B" stamping. Both the lamp body and the lens door were made of rustless steel.

The lens was made of high transmission Ruby colored glass with its back face covered with cubical reflecting prisms and a $^{3}/_{4}$ inch diameter bulls eye in the center.

A steel bracket painted to match the fender, was used to

mount the lamp to the fender. In April 1933, the deck step was added to all right side lamp brackets mounted to bodies with a rumble seat. The 1933 tail lamps and mounting brackets were carried over on all 1934 models except the Victoria which had a longer unique mounting bracket, placing the rear lamp $7^{7}/_{16}$ inches behind the rear fender.

The rear license plate bracket was also new. It was painted black, and similar to the tail lamp, it was stamped "Duo-lamp-B." In October 1933, a special license plate bracket, five inches higher, was required for cars sold in Mississippi.

Door and Window Regulator Handles

The outside door handles on all closed passenger car bodies, were a carry-over of the 1932 flat "S" style handle, except the metal was changed from rustless steel to brass with bright chrome plating. In June, this handle was also used on the Station Wagon which had been using the Model A scroll design.

Exterior door handles on the Roadster and Phaeton were also a carry-over of the 1932 style until the 1934 model change. A new scroll type handle made of chrome plated brass was introduced with Job-one 1934. The 1932 rear deck door handle was a carry-over for use on Roadsters with or without the rumble seat as well as on Coupes without rumble seat. Coupe and Cabriolet bodies with rumble seats were equipped with a new remote control latch operated by a handle inside the car, just below the back window.

New L-shaped interior door handles were used on all passenger cars except the Fordor Sedans, Roadsters and Phaetons. These handles were made of zinc die casting with a bright nickel finish. Rotating the end of the handle down opened the door; rotating the handle up locked the door. Leftover 1932 deluxe Coupe door handles were installed on the early production Fordor Sedans until stock ran out. Use of these handles was coordinated with identical 1932 deluxe Coupe window regulator handles and rear window handles. The Roadsters and Phaetons were equipped with the carry-over Station Wagon handle.

The rumble seat latch on the Cabriolet and Coupe bodies was operated by a handle inside the car.

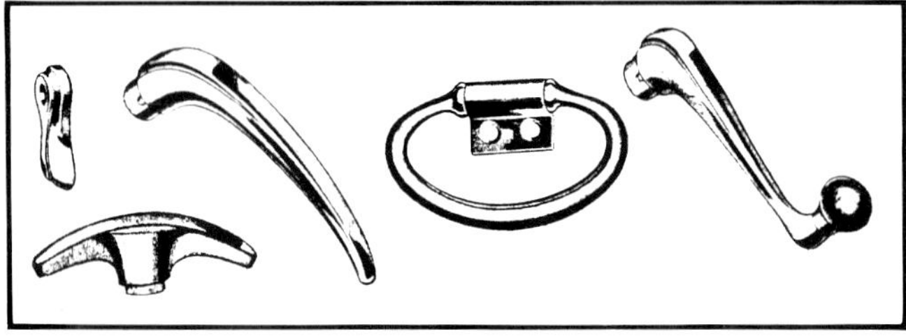

Typical interior hardware.

Because the rear hinged doors of the 1933 style were much larger than previous doors, a "pull-to" handle was considered necessary to close the doors. Two designs were used. On the standard models the handle consisted of a bright nickel plated ring and mounting bracket, while on the deluxe cars, the pull-to handle was a cord, carried over from 1932. A Russet Brown leather cord was installed on bodies with cloth trim schemes and a Copra Drab leather cord was on bodies with the leather trim schemes. When the 1932 stock was used up, the deluxe models were converted to the metal ring pull-to handle, identical to those on the standard models. The ring pull-to handle was obsoleted in September 1933. On standard bodies, it was replaced by a new window finish strip with a raised finger grip. On the deluxe bodies it was replaced with a pull-to cord with new mounting end pieces.

With the introduction of the 1934 models the locking mechanism of the closed cars was changed. To lock the door the handle was rotated down, and to open the door the handle was rotated up. The change was made as stock of the new locks became available, therefore, some 1933 locks were installed on early production 1934 models. In March 1934, a new Victoria body was introduced which featured a new lock and remote control rod. This feature permitted the inside door handle to be located near the center of the door, thus eliminating the need for the pull-to cord. Later that month, a similar change was made to all the deluxe closed bodies, including the Cabriolet.

The window regulator handles on the 1933 closed cars were also new. They were made of zinc die casting finished with bright nickel plating. The knob on the standard models was a matching zinc die casting, but on the deluxe bodies the knob was made of a mixed Maroon and Thorn Brown plastic. A small curved "T" type regulator handle was used on the rear quarter windows, the back window, and for operating the windshield opening mechanism.

Interior Visors

The 1933 sun visors were the internal end mounting type similar to 1932—covered with headlining material to match the interior trim. The visors on passenger car bodies with the cloth trim had a Russet Brown Fine Colonial Grain artificial leather binding, while bodies with leather trim had a Copra Drab Fine Colonial Grain artificial leather binding. The binding on the sedan delivery visor was made of two-tone Black Brown Fine Colonial Grain artificial leather. Two visors were installed on deluxe bodies, but only one, on the driver's side, was installed on standard bodies.

A new visor with a single pivot mounting bracket which could be adjusted to the front or side was released in September 1933, for use only on deluxe bodies with the cloth trim schemes. By November, this visor was installed on all deluxe bodies. The standard models continued to use the original design, but the second style was released starting with the 1934 models.

Floor Mats and Carpets

A tan rubber floor mat with a "Kirsey pad" was installed in the front compartment of all V-8 bodies for 1933. The pattern, a simulated tapestry carpet weave, was similar to that used in 1932. The floor mat had an oval-shaped opening in the center to fit around the raised transmission tunnel. A matching tan rubber mat covered the tunnel. For the four cylinder cars, the mat had a sunburst pattern. Identical mats were used on the Tudor and Victoria, Roadster and Phaeton, Fordors, Coupes and Cabriolet. Except for the seat mounting slots, the Sedan Delivery mat was similar to the Tudor, while the Station Wagon had its own unique mat with the sunburst pattern.

The Kirsey pad was eliminated from all mats in July 1933 to avoid a patent infringement. Other changes also followed. In October the Tudor and Victoria mats were changed as the result of a modification on the front seat mounting mechanism. When the new Victoria body was introduced in March 1934, it had a unique floor mat that was not interchangeable with any other. In May 1934 a black rubber waffle pattern was molded to the bottom of the mats to provide a cushion effect similar to that of the Kirsey pad.

In the rear compartment, the deluxe sedans had a one piece brown carpet but the standard sedans had a three piece tan rubber mat. However, due to a surplus of carpets from 1932, the standard bodies also had carpets until stock ran out in April 1933. The Phaeton had a tan rubber mat throughout. In September 1933, that one piece mat was changed to three pieces, one piece on the tunnel and the others on each side. However, with Job-one 1934 the mat was changed back to the one piece design. In addition, the Phaeton mat was increased five inches in length.

The Tudor and Victoria bodies had an additional center floor mat located under the front seat, between the front and rear mats. On the 1933 models, this mat was made of tan rubber identical to the front mat. When the front seat mounting brackets were changed, the center mat was changed to brown carpet on deluxe bodies only.

The commercial vehicles had two variations of rear mats. The Sedan Delivery used a one piece mat with the sunburst pattern, while the Station Wagon had a three piece mat with a pyramid pattern on the main piece and a sunburst pattern on the side pieces. Similar to the passenger cars, the early mats had the Kirsey pad on the bottom until July 1933, then a waffle mat from May 1934 to the end of production.

Miscellaneous Interior Items

The metal frames around the door windows, quarter windows and back window of closed bodies were identified as the window finish strip. On the standard bodies, these items were painted gray enamel until May 1933, when they were changed to maroon. On the deluxe bodies they were finished in a walnut grain pattern. These items received few changes. In September 1933, the door finish strips on the standard bodies and Sedan Delivery were modified to include a raised pull grip for closing the door. However, the raised portion was eliminated in March 1934 when the door handle was relocated. With the model change in 1934, the lower flange of the finish strip was increased from $1^1/_4$ to $2^1/_8$ inches and a stylized embossed oval was added.

Both the assist loops and curtain cords on the deluxe Tudor, Fordor and Victoria bodies were a direct carry over from the 1932 models.

The door sill scuff plates were made of aluminum or zinc embossed on the top surface with a fine dimple pattern.

The shape of the headlining material for all 1934 closed bodies was made with cove corners which terminated on top of the windows, thus eliminating the roof rail side piece.

Tudor (40-700) Standard and Deluxe

Beginning with 1933 the Tudor became the basic body. Any part from the Tudor that was used on other body styles

An early 1934 Deluxe Tudor.

A mid-year 1934 Deluxe Tudor with bumper guards which became available on special order in 1934.

Front interior trim of a 1933 Deluxe Tudor. Note the stitch pattern and the pull-to cord mounting on the door panel.

retained the Tudor part number.

The standard body was equipped with an adjustable driver's seat, glove box, sun visor on driver's side, dome light and a choice of three interior trim schemes—Thorn Brown Mohair, Tan Pinstripe Broadcloth, and Copra Drab Fine Colonial Grain artificial leather.

The deluxe body was equipped with all the items of the standard body plus a cigar lighter and ashtrays, arm rests on driver's door and rear quarter, and a second visor on

Rear compartment of the 1933 Deluxe Tudor.

the passenger side. Interior trim scheme selections were Rose Beige Mohair, Brown Bedord Cord, Brown Stripe Broadcloth and Copra Drab Fine Colonial Grain leather. The distinquishing features on the outside were the cowl lights, dual horns, and dual tail lamps.

There were subtle body changes between 1933 and 1934 models. The most significant were the window ventilation system and new front bucket seats. In March 1934, a counterbalance spring and bracket was added to the front seat to prevent its top section from hitting the front belt rail finish panel when the seat was tilted forward.

In comparison with the 1932, the striping of the 1933 Tudor was very simple. Two fine stripes started at a point at the beginning of the belt molding on the hood and went completely around the body. The stripes were $^{1}/_{32}$ inch wide and were 0.30 inch from the edges of the molding. On the 1934 models, a $^{3}/_{32}$ inch stripe was added between the two pin stripes. In addition, a $^{1}/_{32}$ inch stripe was added to the hood louvers of the deluxe Tudor.

Shipping weight for the standard Tudor car was 2,675 pounds, but the deluxe Tudor weighed 2,684 pounds.

Redesigned front seats of the 1934 Deluxe Tudor.

The full tilting style front seat of the Deluxe Tudor. Compare the pull-to cord mounting bracket to the 1933 design.

1933 STANDARD TUDOR SEDAN INTERIOR TRIM SCHEMES

Thorn Brown Mohair Trim Scheme
Seats, doors, quarter: Thorn Brown Mohair.
Back, upper hinge pillar, roof side rail, headlining, windshield header, visor: Thorn Brown Napped Cotton.
Rear curtain: Brown Poplin with Tab.
Windlace: Brown Worsted Cloth.

Tan Pinstripe Trim Scheme
Seats: Tan Pinstripe Broadcloth.
Back, door, quarter, hinge pillar, roof side rail: Brown Sidewall Cloth.
Headlining, windshield header, visor: Brown Napped Cotton.
Rear curtain: Brown Poplin with Tab.
Windlace: Tan Worsted Cloth.

Copra Drab Imitation Leather Trim Scheme (Adopted April 1933)
Seats, back, door, quarter, hinge pillar, roof side rail, headlining, windshield header, visor, windlace: Copra Drab Fine Colonial Grain Artificial Leather.
Rear curtain: Copra Drab Fine Colonial Grain Artificial Leather with Tab.

Items which were identical on each trim scheme
Cowl, seat bottom: Two-tone Black Maroon Fine Colonial Grain Cardboard.
Finish moldings, front belt rail, glove box door: Gray Enamel until May 1933 then changed to Maroon Enamel.
Front and center floor mat: Tan Rubber.
Rear floor mat: Tan Rubber or Brown Carpet with matching trim scheme.
Front belt molding: Rustless Steel.
Body hardware: Bright Nickel Plate.
Windshield frame: Painted body color.

1933 DELUXE TUDOR SEDAN INTERIOR TRIM SCHEMES

Rose Beige Mohair Trim Scheme
Seats, back, doors, quarter, arm rest, roof side rail, hinge pillar, windlace: Rose Beige Mohair.
Headlining, windshield header, visor: Brown Napped Cotton.
Rear curtain: Brown Leona Weave Cloth with Tab.

Brown Bedford Cord Trim Scheme
Seats: Brown Bedford Cord.
Back, doors, quarter, arm rest, roof side rail, hinge pillar, windlace: Brown Broadcloth.
Headlining, windshield header, visor: Brown Napped Cotton.
Rear curtain: Brown Leona Weave Cloth with Tab.

Brown Stripe Trim Scheme
Seats: Brown Stripe Broadcloth.
Back, doors, quarter, arm rest, roof side rail, hinge pillar, windlace: Brown Broadcloth.
Headlining, windshield header, visor: Brown Napped Cotton.
Rear curtain: Brown Leona Weave Cloth with Tab.

Copra Drab Leather Trim Scheme (Released April 1933)
Seats, back, doors, quarter, arm rest, roof side rail, hinge pillar, windlace, headlining, windshield header, visor: Copra Drab Fine Colonial Grain Leather.
Rear curtain: Copra Drab Fine Colonial Grain Artificial Leather with Tab.

Items which were identical on each trim scheme
Cowl, seat bottom: Two-tone Black Maroon Fine Colonial Grain Cardboard.
Front belt rail, glove box door: Walnut Burl Grain.
Finish moldings: Walnut Grain.
Front and center floor mat: Tan Rubber.
Rear floor mat: Brown Carpet with binding to match trim scheme.
Rear seat heel board: Brown Carpet added September 1933.
Front belt molding: Rustless Steel.
Body hardware: Bright Nickel Plate.
Windshield frame: Bright Chrome Plate.

1934 STANDARD TUDOR SEDAN INTERIOR TRIM SCHEMES

Thorn Brown Mohair Trim Scheme
Seats, doors, quarter, arm rest, hinge pillar: Thorn Brown Mohair.
Back, headlining, windshield header, visor: Thorn Brown Napped Cotton.
Rear curtain: Brown Proxylin with Tab.
Windlace: Brown Worsted Cloth.

Tan Pinstripe Trim Scheme
Seats: Tan Pinstripe Broadcloth.
Back, doors, quarter, arm rest, hinge pillar: Brown Sidewall Cloth.
Headlining, windshield header, visor: Brown Napped Cotton.
Rear curtain: Brown Proxylin with Tab.
Windlace: Brown Worsted Cloth.

Copra Drab Leather Trim Scheme (Discontinued May 1934)
Seats: Copra Drab Fine Colonial Grain Leather.
Back, doors, hinge pillar, quarter, arm rest, headlining, windshield header, visor, windlace: Copra Drab Fine Colonial Grain Artificial Leather.
Rear curtain: Copra Drab Fine Colonial Grain Artificial Leather with Tab.

Copra Drab Imitation Leather Trim Scheme (Discontinued May 1934)
Seats, back, doors, hinge pillar, quarter, arm rest, headlining, windshield header, visor, windlace: Copra Drab Fine Colonial Grain Artificial Leather.
Rear curtain: Copra Drab Fine Colonial Grain Artificial Leather with Tab.

Taupe Leather Trim Scheme (Introduced May 1934)
Seats: Taupe Fine Colonial Grain Leather.
Back, doors, hinge pillar, quarter, arm rest, headlining, windshield header, windlace: Taupe Fine Colonial Grain Artificial Leather.
Visor: Covered with Embossed Cardboard to match headlining material.
Rear curtain: Taupe Fine Colonial Grain Artificial Leather with Tab.

Taupe Imitation Leather Trim Scheme (Introduced May 1934)
Seats, back, doors, hinge pillar, quarter, arm rest, headlining, windshield header, windlace: Taupe Fine Colonial Grain Artificial Leather.
Visor: Covered with Embossed Cardboard to match headlining material.
Rear curtain: Taupe Fine Colonial Grain Artificial Leather with Tab.

Items which were identical on each trim scheme
Cowl, seat bottom: Two-tone Black Maroon Fine Colonial Grain Cardboard.
Finish moldings, front belt rail, glove box door: Maroon Enamel.
Front, center, and rear floor mats: Tan Rubber.
Body hardware: Bright Nickel Plate.
Windshield frame: Painted body color.

1934 DELUXE TUDOR SEDAN INTERIOR TRIM SCHEMES

Rose Beige Mohair Trim Scheme
Seats, doors, arm rest, quarter, hinge pillar, windlace: Rose Beige Mohair.
Back, headlining, windshield header, visor: Rose Beige Napped Cotton.
Rear curtain: Brown Poplin with Tab.

Brown Stripe Trim Scheme
Seats: Brown Stripe Broadcloth.
Back, headlining, windshield header, visor: Brown Napped Cotton.
Doors, arm rest, quarter, hinge pillar, windlace: Brown Broadcloth.
Rear curtain: Brown Poplin with Tab.

Copra Drab Leather Trim Scheme (Discontinued May 1934)
Seats, back, doors, arm rest, quarter, hinge pillar, headlining, windshield header, visor, windlace: Copra Drab Fine Colonial Grain Leather.
Rear curtain: Copra Drab Fine Colonial Grain Artificial Leather with Tab.

Taupe Leather Trim Scheme (Introduced May 1934)
Seats, back, door, arm rest, quarter, hinge pillar, headlining, windshield header, windlace: Taupe Fine Colonial Grain Leather.
Visor: Covered with Embossed Cardboard of same color and grain.
Rear curtain: Taupe Fine Colonial Grain Artificial Leather with Tab.

Items which were identical on each trim scheme
Cowl, seat bottom: Two-tone Black Maroon Fine Colonial Grain Cardboard.
Front belt rail, glove box door: Walnut Burl Grain.
Finish moldings: Walnut Grain.
Front floor mat: Tan Rubber.
Rear and center floor mat, rear seat heel board: Brown Carpet with binding to match trim scheme.
Body hardware: Bright Nickel Plate.
Windshield frame: Bright Chrome Plate.

The 1934 Deluxe Roadster with rumble seat and side curtains.

The 1933 Roadster with top down.

Roadster (40-710) Standard and Deluxe

With a shipping weight of only 2,461 pounds, the 1933 Roadster was probably the peppiest V-8 ever produced by Ford. The standard model was bare of frills, but special equipment options included cigar lighter and ash tray, windwings, dust boot and rumble seat. Its interior trim scheme consisted of the two-tone Black Brown Fine Colonial Grain Artificial leather. The top material was made of a double rubber interlined fabric, black and white on the outside and Gray Drab on the inside. After the 1933 production this standard Roadster was discontinued.

In contrast with the standard Roadster, the deluxe Roadster of 1933 was equipped with a chrome windshield frame, cowl lights, dual horns and tail lamps, lighter and ashtray, glove box, rumble seat, and genuine Copra Drab Fine Colonial Grain leather in the front compartment with matching artificial leather in the rumble seat. The top material was a double rubber interlined fabric, drab inside and out. Special equipment included the wind wings and dust boot which ultimately became standard equipment on the 1934 models.

In January 1934, the contour of the Roadster seat cushion and back was modified so as to conform with the shape of the Tudor seat. Another 1934 change was made in May when the Copra Drab trim scheme was replaced with Taupe.

The striping consisted of two stripes which began at the front of the hood similar to the Tudor, then followed the belt line to the rear corner of the body and across the lower portion of the back deck to the other side. A third stripe painted between the two pin stripes, as well as louver stripes were added to the 1934 models.

Early 1934 Deluxe Roadster with the chrome plated windshield frame and stantions. This view shows the proper location of the rear fender step plate, common to all cars with rumble seat.

1933 STANDARD ROADSTER INTERIOR TRIM SCHEME

Black Brown Imitation Leather Trim Scheme

Seat, seat side, package tray, seat heel board, windlace: Two-tone Black Brown Fine Colonial Grain Artificial Leather.

Doors, quarter hinge pillar: Two-tone Black Brown Fine Colonial Grain Cardboard.

Cowl panel: Two-tone Black Maroon Fine Colonial Grain Cardboard.

Glove box door, front belt rail: Gray Enamel until May 1933, then changed to Walnut Burl Grain.

Floor: Tan Rubber.

Top, side curtains: outside - Black White; inside - Gray Drab. Rubber Interlined Fabric.

Rumble seat: seat - Two-tone Black Brown Fine Colonial Grain Artificial Leather; deck side - Two-tone Black Brown Fine Colonial Grain Cardboard; deck floor - Tan Rubber.

Dust hood: Black White Fabric.

Backlight frame: Black Enamel outside; Gray Enamel inside.

Top irons: Black Enamel.

Body hardware: Bright Nickel Plate.

Front belt moldings: Rustless Steel.

Windshield frame, windshield stantions: Black Enamel.

1933 DELUXE ROADSTER INTERIOR TRIM SCHEME

Copra Drab Leather Trim Scheme

Seat, door with binding to match, quarter hinge pillar, package tray, heel board, windlace: Copra Drab Fine Colonial Grain Leather.

Glove box door, front belt molding: Walnut Burl Grain.

Cowl: Two-tone Black Maroon Fine Colonial Grain Cardboard.

Floor: Tan Rubber.

Top, side curtains: outside - Black White; inside - Gray Drab Rubber Interlined Fabric.

Rumble seat: seat - Copra Drab Fine Colonial Grain Artificial Leather; deck side - Copra Drab Fine Colonial Grain Cardboard; deck floor - Tan Rubber.

Dust hood: Drab Fabric.

Outside backlight frame, inside backlight frame, top irons, windshield frame and windshield stantions: Bright Chrome Plate.

Body hardware: Bright Nickel Plate.

1934 DELUXE ROADSTER INTERIOR TRIM SCHEME

Copra Drab Trim Scheme (Used until May 1934)

Seat, door with binding to match, quarter hinge pillar, heel board, windlace: Copra Drab Fine Colonial Grain Leather.

Rumble seat: seat - Copra Drab Fine Colonial Grain Artificial Leather; deck side, package tray - Copra Drab Fine Colonial Grain Cardboard; deck floor - Tan Rubber.

Taupe Trim Scheme (Introduced May 1934)

Seat, door, quarter hinge pillar, heel board, windlace: Taupe Fine Colonial Grain Leather.

Rumble seat: seat - Taupe Fine Colonial Grain Artificial Leather; deck side, package tray - Taupe Fine Colonial Grain Cardboard; deck floor - Tan Rubber.

Items which were identical on each trim scheme

Front belt rail finish panel, glove box door: Walnut Burl Grain.

Floor: Tan Rubber.

Cowl: Two-tone Black Maroon Fine Colonial Grain Cardboard.

Top, side curtains: inside and out - Drab Rubber Interlined Fabric.

Dust hood: Drab Fabric.

Outside backlight frame, inside backlight frame, top irons, windshield frame and windshield stantions: Bright Chrome Plate.

Body hardware: Bright Nickel Plate.

The 1933 Deluxe Three Window Coupe.

An early 1934 Deluxe Three Window Coupe. The chrome windshield frame was installed on deluxe models only.

Coupes, Three Window (40-720)-Five Window (40-770) Standard and Deluxe

In 1932, the three window Coupe was available only as a deluxe, but for 1933 it came in either the standard or deluxe version, similar to the five window coupe. Other than the added quarter window and extra space behind the seat of the five window body, the two models were identical. Both styles were very popular with salesmen and fleet buyers. The standard bodies were equipped with an adjustable seat, glove box, driver's side sun visor, dome light and roll down rear window. The rumble seat, cigar lighter and ashtray were available as special equipment. Only two interior trim schemes were available at introduction, Thorn Brown Mohair and Tan Pinstripe. Two more, Copra Drab Fine Colonial Grain genuine leather or artificial leather were added in April 1933.

The deluxe bodies had all the items of the standard models plus a chrome windshield frame, cowl lights, dual horns

The 1933 Standard Five Window Coupe.

A preproduction 1934 Deluxe Five Window Coupe.

Interior compartment of the 1933 Standard Five Window Coupe.

and tail lamps, two sun visors, lighter, ash tray and a driver's door arm rest. Similar to the standard model, the rumble seat was available as an option at extra cost. Upholstery options were Rose Beige Mohair, Brown Bedford Cord and Brown Stripe Broadcloth. The Copra Drab Fine Colonial Grain leather trim was released in April 1933.

With the end of the 1933 production the standard three window Coupe body was discontinued, but the others were carried into 1934 virtually unchanged. A passenger side arm rest was added at model change-over and the Brown Bedford Cord trim was dropped. In May 1934, the Copra Drab leather trim scheme was changed to Taupe leather.

Striping of the Coupes was identical to the Roadster.

Interior of the 1934 Deluxe Five Window Coupe.

1933 STANDARD THREE AND FIVE WINDOW COUPE INTERIOR TRIM SCHEMES

Thorn Brown Mohair Trim Scheme
Seat, seat back bellows, package tray, doors: Thorn Brown Mohair.
Headliner, windshield header, roof side rail, back, visor: Thorn Brown Napped Cotton.
Rear curtain: Brown Poplin with Tab.
Windlace: Brown Worsted Cloth.

Tan Pinstripe Trim Scheme
Seat: Tan Pinstripe Broadcloth.
Seat back bellows, package tray, back, doors: Brown Sidewall Cloth.
Headliner, windshield header, roof side rail, visor: Brown Napped Cotton.
Rear curtain: Brown Poplin with Tab.
Windlace: Brown Worsted Cloth.

Copra Drab Leather Trim Scheme (Introduced April 1933)
Seat: Copra Drab Fine Colonial Grain Leather.
Seat back bellows, package tray, door, headliner, back, windshield header, roof side rail, visor, windlace: Copra Drab Fine Colonial Grain Artificial Leather.
Rear curtain: Copra Drab Fine Colonial Grain Artificial Leather with Tab.

Copra Drab Imitation Leather Trim Scheme (Introduced April 1933)
Seat, seat back bellows, package tray, door, headliner, back, windshield header, roof side rail, visor, windlace: Copra Drab Fine Colonial Grain Artificial Leather.
Rear curtain: Copra Drab Fine Colonial Grain Artificial Leather with Tab.

Items which were identical on each trim scheme
Cowl: Two-tone Black Maroon Fine Colonial Grain Cardboard.
Finish moldings, front seat rail, glove box door: Gray Enamel until May 1933 then changed to Maroon.
Floor: Tan Rubber.
Rumble seat: seat - Two-tone Black Brown Fine Colonial Grain Leather; deck side - Two-tone Black Brown Fine Colonial Grain Cardboard; deck floor - Tan Rubber.
Front belt molding: Rustless Steel.
Body hardware: Bright Nickel Plate.
Windshield frame: Painted body color.

1933 DELUXE THREE AND FIVE WINDOW COUPE INTERIOR TRIM SCHEMES

Rose Beige Mohair Trim Scheme
Seat, seat back bellows, package tray, doors, back, windlace: Rose Beige Mohair.
Headlining, windshield header, roof side rail, visor: Brown Napped Cotton.
Rear curtain: Brown Leona Weave Cloth with Tab.

Brown Bedford Cord Trim Scheme
Seat: Brown Bedford Cord.
Back, seat back bellows, package tray, doors, windlace: Brown Broadcloth.
Headlining, windshield header, roof side rail, visor: Brown Napped Cotton.
Rear curtain: Brown Leona Weave Cloth with Tab.

Brown Stripe Trim Scheme
Seat: Brown Stripe Broadcloth.
Back, seat back bellows, package tray, door, windlace: Brown Broadcloth.
Headlining, windshield header, roof side rail, visor: Brown Napped Cotton.
Rear curtain: Brown Leona Weave Cloth with Tab.

Copra Drab Leather Trim Scheme (Introduced April 1933)
Seat, back, seat back bellows, package tray, doors, windlace, headlining, windshield header, roof side rail, visor: Copra Drab Fine Colonial Grain Leather.
Rear curtain: Copra Drab Fine Colonial Grain Artificial Leather with Tab.

Items which were identical on each trim scheme
Cowl: Two-tone Black Maroon Fine Colonial Grain Cardboard.
Finish moldings: Walnut Grain.
Front belt rail, glove box door: Walnut Burl Grain.
Floor: Tan Rubber.
Rumble seat: seat and deck side - Copra Drab Fine Colonial Grain Artificial Leather; deck floor - Tan Rubber.
Front belt molding: Rustless Steel.
Body hardware: Bright Nickel Plate.
Windshield frame: Bright Chrome Plate.

1934 STANDARD FIVE WINDOW COUPE INTERIOR TRIM SCHEMES

Thorn Brown Mohair Trim Scheme

Seat, seat back bellows, doors, hinge pillar, quarter, package tray: Thorn Brown Mohair.
Headlining, windshield header, visor: Thorn Brown Napped Cotton.
Cowl: Two-tone Black Maroon Fine Colonial Grain Cardboard.
Rear curtain: Brown Proxylin with Tab.
Windlace: Brown Worsted Cloth.
Rumble seat: deck seat - Copra Drab Fine Colonial Grain Artificial Leather until April, then changed to Taupe; deck side - matching cardboard; deck floor - Tan Rubber.

Tan Pinstripe Trim Scheme

Seat: Tan Pinstripe Broadcloth.
Seat, seat back bellows, doors, hinge pillar, quarter, package tray: Brown Sidewall Cloth.
Headlining, windshield header, visor: Brown Napped Cotton.
Cowl: Two-tone Black Maroon Fine Colonial Grain Cardboard.
Rear curtain: Brown Proxylin with Tab.
Windlace: Brown Worsted Cloth.
Rumble seat: deck seat - Copra Drab Fine Colonial Grain Artificial Leather until April, then changed to Taupe; deck side - matching cardboard; deck floor - Tan Rubber.

Copra Drab Leather Trim Scheme (Used until May 1934)

Seat: Copra Drab Fine Colonial Grain Leather.
Seat back bellows, doors, hinge pillar, quarter, package tray, windlace, headlining, windshield header, visor: Copra Drab Fine Colonial Grain Artificial Leather.
Cowl: Two-tone Black Maroon Fine Colonial Grain Cardboard.
Rear curtain: Copra Drab Fine Colonial Grain Artificial Leather with Tab.
Rumble seat: seat - Copra Drab Fine Colonial Grain Artificial Leather; deck side - Copra Drab Fine Colonial Grain Cardboard; deck floor - Tan Rubber.

Copra Drab Imitation Leather Trim Scheme (Used until May 1934)

Seat, seat back bellows, doors, hinge pillar, quarter, package tray, windlace, headlining, windshield header, visor: Copra Drab Fine Colonial Grain Artificial Leather.
Cowl: Two-tone Black Maroon Fine Colonial Grain Cardboard.
Rear curtain: Copra Drab Fine Colonial Grain Artificial Leather with Tab.
Rumble seat: seat - Copra Drab Fine Colonial Grain Artificial Leather; deck side - Copra Drab Fine Colonial Grain Cardboard; deck floor - Tan Rubber.

Taupe Leather Trim Scheme (Released May 1934)

Seat: Taupe Fine Colonial Grain Leather.
Seat back bellows, door, hinge pillar, quarter, package tray, windlace, headlining, windshield header: Taupe Fine Colonial Grain Artificial Leather.
Visor: Covered with Embossed Cardboard.
Cowl: Two-tone Black Maroon Fine Colonial Grain Cardboard.
Rear curtain: Taupe Fine Colonial Grain Artificial Leather with Tab.
Rumble seat: seat - Taupe Fine Colonial Grain Artificial Leather; deck side - Taupe Fine Colonial Grain Cardboard; deck floor - Tan Rubber.

Taupe Imitation Leather Trim Scheme (Released May 1934)

Seat, seat back bellows, door, hinge pillar, quarter, package tray, windlace, headlining, windshield header: Taupe Fine Colonial Grain Artificial Leather.
Visor: Covered with Embossed Cardboard.
Cowl: Two-tone Black Maroon Fine Colonial Grain Cardboard.
Rear curtain: Taupe Fine Colonial Grain Artificial Leather with Tab.
Rumble seat: seat - Taupe Fine Colonial Grain Artificial Leather; deck side - Taupe Fine Colonial Grain Cardboard; deck floor - Tan Rubber.

Items which were identical on each trim scheme

Finish moldings, front belt rail, glove box door: Maroon Enamel.
Floor: Tan Rubber.
Body hardware: Bright Nickel Plate.
Windshield frame: Painted body color.

1934 DELUXE THREE AND FIVE WINDOW COUPE INTERIOR TRIM SCHEMES

Rose Beige Mohair Trim Scheme

Seat, back, doors, door pillar, arm rest, windlace: Rose Beige Mohair.
Headlining, windshield header, package tray, seat back bellows, visor: Rose Beige Napped Cotton.
Rear curtain: Brown Poplin with Tab.
Rumble seat: seat - Copra Drab Fine Colonial Grain Artificial Leather until April 1934, then changed to Taupe Fine Colonial Grain Artificial Leather; deck side - Copra Drab Fine Colonial Grain Cardboard until April 1934, then changed to Taupe Fine Colonial Grain Cardboard; deck floor - Tan Rubber.

Brown Stripe Trim Scheme

Seat: Brown Stripe Broadcloth.
Back, door, door pillar, arm rest, windlace: Brown Broadcloth.
Headlining, windshield header, package tray, seat back bellows, visor: Brown Napped Cotton.
Rear curtain: Brown Poplin with Tab.
Rumble seat: seat - Copra Drab Fine Colonial Grain Artificial Leather until April 1934, then changed to Taupe Fine Colonial Grain Artificial Leather; deck side - Copra Drab Fine Colonial Grain Cardboard, until April 1934, then changed to Taupe Fine Colonial Grain Cardboard; deck floor - Tan Rubber.

Copra Drab Leather Trim Scheme (Used until May 1934)

Seat, back, seat back bellows, door, door pillar, arm rest, windlace, headlining, windshield header, package tray, visor: Copra Drab Fine Colonial Grain Leather.
Rear curtain: Copra Drab Fine Colonial Grain Artificial Leather.
Rumble seat: seat - Copra Drab Fine Colonial Grain Artificial Leather; deck side - Copra Drab Fine Colonial Grain Cardboard; deck floor - Tan Rubber.

Taupe Leather Trim Scheme (Introduced May 1934)

Seat, back, seat back bellows, door, door pillar, arm rest, windlace, headlining, windshield header, package tray: Taupe Fine Colonial Grain Leather.
Visor: Covered with Embossed Cardboard matching headlining.
Rear curtain: Taupe Fine Colonial Grain Artificial Leather.
Rumble seat: seat - Taupe Fine Colonial Grain Artificial Leather; deck side - Taupe Fine Colonial Grain Cardboard.

Items which were identical on each trim scheme

Cowl: Two-tone Black Maroon Fine Colonial Grain Cardboard.
Finish moldings: Walnut Grain.
Front belt rail, glove box door: Walnut Burl Grain.
Floor: Tan Rubber.
Body hardware: Bright Nickel Plate.
Windshield frame: Bright Chrome Plate.

This Fordor is demonstrating the flexibility of the Ford transverse spring suspension, a system the company used to the end of the 1948 production.

The 1933 Deluxe Fordor Sedan.

A preproduction 1934 Deluxe Fordor at Ford's Engineering Lab. The striping had not been done.

Fordor (40-730) Standard and Deluxe

Standard equipment on the Fordor bodies followed the motif of the Tudor. The standard Fordor body came equipped with an adjustable front seat, glove box, sun visor on driver's side, dome light and a choice of three interior upholstering materials—Mohair, Pinstripe Broadcloth, and genuine leather or artificial leather. The cigar lighter and ash tray were available at extra cost.

In addition to the above, standard items on the deluxe Fordor included cowl lights, dual horns and tail lamps, two sun visors, cigar lighter, ash trays, and arm rests in the rear and on the driver's door. An additional trim scheme, Bedford Cord, was available.

Some of the features on 1934 models were the window ventilation system, coved headlining and the addition of an

An early 1934 Deluxe Fordor showing the rear quarter glass in the ventilating position.

Front compartment of a 1933 Standard Fordor Sedan. Note the single sun visor, the pull-to door handle and the installation of the floor mat at the tunnel.

Rear compartment of a 1933 Standard Fordor Sedan. Note the color difference between the mohair side panel and the napped cotton on the back panel and the upper hinge pillar.

Rear compartment of a 1933 Deluxe Fordor Sedan.

arm rest on the front passenger door. In May 1934 the Copra Drab leather trim was changed to Taupe leather.

Striping on the Fordor was identical to the Tudor, with two fine pin stripes starting at the front of the hood molding and going around the body. A $^3/_{32}$ inch center stripe was added to the 1934 models.

Shipping weight of the Fordor was 2,675 pounds for the standard and 2,684 pounds for the deluxe.

1933 STANDARD FORDOR SEDAN INTERIOR TRIM SCHEMES

Thorn Brown Mohair Trim Scheme
Seats, doors, quarter, center body pillar, hinge pillar, arm rests: Thorn Brown Mohair.
Back, sides, headlining, roof side rail, windshield header, visors: Thorn Brown Napped Cotton.
Rear curtain: Brown Poplin with Tab.
Windlace: Brown Worsted Cloth.

Tan Pinstripe Trim Scheme
Seats: Tan Pinstripe Broad Cloth.
Doors, quarter, center body pillar, hinge pillar, back, sides, roof side rail: Brown Sidewall Cloth.
Headlining, windshield header, visors: Brown Napped Cotton.
Rear curtain: Brown Poplin with Tab.
Windlace: Brown Worsted Cloth.

Copra Drab Leather Trim Scheme (Introduced in April)
Seats: Copra Drab Fine Colonial Grain Leather.

Copra Drab Imitation Leather Trim Scheme (Introduced in April)
Seats: Copra Drab Fine Colonial Grain Artificial Leather.
Other items such as doors, quarters, center body pillar, hinge pillar, back, sides, roof side rail, headlining, windshield header, visors, rear curtain, and windlace were Copra Drab Imitation Leather on both trim schemes.

Items which were identical on each trim scheme
Finish moldings, front belt rail, glove box door: Gray Enamel until May 1933, then changed to Maroon.
Cowl panels: Two-tone Black Maroon Fine Colonial Grain Cardboard.
Floor: front - Tan Rubber; rear - Tan Rubber or Brown Carpet with binding matching the trim.
Windshield frame: Painted body color.
Front belt molding: Rustless Steel.
Body hardware: Bright Nickel Plated.

1933 DELUXE FORDOR SEDAN INTERIOR TRIM SCHEMES

Rose Beige Mohair Trim Scheme
Seats, doors, quarters, back, center body pillar, hinge pillar, roof side rail, arm rests, windlace: Rose Beige Mohair.
Headlining, windshield header, sun visors: Brown Napped Cotton.
Rear curtain: Brown Leona Weave Cloth with Tab.

Brown Bedford Cord Trim Scheme
Seats: Brown Bedford Cord.
Doors, quarters, back, center body pillar, hinge pillar, roof side rail, arm rests, windlace: Brown Broadcloth.
Headlining, windshield header, sun visors: Brown Napped Cotton.
Rear curtain: Brown Leona Weave Cloth with Tab.

Brown Stripe Trim Scheme
Seats: Brown Stripe Broadcloth.
Doors, quarters, back, center body pillar, hinge pillar, roof side rail, arm rests, windlace: Brown Broadcloth.
Headlining, windshield header, sun visors: Brown Napped Cotton.
Rear curtain: Brown Leona Weave Cloth with Tab.

Copra Drab Leather Trim Scheme (Released April 1933)
All items - seats, doors, quarters, back, center body pillar, hinge pillar, roof side rail, arm rests, windlace, headlining, windshield header, and sun visors were Copra Drab Fine Colonial Grain Leather.
Rear curtain: Copra Drab Fine Colonial Grain Artificial Leather with Tab.

Items which were identical on each trim scheme
Cowl panels: Two-tone Black Maroon Fine Colonial Grain Cardboard.
Finish moldings: Walnut Grain.
Floor: front - Tan Rubber; rear - Brown Carpet with binding matching the trim.
Windshield frame and body hardware: Bright Chrome Plated.
Front belt rail and glove box: Walnut Burl Grain.
Front belt molding: Rustless Steel.

1934 STANDARD FORDOR SEDAN INTERIOR TRIM SCHEMES

The 1933 interior trim schemes were a carry over into 1934 except as follows:
Copra Drab Leather and Imitation Leather trim schemes were discontinued in May 1934, and replaced with Taupe Leather.
The roof side rail was eliminated and the brown carpet rear floor mat was discontinued.

Taupe Leather Trim Scheme (Released in May 1934)
Seats: Taupe Fine Colonial Grain Leather.

Taupe Imitation Leather Trim Scheme (Released in May 1934)
Seats: Taupe Fine Colonial Grain Artificial Leather.
Other items such as doors, quarters, center body pillar, hinge pillar, back, sides, headlining, windshield header, rear curtain, and windlace were finished in Taupe Imitation Leather on both trim schemes.
Sun visors: Embossed Cardboard matching the headlining material.

1934 DELUXE FORDOR SEDAN INTERIOR TRIM SCHEME

The 1933 interior trim schemes were a carry over into 1934 except as follows:
The Brown Bedford Cord trim scheme was not used in 1934.
The Copra Drab Leather trim scheme was discontinued in May 1934, and replaced with Taupe Fine Colonial Grain Leather.
The sun visors were made of Embossed Cardboard matching the headlining material.

The bustle back 1933 Victoria.

Introduction of the new slant back 1934 Victoria with the exterior luggage compartment door.

Victoria (40-740)

The 1933 Victoria retained the bustle back characteristic until May 1934, when a new body was introduced. The distinguishing features of this new body was the sloping back, which would characterize the 1935 models, and luggage space neatly concealed behind the back seat that was accessible from the outside through a luggage door. This body style was available only in the deluxe version with the same items, trim schemes, and striping as the deluxe Tudor.

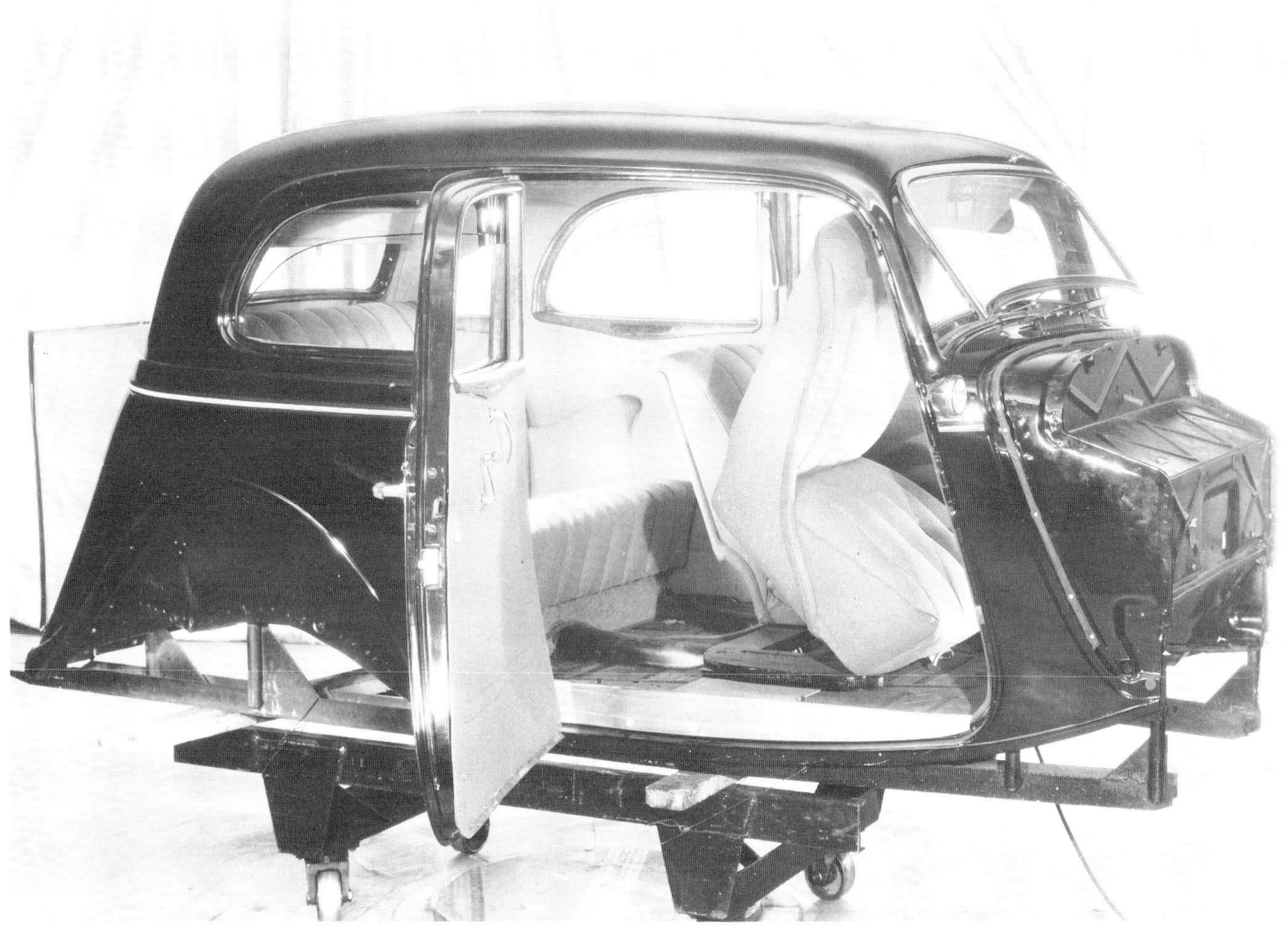

A 1934 Victoria body ready to be shipped to the assembly line.

1933 VICTORIA INTERIOR TRIM SCHEMES

(Used until March 1934)

Rose Beige Mohair Trim Scheme
Seats, back, doors, roof side rail, quarter, hinge pillar, arm rest, windlace: Rose Beige Mohair.

Brown Bedford Cord Trim Scheme
Seats: Brown Bedford Cord.
Back, doors, roof side rail, quarter, hinge pillar, arm rest, windlace: Brown Broadcloth.

Brown Stripe Trim Scheme
Seats: Brown Stripe Broadcloth.
Back, doors, roof side rail, quarter, hinge pillar, arm rest, windlace: Brown Broadcloth.

Items which were identical on each trim scheme
Headlining, windshield header, visor: Brown Napped Cotton.
Front belt rail, glove box door: Walnut Burl Grain.
Finish moldings: Walnut Grain.
Cowl, seat bottom: Two-tone Black Maroon Fine Colonial Grain Cardboard.
Floor front, floor center: Tan Rubber.
Floor rear: Brown Carpet with binding to match trim.
Front belt molding: Rustless Steel.
Body hardware: Bright Nickel Plate.
Windshield frame: Bright Chrome Plate.
Rear seat heel board: Brown Carpet added September 1933.

1934 VICTORIA INTERIOR TRIM SCHEMES

Rose Beige Mohair Trim Scheme
Seats, back, doors, arm rests, hinge pillar, quarter, package tray, windlace: Rose Beige Mohair.
Headlining, windshield header, visor: Rose Beige Napped Cotton.
Rear curtain: Brown Poplin with Tab.

Brown Stripe Trim Scheme
Seats: Brown Stripe Broadcloth.
Back, doors, arm rest, hinge pillar, quarter, package tray, windlace: Brown Broadcloth.
Headlining, windshield header, visor: Brown Napped Cotton.
Rear curtain: Brown Poplin with Tab.

Copra Drab Leather Trim Scheme (Used until May 1934)
Seats, back, doors, arm rests, hinge pillar, quarter, package tray, headlining, windshield header, visor, windlace: Copra Drab Fine Colonial Grain Leather.
Rear curtain: Copra Drab Fine Colonial Grain Artificial Leather with Tab.

Taupe Leather Trim Scheme (Released May 1934)
Seats, back, doors, arm rest, hinge pillar, quarter, package tray, headlining, windshield header, windlace: Taupe Fine Colonial Grain Leather.
Visor: Covered with Embossed Cardboard to match headlining material.
Rear curtain: Taupe Fine Colonial Grain Artificial Leather with Tab.

Items which were identical on each trim scheme
Cowl, seat bottom: Two-tone Black Maroon Fine Colonial Grain Cardboard.
Front belt rail, glove box door: Walnut Burl Grain.
Finish moldings: Walnut Grain.
Floor front: Tan Rubber.
Floor center, floor rear with rear seat heel board: Brown Carpet with binding to match trim.
Body hardware: Bright Nickel Plate.

The 1934 Deluxe Phaeton.

Phaeton (40-750) Standard and Deluxe

Both a standard and deluxe Phaeton was produced in 1933, but only the deluxe style was carried over to 1934. This body style had an unusual feature, in that both doors opened toward each other—hinged in the center to a semi-concealed post fastened to the front seat for stiffness. Black Brown imitation leather was the only trim scheme available on the 1933 standard body, while Copra Drab leather was available on the deluxe. In May 1934, Taupe leather replaced the Copra Drab. The top and side curtains were made of double rubber interlined fabric, black-white on the outside and gray drab on the inside.

The deluxe model came equipped with cowl lights, dual horns and tail lamps, chromed windshield assembly, glove box, cigar lighter and ash trays. Of these items, only the glove box came with the standard Phaeton. All the other items were classified as special equipment at extra cost. The wind wings and dust boot were special equipment in 1933, but became standard items on the 1934 deluxe body.

To provide additional toe room for the back seat passengers, a depression was added to the lower end of the front seat panel. At the same time the contour of the seat cushions and back were reshaped to match those of the Tudor.

Striping was identical to the Tudor.

1933 STANDARD PHAETON INTERIOR TRIM SCHEME

Black Brown Imitation Leather Trim Scheme

Seat, quarter, lock pillar, rear belt, windlace: Two-tone Black Brown Fine Colonial Grain Artificial Leather.
Door: Two-tone Black Brown Fine Colonial Grain Cardboard.
Cowl: Two-tone Black Maroon Fine Colonial Grain Cardboard.
Front belt rail, glove box door: Gray Enamel until May 1933, then changed to Walnut Burl Grain.
Floor front, floor rear: Tan Rubber.
Top, side curtains: outside - Black White; inside - Drab Rubber Interlined Fabric.
Dust hood: Black White Fabric.
Outside backlight frame, top irons, windshield frame, windshield stantions: Black Enamel.
Inside backlight frame: Gray Enamel.
Body hardware: Bright Nickel Plate.
Front belt molding: Rustless Steel.

1933 DELUXE PHAETON INTERIOR TRIM SCHEME

Copra Drab Leather Trim Scheme

Seat, quarter, lock pillar, rear belt, windlace: Copra Drab Fine Colonial Grain Leather.
Doors: Copra Drab Fine Colonial Grain Leather with binding to match.
Front belt rail, glove box door: Walnut Burl Grain.
Floor front, floor rear: Tan Rubber.
Cowl: Two-tone Black Maroon Fine Colonial Grain Cardboard.
Top, side curtains: Drab Rubber Interlined Fabric.
Dust hood: Drab Fabric.
Outside backlight frame, inside backlight frame, top irons, windshield frame, windshield stantions: Bright Chrome Plate.
Body hardware: Bright Nickel Plate.

1934 DELUXE PHAETON INTERIOR TRIM SCHEMES

Copra Drab Leather Trim Scheme (Used until May 1934)

Seat, quarter, lock pillar, rear belt, front belt rail, windlace: Copra Drab Fine Colonial Grain Leather.
Doors: Copra Drab Fine Colonial Grain with binding to match.

Taupe Leather Trim Scheme (Adopted May 1934)

Seat, quarter, lock pillar, rear belt, front belt rail, windlace: Taupe Fine Colonial Grain Leather.
Doors: Taupe Fine Colonial Grain Leather with binding to match.

Items which were identical on each trim scheme

Front belt rail, glove box door: Walnut Burl Grain.
Floor front, floor rear: Tan Rubber.
Cowl: Two-tone Black Maroon Colonial Grain Cardboard.
Top, side curtains: Drab Rubber Interlined Fabric.
Dust hood: Drab Fabric.
Outside backlight frame, inside backlight frame, top irons, windshield frame, windshield stantions: Bright Chrome Plate.
Body hardware: Bright Nickel Plate.

A 1933 Cabriolet. The rumble seat and the Tacoma Cream wheels were standard items.

An early 1933 Cabriolet with top down and dust hood in place. The tail light bracket step plate was not released until April 1933.

Cabriolet (40-760)

The 1933–34 Cabriolet body was available only with the deluxe features. Included were a chrome plated windshield frame, cowl lamps, dual horns and tail lamps, adjustable seat, glove box, two sun visors, cigar lighter, ash tray, rumble seat and dust hood. For the upholstering, a buyer could choose either Brown Bedford Cord or genuine Copra Drab Fine Colonial Grain leather, the latter being changed to Taupe leather in May 1934.

The striping on the belt was identical to that of the Roadster and Coupes.

Rear quarter of a 1933 Cabriolet, an excellent reference for the top installation, stripe location and spare tire cover.

The 1934 Cabriolet.

A 1933 Cabriolet cloth trimmed body ready for shipment to the assembly line. The floor mat was not installed until the body was bolted to the chassis.

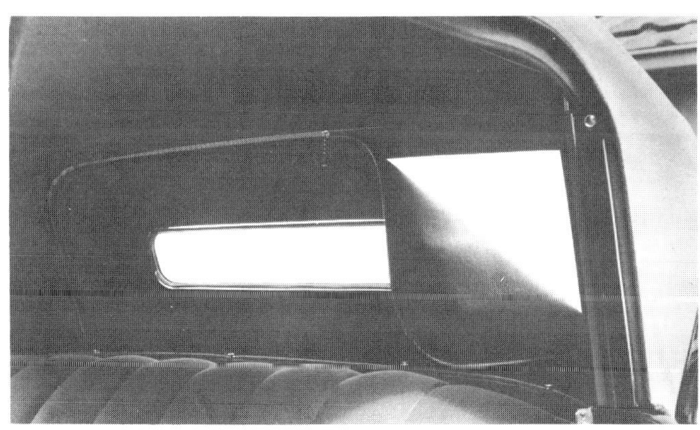

Installation of the back curtain on a 1933-34 Cabriolet.

1933 CABRIOLET INTERIOR TRIM SCHEMES

Brown Bedford Cord Trim Scheme

Seat, doors, quarter, hinge pillar, package tray, back belt, seat side shield: Brown Bedford Cord.
Windlace: Brown Broadcloth.

Copra Drab Leather Trim Scheme

Seat, door, quarter, hinge pillar, package tray, back belt, seat side shield: Copra Drab Fine Colonial Grain Leather.
Windlace: Copra Drab Fine Colonial Grain Leather.

Items which were identical on each trim scheme

Cowl: Two-tone Black Maroon Fine Colonial Grain Cardboard.
Front belt rail, glove box door: Walnut Burl Grain.
Finish moldings: Walnut Grain.
Floor: Tan Rubber.
Top: Drab Rubber Interlined Fabric.
Rumble seat: seat - Copra Drab Fine Colonial Grain Artificial Leather; deck side - Copra Drab Fine Colonial Grain Cardboard; deck floor: Tan Rubber.
Dust hood: Drab Fabric.
Outside backlight frame, inside backlight frame, top irons, windshield frame: Bright Chrome Plate.
Body hardware: Bright Nickel Plate.
Front belt molding: Rustless Steel.

1934 CABRIOLET INTERIOR TRIM SCHEMES

Brown Bedford Cord Trim Scheme

Seat, doors, arm rest, quarter, hinge pillar, package tray, back belt, seat side shield: Brown Bedford Cord.
Rumble seat: seat - Copra Drab Fine Colonial Grain Artificial Leather until April 1934, then changed to Taupe; deck floor - Tan Rubber.
Windlace: Brown Broadcloth.

Copra Drab Leather Trim Scheme (Dropped May 1934)

Seat, doors, arm rest, quarter, hinge pillar, package tray, back belt, seat side shield: Copra Drab Fine Colonial Grain Leather.
Rumble seat: seat - Copra Drab Fine Colonial Grain Artificial Leather; deck side - Copra Drab Fine Colonial Grain Cardboard; deck floor - Tan Rubber.
Windlace: Copra Drab Fine Colonial Grain Leather.

Taupe Leather Trim Scheme (Adopted May 1934)

Seat, door, arm rest, quarter, hinge pillar, package tray, back belt, seat side shield: Taupe Fine Colonial Grain Leather.
Rumble seat: seat - Taupe Fine Colonial Grain Artificial Leather; deck side - Taupe Fine Colonial Grain Cardboard; deck floor - Tan Rubber.
Windlace: Taupe Fine Colonial Grain Leather.

Items which were identical on each trim scheme

Cowl: Two-tone Black Maroon Fine Colonial Grain Cardboard.
Front belt rail, glove box door: Walnut Burl Grain.
Finish moldings: Walnut Grain.
Floor: Tan Rubber.
Top: Drab Rubber Interlined Fabric.
Dust hood: Drab Fabric.
Outside backlight frame, inside backlight frame, top irons, windshield frame: Bright Chrome Plate.
Body hardware: Bright Nickel Plate.

Commercial Vehicles

The 1933–34 commercial vehicles included the Open and Closed Cab, Sedan Delivery, Panel Delivery and Station Wagon—all produced on the 112 inch wheel base passenger chassis, but with two distinct styles of front end treatment. The Station Wagon and Sedan Delivery were designed with the new passenger car hood, grill, fenders, headlights and bumpers, while the Panel Delivery, Open Cab and Closed Cab Trucks retained the 1932 style. On the latter, the front end sheet metal items seem to be a carry over, but were actually modified to compensate for the longer wheel base and a slight slant in the grill. The headlights, though shaped like those of 1932, were slightly deeper and $^{1}/_{2}$ inch smaller in diameter. The horn which was carried over, was hung back on the headlight bar, identical to the Model A.

The model change from 1933 and 1934 was less noticeable, but more confusing on the Commercial vehicle. On the Station Wagon and Sedan Delivery the change took place in November and December, the same as the passenger cars, but on the other Commercial vehicles, it occurred in March 1934. The most visible changes were the restyling of the radiator shell, radiator cap, hood, and the addition of a hood side name plate.

Open Cab (46-800) Closed Cab (46-810) and Pickup Box (46-830)

The Open and Closed Cab bodies were basically a carry-over from 1932 with minor changes. In November 1933, the seat cushion and seat back were restyled to increase the leg room and provide better seating comfort. With the model change in March 1934, the seat cushion was further improved by making its front higher and the back lower. Only one interior trim scheme was used, Black Brown imitation leather. The top material on the Open Cab body was made of black Short Long Grain rubber coated fabric.

The 1933 Open Cab Pickup Truck.

Top and instrument panel of a 1933-34 Open Cab Truck.

The 1933 Closed Cab Pickup with the four cylinder chassis. The spare tire was installed by the dealer.

The 1934 Pickup Truck. The Ford emblem on the side of the hood and the new style hub caps were the distinguishing features of the 1934 commercial vehicles.

Typical fleet order of 1933 commercial vehicles including a cowl with a special body.

Although striping was not provided, it was available on special single orders and for fleet sales. Similar to 1932, two stripes started at the hood molding and went around the body.

The pickup box was a direct carry over from 1932. A minor modification was made to the side panels to match the new location of the rear fenders, and a new tail gate chain hook safety spring was added.

1933-34 OPEN CAB INTERIOR TRIM SCHEME

Black Brown Imitation Leather Trim Scheme

Seat, windlace, back belt rail: Two-tone Black Brown Fine Colonial Grain Artificial Leather.
Cowl, seat side: Two-tone Black Brown Fine Colonial Grain Cardboard.
Door: Black Painted Masonite.
Finish moldings: Black Enamel or Pyroxylin.
Front belt molding: Rustless Steel.
Floor: Tan Rubber.
Top, curtains: Black Short Long Grain Rubber Coated Fabric.
Body hardware: Nickel Plate Butler Finish.

1933-34 CLOSED CAB INTERIOR TRIM SCHEME

Black Brown Imitation Leather Trim Scheme

Seat, windlace: Two-tone Black Brown Fine Colonial Grain Artificial Leather.
Doors: Painted (no paneling).
Cowl: Two-tone Black Brown Fine Colonial Grain Cardboard.
Finish moldings: Black Enamel or Pyroxylin.
Front belt molding: Rustless Steel.
Floor: Tan Rubber.
Body hardware: Nickel Plate Butler Finish.

Interior of the 1933-34 Closed Cab. Note that the door has no trim panel.

A 1933 Sedan Delivery body on a four cylinder chassis.

The 1934 Sedan Delivery. The special paint combination indicates a fleet sale.

Sedan Delivery (46-850)

The Sedan Delivery was basically a stretched Tudor body with the Fordor front door. It was equipped with all the deluxe features of the Tudor Sedan except the dual horns and tail lamps. The interior trim was Black Brown Colonial Grain imitation leather in the front compartment with Masonite in the delivery compartment. Striping was identical to the Tudor.

The 1933 Sedan Delivery front compartment.

Front seats of the Sedan Delivery. The hole under the floor was for the tool box.

Rear compartment of the Sedan Delivery.

1933-34 SEDAN DELIVERY INTERIOR TRIM SCHEME

Black Brown Imitation Leather Trim Scheme

Seats, windlace, headlining, visor: Two-tone Black Brown Fine Colonial Grain Artificial Leather. Visor changed to Embossed Cardboard April 1934.

Cowl, doors, door header, side roof rail, rear door, rear door header: Two-tone Black Brown Fine Colonial Grain Cardboard.

Quarter lining: Masonite.

Front belt molding: Rustless Steel.

Finish moldings: Gray Enamel until May 1933, then changed to Maroon.

Body hardware: Bright Nickel Plate.

Windshield frame: Black Enamel.

Floor: Front compartment - Tan Rubber: rear mat (under seat) - Tan Rubber.

The 1933 preproduction Panel Delivery.

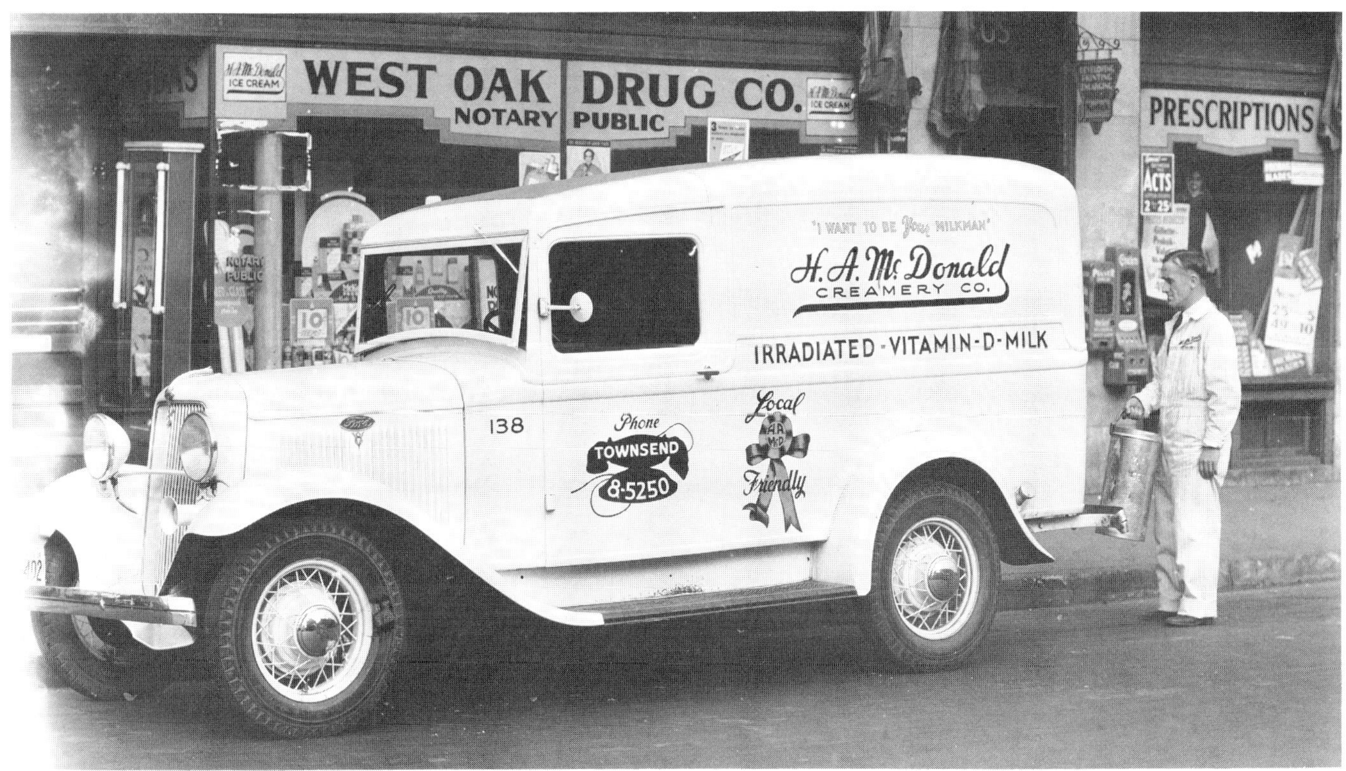

A 1934 Panel Delivery with special commercial paint combination.

Panel Delivery (46-820) Standard and Deluxe

The Panel Delivery body was a carry over of the 1932 body shell, but, because of the longer 1933 chassis it was located further forward, resulting in less overhang and a better load balance. This change also required the relocation of the wheelhouse and fender. Only the driver's seat was provided, but the passenger's seat was available. Cowl lights, chromed bumpers and a highly polished exterior finish were the only additional exterior features of the Deluxe model. Model change to the 1934 style occurred in March 1934, and consisted of restyling the radiator shell, radiator cap, and hood, similar to the Closed Cab Truck.

Front compartment of the 1933-34 Panel Delivery. Note the tool box behind the seat.

The package compartment of the 1933-34 Panel Delivery.

1933-34 PANEL DELIVERY INTERIOR TRIM SCHEME (Standard and Deluxe)

Black Brown Imitation Leather Trim Scheme

Seat and windlace: Two-tone Black Brown Fine Colonial Grain Artificial Leather.

Cowl panels, seat bottom, seat back, roof rail: Two-tone Black Brown Fine Colonial Grain Cardboard.

Doors: Standard models - Black Paint (no panels); Deluxe models - Two-tone Black Brown Fine Colonial Grain Cardboard.

Headlining: Standard models - None; Deluxe models - Two-tone Black Brown Fine Colonial Grain Artificial Leather.

Finish moldings: Painted Black Enamel or Pyroxylin.

Floor: Front compartment - Tan Rubber; rear mat (under seat) - Tan Rubber.

Front belt molding: Rustless Steel.

Body hardware: Nickel Plated Butler Finish.

Windshield frame: Black Enamel.

The 1933 Station Wagon. For 1934, the front end sheet metal changed at the same time as the passenger cars, but the body was a direct carry-over.

Right side of the 1933 Station Wagon showing the spare tire location.

Station Wagon (46-860)

Though similar in appearance to the 1932 model, the 1933 Station Wagon was all new. It featured the passenger car front end appointments, including the forward opening doors and the cowl lights. The Wagon's interior was finished in two-tone Black Brown Colonial Grain artificial leather. While the sheet metal was painted Mountain Brown, the wood was finished natural with Spar Varnish.

Interior of the 1933 Station Wagon. Note the angle of the grooves on the posts for installation of the side curtains.

1933-34 WINDSHIELD WIPER DATA

B = Black Paint C = Chrome Plated K = Cadmium Plated

Body Styles	Wiper Number	Mounting Method	Finish	Wiper Arm Length	Wiper Arm Finish	*Blade Finish
Standard Tudor, Coupes and Fordor	40-17508-A	Threaded shaft sleeve	K	8¼	B	B
Deluxe Tudor, Coupes and Fordor	40-17508-A	Threaded shaft sleeve	K	8¼	C	C
Standard Phaeton and Roadster	B-17508-D	Two screws	B	6	B	B
Deluxe Phaeton and Roadster	B-17508-E	Two screws	C	6	C	C
Victoria and Sedan Delivery	40-17508-A	Threaded shaft sleeve	K	8¼	C	C
Cabriolet	40-17508-B	Threaded shaft	C	6	C	C
Station Wagon	46-17508	Two holes and threaded shaft	B	9½	B	B
Open Cab	B-17508-H	Two screws	B	8¼ †	B	B
Closed Cab	B-17508-H	Two screws	B	9½	B	B
Standard Panel Delivery	B-17508-J	Two holes and threaded shaft	None	9½	B	B
Deluxe Panel Delivery	B-17508-J	Two holes and threaded shaft	None	9½	C	C

*All blades were 8 inches long with two black rubbed outer strips and one red rubber center strip.

†Wiper arm was 8¼ inches long until January 1934 then changed to 6 inches long.

Wiper arms were the spring, rod and clip design.

The shafts on all wipers were nickel plated except on the Standard Roadster, Open Cab Truck and Closed Cab Truck which were painted black.

1933-34 STATION WAGON INTERIOR TRIM SCHEME

Black Brown Imitation Leather Trim Scheme

Seats: Two-tone Black Brown Fine Colonial Grain Artificial Leather.
Cowl panels: Two-tone Black Brown Fine Colonial Grain Cardboard.
Front belt rail: Gray Enamel until May 1933, Maroon until September 1933, Winterleaf Brown until February 1934, Cordova Gray to end of production.
Glove box door: Gray Enamel.
Front belt molding: Rustless Steel.
Body pillar finish: Walnut Grain.
Door locks: Brown Pyroxylin.
Tailgate chain cover: Black Short Long Grain Artificial Leather.
Curtains: Tan Fabric.
Floor: Tan Rubber.
Body hardware: Nickel Plate Butler Finish.
Windshield frame: Painted body color.

DOMESTIC PRODUCTION OF 1933 CARS

Body Style	V-8	4 Cyl.	Total
Tudor Sedan, Standard (40-700)	95,561	2,875	98,436
Deluxe (40-700)	42,433	79	42,512
Roadster, Standard (40-710)	128	107	235
Deluxe (40-710)	4,114	93	4,207
Coupe (3W), Standard (40-720)	6,595	191	6,786
Deluxe (40-720)	13,887	24	13,911
Fordor Sedan, Standard (40-730)	17,798	594	18,392
Deluxe (40-730)	40,540	133	40,673
Victoria (40-740)	4,856	23	4,879
Phaeton, Standard (40-750)	214	337	551
Deluxe (40-750)	1,450	175	1,625
Cabriolet (40-760)	10,256	21	10,277
Coupe (5W), Standard (40-770)	27,473	2,107	29,580
Deluxe (40-770)	11,731	27	11,758
Panel Delivery, Standard (46-820)	1,628	2,821	4,449
Deluxe (46-820)	1,212	1,293	2,505
Sedan Delivery (46-850)	1,752	1,914	3,666
Station Wagon (46-860)	1,486	314	1,800

DOMESTIC PRODUCTION OF 1934 CARS

Body Style	V-8	4 Cyl.	Total
Tudor Sedan, Standard (40-700)	136,355	221	136,576
Deluxe (40-700)	127,586	18	127,604
Roadster, Deluxe (40-710)	5,145	40	5,185
Coupe (3W), Deluxe (40-720)	27,949	7	27,956
Fordor Sedan, Standard (40-730)	24,509	469	24,978
Deluxe (40-730)	107,525	431	107,956
Victoria (40-740)	20,066	3	20,069
Phaeton, Deluxe (40-750)	3,657	1,005	4,662
Cabriolet (40-760)	15,075	25	15,100
Coupe (5W), Standard (40-770)	51,847	61	51,908
Deluxe (40-770)	28,393	4	28,397
Panel Delivery, Standard (46-820)	5,840	76	5,916
Deluxe (46-820)	3,074	6	3,080
Sedan Delivery (46-850)	9,189	373	9,562
Station Wagon (46-860)	2,899	104	3,003

Ford's Model "44"

In 1934 Ford Motor Company almost introduced two models, one with the 112 inch wheel base and the other with a 105 inch wheel base. The idea started in early 1932, shortly after the design and development of the 112 inch wheel base Model "40" was underway. As was customary with him, one day Henry Ford walked in to the design room and expressed the opinion that due to the depressed economic condition the public ought to have the choice of a smaller, less expensive V-8 automobile. As a result, the design and development of the 105 inch wheel base "Model 44" was launched. Other than for size differences, Models 40 and 44 progressed along the same lines except that Model 40 got the priority.

By November that year, engineering and tooling drawings were completed and production quotations were received from Briggs and Murray. A production schedule and announcement date were established for the Model 40, but delayed for the Model 44. Although the hand built prototypes of the 44 were scheduled, in January it was decided to make the prototypes from the production tools in order to save cost. Ford would build the Tudor and Fordor bodies, while Murray would make the Roadster and Phaeton, and Briggs the Coupe. A total of 60,000 units were planned.

By March 1933, tooling was complete and production could be implemented in 8 to 10 weeks. With the Model 40 already in dealer showrooms, Henry Ford called a meeting of his key personnel to discuss plans for an introduction date for the 44. However, after a review of the effects of a strike at Briggs which had delayed introduction of the Model 40, and obviously disturbed by the closing of banks across the country, Ford postponed any decision until April. This delay was the first in a series of postponements which ultimately lead to the cancellation of Ford's plans to introduce a U.S. built small car.

In February 1934, the company decided to build a similar model in France, but there is no indication if the tools prepared for the 44 in Dearborn were transferred abroad. Nevertheless, records at the archives show that three 44 blocks were built on February 16, and an experimental car was brought into the garage for brake and clutch analysis as late as April 18. Henry Ford made the final announcement to abandon the project on June 28, giving Edsel Ford the responsibility for gradually phasing out all outstanding orders through the remainder of 1934 to avoid arousing poor publicity from the press.

One item, however, was carried over into 1935. The 24,000 yards of brown checked cloth was re-scheduled to trim approximately 5,600 Standard Coupe bodies of the 1935 models.

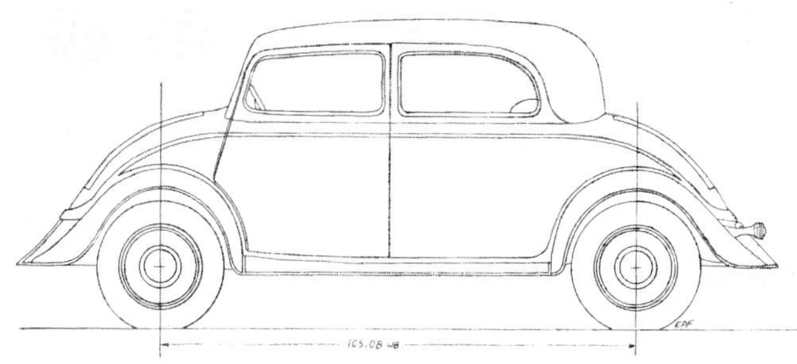

This sketch from the Ford Engineering file was made in 1933 when Henry Ford was considering a small car. A prototype, built late in 1933, utilized the rear sheet metal (quarter, deck lid, back and rear fenders) from a Model 40 Coupe. Its V-8 power plant was mounted behind the rear seat. In 1936 when Dr. Ferdinand Porsche visited Henry Ford, he was shown this vehicle. We can only wonder what ideas were exchanged between the two auto magnates about the car since Porsche was developing the Volkswagen "Beetle" about the same time.

The U.S. built Model "44".

Real comfort in the back seat

THE WOMAN who rides in the back seat, as well as the woman who drives, will have some nice things to say about the New Ford V-8 for 1935. It has been built to give all passengers a new kind of modern comfort. . . . New weight distribution, new seat position and new longer springs of unusual flexibility give you an exceptionally smooth ride on every type of road. . . . There are many other important features which show the modern manner of the 1935 Ford. . . . You see it in its distinctive lines and the richness of its upholstery and appointments. . . . You find it also in the outstanding performance of its V-8 engine. This is unquestionably the finest engine ever built into a low-price car and it has made an exceptional record for reliability and economy. . . . You drive with greater confidence in the Ford V-8 because it is such a dependable, obedient car. You have a further feeling of security because of ease of handling, the substantial all-steel body and the added protection of Safety Glass all around. There is no extra charge for this.

IX—The 1935-36 Models

The 1935 cars were almost totally new with very few parts carried over from 1934. Prior to the public introduction on December 27, 1923, Henry Ford invited the news media to the Dearborn Assembly Plant to view the production of the new cars. Following the tour of the plant, the news men were taken to the Edison Institute Theater (part of the Henry Ford Museum) for a formal introduction and an opportunity to drive the new cars around the Ford Airport road. The Company boasted, "The new car has been built to give the passengers a new kind of comfort. New weight distribution, new seat position and new longer springs of unusual flexibility give you an exceptionally smooth ride on every type of road."

Even though built on the same 112 inch wheel base as the 1934, the new car was 6.65 inches longer. By redesigning the frame with the front spring overhanging the front axle, the engine, transmission and passenger seats could be moved forward creating the mid-ship seating concept for the passengers. In addition, the body width was increased 2.1 inches and the weight of a standard Fordor was 2849 pounds, 174 pounds more than its 1934 counterpart. In appearance, it had a longer streamlined look, featuring a narrow full length grille, longer bullet-shaped headlamps, sloping windshield, completely skirted fenders and the sloping back which had been introduced on the 1934 Victoria. Also, the front doors were returned to the front hinge design. In addition, the touring body style, featuring a rear trunk, was added to the Tudor and Fordor Sedan line. These body styles were available only with the deluxe decor.

By 1935 the country was recovering from the depression and car sales were on the rise. For the first time since the introduction of the V-8, Ford cars would outsell Chevrolet. As a result, the high volume production exhausted some of the upholstering materials before the end of the year and new trim schemes had to be introduced.

Most of the body changes for the 1935 passenger cars were improvements related to squeaks, weather strips, or sound insulation problems. One or more changes were directed for each of the first seven months of production. In January, the anti-squeak material at the front end of the bodies at the "X" member joint was made longer, and an anti-squeak piece was placed between the rear outrigger frame bracket and the body. Also, two ¼ inch drain holes were added to the cowl top panel to prevent water from entering at the windshield opening.

Improved windshield frame and cowl vent weather strips were released in February as additional water leak deterrents in those areas. Also in that month, a sponge rubber dust sealer was added to the bottom edge of the floor boards to eliminate possible squeaks and to seal out dust. Two springs were added to the glove compartment door to keep it from opening.

In March, two silencer-insulation packets were released. After the body was painted, but before trimming, "Seapak Asphaltum insulation" pads were rubber cemented to the back panel, quarter panel, front end, cowl, and floor extensions, and "kimpack burlap insulation" sheeting pads were cemented and tacked between the wood framing on the upper back. In addition, new rubber silencer pads were cemented to the body floor after the body was installed on the chassis and all the body bolts were tightened. The changes in May consisted of new weather strip at the front door hinge pillar to prevent leaking at the hinge, and the windshield retaining strip material of a cork composition became an uncured gum rubber composition. An improved luggage compartment weather strip was also released in July.

Production of the 1935 models terminated at all assembly plants on September 9, 1935, and the change over to the 1936 models was completed within a week. With the exception of the facelift to the front end sheet metal, most modifications were very slight. Some items such as the finish moldings and knobs which had a surface finish change from dark Taupe to Benton Gray, and the bezels around the instruments which went from Butler Chrome to bright chrome did not take place with Job-one at every plant. Therefore, some early 1936 models had a few items with the 1935 finish. The change from 1935 to 1936 was actually so slight that the Company offered the dealers a 1936 front end sheet metal package which permitted them to convert the exterior appearance of an owner's 1935 car to a 1936. It is interesting to note that the package of parts cost the dealers $213.28 and they would charge $69.00 to install it.

The interior trim sewing room at Briggs Manufacturing Company.

As part of a summer sales campaign, in May 1936, the finish on most of the interior items were changed simultaneously on all body styles. The changes were listed by the company as follows:

STANDARD PASSENGER CARS AND SEDAN DELIVERY

New trim sewing patterns and alternate trims.
All interior body hardware changed to bright chrome.
Finish moldings changed to Mahogany Grain.
Gear shift lever, knob, and hand brake lever changed to black.
Standard (5W) Coupe without rumble seat changed to fixed rear window (not adjustable).

DELUXE PASSENGER CARS AND STATION WAGON

New trim on doors and Tudor quarters.
Finish strips changed to Walnut Grain.
All interior hardware, knobs, steering wheel, gear shift lever, hand brake lever, and all instrument panel bezels, etc., changed to Brown to match the Walnut Grain.

Hood, Grille and Fenders

The new 1935 front end styling featured a full length vee-shaped grille and large full skirted fenders with leading edges extending down to the bumper. For the first time, the finish of the grille and shell distinguished the difference between the deluxe and standard models. According to the engineering specs, the one piece grille-shell part for the deluxe cars was entirely chrome plated while on the standard cars the grille area was painted black with the outer shell painted body color. For both, the clip-on horizontal strips and the outline molding were made of rustless steel. The radiator cap was tucked under the hood and the V-8 grille ornament was moved to the top of the shell to form a new hood ornament. The louvers on the side of the hood were shortened and accentuated with four horizontal metal strips. In April, the hood corner pads were re-designed to reduce the possibility of scratching the fenders when the hood was raised.

One left front fender design was used on all passenger cars, but two variations were necessary on the right side. The difference was the horn mounting hole. Because of the dual horns, the right fender on deluxe cars had the hole while the fenders for the standard cars did not. In June 1935 the deluxe left front fender appeared on all cars and a carriage bolt was used to seal the unrequired hole on the standard models. Also in June, eight louvers were added to the passenger car front fender aprons to improve engine compartment cooling.

The rear fenders were made in four styles — one for use on the Tudor, Fordor, Phaeton, and Convertible Sedan, another for the Roadster, Coupe, and Cabriolet, a third for the Station Wagon, and a fourth for the Sedan Delivery. The left hand fender in each group was common to each body, but the right rear fender had additional variations to accommodate the dual tail lamps on the deluxe cars and the step plate mounting hole for those vehicles with a rumble seat.

Styling refinements for 1936 were the wrap-around grille and the elimination of the radiator shell which had been gradually shrinking since 1932. The grill was chrome plated on deluxe cars and painted black on the standard models. On both, the outer edge of the grille was trimmed with a rustless steel molding. The hood ornament was made larger with high tips on the "V" which often broke off.

The 1935 front end design.

Grille chrome plating operation.

Fenders and miscellaneous parts conveyer line, prior to painting.

Deburring the 1936 grilles.

The hood itself was redesigned to fit the new shape of the grille, while the four horizontal metal strips on the hood louvers were reduced to three.

The 1936 front fender was a two piece assembly with a chromed molding covering the joint. A small grilled opening on each fender indicated the horn location, even though only one horn was used on the standard cars. The rear fenders were fuller at the back and without the reverse curve, except on the Station Wagon and Sedan Delivery which had carry-over.

Lights

In contrast to those of the previous year, the headlights for 1935 passenger cars were made 1¾ inches longer as well as smaller in diameter, and with their spherical lens, created more of a tear drop effect. The cold rolled steel case was painted the same color as the fenders while the headlamp door was made of rustless steel. Similar to previous years, the Ford trademark and "Twolite Headlamp" was stamped on the case. The crystal clear glass lens had a seven focus zone pattern and the word "Top" cast at the top of the lens face, along with the Ford trademark and the words "Twolite Headlamp" cast near the bottom. A new pre-focus 33-32 CP bulb was installed in the headlamp. This bulb was used on all Ford vehicles through 1938.

For 1936, the headlight length was increased another 1½ inches by widening the lens door and adding more curvature to the lens.

The 1935-36 passenger car tail lamps, lens and license plate bracket were all a carry over from 1934. However, instead of rustless steel, the rear lamp case was made of cold rolled steel and painted to match the fender. The left rear lamp bracket was redesigned with the addition of a new feature — the fuel filler pipe on its top surface. In addition, the bracket for the Tudor and Fordor Touring was four inches longer. These, too, were made of a steel stamping and painted the same as the fender. Similar to previous years, dual rear lamps were standard equipment on the deluxe vehicles, but were not installed on the standard vehicles unless ordered as special equipment. The step plate right hand bracket was used on deluxe vehicles with rumble seat. The Standard Coupe with rumble seat but without a right side tail lamp bracket, was equipped with a second step plate in addition to the one on top of the fender. In March 1935, the large tail lamp wire hole in the pad between rear lamp bracket and fender was reduced to prevent mud under the fender from coming through and running down the outside of the fender.

In 1936, the tail lamp brackets were restyled with a lower slope placing the tail lamps closer to the bumpers.

Door and Window Regulator Handles

The 1935 outside door handles were a simple straight design, departing from the graceful "S" style of 1934. These handles were made of either rustless steel or chrome plated zinc die castings. With both materials, the escutcheon plate was chrome plated brass. The same style handle was used on all passenger cars and commercial vehicles. The only difference was the length of the shaft which varied according to body style. A rustless steel "T" handle was used on the deck lid of cars with a rumble seat or trunk.

The handles were modified slightly and made thicker for the early production of 1936 passenger cars, Station Wagons and Sedan Deliveries, while the commercial vehicles continued to use the 1935 style. In January 1936, a new semicircle style handle was released for use on passenger cars, Station

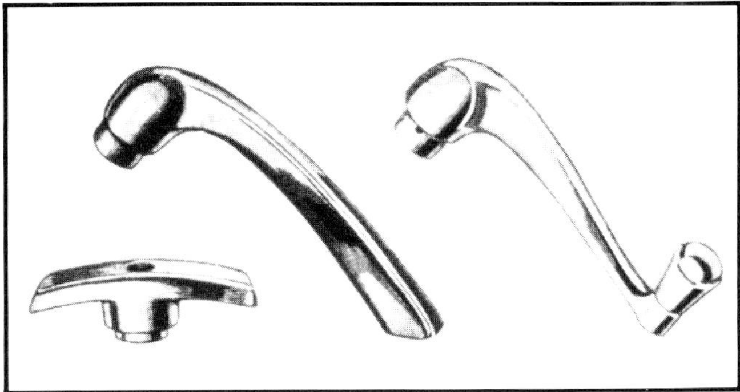

The 1935 style interior handles.

Wagons and Sedan Deliveries. However, in March, this curved handle was designated for use on deluxe passenger cars only and the standard cars were equipped with the earlier 1936 style handle. By September it was changed back to the curved style again.

On cars with a rumble seat, the 1934 remote control lock and handle was replaced with the outside "T" deck lid handle, but this change was not made with Job-one at every plant.

The interior hardware, consisting of door handles, window regulator handles and pull-to-cord, was also new for 1935. The door handles were made in two designs: one style for the closed cars and the other for the open cars. The handles used on the standard bodies were a zinc die casting finished with butler nickel plate, while those used on deluxe bodies were aluminum die castings finished with dark Taupe oxide. In January the aluminum handles were made thicker for added strength, with branches and dealers being instructed to replace the earlier handles on any cars in stock. Dealers were further advised to replace the handles on earlier production cars when they were brought in for service.

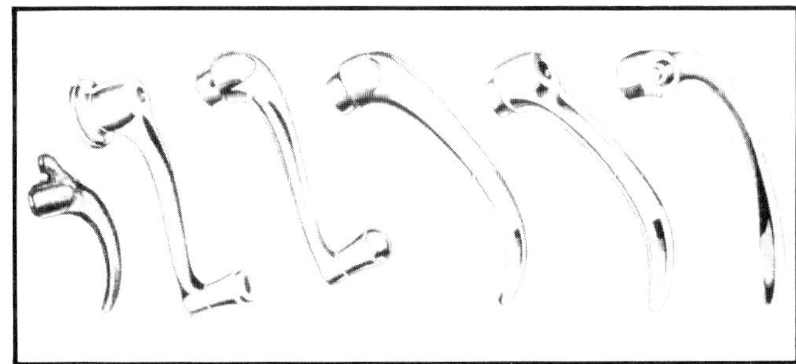

The 1936 style interior handles.

In February, the finish on handles for the Tudor and Fordor Touring bodies was changed to a new etched cellulose-ester coated Taupe. Later, in June, the same change was made on all deluxe body styles.

There were four variations of the window regulator handles. The standard bodies were equipped with a zinc die casting handle finished with butler nickel plating. Its knob was either a matching die cast or plastic. The handle for the deluxe cars was made of aluminum and finished in dark Taupe oxide. The quarter window regulator handle was a "T" design finished to match the other window regulator handles. The Station Wagon had a unique design handle which was zinc die cast and finished with butler nickel plating. Similar to the door handles, in February the finish on the window regulator handles for the deluxe touring sedans was changed to etched cellulose-ester coated Taupe. In October the front door regulator handle on closed cars was moved forward four inches.

Care was taken during production to insure that all interior handles on each body matched.

All interior door handles and window regulator handles were restyled for the 1936 production. The door handles were thinner with a tapered end which curved toward the door panel. Two styles were used — one for closed cars and a second for open cars. The handles on the standard cars and all open cars were finished in butler nickel plate, while the deluxe closed cars had a finish of etched cellulose-ester coated Benton Gray. In May the handle finish was changed to bright chrome plate on standard and open cars, and etched cellulose-ester coated brown appeared on deluxe closed cars. The Station Wagon used the same handle as the open cars until June when the handle was redesigned, but with the same finish. Convertibles used the closed car handles.

The slight change to the 1936 window regulator handle was made at the mounting end. The finish followed the same changes made to the door handles.

A pull-to cord and bracket assembly was released for all deluxe closed cars starting with Job-one, but was not released for the standard closed cars until January 1935, and then, only for the front doors. The cord mounting brackets were butler nickel plated on the standard cars and painted Taupe color on the deluxe ones. For the standard, the cord was made of Russet Brown Fine Colonial Grain artificial leather; for the deluxe, it was Taupe worsted cloth; and for the leather trim cars it was Gray Brown Fine Colonial Grain artificial leather. These pull-to cords were eliminated in March when the door handles were relocated farther back, making the cords unnecessary. The front door handle was moved back approximately 15¾ inches from the door's front edge; the rear handle moved approximately eight inches; and on the open cars the handles were moved back 11½ inches, even though they did not have the pull-to cord.

Door and regulator handles on the 1935-36 Pickup Truck were a carry over from the 1934 closed passenger cars. Handles for the Panel Delivery were a carry over from the 1934 open passenger cars.

Sun Visors

The 1935-36 closed body styles were equipped with sun visors similar to those used in 1934. Two visors were installed on the deluxe bodies while one was installed on the driver's side on the standard bodies. A second visor was available as special equipment for the standard cars and commercial vehicles. The visors were covered with either embossed cardboard or a variety of napped cotton with a gimp binding, depending upon the trim schemes. The mounting brackets were either painted or nickel plated. For specific details see the interior trim scheme charts for a particular body style.

The 1935 style sun visor and two-way pivot mounting bracket.

Floor Mats and Carpets

Front floor mats for all 1935-36 passenger cars and commercial vehicles were made of rubber — Tan Rubber for 1935 models and Benton Gray after October 1935. A jute pad backing was added in February 1935. Even though the shape of the mats differed with various body styles, the texture was identical with each mat. In 1935 the body of the mat for all passenger cars, Station Wagons and Sedan Deliveries consisted of a pyramid pattern framed by a rope effect bead and a pebble grain outer border. In February the rope bead and pebble grain border was also added around the transmission opening. The mat for the other commercial vehicles and trucks had a sunburst pattern with a herringbone border and a plain outer edge.

With the start of the 1936 models the mat pattern for the passenger cars, including Station Wagons and Sedan Deliveries, was changed. The main part of the mat had a ribbed design framed by two rope effect beads with a strip of angular seration between them and a duck weave outer border. The commercial mat pattern was not changed but in December its composition was changed from tan rubber to black rubber.

For the purpose of interchangeability, the Roadster and Phaeton had a common front mat, as did also the Coupes, Fordors, Cabriolet and Convertible Sedan. However, the Tudors, Station Wagon and Sedan Delivery each had a unique mat.

The rear floor mat for the 1935-36 Deluxe Tudors, Fordors, Convertible Sedan, and Club Cabriolet bodies was made of Brown carpet with a binding to match the trim scheme color. In December 1935, the binding was changed to brown for all trim schemes. This one piece mat was used until July 1936 when it was changed to a three piece design to obtain a better fit around the tunnel area.

The rear floor mat for all other 1935-36 body styles, including the rumble seat mats, was made of Tan Rubber with a pattern to match the front mat. The only exception was the Station Wagon rear mat which had a pyramid pattern.

Interior Finish Strips

The interior windshield frame, door window frames, and rear window frame were identified as finish strips and were painted to complement the trim schemes. The finish strips on the 1935 cars were painted Maroon on the standard bodies and metallic Taupe on the deluxe bodies. As a result of Ford's soybean plastic development, in June 1935 plastic finish strips of the same color were introduced for use on all Tudor and Coupe body styles. However, these were discontinued at the end of the 1935 production. Vermillion stripes on each side of the finish panel on the dash was eliminated in December 1934.

With the beginning of 1936 models, the color of these items, plus a new garnish panel on the deluxe Tudors, Fordors and Coupe bodies, was changed to dark Taupe for the standard bodies and Benton Gray Metallic for the deluxe bodies. The change was to be effective with Job-one, but some early production cars came through with 1935 items. Another color change was made on these items in May 1936. Mahogany grain finish was used for the standard trim schemes, while walnut grain was used for the deluxe ones.

The inside and outside rear light frames on both 1935 and

1936 open body tops were finished with bright chrome plating. These frames on the new 1936 Club Cabriolet and Convertible Sedan were painted Cordoba Tan.

Exterior Body Colors

A new series of exterior body colors was released with the introduction of the 1935 models. The charts list the regular production combinations which were used to fill stock orders and were the basis for assembly scheduling. Other combinations were possible through fleet sales or single special orders at extra cost. Ford policy was "do not lose a sale because of color combination."

At introduction, only two color combinations were available for the standard body style, but five combinations were available for the deluxe. However, two unique color combinations were used on cars build for export which were also available for domestic production at extra cost. Wheel color for the standard cars was normally black, but colored wheels were available as special equipment. Those who purchased the deluxe cars had an option of black wheels or any one of the colors listed.

Some plants apparently had not been following the color specifications because in December 1935 the home office issued the following directive: "It has been found that some assembly branches are not strictly adhering to the color combinations as specified for standard passenger cars, but instead are painting some standard passenger cars in deluxe passenger car colors. Only when extra cost orders are received should this be done."

1935 STANDARD PASSENGER CAR COLORS

Body Color	Stripe Color	Wheels Color (1)
Medium Luster Black* †	Bright Apple Green	Black
Vineyard Green*	Bright Apple Green	Black
Cordoba Gray †	Medium Bright Poppy Red	Black
Light Gunmetal Gray (2)	Bright Apple Green	Black

* For Standard Tudor and Fordor Sedans

† For Standard Coupe (5W)

(1) Color wheels available on special order.

(2) Available June 1935 for Standard Tudor, Fordor and Coupe (5W)

1935 DELUXE PASSENGER CAR COLORS

(Includes Sedan Delivery and Panel Delivery)

Body Color	Stripe Color	Wheels Color (1)
Medium Luster Black	Bright Apple Green	Black or Medium Apple Green
Vineyard Green	Bright Apple Green	Vineyard Green or Medium Apple Green
Cordoba Gray	Medium Bright Poppy Red	Cordoba Cream or Medium Poppy Red
Dearborn Blue	Medium Bright Poppy Red	Medium Poppy Red
Light Gunmetal Gray	Bright Apple Green	Light Gunmetal Gray
Duncan Blue*	Medium Bright Poppy Red	Medium Poppy Red
Coach Maroon*	Medium Bright Poppy Red	Medium Poppy Red

* For cars built for export. Available for U.S. production on special order.

(1) Black wheels were also available with any color scheme.

1935 PICKUP (and other trucks) COLORS

Body Color	Stripe Color	Wheel Color (1)
Light Gunmetal Gray	Bright Apple Green	Black
Dearborn Blue	Medium Bright Poppy Red	Black
Medium Luster Black	Bright Apple Green	Black
Cordoba Gray	Medium Bright Poppy Red	Black
Vineyard Green	Bright Apple Green	Black
Vermillion Red*	Black	Black

* This color was also used on Sedan Delivery with Tacoma Cream wheels and stripe.

(1) Color wheels were available as special equipment.

NOTE: Other color combinations were available as special equipment.

In March 1935, in order to help dealers in the repainting business, Ford Engineering approved five lacquer colors for use over specific Ford standard colors. The colors were: Washington Blue, Slate Green, and Rusk Brown Metallic over Vineyard Green; Gunmetal Light Metallic over Light Gunmetal Gray; and Palm Beach Gray over Cordoba Gray.

Six exterior colors were available as regular production for commercial vehicles, but any combination of passenger car colors was also available through fleet orders or as special equipment at extra cost.

A new series of colors were announced for 1936. In addition, in April 1936, five new "Easter" colors were introduced to stimulate sales during the Easter season. Of these, two were retained as regular production colors for the deluxe body styles.

1936 STANDARD PASSENGER CAR COLORS

Body Color	Stripe Color (1)	Wheels and Hub Cap Ring (1)
Black	Bright Apple Green	Black
Gunmetal Gray	Medium Bright Poppy Red	Black
Washington Blue (2)	Tacoma Cream	Black
Coach Maroon*	Medium Bright Poppy Red	Black
Gray Vineyard Green*	Silver	Black
Cordoba Tan*	Medium Bright Poppy Red	Black

(1) Color wheels were available as special equipment. New optional stripe and wheel colors were introduced in November 1935: Tacoma Cream stripe and wheels; Bright Apple Green stripe with Medium Apple Green wheels; Medium Bright Poppy Red stripe with Medium Poppy Red wheels.

(2) Originally for export cars but became U.S. production color February 1936.

* For export cars. Available for U.S. production on special order.

1936 DELUXE PASSENGER CAR COLORS

(Includes Sedan Delivery and Panel Delivery)

Body Color	Stripe Color	Wheels and Hub Cap Ring
Black	Bright Apple Green	Black
Gunmetal Gray	Medium Bright Poppy Red	Gunmetal Gray
Gray Vineyard Green (1)	Silver	Gray Vineyard Green
Bright Vineyard Green (2)	Silver	Bright Vineyard Green
Washington Blue	Tacoma Cream	Washington Blue
Cordoba Tan	Medium Bright Poppy Red	Cordoba Tan
Coach Maroon*	Medium Bright Poppy Red	Coach Maroon

(1) Discontinued April 1936.

(2) Available April and discontinued May 1936.

* For cars built for export. Available for U.S. production on special order.

EASTER COLORS FOR DELUXE PASSENGER CARS

(Available only during April 1936)

Body Colors	Stripe Colors	Wheels and Hub Cap Ring
Desert Sand	Red	Desert Sand
Armory Green*	Silver	Armory Green
Light Fast Maroon*	Gold	Light Fast Maroon
Bambalina Blue	Cream	Bambalina Blue
Coach Maroon	Bright Poppy Red	Coach Maroon

Red or Cream wheels and hub cap rings were optional colors for all of the above body colors.

* These two became regular production colors for the deluxe body styles for the remainder of 1936.

1936 PICKUP (and other trucks) COLORS

Body Color	Stripe Color	Wheel Color (1)
Black	Bright Apple Green	Black
Gunmetal Gray	Medium Bright Poppy Red	Black
Gray Vineyard Green (2)	Silver	Black
Bright Vineyard Green (3)	Silver	Black
Armory Green (4)	Silver	Black
Washington Blue	Tacoma Cream	Black
Cordoba Tan	Medium Bright Poppy Red	Black
Vermillion Red*	Black	Black

* This color was also used on Sedan Delivery with Tacoma Cream wheels and stripe.

(1) Color wheels were available as special equipment.

(2) Discontinued April 1936.

(3) Available April and discontinued in May 1936.

(4) Available May 1936.

Grilles painted black or body color.

NOTE: Other color combinations were available as special equipment.

The 1935 Standard Tudor Sedan with the black painted grille, single horn, painted windshield frame and black windshield wiper arm.

A 1935 Deluxe Tudor Sedan.

Tudor (48-700 and 68-700) Standard, Deluxe and Touring

The Tudor Sedan was the base body of the 1935 models. Any Tudor part which was used on other body styles still retained the Tudor part number. Production was in three body styles, the Standard Tudor, Deluxe Tudor and Touring Tudor. Each of these was equipped with the adjustable driver's seat, glove box, sun visors (one for standard models and two

The rear trunk was the distinctive feature of the 1935 Touring Tudor Sedan. The rustless steel running board molding was a standard item on Touring models and Convertible Sedans.

The 1936 Deluxe Tudor Sedan. In addition to the grille, other 1936 features included the horn grilles in the fenders and the stamped metal wheels.

for deluxe), dome light, ash tray and rear arm rests. The Deluxe Tudor and the Touring Tudor, also had an arm rest on the driver's door starting with Job-one, but the standard body did not receive it until April 1935. The main difference between the standard and deluxe was the color of the grille along with the better quality of upholstering materials installed in the deluxe and touring bodies.

Three interior trim schemes were available on the deluxe

A 1936 Standard Touring Sedan. Its standard features consisted of the painted radiator grille, painted horn grilles, and painted windshield frame.

Rear view of the 1936 Standard Touring Sedan with its integral rear trunk and the spare tire cover.

A 1936 Deluxe Touring Tudor Sedan showing the limited access to the trunk compartment.

models while only two could be selected for the standard. However, due to sales improvement during the year, two new trim schemes were added to the standard model to cope with the increased production schedule.

Some changes to these bodies were made early in 1935, but more were made during 1936. Back in December 1934, the vermillion stripes on each side of the center finish panel on the dash panel were eliminated. On the standard model, the Bedford Cord interior trim was changed to plain side wall cloth. In April, the headlining was redesigned and extended to include the back panels. By May, a water resistant cardboard water deflector was cemented below the rear quarter window, above the wheel house, and between the quarter panel and the package tray strainer to keep water from leaking in at that point.

Production change-over to the 1936 model was started the third week in September 1935. With the change, some new exterior color combinations were introduced, and, in addition to new interior trim patterns, the quality of the upholstering cloths for the Deluxe and Touring bodies was improved. However, some leftover 1935 cloths were used up on early 1936 models. In December 1935, the Touring Tudor Sedan, previously available only in the deluxe style, became available in either the deluxe or standard.

Front compartment of the 1935 Deluxe Tudor Sedan. The presence of the pull-to cord indicates this to be an early production car.

In addition, the finish of the package tray and luggage compartment cardboards was changed in December and January. The rear support of the front seat was shortened 0.4 inches in January, tilting the seat back for more comfort. By February the front seat springs were made softer and the seat reshaped to a common contour for all closed cars. Additional upholstery material changes, including new sewing patterns on door and quarter panels, were made in May, June, and July.

Striping consisted of a single pin stripe 3/32 inch wide, starting with a slight curve at the front edge of the hood and continuing around the body 5/8 inch below the belt line.

Shipping weight of the 1935 Standard Tudor was 2,806 pounds, Deluxe Tudor weighed 2,826 pounds and the Touring Tudor was 2,861 pounds.

Rear compartment of a 1935 Deluxe Tudor. Note the shade difference between the rear quarter panel and the back panel.

A 1936 pre-production Deluxe Tudor Sedan interior. The arm rest was only on the driver's door. An assist loop was added to production cars.

Rear compartment of the 1936 Tudor Sedan.

1935 STANDARD TUDOR SEDAN INTERIOR TRIM SCHEMES

Light Brown Wide Wale Bedford Cord Trim Scheme

Seats, arm rests: Light Brown Wide Wale Bedford Cord.

Door panel, quarter, lock pillar: Light Brown Wide Wale Bedford Cord until February 1935, then changed to Light Brown Plain Sidewall Cloth.

Door pillar and header: Light Brown Plain Side Wall Cloth.

Headlining, back (became one piece in April 1935): Light Brown Napped Cotton.

Visor: Light Brown Napped Cotton with Light Brown Fine Colonial Grain artificial leather binding.

Windlace: Light Brown Worsted Cloth.

Door pull-to cord: Russet Brown Fine Colonial Grain artificial leather.

Gray Brown Imitation Leather Trim Scheme

Seats, door panels, quarter, lock pillar, arm rests, door pillar and header, headlining, back, door pull-to cord, windlace: Gray Brown Veal Grain artificial leather, (Headlining and back became one piece in April 1935).

Visor: Gray Brown Veal Grain Embossed Cardboard with Gray Brown Fine Colonial Grain artificial leather binding.

Taupe Worsted Suede (Introduced August 1935)

Seats, door panels, quarter, lock pillar, arm rests, door pillar and header: Taupe Worsted Suede.

Headlining: Taupe Napped Cotton.

Visor: Taupe Napped Cotton with Taupe Fine Colonial Grain artificial leather binding.

Windlace: Taupe Worsted Cloth.

Brown Wide Wale Bedford Cord (Introduced August 1936)

Seats, door panels, quarter, lock pillar, arm rests: Brown Wide Wale Bedford Cord.

Door pillar and header: Brown Plain Side Wall Cloth.

Headlining: Light Brown Napped Cotton.

Visor: Light Brown Napped Cloth with Light Brown Fine Colonial Grain artificial leather binding.

Windlace: Brown Worsted Cloth.

Items which were identical on each trim scheme

Front and rear floor mat: Tan Rubber.

Cowl, seat bottom: Gray Brown Fine Colonial Grain Cardboard.

Instrument panel, finish strips: Maroon Paint.

Glove compartment door interior: Taupe Napped Cotton.

Windshield frame: Painted body color.

Interior hardware: Butler Nickel Plated.

Windshield regulator handle, glove compartment lock: Satin Finish Chrome.

Glove compartment handle: Maroon Plastic.

1935 DELUXE TUDOR SEDAN INTERIOR TRIM SCHEMES

Taupe Mohair Trim Scheme
Seats, door panels, quarter, quarter lock pillar, arm rests, door pillar and header: Taupe Mohair.
Headlining, back (became one piece in April 1935): Taupe Napped Cotton.
Visors: Taupe Napped Cotton with Taupe Fine Colonial Grain artificial leather binding.
Windlace: Taupe Worsted Cloth.
Assist loop: Taupe Worsted Cloth with Taupe Fine Colonial Grain artificial leather binding.
Rear curtain: Brown Poplin.
Door pull-to cord: Taupe Fine Colonial Grain artificial leather.

Taupe Pinstripe Broadcloth Trim Scheme
Seat, door panels, quarters, door pillar and header, lock pillar, arm rests: Taupe Pinstripe Broadcloth.
Headlining, back (became one piece in April 1935): Taupe Napped Cotton.
Visors: Taupe Napped Cotton with Taupe Fine Colonial Grain artificial leather binding.
Windlace: Taupe Worsted Cloth.
Assist loop: Taupe Worsted Cloth with Taupe Fine Colonial Grain artificial leather binding.
Rear curtain: Brown Poplin.
Door pull-to cord: Taupe Fine Colonial Grain artificial leather.

Gray Brown Leather Trim Scheme
Seats, door panels, quarter, front arm rest: Gray Brown Veal Grain leather.
Seat back, door pillar and header, lock pillar, rear arm rests, assist loop, headlining, back, windlace, door pull-to cord: Gray Brown Veal Grain artificial leather, (headlining and back became one piece in April 1935).
Visors: Gray Brown Veal Grain Embossed Cardboard with Gray Brown Fine Colonial Grain artificial leather binding.
Rear curtain: Gray Brown Pyroxylin.

Items which were identical on each trim scheme
Front floor mat: Tan Rubber.
Rear floor mat, rear seat heel board: Brown Carpet.
Cowl panels, seat bottom: Gray Brown Fine Colonial Grain Cardboard.
Instrument panel, finish strips: Metallic Taupe.
Glove compartment door interior: Taupe Napped Cotton.
Windshield frame: Bright Chrome Plated.
Interior hardware: Oxidized Dark Taupe until June 1935, then changed to Ester Coated Taupe.
Windshield regulator handle: Ester Coated Taupe.
Escutcheons: Dark Taupe Plastic.
Glove compartment handle: Light Taupe Plastic.
Window regulator knob: Light Taupe Plastic until June 1935, then changed to Chrome Plated Zinc.
Instrument center finish panel trim: Bright Chrome Plated.

1935 TOURING TUDOR SEDAN INTERIOR TRIM SCHEMES

Taupe Bedford Cord Trim Scheme
Seat, door panels, quarter, arm rests, door pillar and header, lock pillars: Taupe Bedford Cord.
Headlining, back (Became one piece in April 1935): Taupe Napped Cotton.
Visors: Taupe Napped Cotton with Taupe Fine Colonial Grain artificial leather binding.
Windlace: Taupe Worsted Cloth.
Assist loop: Taupe Worsted Cloth with Taupe Fine Colonial Grain artificial leather binding.
Rear curtain: Brown Poplin.
Door pull-to cord: Taupe Fine Colonial Grain artificial leather.

Taupe Worsted Suede Trim Scheme
Seats, door panels, quarter, arm rests, lock pillar, door pillar and header: Taupe Worsted Suede.
Headlining, back (Became one piece in April 1935): Taupe Napped Cotton.
Visors: Taupe Napped Cotton with Taupe Fine Colonial Grain artificial leather binding.
Windlace: Taupe Worsted Cloth.
Assist loop: Taupe Worsted Cloth with Taupe Fine Colonial Grain artificial leather binding.
Rear curtain: Brown Poplin.
Door pull-to cord: Taupe Fine Colonial Grain artificial leather.

Gray Brown Leather Trim Scheme
Seats, door panels, quarter, front arm rest: Gray Brown Veal Grain Leather.
Seat back, door pillar and header, lock pillar, rear arm rests, assist loop, headlining, back, windlace, door pull-to cord: Gray Brown Veal Grain artificial leather.
Visors: Gray Brown Veal Grain Embossed Cardboard with Gray Brown Fine Colonial Grain artificial leather binding.
Rear curtain: Gray Brown Pyroxylin.

Items which were identical on each trim scheme
Front floor mat: Tan Rubber.
Rear floor mat, rear seat heel board: Brown Carpet.
Cowl panels, seat bottom, package tray, luggage compartment: Gray Brown Fine Colonial Grain Cardboard.
Instrument panel, finish strips: Metallic Taupe.
Glove compartment door interior: Taupe Napped Cotton.
Windshield frame: Bright Chrome Plated.
Interior hardware: Oxidized Dark Taupe until June 1935, then changed to Ester Coated Taupe.
Windshield regulator handle: Ester Coated Taupe.
Escutcheons: Dark Taupe Plastic.
Glove compartment handle: Light Taupe Plastic.
Window regulator knob: Light Taupe Plastic until June 1935, then changed to Chrome Plated Zinc.
Instrument center finish panel trim: Bright Chrome Plated.

1936 STANDARD TUDOR SEDAN INTERIOR TRIM SCHEMES

Light Brown Wide Wale Bedford Cord Trim Scheme (Discontinued June 1936)
Seats, arm rests: Light Brown Wide Wale Bedford Cord.
Door panels, door pillar and header, quarter, lock pillar: Light Brown Side Wall Cloth.
Headlining: Light Brown Napped Cotton.
Visor: Light Brown Napped Cotton with Brown Fine Colonial Grain artificial leather binding.
Windlace: Light Brown Worsted Cloth.

Brown Imitation Leather Trim Scheme
Seats, door panels, door pillar and header, lock pillar, quarter, arm rest, headlining, windlace: Brown Fine Colonial Grain artificial leather.
Visor: Brown Fine Colonial Grain Embossed Cardboard with matching artificial leather binding.

Two-tone Brown Mohair Trim Scheme (May and June 1936)
Seats, door panels, door pillar and header, quarter, lock pillar, arm rests: Two-tone Brown Mohair.
Headlining: Light Brown Napped Cotton.
Visor: Light Brown Napped Cotton with Brown Fine Colonial Grain artificial leather binding.
Windlace: Light Brown Worsted Cloth.

Two-tone Light Taupe Mohair Trim Scheme (June and July 1936)
Seats, door panels, door pillar and header, quarter, lock pillar, arm rests: Two-tone Light Taupe Mohair.
Headlining: Light Brown Napped Cotton.
Visor: Light Brown Napped Cotton with Brown Fine Colonial Grain artificial leather binding.
Windlace: Two-tone Light Taupe Worsted Cloth.

Dark Brown Wide Wale Bedford Cord Trim Scheme (Introduced July 1936)
Seats, arm rests: Dark Brown Wide Wale Bedford Cord.
Door panels, door pillar and header, lock pillar, quarter, seat face sides and back: Dark Brown Side Wall Cloth until August 1936, then changed to Dark Brown Wide Wale Bedford Cord.
Headlining: Light Brown Napped Cotton.
Visor: Light Brown Napped Cotton with Brown Fine Colonial Grain artificial leather binding.
Windlace: Dark Brown Worsted Cloth.

Items which were identical on each trim scheme
Front floor mat: Tan Rubber until November 1935, then changed to Benton Gray Rubber.
Rear floor mat: Matched front mat until July 1936, changed to Brown Carpet.
Cowl panels, seat bottom: Brown Fine Colonial Grain Cardboard until May 1936, then cowl panels changed to Dark Taupe Fine Colonial Grain Cardboard and seat bottom changed to Dark Taupe no grain cardboard.
Instrument panel, finish strips: Benton Gray Metallic until May 1936, then changed to Mahogany Grain.
Glove compartment door interior: Taupe Napped Cotton until May 1936, then changed to Black Cardboard.
Windshield frame: Painted body color.
Interior hardware: Butler Finish Nickel Plate until May 1936, then changed to Bright Chrome Plate.
Windshield regulator handle: Benton Gray Metallic until May 1936, then changed to Bright Chrome Plate.
Glove compartment handle: Benton Gray Plastic until May 1936, then changed to Chrome Plated Zinc Die Casting.

1936 STANDARD TOURING TUDOR SEDAN INTERIOR TRIM SCHEMES

Same trim as Standard Tudor Sedan except as follows:
Front floor mat: Benton Gray Rubber.
Rear floor mat: Benton Gray Rubber until July 1936, then changed to Brown Carpet.
Windshield regulator handle, glove compartment handle: Benton Gray Metallic until May 1936, then changed to Bright Chrome Plate.
Package tray, luggage compartment: Black Dash Grain Cardboard until January 1936, then changed to Black Seal Grain Cardboard for January, then changed to Black Morocco Grain in February 1936.

1936 DELUXE TUDOR SEDAN AND DELUXE TOURING TUDOR SEDAN INTERIOR TRIM SCHEMES

Taupe Mohair Trim Scheme*

Seats, door panels, door pillar and header, quarter, lock pillar, arm rests: Taupe Mohair.
Headlining: Taupe Napped Cotton.
Visors: Taupe Napped Cotton with Taupe Fine Colonial Grain artificial leather binding.
Windlace: Taupe Worsted Cloth.
Rear curtain: Brown Poplin.
Assist loop: Taupe Worsted Cloth with Taupe Fine Colonial Grain artificial leather binding.

Taupe Bedford Cord Trim Scheme

Seats, door panels, door pillar and header, quarter, lock pillar, arm rests: Taupe Bedford Cord.
Headlining: Taupe Napped Cotton.
Visors: Taupe Napped Cotton with Taupe Fine Colonial Grain artificial leather binding.
Windlace: Taupe Worsted Cloth.
Rear curtain: Brown Poplin.
Assist loop: Taupe Worsted Cloth with Taupe Fine Colonial Grain artificial leather binding.

Brown Broadcloth Trim Scheme (Discontinued November 1935)

Seats, door panels, door pillar and header, quarter, lock pillar, arm rests: Brown Broadcloth.
Headlining: Taupe Napped Cotton.
Visors: Taupe Napped Cotton with Taupe Fine Colonial Grain artificial leather binding.
Windlace: Brown Worsted Cloth.
Rear curtain: Brown Poplin.
Assist loop: Brown Worsted Cloth with Brown Fine Colonial Grain artificial leather binding.

Brown Leather Trim Scheme

Seats, door panels, quarter, arm rests: Brown Fine Colonial Grain Leather.
Door pillar and header, lock pillar, headlining, windlace, assist loop: Brown Fine Colonial Grain artificial leather.
Visors: Brown Fine Colonial Grain Embossed Cardboard with matching artificial leather binding.
Rear curtain: Brown Pyroxylin.

Gray Brown Broadcloth Trim Scheme (Introduced November 1935)

Seats, door panels, door pillar and header, quarter, lock pillar, arm rests: Gray Brown Broadcloth.
Headlining: Taupe Napped Cotton.
Visors: Taupe Napped Cotton with Taupe Fine Colonial Grain artificial leather binding.
Windlace: Gray Brown Worsted Cloth.
Rear curtain: Brown.
Assist loop: Gray Brown Worsted Cloth with Gray Brown Fine Colonial Grain artificial leather binding.

Items which were identical on each trim scheme

Front floor mat: Tan Rubber until November 1935, then changed to Benton Gray Rubber.
Rear floor mat, rear seat heel board: Brown Carpet.
Cowl panel: Brown Fine Colonial Grain Cardboard until May 1936, then changed to Dark Taupe Fine Colonial Grain Cardboard.
Seat bottom: Brown Fine Colonial Grain Cardboard until May 1936, then changed to Dark Taupe no grain cardboard.
Instrument panel, finish strips: Benton Gray Metallic until May 1936, then changed to Walnut Grain.
Glove compartment door interior: Taupe Napped Cotton until May 1936, then changed to Black Cardboard.
Windshield frame: Bright Chrome Plate.
Interior hardware: Ester Coated Benton Gray until May 1936, then changed to Ester Coated Brown.
Escutcheons: Benton Gray Plastic until January 1936, then changed metal painted Benton Gray Metallic until May 1936, then changed to Brown Paint.
Window regulator handle knob, ash tray knob: Light Gray Plastic until May 1936, then changed to Brown.
Glove compartment handle: Light Gray Plastic until May 1936, then changed to Chrome Plated Zinc Die Casting.
Touring body only: package tray, luggage compartment – Gray Brown Fine Colonial Grain Cardboard until December 1935, then Black Seal Grain Cardboard during January 1936, then changed to Black Morocco Grain Cardboard.

*Left over cheaper quality 1935 Taupe Mohair was used on early production at the Dearborn and Cincinnati Assembly Plants.

The 1935 Roadster with top down and dust hood installed.

Roadster (48-710 and 68-710) Deluxe

The 1935 Roadster was available only in deluxe style. It came equipped with wind wings, glove box, and ash tray. The front compartment was trimmed with Gray Brown Veal Grain leather, while the rumble seat compartment was trimmed with matching artificial leather. The top as well as the side curtains were made of Drab Rubber interlined fabric. The back light frame, windshield frame, stanchions and top bows were finished with bright chrome plate. The outside dimensions of the rear light frame were 25 × 5-3/8 and changed to 25 × 7 in June 1935.

The 1936 Roadster with top up. The windshield frame, stantions and wind wing mounting brackets were all chrome plated. White wall tires were special order.

In November 1934, the seat was redesigned to provide a larger tool compartment underneath. At the same time, the inside remote control deck lid lock was replaced with the former "T" handle. At some plants these changes were made on Job-one for 1935.

For 1936 the trim material was changed to Brown Fine Colonial Grain leather in the front with matching artificial leather in the rumble seat compartment. The finish on the top bows was changed in April from chrome plating to Cordoba Tan paint, and in May the finish panel became Walnut Grain.

The pin stripe on the Roadster started at the front edge of the hood, similar to that on the Coupe, and followed the belt line to the rear quarter, where it went down to the rear corner of the body and around the back just below the deck lid.

1935 ROADSTER INTERIOR TRIM SCHEME

Gray Brown Leather Trim Scheme

Seat: Gray Brown Veal Grain Leather.

Door panels: Gray Brown Veal Grain artificial leather until January 1935, then changed to Genuine Leather.

Cowl panels: Gray Brown Fine Colonial Grain Cardboard.

Windlace, rumble seat: Gray Brown Veal Grain artificial leather.

Rear belt, front belt rail, package tray, seat sides, deck sides: Gray Brown Veal Grain Cardboard.

Front floor mat, deck floor mat: Tan Rubber.

Top and side curtain: Drab Rubber interlined fabric.

Dust hood: Drab Fabric.

Glove compartment door interior: Taupe Napped Cotton.

Front belt rail panel, finish strips: Metallic Taupe.

Interior hardware: Nickel Plated, Butler Finish.

Top bows: Wood – varnished; steel – painted Taupe; steel top irons – Chrome Plated.

1936 ROADSTER INTERIOR TRIM SCHEME

Brown Leather Trim Scheme

Seat, door panels: Brown Fine Colonial Grain Leather.

Cowl panel, front belt, rear belt, package tray, seat sides, deck sides: Brown Fine Colonial Grain Cardboard.

Windlace, rumble seat: Brown Fine Colonial Grain artificial leather.

Front floor mat and deck floor mat: Tan Rubber until November 1935, then changed to Benton Gray Rubber.

Top and side curtains: Drab Rubber interlined fabric.

Dust hood: Drab Fabric.

Glove compartment door interior: Taupe Napped Cotton.

Front belt rail panel, finish strips: Benton Gray Metallic until May 1936, then changed to Walnut Grain.

Interior hardware: Nickel Plated Butler Finish until May 1936, then changed to Bright Chrome Plate.

Glove compartment handle: Light Gray Plastic until May 1936, then changed to Chrome Plated Zinc Die Casting.

Top bows: Wood – varnished; steel – painted Taupe until May 1936 then changed to Cordoba Tan; steel top irons – Chrome Plated until May then changed to Cordoba Tan.

The 1935 Three Window Coupe — available only in the deluxe decor.

A 1935 Three Window Coupe with rumble seat which was not a standard item, but available at extra cost.

Coupe, Three Window (48-720 and 68-720) Deluxe

The three window Coupe came equipped with an adjustable seat, glove box, sun visors, dome light, arm rest on driver's door, and a roll down rear window. Regular production upholstering consisted of two schemes: taupe mohair and taupe pin stripe broadcloth, but a gray brown leather trim scheme was also available as special equipment. Although the rumble seat was not a regular item, it was available on special order.

The 1936 Three Window Coupe.

An early production model of the 1935 Three Window Coupe with the pull-to cord which was discontinued in March 1935.

The windshield frame was finished bright chrome plate throughout its 1935-36 production.

Three changes were made early in production. In November 1934, the package tray was made larger and the inside remote control deck lock and handle were replaced by the former deck lid "T" handle. In December the vermillion stripe on each side of the center finish panel on the dash was eliminated. Another change was made in February 1935 when a drain tube was added to the left and right rear corner of the deck drain trough to eliminate a leak. Then in April the headlining was redesigned to include the back trim pieces.

No body changes were made during the 1935 to 1936 model change, but shortly after introduction two of the interior trim schemes were changed. Later, in February 1936, the seat was moved back 3/4 inch to provide additional leg room.

The stripe on the Coupe was identical to the Roadster.

Interior of a 1936 Three Window Coupe. Note the new door panel sew pattern which became effective May 1936.

1935 THREE WINDOW COUPE INTERIOR TRIM SCHEMES

Taupe Mohair Trim Scheme
Seat, door panels, lock pillar, seat side arm, seat bellows, arm rest: Taupe Mohair.
Headlining, back (one piece after April 1935): Taupe Napped Cotton.
Visors: Taupe Napped Cotton with Taupe Fine Colonial Grain artificial leather binding.
Windlace: Taupe Worsted Cloth.
Rear curtain: Brown Poplin.
Door pull-to cord: Taupe Fine Colonial Grain artificial leather.

Taupe Pinstripe Broadcloth Trim Scheme
Seat, door panel, lock pillar, seat sides arm, seat bellows, arm rest: Taupe Pinstripe Broadcloth.
Headlining, back (one piece after April 1935): Taupe Napped Cotton.
Visors: Taupe Napped Cotton with Taupe Fine Colonial Grain artificial leather binding.
Windlace: Taupe Worsted Cloth.
Rear curtain: Brown Poplin.
Door pull-to cord: Taupe Fine Colonial Grain artificial leather.

Gray Brown Leather Trim Scheme
Seat, door panels, arm rest: Gray Brown Veal Grain Leather.
Lock pillar, seat side arm, seat bellows, headlining, back, windlace, door pull-to cord: Gray Brown Veal Grain artificial leather.
Visors: Gray Brown Veal Grain Embossed Cardboard with Gray Brown Fine Colonial Grain artificial leather binding.
Rear curtain: Gray Brown Pyroxylin.

Items which were identical on each trim scheme
Front floor mat: Tan Rubber.
Cowl panels: Gray Brown Fine Colonial Grain Cardboard.
Instrument panel, finish strips: Metallic Taupe.
Glove compartment door interior: Taupe Napped Cotton.
Windshield regulator handle: Ester Coated Taupe.
Escutcheons: Dark Taupe Plastic.
Rumble seat: deck seat - Gray Brown Veal Grain artificial leather; deck sides - matching cardboard; deck floor - Tan Rubber.
Interior hardware: Oxidized Dark Taupe until June 1935, then changed to Ester Coated.
Glove compartment handle: Bright Chrome Plated.
Window regulator knob: Light Taupe until June 1935, then changed to Chrome Plated Zinc Die Casting.

Body installation at Dearborn Assembly Plant.

1936 THREE WINDOW COUPE INTERIOR TRIM SCHEMES

Taupe Mohair Trim Scheme
Seat, door panels, lock pillar, seat side arm, seat bellows, arm rest: Taupe Mohair.
Headlining: Taupe Napped Cotton.
Visors: Taupe Napped Cotton with Taupe Fine Colonial Grain artificial leather binding.
Windlace: Taupe Worsted Cloth.
Rear curtain: Brown Poplin.

Brown Broadcloth Trim Scheme (Discontinued November 1935)
Seat, door panels, lock pillar, seat side arm, seat bellows, arm rest: Brown Broadcloth.
Headlining: Taupe Napped Cotton.
Visors: Taupe Napped Cotton with Taupe Fine Colonial Grain artificial leather binding.
Windlace: Brown Worsted Cloth.
Rear curtain: Brown Poplin.

Gray Brown Broadcloth (Introduced November 1935)
Seat, door panels, lock pillar, seat side arm, seat bellows, arm rest: Gray Brown Broadcloth.
Headlining: Taupe Napped Cotton.
Visors: Taupe Napped Cotton with Fine Colonial Grain artificial leather binding.
Windlace: Brown Worsted Cloth.
Rear curtain: Brown Poplin.

Brown Leather Trim Scheme
Seat, door panels, arm rests: Brown Fine Colonial Grain Leather.
Door pillar and header, lock pillar, seat side arm, seat bellows, headlining, windlace: Brown Fine Colonial Grain artificial leather.
Visors: Brown Fine Colonial Grain Embossed Cardboard with Brown Fine Colonial Grain artificial leather binding.
Rear curtain: Brown Pyroxylin.

Items which were identical on each trim scheme
Cowl panels: Brown Fine Colonial Grain Cardboard until May 1936, then changed to Dark Taupe Fine Colonial Grain Cardboard.
Front floor mat: Tan Rubber until November 1935, then changed to Benton Gray Rubber.
Instrument panel, finish strips: Benton Gray Metallic until May 1936, then changed to Walnut Grain.
Glove compartment door interior: Taupe Napped Cotton until May 1936, then changed to Black Cardboard.
Windshield regulator handle: Ester Coated Taupe.
Escutcheons: Dark Taupe Plastic.
Interior hardware: Oxidized Dark Taupe until June 1935, then changed to Ester Coated.
Rumble seat: deck seat - Gray Brown Veal Grain artificial leather; deck sides - Gray Brown Veal Grain Cardboard; floor mat - Tan Rubber.
Glove compartment handle: Light Gray Plastic until May 1936, then changed to Chrome Plated Zinc Die Casting.
Window regulator knob, ash tray knob: Light Gray Plastic until May 1936, then changed to Brown.

1936 THREE WINDOW COUPE INTERIOR TRIM SCHEMES

Taupe Mohair Trim Scheme
Same as 1935 model.

Right front view of a 1935 Deluxe Fordor Sedan with deluxe features identical to the Deluxe Tudor.

Left side of a 1935 Deluxe Fordor Sedan.

Fordor (48-730 and 68-730) Standard, Deluxe and Touring

Similar to the Tudor, the Fordor Sedan was available in three body styles, Standard, Deluxe and Touring. The Touring Fordor came only with deluxe trim until December 1935, at the time the Standard Touring Fordor was introduced. These bodies were equipped with an adjustable front seat, glove box, sun visors (one for the standard body and two for

The 1936 Deluxe Fordor Sedan. Note the pivot style rear quarter window, introduced with the 1936 models.

A 1935 Deluxe Touring Fordor Sedan. Evident in this view is the longer tail light mounting bracket, a unique feature of the Touring bodies.

the deluxe), dome light, ash tray and rear seat arm rests. The Deluxe Tudor and Touring Tudor also had an armrest on the driver's door, while the standard body did not get one until April 1935. Other than the grille color, the main difference between the standard and deluxe cars was the better quality of upholstery material installed in the latter.

During the 1935 production, three interior trim schemes were available for each of these body styles. Then, new trim

A 1936 Standard Touring Fordor Sedan as evident by the lack of a right hand tail lamp and no rustless steel molding on the running board.

The 1936 Deluxe Touring Fordor Sedan.

An early 1935 Deluxe Fordor Sedan interior.

schemes were introduced during the early production of the 1936 models, with additional running changes being made to the trim schemes, floor mats, and interior finish strips through July 1936.

A significant alteration was made to the rear quarter window, starting with the 1936 production. It was changed from the roll up type to the pivot type. In February 1936, the chrome plated frame which went only part way around the rear quarter window glass was extended completely around the glass.

A single pin stripe was on the body 5/8 inch below the belt line, similar to the Tudor Sedan.

Front compartment of a 1936 Deluxe Fordor showing the May 1936 sew pattern on the door panel.

Rear compartment of the 1936 Deluxe Fordor Sedan showing how the headlining was extended to include the back panel. Compare it to the headlining of the 1935 model.

A pre-production rear compartment of the Deluxe Fordor Sedan with the early 1936 sew pattern on the door. An assist loop was installed on regular production.

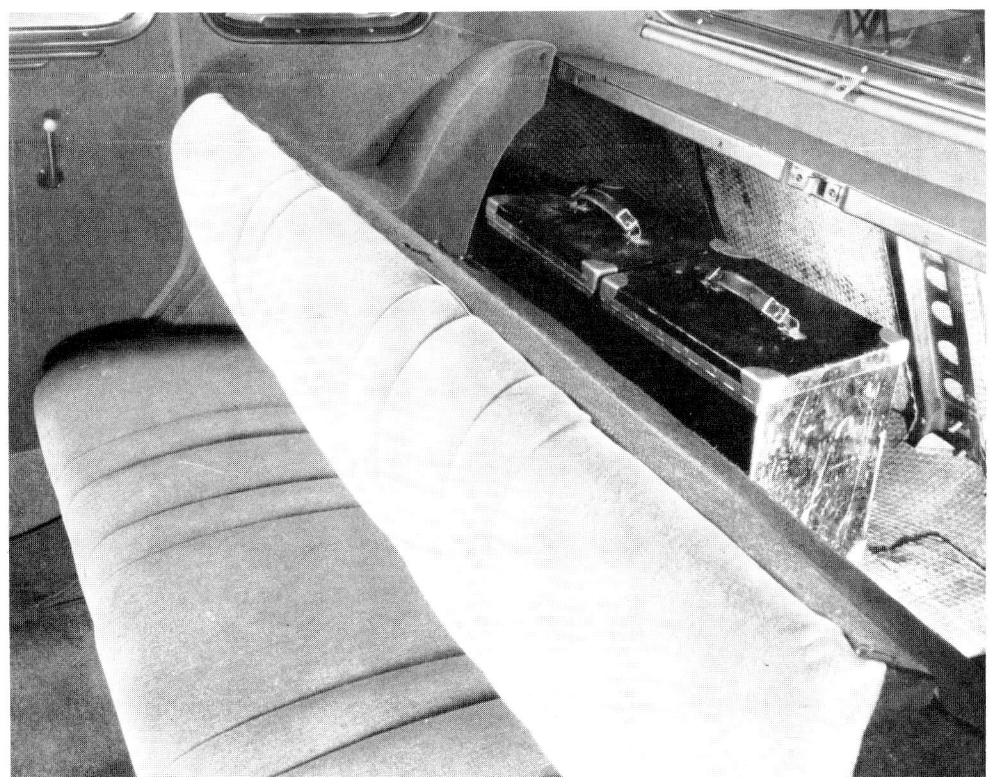

Typical rear compartment of 1936 Fordor Sedan with the seat back pulled forward revealing the storage compartment.

1935 STANDARD FORDOR SEDAN INTERIOR TRIM SCHEMES

Light Brown Wide Wale Bedford Cord Trim Scheme

Door panel, center pillar, quarter hinge pillar, quarter: Light Brown Wide Wale Bedford Cord until February 1935, then changed to Light Brown Plain Sidewall Cloth.
Seats, arm rests: Light Brown Wide Wale Bedford Cord.
Door pillar and header: Light Brown Plain Sidewall Cloth.
Headlining, back (became one piece in April 1935): Light Brown Napped Cotton.
Visor: Light Brown Napped Cotton with Light Brown Fine Colonial Grain artificial leather binding.
Windlace: Light Brown Worsted Cloth.
Door pull-to cord: Russet Brown Fine Colonial Grain artificial leather.

Gray Brown Imitation Leather Trim Scheme

Door panels, center pillar, quarter hinge pillar, quarter, seats, arm rests, door pillar and header, headlining, back, door pull-to cord, windlace: Gray Brown Veal Grain artificial leather.
Visor: Gray Brown Veal Grain Embossed Cardboard with Gray Brown Fine Colonial Grain artificial leather binding.

Thorn Brown Mohair (Introduced February 1935)

Door panels, center pillar, quarter hinge pillar, quarter, door pillar and header, arm rests: Thorn Brown Mohair.
Headlining, back (became one piece April 1935): Thorn Brown Napped Cotton.
Visor: Thorn Brown Napped Cotton with Brown Fine Colonial Grain artificial leather binding.
Windlace: Thorn Brown Worsted Cloth.

Items which were identical on each trim scheme

Cowl panels: Gray Brown Fine Colonial Grain Cardboard.
Floor mats: Tan Rubber.
Instrument panel, finish strip: Maroon.
Glove compartment door interior: Taupe Napped Cotton.
Windshield frame: Painted body color.
Interior hardware: Nickel Plated, Butler Finish.
Glove compartment handle: Maroon Plastic.

1935 DELUXE FORDOR SEDAN INTERIOR TRIM SCHEMES

Taupe Mohair Trim Scheme

Seats, door panels, door pillar and header, center pillar, quarter hinge pillar, quarter, arm rests: Taupe Mohair.
Headlining, back (became one piece April 1935): Taupe Napped Cotton.
Visors: Taupe Napped Cotton with Taupe Fine Colonial Grain artificial leather binding.
Windlace: Taupe Worsted Cloth.
Assist loop, robe cord: Taupe Worsted Cloth with Taupe Fine Colonial Grain artificial leather binding.
Rear curtain: Brown Poplin.
Door pull-to cord: Taupe Fine Colonial Grain artificial leather.

Taupe Pinstripe Broadcloth Trim Scheme

Seats, door panels, door pillar and header, center pillar, quarter hinge pillar, quarter, arm rest: Taupe Pinstripe Broadcloth.
Headlining, back (became one piece April 1935): Taupe Napped Cotton.
Visors: Taupe Napped Cotton with Taupe Fine Colonial Grain artificial leather binding.
Windlace: Taupe Worsted Cloth.
Assist loop, robe cord: Taupe Worsted Cloth with Taupe Fine Colonial Grain artificial leather binding.
Rear curtain: Brown Poplin.
Door pull-to cord: Taupe Fine Colonial Grain artificial leather.

Gray Brown Leather Trim Scheme

Seats, door panels, quarter, front door arm rest: Gray Brown Veal Grain Leather.
Door pillar and header, center pillar, quarter hinge pillar, rear arm rests, front seat back, assist loop, headlining, back, windlace, door pull-to cord: Gray Brown Veal Grain artificial leather.
Visors: Gray Brown Veal Grain Embossed Cardboard with Gray Brown Fine Colonial Grain artificial leather binding.
Rear curtain: Gray Brown Pyroxylin.

Items which were identical on each trim scheme

Cowl panel: Gray Brown Fine Colonial Grain Cardboard.
Front floor mat: Tan Rubber.
Rear floor mat, rear seat heel board: Brown Carpet.
Instrument panel, finish strips: Metallic Taupe.
Glove compartment door interior: Taupe Napped Cotton.
Windshield frame: Bright Chrome Plating.
Interior hardware: Oxidized Dark Taupe until June 1935, then changed to Ester Coated Taupe.
Escutcheons: Dark Taupe Plastic.
Glove compartment handle: Light Taupe Plastic.
Window regulator knob: Light Taupe Plastic until June 1935, then changed to Chrome Plated Zinc.

1935 TOURING FORDOR SEDAN INTERIOR TRIM SCHEMES

Taupe Bedford Cord Trim Scheme

Seats, door panels, door pillar and header, center pillar, quarter hinge pillar, quarter, arm rests: Taupe Bedford Cord.
Headlining, back (became one piece April 1935): Taupe Napped Cotton.
Visors: Taupe Napped Cotton with Taupe Fine Colonial Grain artificial leather binding.
Windlace: Taupe Worsted Cloth.
Assist loop: Taupe Worsted Cloth with Taupe Fine Colonial Grain artificial leather binding.
Rear curtain: Brown Poplin.
Door pull-to cord: Taupe Fine Colonial Grain artificial leather.

Taupe Worsted Suede Trim Scheme

Seats, door panels, door pillar and header, center pillar, quarter hinge pillar, quarter, arm rests: Taupe Worsted Suede.
Headlining, back (became one piece April 1935): Taupe Napped Cotton.
Visors: Taupe Napped Cotton with Taupe Fine Colonial Grain artificial leather binding.
Windlace: Taupe Worsted Cloth with Taupe Fine Colonial Grain artificial leather binding.
Rear curtain: Brown Poplin.
Door pull-to cord: Taupe Fine Colonial Grain artificial leather.

Gray Brown Leather Trim Scheme

Same as Deluxe Tudor Sedan.

Items which were identical on each trim scheme

Cowl panels, seat bottom, package tray, luggage compartment: Gray Brown Fine Colonial Grain Cardboard.
Front floor mat: Tan Rubber.
Rear floor mat and rear seat heel board: Brown Carpet.
Instrument panel, finish strips: Metallic Taupe.
Glove compartment door interior: Taupe Napped Cotton.
Windshield frame: Bright Chrome Plated.
Interior hardware: Oxidized Dark Taupe until June 1935, then changed to Ester Coated Taupe.
Escutcheons: Dark Taupe Plastic.
Windshield regulator handle: Ester Coated Taupe.
Glove compartment handle: Light Taupe Plastic.

1936 STANDARD FORDOR SEDAN INTERIOR TRIM SCHEMES

Light Brown Wide Wale Bedford Cord (Dropped June 1936 and reinstated August 1936)

Seats, arm rests: Light Brown Wide Wale Bedford Cord.
Door panels, quarter, door pillar and header, center pillar, quarter hinge pillar: Light Brown Side Wall Cloth.
Headlining: Light Brown Napped Cotton.
Visor: Light Brown Napped Cotton, with Brown Fine Colonial Grain artificial leather binding.
Windlace: Light Brown Worsted Cloth.

Brown Imitation Leather Trim Scheme

Seats, arm rests, door panels, quarter, door pillar and header, center pillar, quarter hinge pillar, headlining, windlace: Brown Fine Colonial Grain artificial leather.
Visor: Brown Fine Colonial Grain Embossed Cardboard with Brown Fine Colonial Grain artificial leather binding.

Two Tone Brown Mohair Trim Scheme (Adopted May 1936 and dropped June 1936)

Seats, arm rests, door panels, quarter, door pillar and header, center pillar, quarter hinge pillar: Two Tone Brown Mohair.
Headlining: Light Brown Napped Cotton.
Visor: Light Brown Napped Cotton with Brown Fine Colonial Grain artificial leather binding.
Windlace: Two Tone Brown Worsted Cloth.

Two Tone Light Taupe Mohair Trim Scheme (Adopted June 1936 and dropped July 1936)

Seats, arm rests, door panels, quarter, door pillar and header, center pillar, quarter hinge pillar: Two Tone Light Taupe Mohair.
Headlining: Light Brown Napped Cotton.
Visor: Light Brown Napped Cotton with Brown Fine Colonial Grain artificial leather binding.
Windlace: Two Tone Light Taupe Worsted Cloth.

Dark Brown Wide Wale Bedford Cord Trim Scheme (Adopted July 1936)

Seats, arm rests: Dark Brown Wide Wale Bedford Cord.
Door panels, quarter, door pillar and header, quarter hinge pillar: Dark Brown Side Wall Cloth until August 1936, then changed to Dark Brown Wide Wale Bedford Cord.
Headlining: Light Brown Napped Cotton.
Visor: Light Brown Napped Cotton with Brown Fine Colonial Grain artificial leather binding.
Windlace: Dark Brown Worsted Cloth.

Items which were identical on each trim scheme

Cowl panels: Brown Fine Colonial Grain Cardboard until May 1936, then changed to Dark Taupe Fine Colonial Grain Cardboard.
Front floor mat: Tan Rubber, changed to Benton Gray Rubber in November 1935.
Rear floor mat: Tan Rubber, changed to Brown Carpet in July 1936.
Instrument panel, finish strips: Benton Gray Metallic, changed to Mahogany Grain in May 1936.

Glove compartment door interior: Taupe Napped Cotton, changed to Black Cardboard in May 1936.
Windshield frame: Painted body color.
Interior hardware: Nickel Plated, Butler Finish, changed to Bright Chrome Plate in May 1936.
Windshield regulator handle: Benton Gray Metallic, changed to Zinc Die Casting Bright Chrome Plate in May 1936.
Glove compartment handle: Light Gray Plastic until May 1936, then changed to Chrome Plated Zinc Die Casting.

1936 STANDARD TOURING FORDOR SEDAN INTERIOR TRIM SCHEMES

Same as Standard Fordor Sedan except as follows:
Front floor: Benton Gray Rubber.
Rear floor: Benton Gray Rubber until July 1936, then changed to Brown Carpet.
Package tray, luggage compartment: Black Dash Grain Cardboard, changed to Black Seal Grain Cardboard in January 1936 and to Morocco Grain in February 1936.

1936 DELUXE FORDOR SEDAN AND DELUXE TOURING FORDOR SEDAN INTERIOR TRIM SCHEMES

Taupe Mohair Trim Scheme
Seats, door panels, quarter, arm rests, door pillar and header, center pillar, quarter hinge pillar: Taupe Mohair.
Headlining: Taupe Napped Cotton.
Visors: Taupe Napped Cotton with Taupe Fine Colonial Grain artificial leather binding.
Windlace: Taupe Worsted Cloth.
Rear curtain: Brown Poplin.
Assist loop, robe cord: Taupe Worsted Cloth with Taupe Fine Colonial Grain artificial leather binding.

Brown Broadcloth Trim Scheme (Dropped in November 1935)
Seats, door panels, quarter, arm rests, door pillar and header, center pillar, quarter hinge pillar: Brown Broadcloth.
Headlining: Taupe Napped Cotton.
Visors: Taupe Napped Cotton with Taupe Fine Colonial Grain artificial leather binding.
Windlace: Brown Worsted Cloth.
Rear curtain: Brown Poplin.
Assist loop, robe cord: Brown Worsted Cloth with Brown Fine Colonial Grain artificial leather binding.

Taupe Bedford Cord Trim Scheme
Seats, door panels, quarter, arm rests, door pillar and header, center pillar: Taupe Bedford Cord.
Headlining: Taupe Napped Cotton.
Visors: Taupe Napped Cotton with Taupe Fine Colonial Grain artificial leather binding.
Windlace: Taupe Worsted Cloth.
Rear curtain: Brown Poplin.
Assist loop, robe cord: Taupe Worsted Cloth with Taupe Fine Colonial Grain artificial leather binding.

Brown Leather Trim Scheme
Seats, door panels, quarter, arm rests: Brown Fine Colonial Grain Leather.
Door pillar and header, center pillar, quarter hinge pillar, headlining, windlace, assist loop, robe cord: Brown Fine Colonial Grain artificial leather.
Visors: Brown Fine Colonial Grain Embossed Cardboard with Brown Fine Colonial Grain artificial leather binding.
Rear curtain: Brown Pyroxylin.

Gray Brown Broadcloth Trim Scheme (Adopted November 1935)
Seats, door panels, quarter, arm rests, door pillar and header, center pillar, quarter hinge pillar: Gray Brown Broadcloth.
Headlining: Taupe Napped Cotton.
Visors: Taupe Napped Cotton with Taupe Fine Colonial Grain artificial leather binding.
Windlace: Gray Brown Worsted Cloth.
Rear curtain: Brown Poplin.
Assist loop, robe cord: Gray Brown Worsted Cloth with Gray Brown Fine Colonial Grain artificial leather binding.

Brown Boucle Trim Scheme (Adopted January 1936)
Seats, door panels, quarter, arm rests, door pillar and header, center pillar, quarter hinge pillar: Brown Boucle.
Headlining: Taupe Napped Cotton.
Visors: Taupe Napped Cotton with Taupe Fine Colonial Grain artificial leather binding.
Windlace: Brown Worsted Cloth.
Rear curtain: Brown Poplin.
Assist loop, robe cord: Brown Worsted Cloth with Brown Fine Colonial Grain artificial leather binding.

Items which were identical on each trim scheme
Cowl panels: Brown Fine Colonial Grain Cardboard, changed to Dark Taupe Fine Colonial Grain Cardboard in May 1936.
Front floor mat: Tan Rubber, changed to Benton Gray Rubber in November 1935.
Rear floor mat, rear seat heel board: Brown Carpet.
Instrument panel, finish strip: Benton Gray Metallic, changed to Walnut Grain in May 1936.
Glove compartment door interior: Taupe Napped Cotton, changed to Black Cardboard in May 1936.
Windshield frame: Bright Chrome Plated.
Interior hardware: Ester Coated Benton Gray, changed to Ester Coated Brown in May 1936.
Escutcheons: Benton Gray Plastic, changed to metal painted Benton Gray Metallic in January 1936, and Brown Paint in May 1936.
Windshield regulator handle: Benton Gray Metallic, changed to Bright Chrome Plate in May 1936.
Window regulator knob, ash tray knob, glove compartment handle: Light Gray Plastic, changed to Brown in May 1936; Glove compartment handle changed to Zinc Die Casting Bright Chrome Plate in May 1936.

Touring Only
Package tray, luggage compartment: Gray Brown Fine Colonial Grain Cardboard, changed to Black Dash Grain Cardboard in December 1935, to Black Seal Grain Cardboard in January 1936, and to Black Morocco Grain Cardboard in February 1936.

Typical assembly line operation.

The 1935 Convertible Sedan. Its running board molding was common with that of the Deluxe Touring Sedan.

The early 1936 Convertible Sedan with top down and dust hood installed.

Convertible Sedan (48-740 and 68-740)

The Convertible Sedan name was a carry over from the 1931-32 two door body style. However, the new version introduced in April 1935, had four doors and its body number was 740, the same as the 1934 Victoria. It was a true convertible with a collapsible top and side windows which rolled down into the lower part of the doors similar to the Cabriolet. The center posts between the front and rear windows were removable when the top was down. Its equipment included all the deluxe features of the closed cars except the sun visors and a choice of two interior trim schemes — Taupe Bedford Cord or Gray Brown Veal Grain Genuine Leather. The top material was made of Drab Rubber interlined fabric. Begin-

The new style 1936 Convertible Sedan with its unique trunk, full length trunk lid and trunk mounted tail lamps. The spare was stowed inside, a feature which became standard on all 1937 cars.

ning in June, a special thumb screw wrench as well as an instruction booklet showing the proper procedure for raising and lowering the top, were provided with each vehicle. The outside dimensions of the rear light frame were 25 × 5-3/8 and changed to 25 × 7 in March 1935.

The 1935 Convertible Sedan body style carried over into 1936 with new interior trim schemes and floor mat color. However, in April 1936 a new body was introduced, featuring a unique built-in luggage compartment trunk with capacity for the spare tire in addition to the luggage. Its full length trunk door was hinged at the top and was designed to stay in the open position when desired. A slight lift of the lid released it for closing. Included with the new body style were shorter tail light brackets which were attached to the trunk lid rather than the fenders.

The stripe on the slant back 1935 and early 1936 cars was identical to that on the Tudor Sedan. On the 1936 model with the trunk, the stripe followed the belt line to the rear quarter, then went down and across the back of the body, just below the trunk lid.

Rear compartment of the 1935 Convertible Sedan showing the seat in the down position revealing the luggage compartment and the folded top storage compartment.

1935 CONVERTIBLE SEDAN INTERIOR TRIM SCHEMES

Taupe Bedford Cord Trim Scheme

Seats, door panels, quarter, front door arm rest, center pillar, quarter and rear belt rail, front seat side arm: Taupe Bedford Cord.

Windlace: Taupe Worsted Cloth.

Gray Brown Leather Trim Scheme

Seats, door panels, quarter, front door arm rest: Gray Brown Veal Grain Leather.

Center pillar, quarter and rear belt rail, front seat side arm, front seat back, windlace: Gray Brown Veal Grain artificial leather.

Items which were identical on each trim scheme

Front floor mat: Tan Rubber.

Rear floor mat, rear seat heel board, front seat back bottom: Brown Carpet.

Cowl panels, folding pillar quarter rail, package tray: Gray Brown Seal Grain Cardboard.

Top: Drab Rubber Interlined Fabric.

Dusthood: Drab Fabric.

Glove compartment door interior: Taupe Napped Cotton.

Instrument panel, finish strip: Metallic Taupe.

Interior hardware: Oxidized Dark Taupe, changed to Ester Coated Taupe in June 1935.

Escutcheons: Dark Taupe Plastic.

Glove compartment handle: Light Taupe Plastic.

Window regulator knob: Light Taupe Plastic, changed to Chrome Plated Zinc in June 1935.

Windshield frame, top back curtain light frame: Bright Chrome Plated.

Top bows: Wood – varnished; steel – painted Taupe; steel top irons – Chrome Plated.

1936 CONVERTIBLE SEDAN INTERIOR TRIM SCHEMES

Taupe Bedford Cord Trim Scheme

Seats, door panels, quarter, arm rests, center pillar, quarter belt rail, rear belt rail, front seat side arm: Taupe Bedford Cord.

Windlace: Taupe Worsted Cloth.

Cowl panels, folding pillar, quarter rail, package tray: Gray Brown Veal Grain Cardboard, changed to Gray Brown Fine Colonial Grain Cardboard in April 1936; Cowl changed to Dark Taupe Fine Colonial Grain Cardboard in May 1936.

Brown Leather Trim Scheme (Dropped June 1936, reinstated August 1936)

Seats, door panels, quarter, arm rests: Brown Fine Colonial Grain Leather.

Center pillar, quarter belt rail, rear belt rail, front seat side arm, front seat back, windlace: Brown Fine Colonial Grain artificial leather.

Cowl, folding pillar, quarter rail, package tray: Brown Fine Colonial Grain Cardboard.

Brown Leather and Cloth Trim Scheme (Adopted June 1936, dropped August 1936)

Seats: Brown Fine Colonial Grain Leather.

Door panels, quarter, arm rests, center pillar, quarter belt rail, rear belt rail: Light Brown Wide Wale Bedford Cord.

Front seat side arm, front seat back: Brown Fine Colonial Grain artificial leather.

Windlace: Light Brown Worsted Cloth.

Cowl panels, folding pillar, quarter rail, package tray: Brown Fine Colonial Grain Cardboard.

Items which were identical on each trim scheme

Front floor mat: Tan Rubber, changed to Benton Gray Rubber in November 1935.

Rear floor mat, rear seat heel board, front seat back bottom: Brown Carpet.

Top: Drab Rubber Interlined Fabric.

Dusthood: Drab Fabric.

Glove compartment door interior: Taupe Napped Cotton, changed to Black Cardboard in May 1936.

Instrument panel, finish strips: Benton Gray Metallic, changed to Walnut Grain in May 1936.

Interior hardware: Ester Coated Benton Gray, changed to Ester Coated Brown in May 1936.

Escutcheons: Benton Gray Plastic, changed to metal painted Benton Gray Metallic in January 1936, painted Brown in May 1936.

Glove compartment handle, window regulator knob, ash tray knob: Light Gray Plastic, changed to Brown in May 1936; Glove compartment handle changed to Zinc Die Casting, Bright Chrome Plated in May 1936.

Windshield frame, top back curtain right frame: Bright Chrome Plate.

Top back curtain frame: Painted Cordoba Tan on trunk models.

Top bows: Wood – varnished; steel – painted Taupe; steel top irons – Chrome Plated on models without trunk; on trunk models, steel bows and top irons, painted Cordoba Tan.

A 1935 Phaeton. The 1935-36 Phaetons were the only body styles with a valance across the top rear window.

Phaeton (48-750 and 68-750) Deluxe

As with the Roadster, the Phaeton was available only in the deluxe style. Its deluxe features included wind wings, glove box, ash tray and dust hood. Only one trim scheme was available, Gray Brown Veal Grain Leather. The door panels, which were finished in artificial leather until January 1935, were covered with genuine leather thereafter. The top and side curtains were made of Drab Rubber interlined fabric. Windshield frame, stanchions and the rear window frame

The 1935 Phaeton, available only with the deluxe features. Note the double white wall on the tires.

The 1936 Phaeton with top up and side curtains installed.

A preproduction photograph of the 1936 Phaeton. Note the valance across the top of the rear curtain.

were all finished in bright chrome plating. A minor change occurred in November 1934 with the redesign of the front seat to provide a larger tool compartment underneath.

The main variation from 1935 to 1936 was the shape of the grille and introduction of new upholstery colors. Other changes during 1936 consisted of painting the top bows Cordoba Tan, starting in April, and the finish on the front belt rail panel and glove box door changed to Walnut Grain in May.

A single pin stripe went around the body 5/8 inch below the belt line, similar to the Tudor Sedan.

Rear seat compartment of 1935 Phaeton.

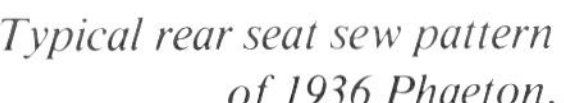

Typical rear seat sew pattern of 1936 Phaeton.

1935 PHAETON INTERIOR TRIM SCHEME

Gray Brown Leather Trim Scheme

Seats: Gray Brown Veal Grain Leather.

Door panels, windlace, rear belt, quarter, center pillar, front seat side, front seat back: Gray Brown Veal Grain artificial leather; Door panels changed to Leather January 1935.

Front belt rail: Gray Brown Veal Grain Cardboard.

Cowl panels: Gray Brown Fine Colonial Grain Cardboard.

Floor (front and rear), front seat back lower: Tan Rubber.

Top and side curtains: Drab Rubber Interlined Fabric.

Dusthood: Drab Fabric.

Glove compartment door interior: Taupe Napped Cotton.

Instrument panel, finish strips: Metallic Taupe.

Interior hardware: Nickel Plate, Butler Finish.

Glove compartment handle: Light Taupe Plastic, changed to Zinc Die Casting Bright Chrome Plate in June 1935.

Windshield frame, stanchions, backlight frame inside and outside: Bright Chrome Plate.

Top bows: Wood – varnished; steel – painted Taupe; steel top irons – Chrome Plated.

1936 PHAETON INTERIOR TRIM SCHEME

Brown Leather Trim Scheme

Seats, door panels: Brown Fine Colonial Grain Leather.

Windlace, center pillar, quarter, back belt rail, front seat back, front seat side: Brown Fine Colonial Grain artificial leather.

Cowl panels, front belt rail: Brown Fine Colonial Grain Cardboard.

Floor (front and rear), front seat lower: Tan Rubber, changed to Benton Gray in November 1935.

Top and side curtains: Drab Rubber Interlined Fabric.

Dust hood: Drab Fabric.

Glove compartment door interior: Taupe Napped Cotton.

Instrument panel, finish strips: Benton Gray Metallic, changed to Walnut Grain in May 1936.

Interior hardware: Nickel Plate, Butler Finish, changed to Bright Chrome Plate in May 1936.

Glove compartment handle: Taupe Plastic changed to Zinc Die Casting Bright Chrome Plate in May.

Ash tray knob: Taupe Plastic, changed to Brown Plastic in May.

Windshield frame, stanchions, back light frame inside and out: Bright Chrome Plate.

Top bows: Wood – varnished; steel – painted Taupe; steel top irons – Chrome Plated.

The 1935 Cabriolet with top up. The rumble seat was a standard item on this model.

A 1936 Cabriolet with top down. The rumble seat step plates were a duplicate of the clutch and brake pedal pads.

Cabriolet and Club Cabriolet (48-760 and 68-760)

Following its introduction in 1929, the Cabriolet was always trimmed in the deluxe style. In 1935 its equipment included an adjustable seat, glove box, ash tray, arm rest on the driver's side, rumble seat, dust hood and a choice of two trim schemes — Taupe Bedford Cord or Gray Brown Veal Grain genuine leather. Its top bows were chrome plated until April 1936, when they were painted Cordoba Tan. Top material was Drab Rubber interlined fabric. Starting with Job-one 1935, the remote control rumble seat lid lock used in 1934 was replaced by the ''T'' handle and lock assembly.

The 1936 Cabriolet showing a good example of the "T" deck lid handle.

An early 1936 Cabriolet front compartment illustrating the windshield header trim, top latching pins, chrome plated windshield wiper, the early style deluxe steering wheel, and unframed rear view mirror.

Prototype version of the 1936 Club Cabriolet. On this body the rear deck compartment was for luggage.

A 1936 Club Cabriolet with top down revealing the new rear passenger compartment. The spare wheel carrier was used on this model only.

For the 1936 model, the Gray Brown Veal Grain Leather was replaced with Brown Fine Colonial Grain Leather. The front seat was moved back 3/4 inch in February to increase leg room. Additional changes occurring on the other deluxe body styles during 1936, were also made to the Cabriolet.

In March 1936 the Club Cabriolet was introduced as an additional Cabriolet body style, featuring a short rear seat compartment instead of the rumble seat. It was equipped with the same deluxe items as the conventional Cabriolet, plus an additional cloth-leather combination interior trim scheme. The outside dimensions of the rear light frame were 25 × 5-3/8 on the 1935 Cabriolet and changed to 25 × 7 in June 1935

Interior of the Club Cabriolet showing the bench style seats with the folding back.

and was a carry over through 1936. On Club Cabriolet it was 21 × 7.

Striping was identical to the Coupe and Roadster bodies.

1935 CABRIOLET INTERIOR TRIM SCHEMES

Taupe Bedford Cord Trim Scheme

Seat, door panels, arm rest, quarter lock pillar, back belt rail, package tray, seat side arm, windbreak, seat back bellows: Taupe Bedford Cord.

Windlace: Taupe Worsted Cloth.

Door pull-to cord: Taupe Fine Colonial Grain artificial leather.

Gray Brown Leather Trim Scheme

Seat, door panels, arm rest: Gray Brown Veal Grain Leather.

Quarter lock pillar, back belt rail, package tray, seat side arm, windbreak, seat back bellows, windlace, door pull-to cord: Gray Brown Veal Grain artificial leather.

Items which were identical on each trim scheme

Cowl panels, package tray bottom, deck side: Gray Brown Veal Grain Cardboard.

Floor (front and deck): Tan Rubber.

Deck seat: Gray Brown Veal Grain artificial leather.

Top: Drab Rubber Interlined Fabric.

Dust hood: Drab Fabric.

Glove compartment door interior: Taupe Napped Cotton.

Instrument panel, finish strip: Metallic Taupe.

Interior hardware: Oxidized Dark Taupe, changed to Ester Coated Taupe in June 1935.

Escutcheons: Dark Taupe Plastic.

Glove compartment handle, window regulator knobs: Light Taupe Plastic; Window regulator knob changed to Zinc, Chrome Plated in June 1935.

Windshield frame, outside door handles, top back curtain frame: Bright Chrome Plate.

Top bows: Wood – varnished; steel – painted Taupe; steel top irons – Chrome Plated.

1936 CABRIOLET INTERIOR TRIM SCHEMES

Taupe Bedford Cord Trim Scheme

Seat, door panels, arm rest, back belt rail, package tray, quarter lock pillar, seat side arm, windbreak, seat back bellows: Taupe Bedford Cord; Back belt rail, package tray changed to Taupe Napped Cotton in January 1936, and to Drab Cloth in June 1936.

Windlace: Taupe Worsted Cloth.

Cowl panels, package tray: Gray Brown Veal Grain Cardboard, changed to Gray Brown Fine Colonial Grain Cardboard in April 1936; Cowl panels changed to Dark Taupe Fine Colonial Grain Cardboard in May 1936.

Brown Leather Trim Scheme

Seat, door panels, arm rest: Brown Fine Colonial Grain Leather.

Back belt rail, package tray, windlace, seat side arm, windbreak, quarter lock pillar, seat back bellows: Brown Fine Colonial Grain artificial leather.

Cowl panels, package tray bottom: Brown Fine Colonial Grain Cardboard.

Items which were identical on each trim scheme

Floor (front and deck): Tan Rubber, changed to Benton Gray in November 1935.

Deck seat: Brown Fine Colonial Grain artificial leather.

Deck side: Brown Fine Colonial Grain Cardboard.

Top: Drab Rubber Interlined Fabric.

Dust hood: Drab Fabric.

Glove compartment door interior: Taupe Napped Cotton, changed to Black Cardboard in May 1936.

Instrument panel, finish strips: Benton Gray Metallic, changed to Walnut Grain in May 1936.

Interior hardware: Ester Coated Benton Gray, changed to Ester Coated Brown in May 1936.

Escutcheons: Benton Gray Plastic, changed to metal painted Benton Gray Metallic in January 1936, and Brown Paint in May 1936.

Glove compartment handle, window regulator knob, ash tray knob: Light Gray Plastic, changed to Brown in May 1936; Glove compartment handle changed to Zinc Die Casting, Bright Chrome Plated in May 1936.

Windshield frame, top back curtain frame: Bright Chrome Plated.

Top bows: Wood – varnished; steel – painted Taupe; steel top irons – Chrome Plated.

1936 CLUB CABRIOLET INTERIOR TRIM SCHEMES

Taupe Bedford Cord Trim Scheme

Seats, door panel, quarter, arm rests: Taupe Bedford Cord.

Windlace: Taupe Worsted Cloth.

Back belt rail, package tray: Taupe Napped Cotton, changed to Drab Cloth in June 1936.

Cowl panels, package tray bottom: Gray Brown Veal Grain Cardboard, changed to Gray Brown Fine Colonial Grain Cardboard in April 1936; Cowl panels changed to Dark Taupe Fine Colonial Grain Cardboard in May 1936.

Brown Leather Trim Scheme

Seats, door panels, quarter, arm rest: Brown Fine Colonial Grain Leather.

Cowl panel, package tray bottom: Brown Fine Colonial Grain Cardboard

Back belt rail, package tray: Brown Fine Colonial Gray artificial leather, changed to Light Brown Wide Wale Bedford Cord in June 1936.

Windlace: Brown Fine Colonial Gray artificial leather.

Front seat back: Light Brown Side Wall Cloth, changed to Light Brown Wide Wale Bedford Cord in June 1936, and to Brown Fine Colonial Grain Leather in August 1936.

Brown Leather and Cloth Trim Scheme (Dropped August 1936)

Seats: Brown Fine Colonial Grain Leather.

Door panels, quarter, arm rests, front seat back: Light Brown Side Wall Cloth, changed to Light Brown Wide Wale Bedford Cord in June 1936.

Cowl panels, package tray bottom: Brown Fine Colonial Grain Cardboard.

Windlace: Light Brown Worsted Cloth.

Back belt rail, package tray: Brown Fine Colonial Grain artificial leather, changed to Light Brown Wide Wale Bedford Cord in June 1936.

Items which were identical on each trim scheme

Floor (front and rear): Benton Gray Rubber; Rear changed to Brown Carpet in July 1936.

Top: Drab Rubber Interlined Fabric.

Dust hood: Drab Fabric.

Glove compartment door interior: Taupe Napped Cotton, changed to Black Cardboard in May 1936.

Instrument panel, finish strips: Benton Gray Metallic, changed to Walnut Grain in May 1936.

Interior hardware: Ester Coated Benton Gray, changed to Ester Coated Brown in May 1936.

Escutcheons: Benton Gray Plastic changed to metal painted Benton Gray Metallic in January 1936, and Brown Paint in May 1936.

Glove compartment handle, window regulator handle knob, ash tray knob: Light Gray Plastic, changed to Brown in May 1936; Glove compartment handle changed to Zinc Die Casting, Bright Chrome Plate in May 1936.

Windshield frame: Bright Chrome Plated.

Top back light frame: Cordoba Tan Paint.

Top bows: Wood – varnished; steel – painted Cordoba Tan; steel top irons – painted Cordoba Tan.

Prototype 1935 Five Window Coupe. The black grille and painted windshield frame designate this a standard model. A grille painted body color was available by special order.

A 1935 Standard Five Window Coupe without rumble seat. The rumble seat was available at extra cost.

Coupe, Five Window (48-770 and 68-770)
Standard and Deluxe

The five window Coupe was produced in two versions, the standard and deluxe body styles. Both bodies were equipped with an adjustable seat, glove box, sun visor on driver's side, roll down rear window and an arm rest on the driver's side. In addition, the deluxe model had a dome light, ash tray and another sun visor on the passenger's side.

Only one trim scheme, Light Brown Wide Wale Bedford Cord was available on the standard car as regular production. However, two additional trim schemes were available for a short period during early production and an imitation leather

The 1935 Deluxe Five Window Coupe.

The 1936 Deluxe Five Window Coupe.

trim was available as special equipment. Three trim schemes were available on the deluxe Coupe, two cloth materials and one genuine leather. The rumble seat was available on special order for both body styles.

Two changes were made in November 1934. The package tray was redesigned and the remote control deck lid lock and inside handle were replaced with the outside deck lid "T" handle. Two more changes were made in early 1935. In February, a drain tube was added to each lower corner of the deck lid trough, and in April the headlining cloth was extended to include the back panels.

The 1935 bodies were carried into 1936 with minimal changes, but included a variety of new interior trim schemes. Other trim changes were made during 1936, (see trim charts). In February the seat was moved back 3/4 inch to increase leg room.

The striping of the Coupe was identical to that of the Roadster.

1935 DELUXE FIVE WINDOW COUPE INTERIOR TRIM SCHEMES

Taupe Mohair Trim Scheme
Seat, door panels, arm rest, door pillar and header, quarter, quarter lock pillar, seat side arm, seat bellows, package tray: Taupe Mohair.
Headlining, back (became one piece April 1935): Taupe Napped Cotton.
Visors: Taupe Napped Cotton with Taupe Fine Colonial Grain artificial leather binding.
Windlace: Taupe Worsted Cloth.
Rear curtain: Brown Poplin.
Door pull-to cord: Taupe Fine Colonial Grain artificial leather.

Taupe Pinstripe Broadcloth Trim Scheme
Seat, door panels, arm rest, door pillar and header, quarter, quarter lock pillar, seat side arm, seat bellows, package tray: Taupe Pinstripe Broadcloth.
Headlining, back (became one piece April 1935): Taupe Napped Cotton.
Visors: Taupe Napped Cotton with Taupe Fine Colonial Grain artificial leather binding.
Windlace: Taupe Worsted Cloth.
Rear curtain: Brown Poplin.
Door pull-to cord: Taupe Fine Colonial Grain artificial leather.

Gray Brown Leather Trim Scheme
Seat, door panels, arm rest: Gray Brown Veal Grain Leather.
Door pillar and header, quarter, quarter lock pillar, seat side arm, seat bellows, package tray, headlining, back, windlace, door pull-to cord: Gray Brown Veal Grain artificial leather. Headlining, back (became one piece in April 1935).
Visors: Gray Brown Veal Grain Embossed Cardboard with Gray Brown Fine Colonial Grain artificial leather binding.
Rear curtain: Gray Brown Pyroxylin.

Items which were identical on each trim scheme
Cowl panels: Gray Brown Fine Colonial Grain Cardboard.
Deck seat: Gray Brown Veal Grain artificial leather.
Deck side: Gray Brown Veal Grain Cardboard.
Floor (front and deck): Tan Rubber.
Instrument panel, finish strip: Metallic Taupe.
Glove compartment door interior: Taupe Napped Cotton.
Windshield frame: Bright Chrome Plate.
Interior hardware: Oxidized Dark Taupe, changed to Ester Coated Taupe June 1935.
Windshield regulator handle: Ester Coated Taupe.
Escutcheons: Dark Taupe Plastic.
Glove compartment handle, window regulator knob: Light Taupe Plastic; Window regulator knob changed to Chrome Plated Zinc in June 1935.

1935 STANDARD FIVE WINDOW COUPE INTERIOR TRIM SCHEMES

Brown Printed Bedford Cord Trim Scheme (only 800 cars)
Seat, door panels, quarter, quarter lock pillar, arm rest, seat side arm, seat bellows, package tray: Brown Printed Bedford Cord.
Door pillar and header: Brown Plain Side Wall Cloth.
Headlining, back: Brown Napped Cotton.
Visor: Brown Napped Cotton with Brown Fine Colonial Grain artificial leather binding.
Windlace: Brown Worsted Cloth.

Brown Check Trim Scheme (used January and February 1935)
Seat, door panel, quarter, quarter lock pillar, arm rest, seat side arm, seat bellows, package tray: Brown Check Cloth.
Door pillar and header: Brown Plain Side Wall Cloth.
Headlining, back: Brown Napped Cotton.
Visor: Brown Napped Cotton with Brown Fine Colonial Grain artificial leather binding.
Windlace: Brown Worsted Cloth.
Door pull-to cord: Russet Brown Fine Colonial Grain artificial leather.

Light Brown Wide Wale Bedford Cord
Seat, seat side arm, seat bellows, arm rest, package tray: Light Brown Wide Wale Bedford Cord.
Door panels, quarter, quarter lock pillar: Light Brown Wide Wale Bedford Cord, changed to Light Brown Plain Side Wall Cloth in February 1935.
Door pillar and header: Light Brown Plain Side Wall Cloth.
Headlining, back (became one piece April 1935): Light Brown Napped Cotton.
Visor: Light Brown Napped Cotton with Brown Fine Colonial Grain artificial leather binding.
Windlace: Light Brown Worsted Cloth.
Door pull-to cord: Russet Brown Fine Colonial Grain artificial leather.

Gray Brown Imitation Leather Trim Scheme
Seat, door panels, quarter, arm rest, quarter lock pillar, seat side arm, seat bellows, package tray, door pillar and header, headlining, back, windlace, door pull-to cord: Gray Brown Veal Grain artificial leather. Headlining, back (became one piece April 1935).
Visor: Gray Brown Veal Grain Embossed Cardboard with Gray Brown Fine Colonial Grain Cardboard binding.

Items which were identical on each trim scheme
Cowl panels: Gray Brown Fine Colonial Grain Cardboard.
Deck seat: Gray Brown Veal Grain artificial leather.
Deck side: Gray Brown Veal Grain Cardboard.
Floor (front and deck): Tan Rubber.
Instrument panel, finish strips: Maroon Paint.
Glove compartment door interior: Taupe Napped Cotton.
Windshield frame: Paint.
Interior hardware: Nickel Plate, Butler Finish.
Windshield regulator handle, glove compartment lock: Chrome Plate, Satin Finish.
Glove compartment handle: Maroon Plastic.

1936 STANDARD FIVE WINDOW COUPE INTERIOR TRIM SCHEMES

Light Brown Wide Wale Bedford Cord Trim Scheme (Dropped June 1936)
Seat, arm rest: Light Brown Wide Wale Bedford Cord.
Door panels, door pillar and header, seat side arm, seat bellows, package tray: Light Brown Side Wall Cloth.
Headlining, quarter lock pillar, quarter, lower back: Light Brown Napped Cotton.
Visor: Light Brown Napped Cotton with Brown Fine Colonial Grain artificial leather binding.
Windlace: Light Brown Worsted Cloth.

Brown Imitation Leather Trim Scheme
Seat, arm rest, door panels, door pillar and header, seat side arm, seat bellows, package tray, headlining, quarter lock pillar, quarter, lower back, windlace: Brown Fine Colonial Grain artificial leather.
Visor: Brown Fine Colonial Grain Embossed Cardboard with Brown Fine Colonial Grain artificial leather binding.

Two Tone Brown Mohair (Adopted May 1936 and dropped June 1936)
Seat, arm rest, door panels, door pillar and header, seat side arm, seat bellows, package trim: Two Tone Brown Mohair.
Headlining, quarter lock pillar, quarter, lower back: Light Brown Napped Cotton.
Visor: Light Brown Napped Cotton with Brown Fine Colonial Grain artificial leather binding.
Windlace: Two Tone Brown Worsted Cloth.

Two Tone Light Taupe Mohair (Adopted June 1936 and dropped July 1936)
Seat, arm rest, door panels, door pillar and header, seat side arm, seat bellows, package tray: Two Tone Light Taupe Mohair.
Headlining, quarter lock pillar, quarter, lower back: Light Brown Napped Cotton.
Visor: Light Brown Napped Cotton with Brown Fine Colonial Grain artificial leather binding.
Windlace: Two Tone Light Taupe Worsted Cloth.

Dark Brown Wide Wale Bedford Cord Trim Scheme (Adopted July 1936)
Seat, arm rest: Dark Brown Wide Wale Bedford Cord.
Door panels, door pillar and header, seat side arm, seat bellows, package tray: Dark Brown Side Wall Cloth, changed to Dark Brown Wide Wale Bedford Cord in August 1936.
Headlining, quarter lock pillar, quarter, lower back: Light Brown Napped Cotton.
Visor: Light Brown Napped Cotton with Brown Fine Colonial Grain artificial leather binding.
Windlace: Dark Brown Worsted Cloth.

Items which were identical on each trim scheme
Cowl panels: Brown Fine Colonial Grain Cardboard, changed to Dark Taupe Fine Colonial Grain Cardboard.
Deck seat: Brown Fine Colonial Grain artificial leather.
Deck side: Brown Fine Colonial Grain Cardboard.
Floor (front and deck): Tan Rubber, changed to Benton Gray Rubber in November 1935.
Instrument panel, finish strips: Benton Gray Metallic, changed to Walnut Grain in May 1936.
Glove compartment door interior: Taupe Napped Cotton, changed to Black Cardboard in May 1936.
Windshield frame: Paint.
Interior hardware: Nickel Plate, Butler Finish, changed to Bright Chrome Plate in May 1936.
Windshield regulator handle: Benton Gray Metallic, changed to Bright Chrome Plate in May 1936.
Glove compartment handle: Benton Gray Plastic, changed to Zinc Die Casting Bright Chrome Plate in May 1936.

1936 DELUXE FIVE WINDOW COUPE INTERIOR TRIM SCHEMES

Taupe Mohair Trim Scheme
Seat, door panels, arm rest, door pillar and header, seat side arm, seat bellows, package tray: Taupe Mohair.
Headlining, quarter, quarter lock pillar, lower back: Taupe Napped Cotton.
Visors: Taupe Napped Cotton with Taupe Fine Colonial Grain artificial leather binding.
Windlace: Taupe Worsted Cloth.
Rear curtain: Brown Poplin.

Brown Broadcloth Trim Scheme (Dropped November 1935)
Seat, door panels, arm rest, door pillar and header, seat side arm, seat bellows, package tray: Brown Broadcloth.
Headlining, quarter, quarter lock pillar, lower back: Taupe Napped Cotton.
Visors: Taupe Napped Cotton with Taupe Fine Colonial Grain artificial leather binding.
Windlace: Brown Worsted Cloth.
Rear curtain: Brown Poplin.

Gray Brown Broadcloth Trim Scheme (Adopted November 1935)
Seat, door panels, arm rest, door pillar and header, seat side arm, seat bellows, package tray: Gray Brown Broadcloth.
Headlining, quarter, quarter lock pillar, lower back: Taupe Napped Cotton.
Visors: Taupe Napped Cotton with Taupe Fine Colonial Grain artificial leather binding.
Windlace: Gray Brown Worsted Cloth.
Rear curtain: Brown Poplin.

Brown Leather Trim Scheme
Seat, door panels, arm rest: Brown Fine Colonial Grain Leather.
Door pillar and header, seat side arm, seat bellows, package tray, headlining, quarter, quarter lock pillar, lower back, windlace: Brown Fine Colonial Grain artificial leather.
Visors: Brown Fine Colonial Grain Embossed Cardboard with Brown Fine Colonial Grain artificial leather binding.
Rear curtain: Brown Pyroxylin.

Items which were identical on each trim scheme
Cowl panels: Brown Fine Colonial Grain Cardboard, changed to Dark Taupe Fine Colonial Grain Cardboard in May 1936.
Deck seat: Brown Fine Colonial Grain artificial leather.
Deck side: Brown Fine Colonial Grain Cardboard.
Floor (front and deck): Tan Rubber, changed to Benton Gray Rubber in November 1935.
Instrument panel, finish strip: Benton Gray Metallic, changed to Walnut Grain in May 1936.
Glove compartment door interior: Taupe Napped Cotton, changed to Black Cardboard in May 1936.
Windshield frame: Bright Chrome Plate.
Interior hardware: Ester Coated Benton Gray, changed to Ester Coated Brown in May 1936.
Escutcheons: Benton Gray Plastic, changed to metal painted Benton Gray Metallic in January 1936, and Brown Paint in May 1936.
Windshield regulator handle: Benton Gray Metallic, changed to Bright Chrome Plate in May 1936.
Window regulator knob, ash tray knob, glove compartment handle: Light Gray Plastic, changed to Brown in May 1936; Glove compartment handle changed to Zinc Die Casting, Bright Chrome Plate in May 1936.

Commercial Vehicles

The 1935-36 commercial vehicles were virtually all newly designed. Since these vehicles were produced on the passenger car chassis, the relocation of the engine and the mid-ship seating concept introduced on the passenger cars had a direct effect on these models. Moving the seat forward provided better weight distribution and reduced the rear overhang. These vehicles were produced in two versions. The Station Wagon and Sedan Delivery were built with the 1935 and 1936 passenger car grille, hood, fenders, headlights and bumpers, described at the beginning of this section. The grille, lights and front end sheet metal for the Closed Cab Trucks and Panel Delivery were all new, but were designed to resemble the 1934 passenger car front end.

The 1935 Sedan Delivery with a special paint combination and lettering, available from the factory with large fleet orders.

Sedan Delivery

The Sedan Delivery, a closed version of the Tudor Sedan body, was equipped with many of the Tudor features. It had the adjustable driver's seat, glove box, a sun visor on driver's side, dome light, tan rubber floor mats, and an artificial leather trim scheme. In addition, the passenger's seat and a roll-down rear window were available as special equipment.

The 1936 Sedan Delivery finished in the conventional factory color combination. The rear bumper was designed to provide easy access to the rear compartment.

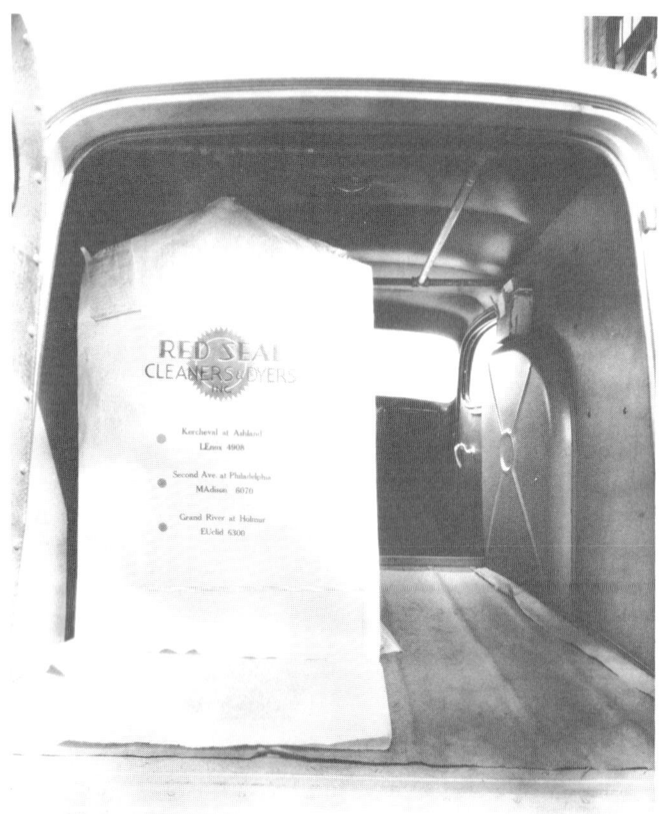

Rear compartment of the 1935 Sedan Delivery, fitted with special racks and the order box mounted on top of the spare tire well.

The 1936 Sedan Delivery interior. The sides were finished with Masonite board while the spare tire well was made of sheet metal.

The front compartment of the 1936 Sedan Delivery.

On the outside it had the standard passenger car features, such as the painted grille and windshield frame, and just one horn.

Most changes occurred during the 1935 to 36 model change over, while others occurred during the 1936 production. These changes are reflected on the interior trim charts.

In June 1936, a new deluxe version of the Sedan Delivery was introduced with all the exterior features of the deluxe passenger car, plus a side view mirror, a passenger seat, dual sun visors and a roll-up rear window. This deluxe vehicle did not have a separate model number until 1937.

A special Tudor Sedan with a rear door entrance was designed for the National Cash Register Company. This model was also made available to other commercial customers on special orders.

The striping for each of these Sedan Deliveries was identical to the Tudor Sedan.

1935-36 SEDAN DELIVERY AND 1936 DELUXE SEDAN DELIVERY INTERIOR TRIM SCHEMES

Gray Black Imitation Leather Trim Scheme (Dropped December 1935)

Seats, windlace, headlining binding, quarter lock pillar: Gray Black Fine Colonial Grain artificial leather.

Cowl and door panels, rear door, headlining: Gray Black Fine Colonial Grain Cardboard.

Instrument panel, finish strips: Maroon, changed to Dark Taupe in September 1935.

Door pull-to cord: Russet Brown Fine Colonial Grain artificial leather.

Front floor: Tan Rubber.

Visor: Gray Black Fine Colonial Grain Embossed Cardboard with Black Fine Colonial Grain artificial leather binding.

Black Imitation Leather Trim Scheme (Adopted December 1935)

Seats, windlace, headlining binding, quarter lock pillar: Black Seal Grain artificial leather.

Door panels, rear door, headlining: Black Seal Grain Cardboard.

Cowl panels: Gray Brown Fine Colonial Grain Cardboard, changed to Dark Taupe in May 1936.

Instrument panel, finish strips: Benton Gray Metallic, changed to Mahogany Grain in May 1936.

Finish strip on rear door: Black.

Front floor mat: Benton Gray Rubber.

Items which were identical both years

Quarter panel: Masonite.

Glove compartment door interior: Taupe Napped Cotton, changed to Black Cardboard in May 1936.

Interior hardware: Nickel Plate, Butler Finish, changed to Bright Chrome Plate in May 1936.

Windshield regulator handle: Chrome Plate, Satin Finish, changed to Dark Taupe in September 1935, changed to Benton Gray Metallic, Job #1, 1936, and to Bright Chrome Plate in May 1936.

Glove compartment handle: Maroon Plastic, changed to Zinc Die Casting Dark Taupe in September 1935, to Benton Gray Metallic Job #1, 1936, and to Bright Chrome Plate in May 1936.

Windshield frame: Paint.

Retouched photograph of the 1935 Station Wagon. Window glass was installed in the front door only.

The 1936 Station Wagon showing the seats arrangement.

Station Wagon (48-790 and 68-790)

The Station Wagon was the only commercial vehicle with passenger car usage. Its all new 1935 body was equipped with the deluxe passenger car front end including the dual horns, chromed grille and chromed windshield frame. For the first time, the Station Wagon front door had a crank operated glass. The rear doors and the other windows, however, continued to use side curtains. The interior trim consisted of Gray Brown Veal Grain artificial leather and Tan Rubber

Interior view of the 1935-36 Station Wagon illustrating the top bows and method for storing the isinglass side curtains.

floor mats. In 1936 this combination was changed to Brown Fine Colonial Grain artificial leather trim with a Benton Gray Rubber floor mat. The first rear bumper for a Ford Station Wagon was released in April 1936.

All exposed wood on the body was finished with clear Spar varnish for both 1935 and 1936 models. The exterior sheet metal items, however, were painted Cordoba Gray in 1935 and Cordoba Tan in 1936. The wheels were painted either Cordoba Gray or Medium Bright Poppy Red in 1935 and Cordoba Tan in 1936.

1935 STATION WAGON INTERIOR TRIM SCHEME

Gray Brown Imitation Leather Trim Scheme

Seats: Gray Brown Veal Grain artificial leather.
Cowl: Gray Brown Fine Colonial Grain Cardboard.
Instrument panel, windshield opening strip: Metallic Taupe.
Floor (front and rear): Tan Rubber.

1936 STATION WAGON INTERIOR TRIM SCHEME

Brown Imitation Leather Trim Scheme

Seats: Brown Fine Colonial Grain artificial leather.
Cowl: Brown Fine Colonial Grain Cardboard.
Instrument panel, windshield opening strip: Benton Gray Metallic, changed to Walnut Grain in May 1936.
Floor (front and rear): Tan Rubber, changed to Benton Gray Rubber in November 1935.

Items which were identical both years

Door locks, mis. interior sheet metal: Brown Pyroxylin.
Tail gate chain cover: Black Short Long Grain artificial leather.
Windshield frame: Bright Chrome Plate.
Interior hardware: Nickel Plate, Butler Finish, changed to Bright Chrome Plate May 1936.
Glove compartment door interior: Taupe Napped Cotton, changed to Black Cardboard in May 1936.
Windshield regulator handle: Ester Coated Taupe, changed to Benton Gray Metallic Job #1, 1936, and to Bright Chrome Plate in May 1936.
Glove compartment handle: Light Taupe Plastic, changed to Light Gray Plastic Job #1, 1936, and to Zinc Die Casting, Bright Chrome Plate in May 1936.

The 1935 Pickup Truck with the 1934 passenger car style front end. The dipped passenger car bumper was available on special order, but became standard equipment in June 1936.

Closed Cab (50-810 and 67-810) and Pickup Box (50-830 and 67-830)

With its new visorless sloping windshield, curved top and rounded pillars, the 1935-36 Closed Cab body finally departed from the 1930 Model A style. The front end sheet metal components were also new, all restyled to resemble the 1934 passenger car. Fender mounted headlights used passenger car items except the case, which was three inches shorter. The wide collar radiator shell was about the only feature retained from the 1932 style.

A 1935 Pickup Truck painted in the special dealer demonstrator color combination.

The 1936 Pickup. Visual differences compared to 1935 are the wheels and location of the hood side medallion.

On early production, the interior trim material was Gray Black Fine Colonial Grain artificial leather, but by April, the trim was changed to Black Dash Grain artificial leather. At the same time, the inside door panels were redesigned to incorporate the door finish strip.

Few visible changes were made to the 1936 models. The hood was redesigned by moving the Ford V-8 side ornament from the center to the front of the hood, and the interior trim scheme became Black Seal Grain artificial leather.

In June 1936 to stimulate sales, the company added a deluxe version of the Closed Cab to its commercial line. It came equipped with chrome plated radiator shell, windshield frame and rear view mirror, dual horns, tandem windshield wipers, dome lamp, ash tray, roll-up back window and a sun visor on the driver's side. Even though sales were slow, this line was continued into 1937.

Typical interior compartment of a 1935-36 Closed Cab.

A single 3/32 inch pin stripe was standard on both units. It started at the front edge of the belt molding and continued around the body.

The Pickup box was a carry-over from 1934 with minor modifications. The side panels required redesign as a result of moving the box forward, a small panel was added between the box and running board, and a center hinge was added to the tail gate. There was no striping on the box.

1935-36 CLOSED CAB AND 1936 DELUXE CLOSED CAB INTERIOR TRIM SCHEMES

Gray Black Imitation Leather Trim Scheme (Dropped April 1935)
Seat, windlace: Gray Black Fine Colonial Grain artificial leather.
Door panels, cowl, quarter, back, headlining, seat back: Gray Black Fine Colonial Grain Cardboard.
Floor: Tan Rubber.

Black Imitation Leather Trim Scheme (Adopted April 1935, dropped December 1935)
Seat, windlace: Black Dash Grain artificial leather.
Door panels, cowl, quarter, back, headlining, seat back: Black Dash Grain Cardboard.
Floor: Tan Rubber.

Black Imitation Leather Trim Scheme (Adopted December 1935)
Seat, windlace: Black Seal Grain artificial leather.
Door panels, cowl, quarter, back, headlining, seat back: Black Seal Grain Cardboard.
Floor: Black Rubber.

Items which were identical on each trim scheme
Finish strips (door, back window, windshield opening): Black Paint.
Instrument panel: Body Color.
Interior hardware: Nickel Plate, Butler Finish.
Windshield frame: Paint.

A 3/4 view of a 1935 Panel Delivery showing details of the rear doors, tail lamp mounting and the location of the spare tire with the accessory cover.

Panel Delivery (50-820 and 67-820) Standard and Deluxe

Similar to the Closed Cab, the 1935-36 Panel Delivery featured an all new body and front end sheet metal. However, the interior construction, which incorporated the wood floor, and wood slat sides with reinforced metal lower panel, was identical to 1934. Two versions were produced. The standard model had a body colored grille, one horn and only the driver's seat. The deluxe, on the other hand, was additionally equipped with a passenger seat, dual horns, aluminum

A 1935 Panel Delivery painted in an optional commercial color.

The 1936 Panel Delivery in typical commercial application.

painted grille, and a chrome plated rear view mirror. Both bodies were trimmed with Gray Black Fine Colonial Grain artificial leather.

In the line of changes, a reinforcement was added to the driver's seat in January, and in April the door window finish strip was eliminated by redesigning the inner door panel. This also caused a change in the cardboard door panel. In May, the inner roof panel in the package compartment was

A 1936 Panel Delivery modified for use as an ambulance.

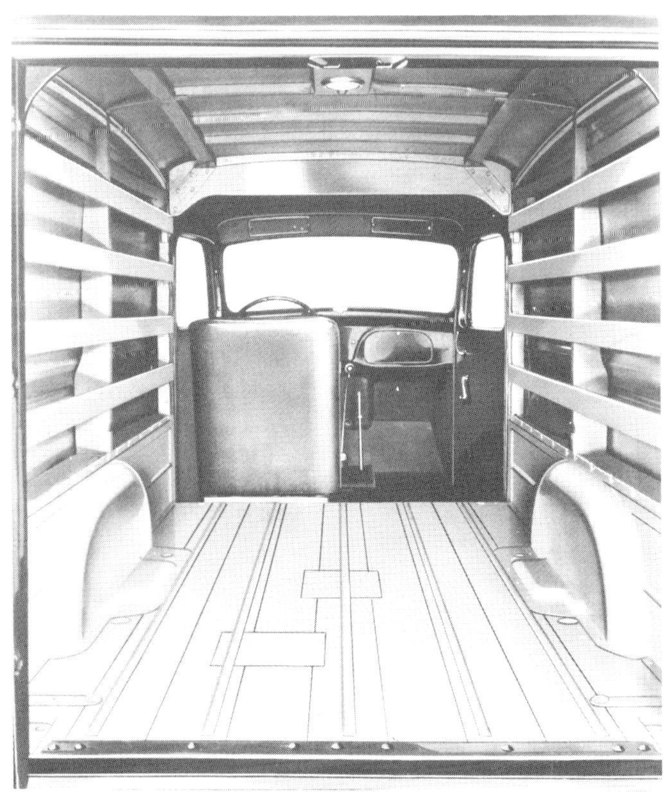

Package compartment of the 1936 Panel Delivery showing the slat sides construction. The Deluxe Panel Delivery had Masonite panel sides.

changed from masonite to hard paper board.

For 1936, the Ford V-8 hood side ornament was relocated and the interior trim became Black Seal Grain artificial leather. Another change occurred in February 1936, when the seat was redesigned for more comfort and a manual adjustment was added. On the previous design the location of the seat could only be altered by relocating the mounting bolts with tools.

Striping consisted of a single pin stripe on the belt molding starting at the front edge of the hood and continuing around the body.

1935-36 STANDARD AND DELUXE PANEL DELIVERY INTERIOR TRIM SCHEMES

Gray Black Imitation Leather Trim Scheme (Dropped April 1935)
Seats, windlace, headlining binding: Gray Black Fine Colonial Grain artificial leather.
Cowl panels, lock pillar, headlining, roof rail, seat back: Gray Black Fine Colonial Grain Cardboard.
Floor (front): Tan Rubber.

Black Imitation Leather Trim Scheme (Adopted April 1935, dropped December 1935)
Seats, windlace, headlining binding: Black Dash Grain artificial leather.
Cowl panels, lock pillar, headlining, roof rail, seat back: Black Dash Grain Cardboard.
Floor (front): Tan Rubber.

Black Imitation Leather Trim Scheme (Adopted December 1935)
Seats, windlace, headlining binding: Black Seal Grain artificial leather.
Cowl panels, lock pillar, headlining, roof rail, seat back: Black Seal Grain Cardboard.
Floor (front): Black Rubber.

Items which were identical on each trim scheme
Finish moldings (door, back doors, windshield opening): Black Paint.
Instrument panel: Body Color.
Interior hardware: Nickel Plate, Butler Finish.
Windshield frame: Paint.

DOMESTIC PRODUCTION OF 1935 CARS

Body Style	Total
Tudor Sedan, Standard (48-700)	228,445
Deluxe (48-700)	76,735
Tudor Touring Sedan (48-700)	76,243
Roadster (48-710)	3,794
Coupe (3W) (48-720)	29,351
Fordor Sedan, Standard (48-730)	39,446
Deluxe (48-730)	64,071
Fordor Touring Sedan (48-730)	91,932
Convertible Sedan (48-740)	3,168
Phaeton (48-750)	3,941
Cabriolet (48-760)	11,712
Coupe (5W), Standard (48-770)	75,914
Deluxe (48-770)	30,832
Sedan Delivery (48-780)	7,687
Station Wagon (48-790)	4,011
Panel Delivery (50-820)	13,732

DOMESTIC PRODUCTION OF 1936 CARS

Body Style	Total
Tudor Sedan, Standard (68-700)	142,430
Deluxe (68-700)	16,010
Tudor Touring Sedan, Standard (68-700)	160,502
Deluxe (68-700)	104,234
Roadster (68-710)	3,028
Coupe (3W) (68-720)	17,630
Fordor Sedan, Standard (68-730)	19,518
Deluxe (68-730)	11,548
Fordor Touring Sedan, Standard (68-730)	35,529
Deluxe (68-730)	120,063
Convertible Sedan (68-740)	5,005
Phaeton (68-750)	3,691
Cabriolet (68-760)	11,274
Club Cabriolet (68-760)	4,647
Coupe (5W), Standard (68-770)	68,437
Deluxe (68-770)	26,004
Sedan Delivery (68-780)	6,648
Station Wagon (68-790)	5,636
Panel Delivery (67-820)	13,502

1935-36 WINDSHIELD WIPER DATA

B = Black Paint C = Chrome Plated R = Rustless Steel

		Housing	Wiper Arm (1)		Blade
Body Style	Wiper Number	Finish*	Length	Finish	Finish (2)
Standard Tudor, Fordor	48-17508-A	None	9½	B	B
and (5W) Coupe			10 (3)	B	B
Deluxe Tudor, Fordor Coupes	48-17508-A	None	9½	C or R	C or R
and Sedan Delivery			10 (3)	C or R	C or R
Roadster and Phaeton	48-17508-C	C	7	C or R	C or R
Convertible Sedan	48-17508-B	C	7	C or R	C or R
Cabriolet	48-17508-B	C	9½	C or R	C or R
			7 (4)	C or R	C or R
Station Wagon	46-17508	None	9½	C or R	C or R
			7 (4)	C or R	C or R
			10 (3)	C or R	C or R
			9¾ (5)	C or R	C or R
Closed Cab and Standard Panel Delivery	50-17508	None	8¼	B	B
Deluxe Panel Delivery	50-17508	None	8½	C or R	C or R

*Mounting was by the threaded shaft sleeve. The shaft on the plain housings were nickel plated; on chrome housings chrome plated. All controls were bright nickel plated.

(1) Wiper Arms 7, 8½ and 9½ inches long were the spring and clip design. All others were stampings and spring steel.

(2) Wiper blades were 8 inches until April 1935, then changed to 8½ inches. Rubber strips were used in 1935 and a molded blade in 1936.

(3) New size released November 1935.

(4) New size released May 1935.

(5) New size released February 1936.

X — The 1937-38 Models

By 1937 the old practice of producing the same model year after year with minor improvements — a system used during the Model T and A years — had been abandoned. Competitive pressure after the depression forced the automobile companies to introduce new passenger car models every year. At Ford, a new passenger car design was introduced every other year while a major face lift was made to that model the following year. Since the 1936 models were a face lift of the 1935's, the 1937 models were all newly designed.

For the first time the closed car bodies were equipped with an all steel top, while all bodies had the luggage compartment built in with access through an outside door. The streamlined styling features included a wedge type grille and split V-type windshield, a styling influence carried over from the novel 1936 Lincoln-Zephyr. In addition, significant improvements were made to the engine and chassis. (See the Engine and Chassis Section for details.) For those desiring better economy, the introduction of the smaller 60 horsepower V-8 was probably the most sensational feature of the 1937 models. Cars with that new engine, previously available in Europe, were an immediate success, and contributed significantly toward making 1937 a good sales year for Ford. Ford outsold Chevrolet on total cars and trucks 945,329 to 941,734, but Chevrolet had a sales edge of 2,087 passenger cars.

Prior to introduction the company announced the following improvements between 1936 and 1937:

New Body Structure — All welded steel construction with steel roof, providing increased strength, rigidity, and a more durable roof. (The 1936 had a welded steel top with a fabric covered roof panel.)

Body Mountings — Body bolts insulated in rubber, insulating chassis noise and providing a quieter body. (Body bolts not insulated on 1936 models.)

Hood — Made with a single hood latch and hinged at the cowl, preventing hood rattles and squeaks. (1936 had a conventional three hinge hood with four latches.)

Spare Wheel Mountings — Inside body at rear, except the Station Wagon. Adds to appearance, and makes car easier to wash and dust. Also provides better protection for spare tire. (Not available on 1936 cars.)

Luggage Compartment — Door on all sedans opens from the bottom edge increasing accessibility. More convenient for large pieces of luggage or bulky articles. (Not available on 1936 cars.)

Seat Adjustment — Seat rises as it is moved forward, providing increased visibility. (Not on 1936 cars.)

Seat Adjustment Lever — Located on left side of seat for more convenience of operation. (Under seat on 1936 cars.)

Instrument Panel Arrangement — Arranged in two groups making them easier to read. (1936 instruments in three groups.)

Provision For Radio Installation — Separate panel, so not necessary to eliminate ash tray. (1936 in ash tray opening.)

Windshield — V-type for better streamlined appearance of car. (1936 had straight windshield.)

Steering Wheel On Standard Type — Two top spokes are widely spaced for increased visibility of instruments. (1936 spokes evenly spaced.)

In addition, all passenger bodies except Roadster and Phaeton had an arm rest on both front doors.

The 1937 passenger cars, while having the same wheel base as 1936, were 3.25 inches longer (179.5 inches overall) and 0.2 inch wider. However, due to the "slant-back" characteristic of the new models, the "greenhouse" area was actually shorter, resulting in an average overall weight reduction of 302 pounds. The body styles offered for 1937 were Standard and Deluxe Tudor; Standard and Deluxe Tudor Touring; Deluxe Roadster; Club Coupe; Standard and Deluxe Fordor; Standard and Deluxe Fordor Touring; Convertible Sedan; Phaeton Touring; Cabriolet; Club Cabriolet; Standard Coupe; and Deluxe Coupe.

Distinguishing features of the standard models were a black grille, body color windshield frame, a single black wiper blade, and single tail light. The deluxe cars could be easily identified by their chrome plated grille and windshield frame, dual wiperblades with bright finish (only one wiper prior to January 1937), and two tail lamps. In addition, the deluxe closed bodies had window curtains while the standards did not (but they were available as special equipment).

In creating the 1938 models, Ford engineers took a new approach to the change over. The 1937 deluxe touring bodies were given a minor face lift in the area of the grille and hood, thus becoming the 1938 standard models. These same bodies with a major face lift consisting of a new grille and hood, became the deluxe line. In addition, the back and rear quarter of the touring sedans were reworked into a fast back style creating the illusion of completely new Deluxe Tudor and Fordor bodies. The wheel base of these new models remained the same, but the overall body length was increased one inch on the standard and eight inches on the deluxe.

Other 1938 differences announced by the company were:

Door Trim Panels, Standard Models — Woodall type embossed board design with carpet at bottom. (No carpet on 1937 models.)

Door Trim Panels, Deluxe Models — Plain pad with vertical metal beads and carpet kick pad. (Woodall type embossed board on 1937 models.)

Cowl Side Panels — Embossed board on standard cars and embossed board with carpet at the bottom, coming to the same height as that on door. (No carpet at bottom of 1937.)

Window Molding (Finish Strip) — Same as 1937 except for color combination rolled section with wainscot panel stamping design welded to same.

Other New Features Not On 1937 Cars — New silent type door locks and striker plates, new instrument board, new lens and finish for dome light, new rubber door opening scuff plates instead of zinc or aluminum. The right hand door arm rest, which was a standard item in 1937, now became available only as an option at extra cost and the back curtain was eliminated.

Five body styles were discontinued after the 1937 production. The slant back Standard and Deluxe Tudor and Fordor Sedans along with the Roadster bodies were eliminated. The standard cars were equipped with a single black windshield wiper blade (changed to bright finish in December 1937), single tail light, and a body colored windshield frame which was changed to bright finish in December 1937. The deluxe models had dual windshield wiper blades brightly finished, and dual tail lights.

At the start of 1938 production, the standard models were

Eight cylinders for smoothness . . . and ECONOMY

MOST people know that eight cylinders make a smoother, quieter, sweeter running engine than any lesser number of cylinders.

But not every one realizes that good design may also make eight cylinders more economical. Ford has proved the fact twice in 1937.

The 85-horsepower Ford V-8 engine — long famous for flashing performance — gives greater gas economy than ever. Owners report averages of 17-21 miles per gallon.

The 60-horsepower Ford V-8 engine — tested for two years in England and France before its American introduction—has established itself as the most economical Ford engine ever built! Careful cost records from owners show averages of 22-27 miles per gallon.

Choose between these modern engines by their power and your purse. Both are built into the same handsome, husky, comfortable car. Both, because of their compact V-type construction, provide extra room for you and your luggage. Both are low priced. In fact, the "60" is available in five standard body types at the lowest Ford price in years!

Ford V-8

trimmed with a pin stripe at the belt line similar to the 1937 cars. However, two months later, on December 29, 1937, an urgent change letter was sent to all assembly plants with instructions to immediately begin using a new rustless steel belt molding. The letter stated in part: *"These standard moldings are now available for shipment and are being expressed or shipped via freight, and are to be used in production at U.S. assembly branches starting 1-3-38. All standard type automobiles shipped by plants starting January 3rd must have these moldings assembled.*

Shipment of hood top and sides, cowls, door and body sides with molding retainer holes incorporated are now going forward to assembly branches. Stock on hand less these holes is to be reworked in accordance with superintendent's letter and sketch 10359."

A follow up letter also made these moldings available upon the request of any owner who had bought an early production car without the molding.

Ford sales in 1938 dropped drastically. Some think it was Henry Ford's reluctance to adapt hydraulic brakes while others point to the unattractive styling of the standard models. The biggest factor, however, was the economic recession of that year which caused the automobile industry to experience its sharpest decline since 1933. Industry wide sales for 1938 were 2,000,985 compared to 3,915,889 for 1937. Ford sales dropped from 945,329 to 363,688.

Exterior Body Colors

Compared with 1936 models, those of 1937 offered a wider range of exterior colors and more customer options. At introduction, three color combinations were used in the regular production of the standard cars, but additional three color combinations were available on special order at extra cost. Customers had an even greater selection in the deluxe models. Seven color combinations were available on regular orders, an eighth color on special order, and four more special spring colors were released in March 1937. During March, approximately one third of the cars were painted with the spring colors. These color combinations were continued into 1938 with minor variations. In addition, these deluxe cars were equipped with factory installed radios and white side wall tires, all at extra cost to buyers.

Wheels and hub cap colors were generally black on standard cars, but at the customer's option, black or body color was on the deluxe cars. All 1937 cars had a single pin stripe at the belt, but in 1938 only the standard cars had a stripe while the deluxe cars were trimmed with a rustless steel belt molding. In January 1938 the stripe on the standard cars was replaced with a rustless steel molding comparable to that on the deluxe cars.

1937-38 STANDARD PASSENGER CAR EXTERIOR COLORS

Body Color	Stripe (1)
Black	Tacoma Cream
Gull Gray (2)	Bright Vermilion
Washington Blue (2)	Tacoma Cream
Coach Maroon Bright*	Gold
Bright Vineyard Green*	Silver
Autumn Brown*	Tacoma Cream

*These colors were for export cars, but also available on U.S. cars as special equipment during 1937 production.

(1) Stripe replaced by rustless steel molding in January 1938.

(2) With these two colors the fenders and tail lights were painted black, but color was available as special equipment.

Wheels and hub caps: Black or color as special equipment.

For a short period, April and May 1937, electric clocks or stem wound clocks were factory installed on all deluxe cars. (See accessory section for details.)

1937 DELUXE PASSENGER CAR SPECIAL SPRING COLORS

Body Color	Stripe, Wheels and Hub Cap
Dalmation Green	Logan Green
Silver Wing Gray	Pomegranate Red
Adobe Tan	Chinese Red
Turquoise Blue	Silver

1937-38 DELUXE PASSENGER CAR EXTERIOR COLORS

Body Color	Stripe (1937 only)
Black	Tacoma Cream
Gull Gray	Bright Vermilion
Washington Blue	Tacoma Cream
Bright Vineyard Green (1)	Silver
Dartmouth Green (1)	None
Wren Building Tan Dark (2)	None
Desert Sand (3)	Bright Vermilion
Coach Maroon Bright	Gold
Washington Blue*	Medium Poppy Red

*Export color, but available for U.S. production as special equipment during 1937 production.

(1) Bright Vineyard Green replaced by Dartmouth Green in March 1938.

(2) Available for 1938 production only.

(3) Used at Richmond and Long Beach plants only.

Wheels and hub caps: Customer option black or color.

1938 DELUXF PASSENGER CAR EASTER COLORS

Body, Wheels and Hub Caps
Avon Blue
Dove Gray

Hood and Fenders

The front end sheet metal for 1937 was all new. The most distinctive lines were those of the wedge type grille, tear-shaped headlights which were molded between the hood and the new highly crowned fenders, and the one piece hood which opened from the front. Long thin horizontal cooling louvers framed by a rustless steel molding extended the wedge shaped styling alongside the hood. The oval Ford nameplate and the V-8 symbol hood ornament were replaced by a rocket style handle which opened the hood from the front. A new arrowhead shaped V-8 ornament, with the Ford script oval as one part of the eight and the horsepower number, either 85 or 60, in the other part of the eight, was located on the right side of the grille. Following the practice of 1936, the finish of the grille was painted black on the standard cars, but was chrome plated on the deluxe. In June 1937, a vertical black shield was placed inside the center bar of the grille to eliminate the "see-through" when viewed from the side.

For 1938, the hood and grille became more massive, but instead of the chrome or paint distinction in the grille, the deluxe passenger cars were restyled with a new grille and hood, while the standard line of bodies simply received a face lift of the 1937 style. In both designs, the grille became part of the

Front end styling of the 1937 passenger car.

The new 1938 deluxe front end.

The 1938 standard front end design, a face-lift of the 1937.

hood and front end sheet metal and, therefore, was painted body color.

On the deluxe grille, the V-8 symbol was incorporated into the center vertical molding and the Ford oval was located on the front edge of the hood. The standard grille also had the Ford oval on the front edge of the hood and above it was the 85 or 60 designation for the engine horsepower. The deluxe hood also had a distinctive arrowhead style V-8 symbol on each side of the hood.

Highly crowned fenders with molded in headlights were part of the styling refinements of the 1937 front end. One type of front fenders was used on all passenger cars, Station Wagon and Sedan Delivery, while three variations were used on the rear — one pair for the Coupe and Roadster bodies, another pair for the slant-back sedans and a third for the touring sedans. However, the Station Wagon and Sedan Delivery continued to use the 1936 fenders. The right hand rear fenders had an additional variation for mounting the dual tail lamps on deluxe cars and the step plate on cars with a rumble seat.

The number of fender variations on the 1938 models was increased, primarily due to the design differences between the standard and deluxe models. The front fenders for the standard models were modified versions of 1937, but those for the deluxe models were redesigned to fit the new style deluxe hood.

With the rear fenders, there were six variations. The Standard Tudor and Fordor Sedan had a reworked 1937 fender, the Deluxe Tudor and Fordor Sedan had a newly designed one, the Coupe and Convertible had a third variation, the Phaeton and Convertible Sedan carried a fourth version, and the Station Wagon had a fifth. The Sedan Delivery, however, continued to use the 1937 fender.

Lights

With the headlights an integral part of the front fenders, the lens and lens door were the only visible portions of the assembly. The lamps were the two light depressed beam type with adjusting screws on each side for right to left movement, and another screw at the top for lowering or raising the beam. The oval shaped clear crystal glass lens was held in place by a rustless steel headlamp door. Light was provided by a prefocused 32-32 CP headlamp bulb introduced in 1935 an used through 1938.

The 1937 lens was modified slightly for use on 1938 models. Even though the two styles looked identical, they were not interchangeable.

The rear lamps were a new bullet shaped design with a short bracket which mounted to the lower part of the fender. The lamp body was made of cold rolled steel while the bracket was a zinc die casting — both painted the same color as the fender. Two sizes of brackets were used. One, 7/8 inch longer than the other, was used on the Convertible Sedan and Phaeton, and the second was used on all other passenger cars. The rear lamp lens, held in place by a rustless steel ring style lens door, was made of high transmission ruby glass. A bull's eye on the inside surface of the lens was surrounded by a 1/8 inch wide cubical prism pattern.

Similar to previous years, the left lamp was standard equipment on all cars, with the right lamp being installed only on the deluxe cars, or on others as special equipment.

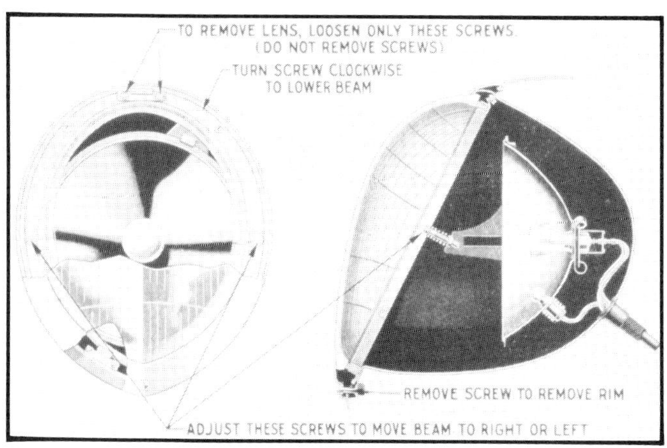

Headlight adjustment.

For 1938, the rear lamps were redesigned as integral parts of the rear fenders. The lamp body was mounted under the fender while a rustless steel rear lamp door held the lens from the outside. All passenger cars were equipped with a right and left rear lamp. With the new design, the license plate bracket, which was mounted on top of the rear lamp in 1937, was moved to the center of the deck lid and made part of the deck handle assembly. The bracket was painted black both years.

Door and Window Regulator Handles

The 1937 exterior door handles were a carry over item from 1936 with the addition of three grooves running the length of the handle. The passenger cars and Sedan Delivery used the same design with variation in shaft length and the shape of the escutcheon plate. The handles were made from one of two materials, rustless steel or bright chrome plated zinc die casting; while the escutcheon plates were made of bright chrome plated brass. On 1938 cars the contour of the handle was retained but the neck of the handle was made thicker to cover the escutcheon mounting screws.

The Station Wagon and other commercial vehicles continued to use the 1936 handles through 1938 with new shaft lengths and escutcheons. A new spearhead style "T" handle with the V-8 symbol embossed on its surface was used on all deck lids and luggage compartment doors during 1937. In 1938, this handle was designed into a new assembly including the license plate bracket and light.

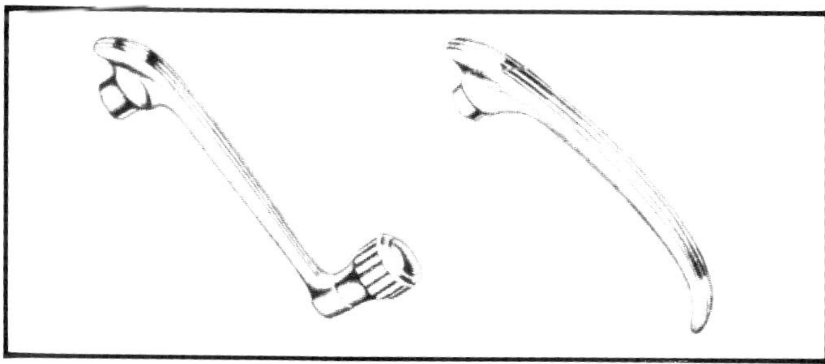

Typical 1937 interior hardware.

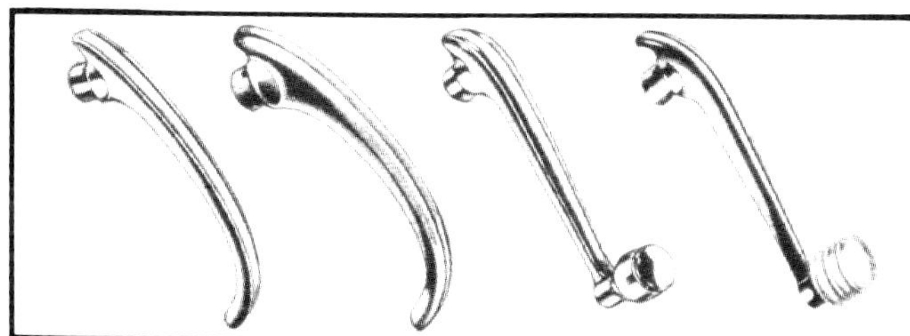

Typical 1938 interior hardware.

The interior door handles and window regulator handles came under the identification of "interior hardware." On the 1937 passenger cars and Sedan Delivery, these items were newly designed, incorporating the three-groove motif of the exterior door handles. Their surface finish was the only distinguishing feature between handles used on the standard body and those used on the deluxe. Bright chrome plating was used on the standard and Rustic Brown Ester coating was used for the deluxe handle. The window regulator handle knob was also chrome plated on the standard bodies, but became Dark Taupe plastic on the deluxe.

These same items, for the Station Wagon and other commercial vehicles, were a carry over from 1936. The Station Wagon hardware was finished in bright chrome, while nickel plating appeared on the commercials.

Except for the Station Wagon, the interior hardware was redesigned for the 1938 models. On the standard and commercial bodies the hardware finish was bright chrome. On the deluxe, it was an Ester dull brass cellulose coating.

Sun Visors

Departing from past policy in 1937, the Company released two sun visors as regular equipment for all passenger cars, Sedan Delivery and Station Wagon. However, in 1938 it reverted back to the former policy of providing two sun visors for the deluxe cars, but only one, on the driver's side, for the standard cars. The second visor, however, was available on special order. On commercial vehicles the visors were special equipment at added cost.

In shape, the visors were identical, but differed with the various interior schemes. On cloth trimmed standard passenger bodies, the visors were covered with headlining cloth and a Brown Taupe or Russet Brown artificial leather binding. Standard passenger car bodies and Sedan Deliveries with artificial leather trim schemes were equipped with visors made of Brown Fine Colonial grain cardboard bound with Brown artificial leather. Visors used on deluxe cars with leather trim schemes were finished with Two-tone Tan Antique surfaced cardboard and a Two-tone Tan artificial leather binding.

The visor hardware consisted of the visor arm bracket, visor arm, visor retaining plug and two corner finish plates. All these items, except the rustless steel corner finish plates were painted to match the trim. The Station Wagon used the carry over 1936 visor equipped with a new design mounting bracket.

For the 1938 standard cars, Engineering released a less expensive "Flock" formed visor cover without binding, but this material proved to the inferior and by May 1938, a change was made reverting back to the Taupe Napped cotton material. An embossed laminated Kraft paper visor for some deluxe cars, however, was successful.

Another design problem arose with the visor mounting bracket on early 1938 production. The mounting holes were not properly located with the result that the visor could not be mounted in a horizontal position with the windshield opening. A fast change letter was sent to the plants in December stating *"Until such time that new stock is received with changes, the rod holding the visor in standard body is to be bent so that the visor is positioned horizontal with the windshield opening.*" The same problem occured on the deluxe bodies even though a new slightly smaller visor had been released.

Floor Mats and Carpets

The front floor mats for all 1937-38 passenger cars, Sedan Deliveries and Station Wagons were made of Benton Gray rubber with the same border pattern as the 1936 mats. Mats for all other vehicles were made of black rubber. One size mat was installed in all vehicles except the Convertible Sedan, Sedan Delivery, Station Wagon and commercial vehicles each of which had individual unique sizes.

The rear compartment mat, rear seat heelboard, front seat foot rest, etc., for the sedans and Club Coupe were made of Brown carpet with a binding to match the trim scheme. Of two qualities used, the better carpet was installed in the deluxe bodies. A cloth binding was used on this, but an artificial leather binding was used on the standard body.

The rear floor mat for the Phaeton as well as the rear deck mat for the Roadster and Cabriolet were made of Benton Gray rubber matching the front.

Instrument Panel and Finish Strips

The inside frames around the door windows, quarter windows, back window and windshield opening came under the heading of finish strips. These parts and the instrument panel had the same finish — Mahogany Grain for the standard cars and Sedan Delivery, and American Walnut Grain for the deluxe cars and Station Wagon. On the commercial vehicles, these items were painted with black enamel. The rear window frame on the open models was not part of the finish strips, but was bright chrome plated on the outside and painted Desert Sand on the inside.

The 1937 Deluxe Coupe, Tudor and Fordor bodies, in addition, had garnish panels on the doors with a dark Taupe plastic inlay. In 1938, these garnish panels were made an integral part of the finish strip with an Oyster Gray plastic insert. The finish strips and instrument panel for the 1938 standard models were Burl Mahogany Grain, while on the deluxe models the finish was straight Walnut Grain.

A 1937 Standard Tudor Sedan. The V-8 grille ornament was installed only on the right side on all cars.

Tudor (74-700, 78-700, 81A-700, 82A-700)
Standard, Deluxe and Touring

As with previous years, the Tudor body style was the basic body for the 1937-38 models, and any of its parts which were used on other body styles retained the Tudor part number. Although four body styles were produced in 1937, there were only two in 1938.

The four 1937 body styles were the Standard and Deluxe Tudor (slant-back), and the Standard and Deluxe Touring Tudor (with trunk). All were equipped with an adjustable front seat, glove box, pair of sun visors, dome lamp, front and rear arm rests, ash tray, and rear window curtain. In ad-

A preproduction 1937 Deluxe Tudor. On regular production a rustless steel strip was added on the side of the running board.

The 1937 Deluxe Tudor Touring Sedan. The bumper guards were regular production items on all body styles; dual windshield wipers were installed on deluxe models starting January 1937; white wall tires were at extra cost.

The 1937 Deluxe Tudor Touring. Note the "see-through" characteristic of the grille, a condition eliminated in June 1937 by the addition of a black shield behind the grille.

The 1938 Standard Tudor Sedan. The chrome windshield frame became a standard item in December 1937 while the belt molding was added in January 1938. Also, note the folded radio antenna.

The 1938 Deluxe Tudor Sedan showing the new grille, hood, fender and the fast-back styling of the body.

A preproduction 1937 Deluxe Tudor interior. On production cars the front floor mat was made of rubber.

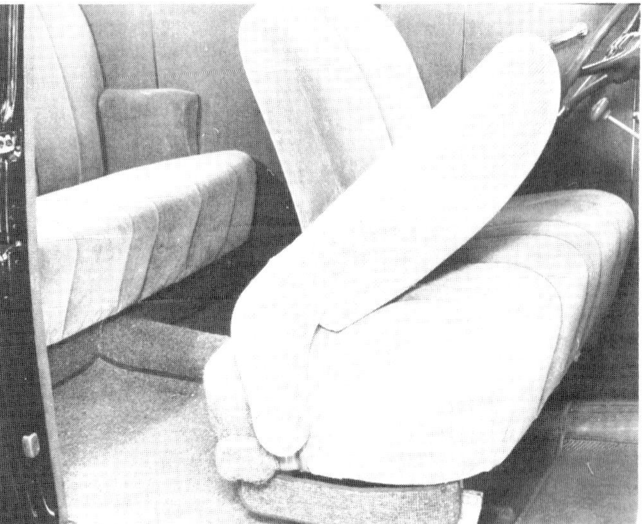

Typical 1938 Standard Tudor interior.

dition to these items, the deluxe body had garnish panels on the door and quarter windows. The main difference between the standard and deluxe cars was the superior quality of upholstering material installed in the deluxe bodies.

Other than the exterior styling changes of the sheet metal, there were minor interior differences between the 1937 and 1938 models. One such difference was the availability of only one sun visor on the standard and one arm rest (driver's side) in the front compartment of both body styles. A single pin stripe, just below the belt line, was applied to both the deluxe

Interior of a 1938 Deluxe Tudor Sedan.

and standard models through the 1937 production. In 1938, only the standard had a stripe, but just until January 1938. This stripe began at the corner of the grille, followed the belt line to the rear corner of the body, and then around the bottom of the trunk opening.

Shipping weight of the 1937 standard body with the 85 HP engine was 2,728 pounds, but only 2,513 pounds with the smaller 60 HP engine.

1937 STANDARD TUDOR SEDAN AND STANDARD TUDOR TOURING SEDAN INTERIOR TRIM SCHEMES

Two-tone Taupe Mohair

Seats, door panels, quarter, arm rests, door pillar, quarter pillar: Two-tone Taupe Mohair.
Headlining, windshield header: Taupe Napped Cotton.
Visors: Taupe Napped Cotton with Brown Taupe or Russet Brown Artificial Leather Binding.
Rear seat back upper, package tray: Gray Brown Fine Colonial Grain Cardboard with Brown Taupe Fine Colonial Grain Artificial Leather Binding.
Windlace: Two-tone Taupe Worsted Cloth.
Rear window curtain: Brown Poplin.

Two-tone Taupe Bark Cord

Seats, door panels, quarter, arm rests, door pillar, quarter pillar: Two-tone Taupe Bark Cord.
Headlining, windshield header: Taupe Napped Cotton.
Visors: Taupe Napped Cotton with Brown Taupe or Russet Brown Artificial Leather Binding.
Rear seat back upper, package tray: Gray Brown Fine Colonial Grain Cardboard with Brown Taupe Fine Colonial Grain Artificial Leather Binding.
Windlace: Two-tone Taupe Worsted Cloth.
Rear window curtain: Brown Poplin.

Two-tone Tan Antique Finish Leather

Seats, door panels, quarter, arm rests, door pillar, quarter pillar, headlining, windlace, windshield header: Two-tone Tan Antique Finish Leather.
Visors: Brown Fine Colonial Grain Cardboard with Brown Fine Colonial Grain Artificial Leather Binding.
Rear seat back upper, package tray: Two-tone Tan Colonial Grain Cardboard with Two-tone Tan Fine Colonial Grain Artificial Leather Binding.
Package tray (74 Model): Brown Fine Colonial Grain Cardboard with Brown Fine Colonial Grain Artificial Leather Binding.
Rear window curtain: Tan Pyroxylin.

Items which were identical on each trim scheme

Cowl panels, glove compartment door interior: Gray Brown Fine Colonial Grain Cardboard.
Front floor: Benton Gray Rubber.
Rear floor, rear seat heelboard: Brown Carpet.
Luggage compartment: Black Morocco Grain Cardboard.
Escutcheons (inside door handle and window regulator handle): Brass, Bright Chrome Plate.
Window regulator handle and knob, inside door handle, glove compartment door handle, windshield regulator handle, windshield regulator handle gromet: Bright Chrome Plate.
Front seat adjuster handle: Bright Nickel Plate.
Ash tray knob: Dark Taupe Plastic.
Finish strips, glove compartment door, instrument panel, etc.: Mahogany Grain.
Rear window curtain brackets: Russet Brown Paint.
Windshield frame: Painted body color.
Door scuff plate: Zinc or Aluminum Basketweave all over.

1937 DELUXE TUDOR SEDAN AND DELUXE TUDOR TOURING SEDAN INTERIOR TRIM SCHEMES

Gray Mohair

Seats, door panels, quarter, arm rests, door pillar, quarter pillar: Gray Mohair.
Headlining, windshield header: Gray Napped Cotton.
Visors: Gray Napped Cotton with Brown Taupe or Russet Brown Artificial Leather Binding.
Rear seat back upper, package tray: Gray Brown Fine Colonial Grain Cardboard with Brown Taupe Fine Colonial Grain Artificial Leather Binding.
Windlace: Gray Worsted Cloth.
Rear curtain with tab: Brown Poplin.
Assist loop: Gray Worsted Cloth with Brown Taupe Colonial Grain Artificial Leather Binding.

Gray Flat Wale Cord

Seats, door panels, quarter, arm rests, door pillar, quarter pillar: Gray Flat Wale Cord.
Headlining, windshield header: Gray Napped Cotton.
Visors: Gray Napped Cotton with Brown Taupe or Russet Brown Artificial Leather Binding.
Rear seat back upper, package tray: Gray Brown Fine Colonial Grain Cardboard with Brown Taupe Fine Colonial Grain Artificial Leather Binding.
Windlace: Gray Worsted Cloth.
Rear window curtain with tab: Brown Poplin.
Assist loop: Gray Worsted Cloth with Brown Taupe Colonial Grain Artificial Leather Binding.

Two-tone Tan Antique Finish Leather

Seats, door panels, quarter, arm rests, door pillar, quarter pillar, headlining, windlace, assist loop, windshield header: Two-tone Tan Antique Finish Leather.
Visors: Two-tone Tan Antique Finish Cardboard with Two-tone Tan Fine Colonial Grain Artificial Leather Binding.
Rear seat back upper, package tray: Two-tone Tan Colonial Grain Cardboard with Two-tone Tan Fine Colonial Grain Artificial Leather Binding.
Rear window curtain with tab: Tan Pyroxylin.

Items which were identical on each trim scheme

Front floor: Benton Gray Rubber.
Rear floor, door bottom, rear seat heelboard: Brown Carpet.
Cowl panel: Gray Brown Fine Colonial Grain Cardboard.
Glove compartment door interior: Brown or Taupe Napped Cotton.
Luggage compartment: Black Morocco Grain Cardboard.
Escutcheons (inside door handle and window regulator handle), window regulator knob, ash tray knob, door and quarter window garnish inlay: Dark Taupe Plastic.
Window regulator handle, inside door handle: Ester Coated Rustic Brown.
Windshield frame, glove compartment door handle, windshield regulator handle, windshield regulator handle gromet: Bright Chrome Plate.
Front seat adjuster handle: Bright Nickel Plate.
Finish strips, glove compartment door, instrument panel, door and quarter window garnish panel, etc: American Walnut Grain.
Rear window curtain brackets: Russet Brown Paint.
Door scuff plate: Zinc or Aluminum, V8 in circle, Background Starburst.

1938 STANDARD TUDOR SEDAN INTERIOR TRIM SCHEMES

Two-tone Taupe Boucle

Seats, door panels, quarter, arm rests, door pillar: Two-tone Taupe Boucle.
Headlining: Taupe Napped Cotton.
Visor: Natural Flock, changed to Taupe Napped Cotton with Brown Taupe or Russet Brown Artificial Leather Binding in May 1938.
Windlace: Two-tone Taupe Worsted Cloth.
Package tray: Gray Brown Fine Colonial Grain Cardboard with Brown Taupe Fine Colonial Grain Artificial Leather Binding.

Brown Striped Mohair

Seats, door panel, quarter, arm rests, door pillar: Brown Striped Mohair.
Headlining: Taupe Napped Cotton.
Visor: Natural Flock, changed to Taupe Napped Cotton with Brown Taupe or Russet Brown Artificial Leather Binding in May 1938.
Windlace: Two-tone Taupe Worsted Cloth.
Package tray: Gray Brown Fine Colonial Grain Cardboard with Brown Taupe Fine Colonial Grain Artificial Leather Binding.

Two-tone Tan Antique Finish Leather

Seats, door panel, quarter, arm rests, door pillar, headlining, windlace: Two-tone Tan Antique Finish Leather.
Visor: Brown Fine Colonial Grain Embossed Kraft Paper, changed to Tan Fine Colonial Grain Cardboard in December 1937.
Package tray: Two-tone Tan Fine Colonial Grain Cardboard with Two-tone Tan Fine Colonial Grain Artificial Leather Binding.

Two-tone Taupe Mohair (with Job-one to use stock on hand)
Seats, door panel, quarter, arm rests, door pillar: Two-tone Taupe Mohair.
Headlining: Taupe Napped Cotton.
Visor: Natural Flock.
Windlace: Two-tone Taupe Worsted Cloth.
Package tray: Gray Brown Fine Colonial Grain Cardboard with Brown Taupe Fine Colonial Grain Artificial Leather Binding.

Brown Broken Stripe Mohair (with Job-one to use stock on hand)
Seats, door panel, quarter, arm rests, door pillar: Brown Broken Stripe Mohair.
Headlining: Taupe Napped Cotton.
Visor: Natural Flock.
Windlace: Two-tone Taupe Worsted Cloth.
Package tray: Gray Brown Fine Colonial Grain Cardboard with Brown Taupe Fine Colonial Grain Artificial Leather Binding.

Items which were identical on each trim scheme
Front floor: Benton Gray Rubber.
Rear floor, door bottom, rear seat heelboard: Brown Carpet.
Cowl panel: Gray Brown Fine Colonial Grain Cardboard.
Luggage compartment: Black Morocco Grain Cardboard.
Escutcheons (inside door handle and window regulator handle): Brass, Bright Chrome Plate.
Window regulator handle and knob, inside door handle, glove compartment door knob, windshield regulator handle: Bright Chrome Plate.
Windshield regulator handle gromet: Bright Chrome Plate, changed to Bright Nickel Plated in June 1938.
Front seat adjuster handle: Black Paint.
Ash tray knob: Oyster Gray Plastic.
Finish strips, instrument panel, etc.: Burl Mahogany Grain.
Windshield frame: Painted body color, changed to Bright Chrome Plate December 1937.

1938 DELUXE TUDOR SEDAN INTERIOR TRIM SCHEMES

Gray Mohair
Seats, door panels, quarter, arm rests, door pillar, package tray: Gray Mohair.
Headlining: Gray Napped Cotton.
Visors: Gray Napped Cotton with Russet Brown Artificial Leather Binding changed to 1937 design in May 1938.
Windlace: Gray Worsted Cloth.
Assist loop: Gray Worsted Cloth with Brown Taupe Fine Colonial Grain Artificial Leather Binding.

Gray Flat Wale Cord
Seats, arm rests: Gray Flat Wale Cord.
Door panels, quarter, door pillar, front seat back: Gray Broadcloth.
Headlining: Gray Napped Cotton.
Visors: Gray Napped Cotton with Russet Brown Artificial Leather Binding changed to 1937 design in May 1938.
Windlace: Gray Worsted Cloth.
Package tray: Gray Mohair.
Assist loop: Gray Worsted Cloth with Brown Taupe Fine Colonial Grain Artificial Leather Binding.

Two-tone Tan Antique Finish Leather
Seats, door panels, quarter, arm rests, door pillar, headlining, windlace, package tray, assist loop: Two-tone Tan Antique Finish Leather.
Visors: Brown Fine Colonial Grain Embossed Kraft Paper, changed to Tan Fine Colonial Grain in December 1937.

Items which were identical on each trim scheme
Front floor: Benton Gray Rubber.
Rear floor, seatside shield, door bottom, rear seat headboard: Brown Carpet.
Cowl panel: Gray Brown Fine Colonial Grain Cardboard.
Luggage compartment: Black Morocco Grain Cardboard.
Escutcheons (inside door handle and window regulator handle), window regulator knob, ash tray knob, window finish strip insert: Oyster Gray Plastic.
Window regulator handle, inside door handle: Cellulose Ester Coated Rich Low Brass.
Windshield frame, glove compartment door knob, windshield regulator handle, windshield regulator handle gromet: Bright Chrome Plate.
Windshield regulator handle gromet: Bright Chrome, changed to Bright Nickel Plate in June 1938.
Front seat adjuster handle: Black Paint.
Finish strips, glove compartment door, instrument panel, etc.: Straight Walnut Grain.

A preproduction Roadster with the running board molding missing. 1937 was the last year for the Roadster body.

Roadster (78-710)

Because of its fixed windshield and post, the 1937 Roadster lost some of its sporty open car look. Sales of this body style were declining while sales of the Cabriolet and Club Cabriolet were on the increase. As a result, the Roadster body style was terminated with the end of 1937 production. The 1937 version came only in the deluxe style — equipped with wind

The production 1937 Roadster. Note the location of the rumble seat step plate on the fender.

wings, adjustable seat, glove box, ash tray, and one interior trim scheme. Its front seat was trimmed with genuine leather while the other components were trimmed with artificial leather. There was one stripe at the belt, identical to the Tudor Sedan.

1937 ROADSTER
INTERIOR TRIM SCHEME

Two-tone Tan Antique Finish Leather

Front seat: Two-tone Tan Antique Finish Leather

Deck seat, door panels, package tray front, windlace, top folding compartment: Two-tone Tan Antique Finish Artificial Leather.

Cowl panels, quarter, package tray bottom, deck side: Two-tone Tan Antique Finish Cardboard.

Top, side curtains: Drab (inside and out) Rubber Interlined Fabric.

Dusthood: Drab Fabric.

Roof bow cover: Drab Cloth.

Front floor mat and rumble seat floor: Benton Gray Rubber.

Escutcheon (inside door handle), ash tray knob: Dark Taupe Plastic.

Inside door handle: Ester Coated Rustic Brown.

Windshield frame, glove compartment door handle: Bright Chrome Plate.

Front seat adjuster handle: Bright Nickel Plate.

Instrument panel, windshield finish strip, etc.: American Walnut Grain.

The 1937 Club Coupe — a new body style for that year. The rear quarter window was the pivot vent type similar to the Fordor.

A 1937 Club Coupe showing the trunk lid and the style of the new trunk lid handle.

Club Coupe (78-720 and 81A-720)

The Club Coupe was a new body style. It featured a rear seat similar to the Club Cabriolet introduced in 1936. Produced only in the deluxe style, its accessories included adjustable front seat, glove box, two visors, front and back arm rests, a dome light, ash tray, door garnish panels, a flip open style quarter window, and rear window curtains (1937 only). Its interior trim schemes consisted of Gray Mohair, Gray Flat Wale Cord and two-tone Tan Antique finish leather. On the outside, a single stripe at the belt was replaced with a rustless steel belt molding for 1938.

The 1938 Club Coupe with a rear seat passenger.

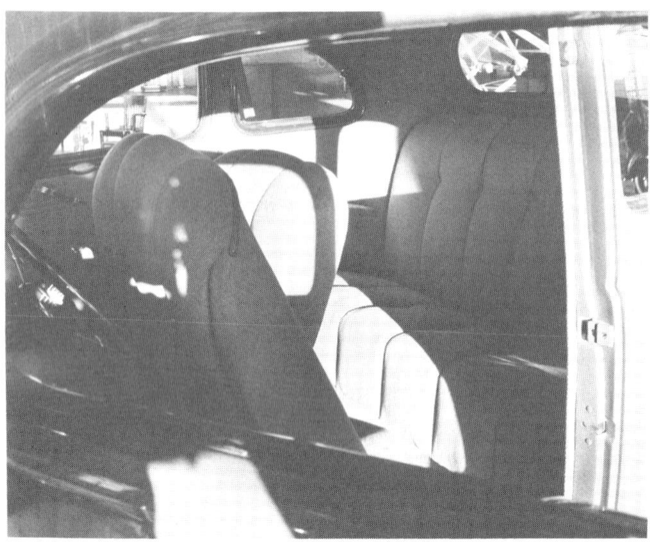

Interior of the 1937 Club Coupe.

1937 CLUB COUPE INTERIOR TRIM SCHEMES

Gray Mohair

Seats, door panels, quarter, arm rests, door pillar, quarter pillar: Gray Mohair.
Headlining, windshield header: Gray Napped Cotton.
Visors: Gray Napped Cotton with Brown Taupe or Russet Brown Antique Leather Binding.
Windlace: Gray Worsted Cloth.
Rear window curtain with tab: Brown Poplin.
Assist loop: Gray Worsted Cloth with Brown Taupe Colonial Grain Artificial Leather Binding.

Gray Flat Wale Cord

Seats, door panels, quarter, arm rests, door pillar, quarter pillar: Gray Flat Wale Cord.
Headlining, windshield header: Gray Napped Cotton.
Visors: Gray Napped Cotton with Brown Taupe or Russet Brown Artificial Leather Binding.
Windlace: Gray Worsted Cloth.
Rear window curtain with tab: Brown Poplin.
Assist loop: Gray Worsted Cloth with Brown Taupe Colonial Grain Artificial Leather Binding.

Two-tone Tan Antique Finish Leather

Seats, door panels, quarter, arm rests, door pillar, quarter pillar, headlining, windshield header, assist loop, windlace: Two-tone Tan Antique Finish Leather.
Visors: Two-tone Tan Antique Finish Cardboard with Two-tone Tan Colonial Grain Artificial Leather Binding.
Rear window curtain with tab: Tan Pyroxylin.

Items which were identical on each trim scheme

Front floor: Benton Gray Rubber.
Rear floor, door bottom, rear seat heelboard: Brown Carpet.
Cowl panels: Gray Brown Fine Colonial Grain Cardboard.
Glove compartment door interior: Brown or Taupe Napped Cotton.
Luggage compartment: Black Morocco Grain Cardboard.
Escutcheons (inside door handle and window regulator handle), window regulator knob, ash tray knob, door garnish inlay: Dark Taupe Plastic.
Window regulator handle, inside door handle: Ester Coated Rustic Brown.
Windshield frame, glove compartment door handle, windshield regulator handle, windshield regulator handle gromet, quarter window handle: Bright Chrome Plate.
Front seat adjuster handle: Bright Nickel Plate.
Finish strips, glove compartment door, instrument panel, door garnish panel, etc.: American Walnut Grain.
Rear window curtain brackets: Russet Brown Paint.
Door scuff plate: Zinc or Aluminum, V8 in circle, Background Starburst.

1938 CLUB COUPE INTERIOR TRIM SCHEMES

Gray Mohair

Seats, door panels, quarter, arm rests, door pillar, quarter pillar: Gray Mohair.
Headlining: Gray Napped Cotton.
Visors: Gray Napped Cotton with Russet Brown Artificial Leather Binding changed to 1937 design in May 1938.
Windlace: Gray Worsted Cloth.
Assist loop: Gray Worsted Cloth with Brown Taupe Fine Colonial Grain Artificial Leather Binding.

Gray Flat Wale Cord

Seats, arm rests: Gray Flat Wale Cord.
Door panel, quarter, door pillar, quarter pillar, front door back: Gray Broadcloth.
Headlining: Gray Napped Cotton.
Visors: Gray Napped Cotton with Russet Brown Artificial Leather Binding, changed to 1937 design in May 1938.
Windlace: Gray Worsted Cloth.
Assist loop: Gray Worsted Cloth with Brown Taupe Fine Colonial Grain Artificial Leather Binding.

Two-tone Tan Antique Finish Leather

Seats, door panels, quarter, arm rests, door pillar, quarter pillar, headlining, windlace, assist loop: Two-tone Tan Antique Finish Leather.
Visors: Brown Fine Colonial Grain Embossed Kraft Paper, changed to Tan Fine Colonial Grain in December 1937.

Items which were identical on each trim scheme

Front floor: Benton Gray Rubber.
Rear floor, seat side shield, door bottom, rear seat heelboard: Brown Carpet.
Cowl panel: Gray Brown Fine Colonial Grain Cardboard.
Luggage compartment: Black Morocco Grain Cardboard.
Escutcheons (inside door handle and window regulator handle), window regulator knob, ash tray knob, window finish strip insert: Oyster Gray Plastic.
Window regulator handle, inside door handle: Cellulose Ester Coated Rich Dull Brass.
Windshield frame, glove compartment door knob, windshield regulator handle, windshield regulator gromet, quarter window handle: Bright Chrome Plate.
Windshield regulator handle gromet: Bright Chrome, changed to Bright Nickel Plate in June 1938.
Front seat adjuster handle: Black Paint.
Finish strips, glove compartment door, instrument panel, etc.: Straight Walnut Grain.

The 1937 Deluxe Fordor Sedan.

Rear view of the 1937 Deluxe Fordor showing the rear tire and luggage space.

Fordor (74-730, 78-730, 81A-730, 82A-730)
Standard, Deluxe and Touring

Similar to the Tudor, four body styles of the Fordor Sedan were produced in 1937, but only two in 1938. Each came equipped with an adjustable front seat, glove box, a pair of sun visors, dome lamp, front and rear arm rests, ash tray and rear window curtain. The deluxe bodies had the additional garnish panels on the door and quarter windows.

A 1937 Fordor Touring Sedan.

Left side of the 1937 Fordor Touring Sedan. Note that on this car, the sheet metal baffle behind the grille has been installed, eliminating the "see-through" characteristic.

Only one sun visor and one arm rest were provided for the 1938 standard cars, while the deluxe cars had two visors, but one arm rest in front. The use of the rear window curtain was discontinued on both body styles.

The body striping pattern precisely followed that of the Tudor.

An early 1938 Standard Fordor Sedan produced before the belt stripe was replaced with a rustless steel molding strip.

The 1938 Deluxe Fordor Sedan.

Front seat of the 1937 Standard Fordor Sedan.

Rear compartment of the 1938 Deluxe Fordor with the new door panels.

Front seat of the 1937 Deluxe Fordor Sedan.

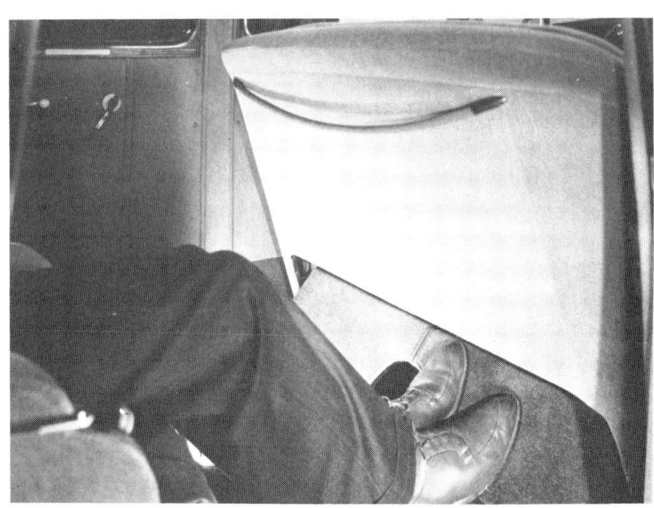

The 1938 rear seat foot rest and robe cord.

Rear compartment of the 1937 Deluxe Fordor Sedan.

1937 STANDARD FORDOR SEDAN AND STANDARD FORDOR TOURING SEDAN INTERIOR TRIM SCHEMES

Two-tone Taupe Mohair

Seats, door panels, quarter, arm rests, door pillar, center pillar, quarter pillar: Two-tone Taupe Mohair.

Headlining, windshield header: Taupe Napped Cotton.

Visors: Taupe Napped Cotton with Brown Taupe or Russet Brown Artificial Leather Binding.

Rear seat back upper, package tray: Gray Brown Fine Colonial Grain Cardboard with Brown Taupe Fine Colonial Grain Artificial Leather Binding.

Windlace: Two-tone Taupe Worsted Cloth.

Rear window curtain: Brown Poplin.

Two-tone Taupe Bark Cord

Seats, door panels, quarter, arm rests, door pillar, center pillar, quarter pillar: Two-tone Taupe Bark Cord.

Headlining, windshield header: Taupe Napped Cotton.

Visors: Taupe Napped Cotton with Brown Taupe or Russet Brown Artificial Leather Binding.

Rear seat back upper, package tray: Gray Brown Fine Colonial Grain Cardboard with Brown Taupe Fine Colonial Grain Artificial Leather Binding.

Windlace: Two-tone Taupe Worsted Cloth.

Rear window curtain: Brown Poplin.

Two-tone Tan Antique Finish Leather

Seats, door panels, quarter, arm rests, door pillar, center pillar, quarter pillar, headlining, windshield header, windlace: Two-tone Tan Antique Finish Leather.

Visors: Brown Fine Colonial Grain Cardboard with Brown Fine Colonial Grain Artificial Leather Binding.

Rear seat back upper, package tray: Two-tone Tan Colonial Cardboard with Two-tone Tan Fine Colonial Grain Artificial Leather Binding.

Package tray (Small Engine 74 Model): Brown Fine Colonial Grain Cardboard with Brown Fine Colonial Grain Artificial Leather Binding.

Rear window curtain: Tan Pyroxylin.

Items which were identical on each trim scheme

Front floor: Benton Gray Rubber.

Rear floor, front seat side, front seat footrest, rear seat heelboard: Brown Carpet.

Cowl panels, glove compartment door interior: Gray Brown Fine Colonial Grain Cardboard.

Luggage compartment: Black Morocco Grain Cardboard.

Escutcheons (inside door handle and window regulator handle): Brass, Bright Chrome Plate.

Window regulator handle and knob, inside door handle, glove compartment door handle, windshield regulator handle, windshield regulator handle gromet: Bright Chrome Plate.

Front seat adjuster handle: Bright Nickel Plate.

Ash tray knob: Dark Taupe Plastic.

Finish strips, glove compartment door, instrument panel, etc.: Mahogany Grain.

Rear window curtain brackets: Russet Brown Paint.

Windshield frame: Painted body color.

Door scuff plate: Zinc or Aluminum Basket Weave all over.

1937 DELUXE FORDOR SEDAN AND DELUXE FORDOR TOURING SEDAN INTERIOR TRIM SCHEMES

Gray Mohair

Seats, door panels, quarter, arm rests, door pillar, center pillar, quarter pillar: Gray Mohair.

Headlining, windshield header: Gray Napped Cotton.

Visors: Gray Napped Cotton with Brown Taupe or Russet Brown Artificial Leather Binding.

Rear seat back upper, package tray: Gray Brown Fine Colonial Grain Cardboard with Brown Taupe Fine Colonial Grain Artificial Leather Binding.

Windlace: Gray Worsted Cloth.

Rear window curtain with tab: Brown Poplin.

Assist loop, cord (robe rail): Gray Worsted Cloth with Brown Taupe Colonial Grain Artificial Leather Binding.

Gray Flat Wale Cord

Seats, door panels, quarter, arm rests, door pillar, center pillar, quarter pillar: Gray Flat Wale Cord.

Headlining, windshield header: Gray Napped Cotton.

Visors: Gray Napped Cotton with Brown Taupe or Russet Brown Artificial Leather Binding.

Rear seat back upper, package tray: Gray Brown Fine Colonial Grain Cardboard with Brown Taupe Fine Colonial Grain Artificial Leather Binding.

Windlace: Gray Worsted Cloth.

Rear window curtain with tab: Brown Poplin.

Assist loop, cord (robe rail): Gray Worsted Cloth with Brown Taupe Colonial Grain Artificial Leather Binding.

Two-tone Tan Antique Finish Leather

Seats, door panel, quarter, arm rests, door pillar, center pillar, quarter pillar, headlining, windshield header, windlace, assist loop, cord (robe rail): Two-tone Tan Antique Finish Leather.

Visors: Two-tone Tan Antique Finish Cardboard with Two-tone Tan Fine Colonial Grain Artificial Leather Binding

Rear seat back upper, package tray: Two-tone Tan Colonial Grain Cardboard with Two-tone Tan Fine Colonial Grain Artificial Leather Binding.

Rear window curtain tab: Tan Pyroxylin.

Items which were identical on each trim scheme

Front floor: Benton Gray Rubber.

Rear floor, door bottom, front seat side, front seat, foot rest, rear seat heelboard: Brown Carpet.

Cowl panels: Gray Brown Fine Colonial Grain Cardboard.

Glove compartment door interior: Brown or Taupe Napped Cotton.

Luggage compartment: Black Morocco Grain Cardboard.

Escutcheons (inside door handle and window regulator handle), window regulator knob, ash tray knob, door garnish inlay: Dark Taupe Plastic.

Window regulator handle, inside door handle: Ester Coated Rustic Brown.

Windshield frame, glove compartment door handle, windshield regulator handle, windshield regulator handle gromet, quarter window glass frame, quarter window handle: Bright Chrome Plate.

Front seat adjuster: Bright Nickel Plate.

Finish strips, glove compartment door, instrument panel, door garnish panel: American Walnut Grain.

Rear window curtain brackets: Russet Brown Paint.

Door scuff plate: Zinc or Aluminum, V8 in circle, Background Starburst.

1938 STANDARD FORDOR SEDAN INTERIOR TRIM SCHEMES

Two-tone Taupe Boucle

Seats, door panels, quarter, arm rests, door pillar, center pillar: Two-tone Taupe Boucle.

Headlining: Taupe Napped Cotton.

Visor: Natural Flock, changed to Taupe Napped with Brown Taupe or Russet Brown Artificial Leather Binding May 1938.

Windlace: Two-tone Taupe Worsted Cloth.

Package tray: Gray Brown Fine Colonial Grain Cardboard with Brown Taupe Fine Colonial Grain Artificial Leather Binding.

Brown Striped Mohair

Seats, door panels, quarter, arm rests, door pillar, center pillar: Brown Striped Mohair.

Headlining: Taupe Napped Cotton.

Visor: Natural Flock, changed to Taupe Napped with Brown Taupe or Russet Brown Artificial Leather Binding in May 1938.

Windlace: Two-tone Taupe Worsted Cloth.

Package tray: Gray Brown Fine Colonial Grain Cardboard with Brown Taupe Fine Colonial Grain Artificial Leather Binding.

Two-tone Tan Antique Finish Leather

Seats, door panels, quarter, arm rests, door pillar, center pillar, headlining, windlace: Two-tone Tan Antique Finish Leather.

Visor: Brown Fine Colonial Grain Embossed Kraft Paper changed to Tan Fine Colonial Grain Cardboard in December 1937.

Package tray: Two-tone Tan Fine Colonial Grain Cardboard with Two-tone Tan Colonial Grain Artificial Leather Binding.

Items which were identical on each trim scheme

Front floor: Benton Gray Rubber.

Rear floor, door bottom, front seat side shield, front seat foot rest, rear seat heelboard: Brown Carpet.

Cowl panels: Gray Brown Fine Colonial Grain Cardboard.

Luggage compartment: Black Morocco Grain Cardboard.

Escutcheons (inside door handle and window regulator handle): Brass, Bright Chrome Plate.

Window regulator handle and knob, inside door handle, glove compartment door knob, windshield regulator handle, windshield regulator handle gromet, quarter glass handle: Bright Chrome Plate.

Windshield regulator handle gromet: Bright Chrome, changed to Bright Nickel Plate in June 1938.

Front seat adjuster handle: Black Paint.

Ash tray knob: Oyster Gray.

Finish strips, instrument panel, etc.: Burl Mahogany Grain.

Windshield frame: Painted body color, changed to Chrome Plate in December 1937.

1938 DELUXE FORDOR SEDAN INTERIOR TRIM SCHEMES

Gray Mohair

Seats, door panels, quarter, arm rests, door pillar, center pillar, front seat back package tray: Gray Mohair.

Headlining: Gray Napped Cotton.

Visors: Gray Napped Cotton with Russet Brown Artificial Leather Binding, changed to 1937 design in May 1938.

Windlace: Gray Worsted Cloth.

Assist loop, cord (robe rail): Gray Worsted Cloth with Brown Taupe Fine Colonial Grain Artificial Leather Binding.

Gray Flat Wale Cord

Seats, arm rests: Gray Flat Wale Cord.

Door panel, quarter, door pillar, center pillar, front seat back: Gray Broadcloth.

Headlining: Gray Napped Cotton.

Visors: Gray Napped Cotton with Russet Brown Artificial Leather Binding, changed to 1937 design in May 1938.

Windlace: Gray Worsted Cloth.

Package tray: Gray Mohair.

Assist loop, cord (robe rail): Gray Worsted Cloth with Brown Taupe Fine Colonial Grain Artificial Leather Binding.

Two-tone Tan Antique Finish Leather

Seats, door panel, quarter, arm rests, door pillar, center pillar, headlining, windlace, package tray, assist loop, cord (robe rail): Two-tone Tan Antique Finish Leather.

Visors: Brown Fine Colonial Grain Embossed Kraft Paper, changed to Tan Fine Colonial Grain in December 1937.

Items which were identical on each trim scheme

Front floor: Benton Gray Rubber.

Rear floor, front seat side shield, front seat, foot rest, rear seat heelboard, door bottom: Brown Carpet.

Cowl panel: Gray Brown Fine Colonial Grain Cardboard.

Luggage compartment: Black Morocco Grain Cardboard.

Escutcheons (inside door handle and window regulator handle), window regulator knob, ash tray knob, window finish strip insert: Oyster Gray Plastic.

Window regulator handle, inside door handle: Cellulose Ester Coated Rich Low Brass.

Windshield frame, glove compartment door knob, windshield regulator handle, windshield regulator handle gromet, quarter glass handle: Bright Chrome Plate.

Windshield regulator handle gromet: Bright Chrome, changed to Bright Nickel Plate in June 1938.

Front seat adjuster handle: Black Paint.

Finish strips, glove compartment door, instrument panel, etc.: Straight Walnut Grain.

The 1937 Convertible Sedan with top down.

A 1937 Convertible Sedan with top up showing the chrome plated frame around the door glass and the removable center pillar panel.

Convertible Sedan (78-740, 81A-740)

The 1937-38 Convertible Sedan body was identical to that first introduced in 1936. It had a fully collapsible top made of drab interlined fabric, roll down windows, and all the deluxe features of the closed cars. Two interior trim schemes were available — Gray Taupe Bedford Cord or Two-tone Tan Antique finish leather. The 1938 Bedford Cord, though identical in styling to that of 1937, was upgraded in quality.

Shipping weight of the 1938 Convertible Sedan was 2,986 pounds, an increase of 13 pounds over the 1937 style.

The 1938 Convertible Sedan. Compare the fender style to those of 1937.

The 1938 Convertible Sedan with top down.

1937 CONVERTIBLE SEDAN INTERIOR TRIM SCHEMES

Gray Taupe Bedford Cord
Seats, door panels, quarter, arm rests, center pillar: Gray Taupe Bedford Cord.
Windlace: Gray Worsted Cloth.
Cowl panels, folding compartment, quarter belt rail: Gray Brown Colonial Grain Cardboard.
Cord (robe rail): Gray Worsted Cloth with Brown Taupe Colonial Grain Artificial Leather Binding.

Two-tone Tan Antique Finish Leather
Seats, door panel, quarter, arm rests, center pillar: Two-tone Tan Antique Finish Leather.
Front seat back rear, front seat side arm, front seat back bellows, windlace, cord (robe rail): Two-tone Tan Antique Finish Artificial Leather.
Cowl panels, folding compartment, quarter belt rail: Two-tone Tan Antique Finish Cardboard.

Items which were identical on each trim scheme
Front floor: Benton Gray Rubber.
Rear floor, front seat footrest, rear seat heelboard: Brown Carpet.
Top: Drab (inside and out) Rubber Interlined Fabric.
Dust hood: Drab Fabric.
Roof bow cover: Drab Cloth.
Luggage compartment, rear seat back rear: Black Morocco Grain Cardboard.
Escutcheons (inside door handle and window regulator handle), windshield regulator knob, ash tray knob: Dark Taupe Plastic.
Window regulator handle, inside door handle: Ester Coated Rustic Brown.
Windshield frame, door glass frame, glove compartment door knob: Bright Chrome Plate.
Front seat adjuster handle: Bright Nickel Plate.
Finish strips, instrument panel, etc.: American Walnut Grain.
Door scuff plate: Zinc or Aluminum, V8 in circle, Background Starburst.

1938 CONVERTIBLE SEDAN INTERIOR TRIM SCHEMES

Gray Taupe Bedford Cord
Seats, door panels, quarter, arm rests, center pillar: Gray Taupe Bedford Cord.
Windlace: Gray Worsted Cloth.
Cowl panels, folding compartment, quarter belt rail: Gray Brown Colonial Grain Cardboard.
Cord (robe rail): Gray Worsted Cloth with Brown Taupe Colonial Grain Artificial Leather Binding.

Two-tone Tan Antique Finish Leather
Seats, door panels, quarter, arm rests, center pillar: Two-tone Tan Antique Finish Leather.
Front seat back rear, front seat side arm, front seat back bellows, windlace, cord (robe rail): Two-tone Tan Antique Finish Artificial Leather.
Cowl panels, folding compartment, quarter belt rail: Two-tone Tan Antique Finish Cardboard.

Items which were identical on each trim scheme
Front floor: Benton Gray Rubber.
Rear floor, front seat foot rest, rear seat heelboard: Brown Carpet.
Top: Drab (inside and out) Rubber Interlined Fabric.
Dust hood: Drab Fabric.
Roof bow cover: Drab Cloth.
Luggage compartment and back of rear seat back: Black Morocco Grain Cardboard.
Escutcheons (inside handle and window regulator handle), window regulator knob, ash tray knob, door garnish insert: Oyster Gray Plastic.
Window regulator handle, inside door handle: Cellulose Ester Coated Rich Dull Brass.
Windshield frame, door glass frame, glove compartment door knob: Bright Chrome Plate.
Front seat adjuster handle: Black Paint.
Instrument panel, finish strips, door garnish, etc.: Straight Walnut Grain.

The 1937 Phaeton. The wind wings were standard items on this model and the Roadster.

Phaeton (78-750, 81A-750)

With its fixed windshield posts and windshield, the 1937 Phaeton became a close facsimile to the Convertible Sedan, but, because of its side curtains, it possessed few of the closed car conveniences. Customer demand for this car dropped drastically during 1938, resulting in the once popular body style being discontinued at the end of that year.

Left side of the 1937 Phaeton. A single stripe at the belt was on the 1937 models only.

The 1938 Phaeton, the last of this body style.

The 1937-38 Phaeton was a deluxe body style, equipped with wind wings, adjustable front seat, glove box, ash tray, dust hood, and a leather interior trim scheme. The seats were trimmed with genuine leather while other components were trimmed with artificial leather.

Shipping weight with the 85 HP engine was 2,803 pounds in 1937, and 2,851 pounds in 1938.

1937 PHAETON INTERIOR TRIM SCHEME

Two-tone Tan Antique Finish Leather

Seats: Two-tone Tan Antique Finish Leather.

Door panels, quarter, windlace, center pillar, back of front seat back, front seat side arm: Two-tone Tan Antique Finish Artificial Leather.

Cowl panels, rear seat back upper: Two-tone Tan Antique Finish Cardboard.

Top, side curtains: Drab (inside and out) Rubber Interlined Fabric.

Dust hood: Drab Fabric.

Roof bow cover: Drab Cloth.

Front and rear floor: Benton Gray Rubber.

Escutcheons (inside door handle), ash tray knob, etc.: Dark Taupe Plastic.

Inside door handle: Ester Coated Rustic Brown.

Windshield frame, glove compartment handle, etc.: Bright Chrome Plate.

Front seat adjuster handle: Bright Nickel Plate.

Instrument panel, finish strips, etc.: American Walnut Grain.

Luggage compartment: Black Morocco Grain.

1938 PHAETON INTERIOR TRIM SCHEME

Two-tone Tan Antique Finish Leather

Seats: Two-tone Tan Antique Finish Leather.

Door panel, quarter, windlace, center pillar, front seat back rear, front seat side arm: Two-tone Tan Antique Finish Artificial Leather.

Cowl panel, rear seat back upper: Two-tone Tan Antique Finish Cardboard.

Top, side curtains: Drab (inside and out) Rubber Interlined Fabric.

Dust hood: Drab Fabric.

Roof bow cover: Drab Cloth.

Floor front, rear: Benton Gray Rubber.

Escutcheon (inside door handle), ash tray knob, etc.: Oyster Gray Plastic.

Inside door handle: Cellulose Ester Rich Low Brass.

Windshield frame, glove compartment knob, etc.: Bright Chrome Plate.

Front seat adjuster handle: Black Paint.

Instrument panel, finish strip, etc.: Straight Walnut Grain.

Luggage compartment: Black Morocco Grain Cardboard.

The 1937 Cabriolet, available only in the deluxe body style.

Cabriolet and Club Cabriolet (78-760A, 78-760B) Convertible Coupe and Convertible Club Coupe (81A-760A, 81A-760B)

The 1937 Cabriolet and the 1938 Convertible Coupe shared the same one-seat convertible body with rumble seat. Likewise, the 1937 Club Cabriolet and the 1938 Convertible Club Coupe had the same two-seat convertible body, without the rumble seat. The main difference between 1937 and 1938 was the front end sheet metal and fenders. Each came with the deluxe decor, being equipped with adjustable front seat, glove box, ash tray, and one arm rest in the front compartment, with an additional pair of arm rests in the rear of the two-seat models. All had optional Gray Taupe Bedford Cord or two-tone Antique finish genuine leather upholstering. In March 1937, the top slat iron pivot bracket on the belt rail was changed to malleable iron casting.

The 1937 Cabriolet with top down and dust hood installed.

Street scene showing the 1938 Convertible Coupe.

The 1937 Club Cabriolet.

A 1938 Convertible Club Coupe.

Interior view of the 1937 Club Cabriolet.

1937 CABRIOLET INTERIOR TRIM SCHEMES

Gray Taupe Bedford Cord

Seat (front), door arm rests, door panels, seat sideshield, quarter belt rail: Gray Taupe Bedford Cord.
Package tray front, top folding compartment: Gray Taupe Colonial Grain Artificial Leather.
Windlace: Gray Worsted Cloth.
Cowl panels, package tray center: Gray Brown Colonial Grain Cardboard.

Two-tone Tan Antique Finish Leather

Seat (front), door arm rests: Two-tone Tan Antique Finish Leather.
Door panel, seat sideshield, quarter belt rail, package tray front, top folding compartment, windlace: Two-tone Tan Antique Finish Artificial Leather.
Cowl panels, package tray center: Two-tone Tan Antique Finish Cardboard.

Items which were identical on each trim scheme

Deck seat: Two-tone Tan Antique Finish Artificial Leather.
Deck side: Two-tone Tan Antique Finish Cardboard.
Front and deck floor: Benton Gray Rubber.
Roof bow cover: Drab Cloth.
Top: Drab Rubber Interlined Fabric.
Dust hood: Drab Fabric.
Escutcheons (inside door handle and window regulator handle), window regulator knob, ash tray knob: Dark Taupe Plastic.
Window regulator handle, inside door handle: Ester Coated Rustic Brown.
Seat adjuster handle: Bright Nickel Plate.
Instrument panel, finish strips, etc.: American Walnut Grain.
Windshield frame, door glass frame, glove compartment handle: Bright Chrome Plate.
Door scuff plate: Zinc or Aluminum, V8 in circle, Background in Starburst.

1937 CLUB CABRIOLET INTERIOR TRIM SCHEMES

Gray Taupe Bedford Cord

Seats, arm rests, door panel, quarter, rear belt rail: Gray Taupe Bedford Cord.
Top folding compartment: Gray Taupe Colonial Grain Artificial Leather.
Windlace: Gray Worsted Cloth.
Cowl panel: Gray Brown Colonial Grain Cardboard.

Two-tone Tan Antique Finish Leather

Seats, arm rests: Two-tone Tan Antique Finish Leather.
Door panel, quarter, rear belt rail, top folding compartment, windlace: Two-tone Tan Antique Finish Artificial Leather.
Cowl panels: Two-tone Antique Finish Cardboard.

Items which were identical on each trim scheme

Front floor: Benton Gray Rubber.
Rear floor: Brown Carpet.
Top: Drab Rubber Interlined Fabric.
Dust hood: Drab Fabric.
Roof bow cover: Drab Cloth.
Luggage compartment: Black Morocco Grain Cardboard.
Escutcheons (inside door handle and window regulator handle), window regulator knob, ash tray knob: Dark Taupe Plastic.
Window regulator handle and inside door handle: Ester Coated Rustic Brown.
Windshield frame, door glass frame, glove compartment handle: Bright Chrome Plate.
Front seat adjuster handle: Bright Nickel Plate.
Instrument panel, finish strips, etc.: American Walnut Grain.
Door scuff plate: Zinc or Aluminum, V8 in circle, Background Starburst.

1938 CONVERTIBLE COUPE INTERIOR TRIM SCHEMES

Gray Taupe Bedford Cord

Seat, door arm rest (l.h.), door panel, seat side shield: Gray Taupe Bedford Cord.
Top folding compartment: Gray Taupe Colonial Grain Artificial Leather.
Windlace: Gray Worsted Cloth.
Cowl panel, belt rail, package tray, quarter: Gray Brown Colonial Grain Cardboard.

Two-tone Tan Antique Finish Leather

Seat, door arm rest (l.h.): Two-tone Tan Antique Finish Leather.
Door panels, seat sideshield, top folding compartment, windlace: Two-tone Tan Antique Finish Artificial Leather.
Cowl panel, belt rail, package tray, quarter: Two-tone Tan Antique Finish Cardboard.

Items which were identical on each trim scheme

Front and deck floor: Benton Gray Rubber.
Deck seat: Two-tone Tan Antique Finish Artificial Leather.
Deck side: Two-tone Tan Antique Finish Cardboard.
Top: Drab Rubber Interlined Fabric.
Dust hood: Drab Fabric.
Roof bow cover: Drab Cloth.
Escutcheons (inside door handle and window regulator handle), window regulator handle knob, ash tray knob, door garnish insert: Oyster Gray Plastic.
Window regulator handle and inside door handle: Cellulose Ester Coated Rich Low Brass.
Windshield frame, door glass frame, glove compartment door knob: Bright Chrome Plate.
Front seat adjuster handle: Black Paint.
Instrument panel, finish strips, etc.: Straight Walnut Grain.

1938 CONVERTIBLE CLUB COUPE INTERIOR TRIM SCHEMES

Gray Taupe Bedford Cord

Seats, door arm rest (l.h.), quarter arm rests, door panel, quarter, rear belt rail: Gray Taupe Bedford Cord.
Top folding compartment: Gray Taupe Colonial Grain Artificial Leather.
Windlace: Gray Worsted Cloth.
Cowl panels: Gray Brown Colonial Grain Cardboard.

Two-tone Tan Antique Finish Leather

Seats, door arm rest (l.h.), quarter arm rests: Two-tone Tan Antique Finish Leather.
Door panels, quarter, rear belt rail, top folding compartment, windlace: Two-tone Tan Antique Finish Artificial Leather.
Cowl panels: Two-tone Tan Antique Finish Cardboard.

Items which were identical on each trim scheme

Front floor: Benton Gray Rubber.
Rear floor: Brown Carpet.
Top: Drab Rubber Interlined Fabric.
Dust hood: Drab Fabric.
Roof bow cover: Drab Cloth.
Luggage compartment: Black Morocco Grain Cardboard.
Escutcheons (inside door handle and window regulator handle), window regulator handle knob, ash tray knobs, door garnish insert: Oyster Gray Plastic.
Window regulator handle and inside door handle: Cellulose Ester Coated Rich Low Brass.
Windshield frame, door glass frame, glove compartment door knob: Bright Chrome Plate.
Front seat adjuster handle: Black Paint.
Instrument panel, finish strips, etc.: Straight Walnut Grain.

A preproduction 1937 Deluxe Five Window Coupe. The running board molding was added to the production model.

The 1937 Standard Five Window Coupe.

Five Window Coupe (74-770, 78-770, 81A-770, 82A-770) Standard and Deluxe

A very popular body style, especially with salesmen, the five window Coupe was available in both the standard and deluxe version. Both 1937 styles were equipped with an adjustable front seat, glove box, two sun visors, two arm rests, dome lamp and a rear window curtain. In addition, the deluxe model had window garnish panels. These same items

The dual tail lamps identify this car as the deluxe model. The rumble seat was no longer available with this body style.

A Standard Five Window Coupe with the 1938 grille and hood.

were carried over into 1938, but only one sun visor on the standard and one arm rest (driver's side) was installed on both models. The most distinguishing feature of the standard and deluxe cars was the individualized treatment of the grille and front end sheet metal.

In February 1937, the spare wheel stowage behind the driver's seat was moved to the floor of the luggage compartment. At the same time, the two-piece seat back in the Deluxe Coupe was redesigned to a one-piece seat.

The 1938 Deluxe Five Window Coupe.

The new 1937 Pickup Coupe — a semi-commercial body introduced in March 1937.

In March 1937, a special slip-on pickup box was released to fit into the luggage compartment of the Standard Coupe body, as a factory installation. With this arrangement, the deck door was not supplied and the spare tire was moved back to its original position behind the driver's seat. In 1938, this body style was assigned body type number 770C.

1937 STANDARD (5W) COUPE INTERIOR TRIM SCHEMES

Two-tone Taupe Mohair

Seat, door panels, quarter, door arm rests, door pillar, quarter pillar, seat bellows, spare wheel cover: Two-tone Taupe Mohair.

Headlining, windshield header: Taupe Napped Cotton.

Visors: Taupe Napped Cotton with Brown Taupe or Russet Brown Artificial Leather Binding.

Windlace: Two-tone Taupe Worsted Cloth.

Rear window curtain: Brown Poplin.

Two-tone Taupe Bark Cord

Seat, door panel, quarter, door arm rests, door pillar, quarter pillar, seat bellows, spare wheel cover: Two-tone Taupe Bark Cord.

Headlining, windshield header: Taupe Napped Cotton.

Visors: Taupe Napped Cotton with Brown Taupe or Russet Brown Artificial Leather Binding.

Windlace: Two-tone Taupe Worsted Cloth.

Rear window curtain: Brown Poplin.

Two-tone Tan Antique Finish Leather

Seat, door panel, quarter, door arm rests, door pillar, quarter pillar, seat bellows, spare wheel cover, headlining, windshield header, windlace: Two-tone Tan Antique Finish Leather.

Seat bellows, seat side arm (small engine 74 model): Two-tone Tan Antique Finish Artificial Leather.

Visors: Brown Fine Colonial Grain Cardboard with Brown Fine Colonial Grain Artificial Leather Binding.

Rear window curtain: Tan Pyroxylin.

Items which were identical on each trim scheme

Floor: Benton Gray Rubber.

Cowl panels, glove compartment door interior: Gray Brown Fine Colonial Grain Cardboard.

Luggage compartment: Black Morocco Grain Cardboard.

Escutcheons (inside door handle and window regulator handle): Brass, Bright Chrome Plate.

Window regulator handle and knob, inside door handle, glove compartment door handle, windshield regulator handle, windshield regulator handle gromet: Bright Chrome Plate.

Front seat adjuster handle: Bright Nickel Plate.

Ash tray knob: Dark Taupe Plastic.

Instrument panel, finish strips, glove compartment door, etc.: Mahogany Grain.

Rear window curtain brackets: Russet Brown Paint.

Windshield frame: Painted body color.

Door scuff plate: Zinc or Aluminum Basket Weave all over.

1937 DELUXE (5W) COUPE INTERIOR TRIM SCHEMES

Gray Mohair

Seat, door panels, quarter, door arm rests, door pillar, quarter pillar, spare wheel cover, seat bellows: Gray Mohair.

Headlining, windshield header: Gray Napped Cotton.

Visors: Gray Napped Cotton with Brown Taupe or Russet Brown Artificial Leather Binding.

Windlace: Gray Worsted Cloth.

Rear window curtain with tab: Brown Poplin.

Gray Flat Wale Cord

Seat, door panels, quarter, door arm rests, door pillar, quarter pillar, spare wheel cover, seat bellows: Gray Flat Wale Cord.

Headlining, windshield header: Gray Napped Cotton.

Visors: Gray Napped Cotton with Brown Taupe or Russet Brown Artificial Leather Binding.

Windlace: Gray Worsted Cloth.

Rear window curtain with tab: Brown Poplin.

Two-tone Tan Antique Finish Leather

Seat, door panels, quarter, door arm rests, door pillar, quarter pillar, spare wheel cover, seat bellows, headlining, windshield header, windlace: Two-tone Tan Antique Finish Leather.

Visors: Two-tone Tan Antique Finish Cardboard with Two-tone Tan Fine Colonial Grain Artificial Leather Binding.

Rear window curtain with tab: Tan Pyroxylin.

Items which were identical on each trim scheme

Floor: Benton Gray Rubber.

Cowl panels: Gray Brown Fine Colonial Grain Cardboard.

Glove compartment door interior: Brown or Taupe Napped Cotton.

Luggage compartment: Black Morocco Grain Cardboard.

Escutcheons (inside door handle and window regulator handle), window regulator knob, ash tray knob, door garnish inlay: Dark Taupe Plastic.

Window regulator handle, inside door handle: Ester Coated Rustic Brown.

Windshield frame, glove compartment door handle, windshield regulator handle, windshield regulator handle gromet: Bright Chrome Plate.

Front seat adjuster handle: Bright Nickel Plate.

Instrument panel, finish strips, glove compartment door, door garnish panel: American Walnut Grain.

Rear window curtain brackets: Russet Brown Paint.

Door scuff plate: Zinc or Aluminum, V8 circle, Background Starburst.

1938 STANDARD (5W) COUPE INTERIOR TRIM SCHEMES

Two-tone Taupe Boucle

Seat, door panels, door arm rest (l.h.), quarter, door pillar, quarter pillar, seat bellows, seat side arm: Two-tone Taupe Boucle.

Headlining: Taupe Napped Cotton.

Visor: Natural Flock changed to Taupe Napped Cotton with Brown Taupe or Russet Brown Artificial Leather Binding in May 1938.

Windlace: Two-tone Taupe Worsted Cloth.

Package tray: Gray Brown Fine Colonial Grain Cardboard with Brown Taupe Fine Colonial Grain Artificial Leather Binding.

Brown Striped Mohair

Seat, door panels, door arm rest (l.h.), quarter, door pillar, quarter pillar, seat bellows, seat side arm: Brown Striped Mohair.

Headlining: Taupe Napped Cotton.

Visor: Natural Flock changed to Taupe Napped Cotton with Brown Taupe or Russet Brown Artificial Leather Binding in May 1938.

Windlace: Two-tone Taupe Worsted Cloth.

Package tray: Gray Brown Fine Colonial Grain Cardboard with Brown Taupe Fine Colonial Grain Artificial Leather Binding.

Two-tone Tan Antique Finish Leather

Seat, door panel, door arm rest (l.h.), quarter, door pillar, quarter pillar, seat bellows, seat side arm, headlining, windlace: Two-tone Tan Antique Finish Leather.

Visor: Brown Fine Colonial Grain Embossed Kraft Paper changed to Tan Fine Colonial Grain Cardboard in December 1937.

Package tray: Two-tone Tan Fine Colonial Grain Cardboard with Two-tone Tan Fine Colonial Grain Artificial Leather Binding.

Items which were identical on each trim scheme

Floor: Benton Gray Rubber.

Cowl panels: Gray Brown Fine Colonial Grain Cardboard.

Luggage compartment: Black Morocco Grain Cardboard.

Escutcheons (inside door handle and window regulator handle): Brass, Bright Chrome Plate.

Window regulator handle and knob, indoor handle, glove compartment door knob, windshield regulator handle: Bright Chrome Plate.

Windshield regulator handle gromet: Chrome Plated, changed to Bright Nickel Plate in June 1938.

Front seat adjuster handle: Black Paint.

Ash tray knob: Oyster Gray Plastic.

Instrument panel, finish strips, etc.: Burl Mahogany Grain.

Windshield frame: Painted to match body until December 1937, then changed to Chrome Plate.

1938 DELUXE (5W) COUPE INTERIOR TRIM SCHEMES

Gray Mohair

Seat, door arm rest (l.h.), door panels, quarter, door pillar, quarter pillar, seat bellows, seat side arm, package tray: Gray Mohair.

Headlining: Gray Napped Cotton.

Visor: Gray Napped Cotton with Russet Brown Artificial Leather Binding changed to 1937 design in May 1938.

Windlace: Gray Worsted Cloth.

Gray Flat Wale Cord

Seat, door arm rest (l.h.): Gray Flat Wale Cord.

Door panels, quarter, door pillar, quarter pillar, seat bellows, seat side arm: Gray Broadcloth.

Headlining: Gray Napped Cotton.

Visor: Gray Napped Cotton with Russet Brown Artificial Leather Binding changed to 1937 design in May 1938.

Windlace: Gray Worsted Cloth.

Package tray: Gray Mohair

Two-tone Tan Antique Finish Leather

Seat, door arm rest (l.h.), door panel, quarter, door pillar, quarter pillar, seat bellows, seat side arm, package tray, headlining, windlace: Two-tone Tan Antique Finish Leather.

Visor: Brown Fine Colonial Grain Embossed Kraft Paper, changed to Tan Fine Colonial Grain in December 1937.

Items which were identical on each trim scheme

Floor: Benton Gray Rubber.

Cowl panel: Gray Brown Fine Colonial Grain Cardboard.

Luggage compartment: Black Morocco Grain Cardboard.

Escutcheons (inside door handle and window regulator handle), window regulator knob, ash tray knob, window finish strip insert: Oyster Gray Plastic.

Window regulator handle and inside door handle: Cellulose Ester Coated Rich Low Brass.

Windshield frame, glove compartment door knob, windshield regulator handle: Bright Chrome Plate.

Windshield regulator handle gromet: Chrome Plated, changed to Bright Nickel Plate in June 1938.

Seat adjuster handle: Black Paint.

Instrument panel, finish strips, etc.: Straight Walnut Grain.

Commercial Vehicles

Ford's 1937-38 commercial vehicles encompassed the Station Wagon, Sedan Delivery, Panel Delivery, and the Pickup truck — all on the passenger car chassis. Of these, the Station Wagon and Sedan Delivery were produced with the passenger car front end sheet metal, while the Panel Delivery and the Pickup had the commercial front end. In appearance these vehicles looked new, but basicaliy they were constructed from modified carry over 1935-36 components. The most notable changes were in the areas of the all steel top, the V-style windshield, new cowl and revised hood and ornamentation. Other features included spare wheel carriers with lock, front and rear bumpers, and ash tray.

Even though the 1937 commercial vehicles were a "facelift" of the previous year, customer acceptance was very high and Ford's commercial vehicles and trucks experienced the best year since 1930. In 1938, however, sales dropped in the same proportion as the rest of the industry.

For 1938, the Sedan Delivery and Station Wagon were restyled to conform with the lines of the passenger cars; but the Closed Cab and the Panel Delivery were all new, with new bodies, grille, hood and fenders.

1937-38 COMMERCIAL AND TRUCK EXTERIOR COLORS

Body Color	Stripe (1937 only)	Wheels (Deluxe)*
Vermilion Red	Black	Tacoma Cream
Black	Tacoma Cream	Tacoma Cream
Gull Gray	Bright Vermilion	Vermilion
Coach Maroon Bright	Gold	Vermilion
Washington Blue	Tacoma Cream	Tacoma Cream
Autumn Brown (1)	Tacoma Cream	None
Desert Sand	Bright Vermilion	Vermilion
Bright Vineyard Green (2)	Silver	Tacoma Cream
Dartmouth Green (2)	None	Tacoma Cream
Wren Building Tan Dark (3)	None	Tacoma Cream

*Regular production wheels were painted black, but color wheels were available as special equipment.

(1) Discontinued at end of 1937 production.

(2) Bright Vineyard Green was replaced with Dartmouth Green in March 1938.

(3) New color with beginning of 1938 production.

Other color combinations were available on special order or fleet sales.

A 1937 Standard Sedan Delivery. The deluxe model had chrome plated grille and windshield frame and dual wipers.

Sedan Delivery (74-780, 78-780, 81A-780, 82A-780)
Standard and Deluxe

The 1937-38 Sedan Delivery was produced in both the standard and deluxe versions. Similar to the passenger cars, the standard style consisted of painted grille and windshield frame, single windshield wiper and a single taillight. In contrast, the deluxe style had a chrome plated grille and windshield frame, two wipers with a bright finish, and dual horns.

In 1938, the Deluxe Sedan Delivery was not equipped with the deluxe passenger car grille and hood, but instead was produced with the standard passenger car grille hood and fenders. Its deluxe features consisted of colored wheels,

The 1937 Standard Sedan Delivery with special paint and lettering, available from the factory as special equipment or on fleet orders.

Rear view of the 1938 Sedan Delivery showing the rear door details.

deluxe style hub caps, chrome plated windshield frame and wiper, and a chrome plated side view mirror.

Interior components were an adjustable driver's seat, glove box, driver's visor, dome lights and artificial leather trim scheme. In addition, a passenger's seat and an adjustable rear window were available as special equipment.

A single stripe was applied just below the belt line similar to the Tudor Sedan. In 1938, the stripe and the rustless steel molding were available at customer option at extra cost.

Rear compartment of the 1937 Sedan Delivery.

1937 AND 1938 STANDARD AND DELUXE SEDAN DELIVERY INTERIOR TRIM SCHEMES

1937 Brown Imitation Leather

Seats, windlace, headlining binding: Brown Fine Colonial Grain Artificial Leather.

Cowl panels, door panels, rear door panel, headlining, glove compartment: Brown Fine Colonial Grain Cardboard.

Quarter lining: Masonite.

Visor: Brown Fine Colonial Grain Cardboard with Brown Fine Colonial Grain Artificial Leather Binding.

Floor (front compartment): Benton Gray Rubber.

Escutcheons (inside door handle and window regulator handle): Brass, Bright Chrome Plate.

Window regulator handle and knob, inside door handle, glove compartment door handle, windshield regulator handle, windshield regulator handle gromet: Bright Chrome Plate.

Instrument panel, finish strips, glove compartment door, etc.: Mahogany Grain.

Windshield frame: Standard - Body Color; Deluxe - Chrome Plated.

Ash tray knob: Dark Taupe Plastic.

1938 Same As 1937 Except

Finish strips: Burl Mahogany Grain.

No glove compartment door trim.

Windshield regulator handle gromet changed to Bright Nickel Plate in June 1938.

Windshield frame standard model changed to Bright Chrome Plate in December 1937.

Ash tray knob: Oyster Gray Plastic.

Visor: Brown Fine Colonial Grain Embossed Kraft Paper.

Interior view of a 1938 Sedan Delivery. The sheet metal panel on the right is for the spare tire.

The 1937 Station Wagon with the deluxe style passenger car front end.

Interior view of the 1937 Station Wagon. The sliding window glass in the rear doors and quarter openings were customer option at extra cost.

Station Wagon (78-790, 81A-790)

Unlike the Sedan Delivery, the Station Wagon was produced only with the deluxe style front end in both 1937 and 1938. Other features included a front, center, and rear seat; glove box with a lock and clock; ash tray; cigar lighter; sun visors; deluxe steering wheel; and an imitation leather trim scheme. The front floor mat was unique to the Station

The 1938 Station Wagon with the regular production deluxe style passenger car front end.

Rear section of a 1938 Station Wagon. Detail of the rear lamp mounting bracket is evident in this view.

Wagon, but had the same border as the other mats. The center and rear mats were made of Benton Gray rubber with an overall pyramid design, but lacked the jute underpad.

The front end sheet metal assembly, cowl, fenders, and wheels were painted in either Autumn Brown or Desert Sand. However, unlike previous years, additional commercial colors were available on special order. All exposed wood parts were finished with clear spar varnish.

Station Wagon spare tire stowage. The cover was a regular production item.

1937 AND 1938 STATION WAGON INTERIOR TRIM SCHEMES

1937 Brown Imitation Leather

Seats, windlace: Brown Fine Colonial Grain Artificial Leather.
Cowl panels, glove compartment: Brown Fine Colonial Grain Cardboard.
Visor: Brown Fine Colonial Grain Cardboard with Brown Artificial Leather Binding.
Front and rear floor: Benton Gray Rubber.
Window regulator handle and knob, inside door handle, glove compartment door handle, windshield frame: Bright Chrome Plate.
Door locks, window regulator covers: Brown Pyroxylin.
Instrument panel, glove compartment door, windshield opening finish: American Walnut Grain.
Ash tray knob: Dark Taupe Plastic.
Curtains (rear door, quarter, back) (Optional): Tan Fabric.
Frame glass (rear door, quarter, back) (Optional): Bright Chrome Plate.
Rear, door, quarter glass handle: Black Rubber changed to Steel Painted in February 1937.

1938 Same As 1937 Except

Instrument panel, glove compartment door, windshield opening finish: Straight Walnut Grain.
No glove compartment trim.
Ash tray knob: Oyster Gray Plastic.
Visor: Brown Fine Colonial Grain Embossed Kraft Paper.
Front door pull to handle: Bright Chrome Plate.
Curtains: Special Equipment.

The 1937 Closed Cab Pickup Truck.

Closed Cab (75-810, 77-810, 81C-810, 22C-810) and Pickup Box (77-830, 81C-830)

In addition to the reworked body features and carry over fenders, headlights and running boards, the 1937 Closed Cab had a longer hood and a new full length grille and shell which gave the new vehicle a massive looking front end. As in 1936, two versions of the Closed Cab were offered — the standard and deluxe. The standard had painted grille and windshield frame, one wiper and one horn, whereas the deluxe had a chrome grille and windshield frame, dual horns, two chrome wipers and chrome strips at the louvers.

Instead of another face lift, the 1938 Closed Cab had many different features, such as a new body, cowl, hood, grille, fenders, running boards and lights. For the first time in the commercial line, styling eliminated the radiator shell and designed the full length hood around the oval shaped grille. The fenders were full skirted, resembling the 1937 passenger car style. The headlights, however, were still mounted separately, but were made longer, resembling the 1936 passenger car lights. Only the standard model was produced.

A 1937 Pickup Truck with the spare tire relocated to provide curb side access for unloading.

The 1938 commercial chassis.

On the 1937 model, a single stripe was applied on the belt molding, while three stripes were applied to the 1938 models, one stripe on each of the three belt moldings.

The 1937 pickup box was a further improvement of the 1935-36 design, with a cargo space four inches longer. A new full length rod style tail gate hinge was the most significant improvement. Released for 1938 was a completely new and larger pickup box 77.75 by 46 inches, and featuring a new all steel floor.

The pickup box was painted the same color as the cab and had no striping.

A 1938 Pickup Truck with the conventional spare tire mounting.

Rear quarter view showing the box and tail gate detail of the 1938 Pickup Truck.

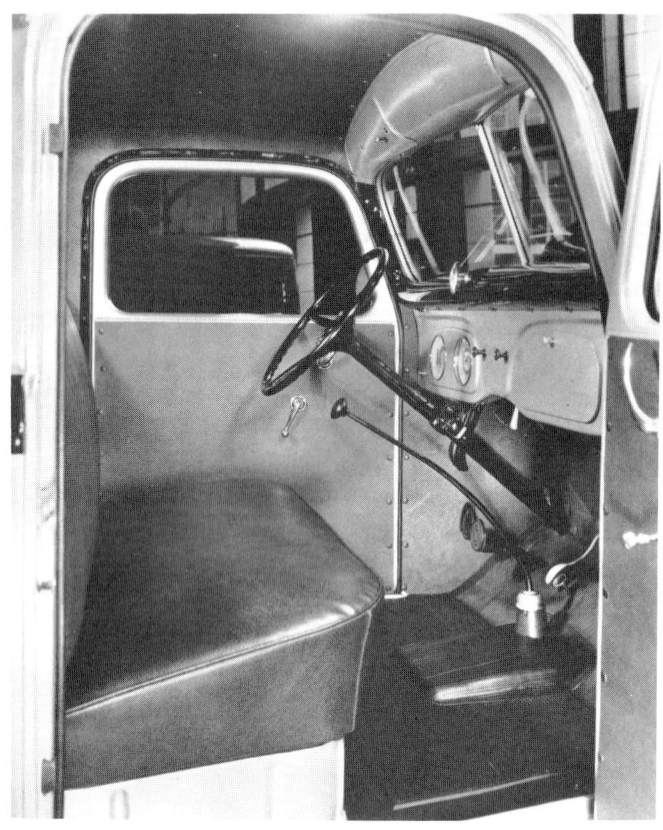

Driver's compartment of a 1938 Closed Cab. Note the change on the door panel and instrument panel compared to 1937.

Interior compartment of the 1937 Closed Cab. The door handles were a carry over from the 1933 passenger car.

1937 STANDARD AND DELUXE CLOSED CAB INTERIOR TRIM SCHEME

Black Imitation Leather

Seats, windlace: Black Seal Grain Artificial Leather.

Door panels, cowl panels, quarter, back, headlining: Black Seal Grain Cardboard.

Finish moldings: Black Enamel.

Visor: Black Seal Grain Cardboard with Colonial Grain Artificial Leather Binding.

Floor (front compartment): Black Rubber.

Inside door handles, window regulator handle and knob, escutcheons: Nickel Plate Butler Finish.

Windshield regulator handle: Bright Chrome Plate.

Windshield regulator handle gromet: Chrome Plated, changed to match instrument panel January 1937.

Windshield frame: Deluxe - Bright Chrome Plate; Standard - Painted Body Color.

1938 CLOSED CAB INTERIOR TRIM SCHEME

Green Imitation Leather

Seats, windlace: Two-tone Green Bedouin Grain Artificial Leather.

Door panel, cowl panel, quarter, back, headlining: Two-tone Green Bedouin Grain Cardboard.

Finish moldings: Black Enamel.

Visor: Green Embossed Kraft Paper.

Floor (front compartment): Black Rubber.

Inside door handle window regulator handle and knob, escutcheons, windshield regulator handle: Bright Chrome Plate.

Windshield frame: Deluxe - Bright Chrome Plate; Standard - Painted Body Color, changed to Chrome Plate in December 1937.

A 1937 Panel Delivery in typical commercial application.

The 1937 Panel Delivery painted in the Ford commercial demonstrator paint scheme for dealers.

Panel Delivery (75-820, 77-820, 81C-820, 82A-820)

The 1937 Panel Delivery was essentially a carry over of the 1936 body, but reworked to include the all steel top, new windshield and cowl, and a new grille and hood similar to the Closed Cab. It was available in standard and deluxe versions. The standard model had a painted grille and windshield frame, one wiper, one horn, and one sun visor. In contrast,

The 1938 Panel Delivery.

The 1938 Panel Delivery with the conventional production color scheme.

the deluxe had a chrome plated grille and windshield frame, chrome plated side view mirror, twin horns, chrome plated dual wipers, two sun visors, and the addition of a passenger's seat. The interior trim scheme was Black Seal Grain artificial leather with a black rubber floor mat.

In 1938, the commercial Panel Delivery was an all new de-

Driver's compartment of the 1937 Panel Delivery. A passenger seat was available as special equipment.

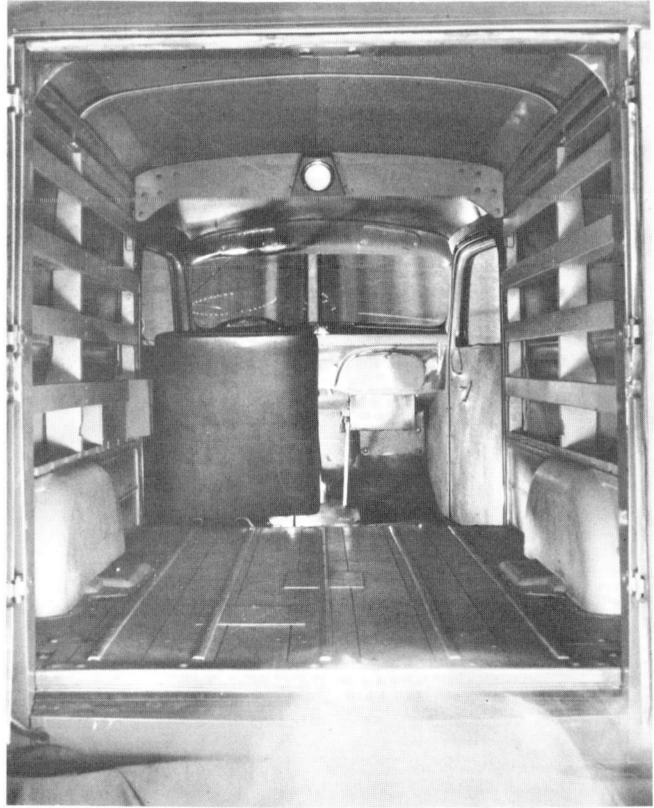

The 1937 Panel Delivery rear compartment. Note the sound deadening material cemented to the inside of the top.

sign with a larger cargo space. Like the Closed Cab, it too had a new grille, hood, cowl, fenders, and lights. This model was available only in the standard version, although deluxe items could be added as special equipment. The interior trim scheme was a two-tone Green Bedouin artificial leather.

A single stripe was on the belt molding of the 1937 model, and three stripes, one on each of the three molding belts, decorated the 1938.

The 1938 Panel Delivery rear compartment with the 1938 style floor and lower side panels.

1937 STANDARD AND DELUXE PANEL DELIVERY INTERIOR TRIM SCHEME

Black Imitation Leather

Seat, windlace: Black Seal Grain Artificial Leather.
Cowl panels, lock pillar, headlining, seat back, door panel: Black Seal Grain Cardboard.
Finish moldings: Black Enamel.
Visor: Black Seal Grain Cardboard with Black Fine Colonial Grain Artificial Leather Binding.
Sidelining: Masonite (Wood Slats Optional).
Floor (front compartment): Black Rubber.
Inside door handles, window regulator handle and knob, escutcheons: Nickel Plate Butler Finish.
Windshield frame: Deluxe - Bright Chrome Plate; Standard - Painted to match body.
Windshield regulator handle: Bright Chrome Plate.
Windshield regulator handle gromet: Chrome Plated, changed to match instrument panel in January 1937.

1938 PANEL DELIVERY INTERIOR TRIM SCHEME

Green Imitation Leather

Seat, windlace: Two-tone Green Bedouin Grain Artificial Leather.
Cowl panels, lock pillar, headlining, seat back, door panel: Two-tone Green Bedouin Grain Cardboard.
Finish moldings: Black Enamel.
Visor: Green Embossed Kraft Paper.
Sidelining: Masonite (Wood Slats Optional).
Floor (front compartment): Black Rubber.
Inside door handles, window regulator handle and knob, escutcheon, windshield regulator handle: Bright Chrome Plate.
Windshield frame: Deluxe - Bright Chrome Plate; Standard - Painted to match body, changed to Chrome Plating in December 1937.

1937 WINDSHIELD WIPER DATA

B = Black Paint C = Chrome Plated R = Rustless Steel

Body Style	Number	Mounting Method*	Wiper Arm Length	Wiper Arm Finish	Blade Finish (1)
Standard Tudor	78-17508-A	Threaded shaft sleeve	8¾	B	B
Deluxe Tudor	78-17508-A	Threaded shaft sleeve	8¾	C or R	C or R
Roadster, Phaeton	78-17508-B	Two screws	7	C or R	C or R
Standard Coupe	78-17508-A	Threaded shaft sleeve	8¾	B	B
Deluxe Coupe, Club Coupe	78-17508-A	Threaded shaft sleeve	8¾	C or R	C or R
Standard Fordor	78-17508-A	Threaded shaft sleeve	8¾	B	B
Deluxe Fordor	78-17508-A	Threaded shaft sleeve	8¾	C or R	C or R
Convertible Sedan, Cabriolet	78-17508-B	Two screws	7	C or R	C or R
Standard Sedan Delivery	78-17508-A	Threaded shaft sleeve	8¾	B	B
Deluxe Sedan Delivery	78-17508-A	Threaded shaft sleeve	8¾	C or R	C or R
Station Wagon	78-17508-B	Two screws	7	C or R	C or R
Standard Closed Cab	77-17508	Threaded shaft sleeve	8¾	B	B
Deluxe Closed Cab	77-17508	Threaded shaft sleeve	8¾	C or R	C or R
Standard Panel Delivery	77-17508	Threaded shaft sleeve	8¾	B	B
Deluxe Panel Delivery	77-17508	Threaded shaft sleeve	8¾	C or R	C or R

*Controls were Cadmium Plated.

(1) Blade length was 8¼ inches.

1938 WINDSHIELD WIPER DATA

B = Black Paint C = Chrome Plated R = Rustless Steel

Body Style	Number	Mounting Method*	Wiper Arm Length	Wiper Arm Finish	Blade Finish (1)
Tudor, Club Coupe (5W) Coupe, Fordor	81A-17508	Threaded shaft sleeve	8¾	C or R	C or R
Convertible Sedan, Phaeton Convertible Coupe	78-17508-B	Two screws	7	C or R	C or R
Sedan Delivery	81A-17508	Threaded shaft sleeve	8¾	C or R	C or R
Station Wagon	78-17508-B	Two screws	7	C or R	C or R
Standard Closed Cab, Standard Panel Delivery	81C-17508	Threaded shaft sleeve	8¾	B	B
Deluxe Closed Cab, Deluxe Panel Delivery	81C-17508	Threaded shaft sleeve	8¾	C or R	C or R

*Controls were Cadmium Plated.

(1) Blade length was 8¼ inches.

Note: The arm and blade on standard cars were painted black until December 1937.

DOMESTIC PRODUCTION OF 1937 CARS

Body Style	85 HP	60 HP	Total
Tudor Sedan, Standard (78-700-A))	147,794	148,467	296,261
Deluxe (78-700-B)	32,651	24	32,675
Tudor Touring Sedan, Standard (78-700-C)	78,895	51,332	130,227
Deluxe (78-700-D)	69,840	62	69,902
Roadster (78-710)	1,032	35	1,067
Club Coupe (78-720)	15,359	70	15,429
Fordor Sedan, Standard (78-730)	20,804	18,541	39,345
Deluxe (78-730)	20,273	148	20,421
Fordor Touring Sedan, Standard (78-730)	19,666	13,976	33,642
Deluxe (78-730)	74,554	809	75,363
Convertible Sedan (78-740)	3,818	42	3,860
Phaeton Touring (78-750)	2,370	175	2,545
Cabriolet (78-760-A)	9,300	41	9,341
Club Cabriolet (78-760-B)	6,169	66	6,235
Coupe (5W), Standard (78-770-A)	45,523	43,866	89,389
Deluxe (78-770-B)	25,486	33	25,519
Sedan Delivery, Standard (78-780)	4,141	3,238	7,379
Deluxe (78-780)	561	103	664
Station Wagon (78-790)	7,555	193	7,748
Panel Delivery, Standard (77-820)	7,144	6,041	13,185
Deluxe (77-820)	903	253	1,156

DOMESTIC PRODUCTION OF 1938 CARS

Body Style	85 HP	60 HP	Total
Deluxe Tudor Sedan (700-B)	82,295	119	82,414
Standard Tudor Sedan (700-C)	58,255	30,850	89,105
Deluxe Club Coupe (720)	5,336	57	5,393
Deluxe Fordor Sedan (730-B)	60,389	674	61,063
Standard Fordor Sedan (730-C)	11,288	5,878	17,166
Deluxe Convertible Sedan (740)	1,963	15	1,978
Deluxe Phaeton (750)	668	67	735
Deluxe Convertible Coupe (760-A)	3,047	22	3,069
Deluxe Convertible Club Coupe (760-B)	3,973	38	4,011
Standard Coupe (5W) (770-A)	17,844	13,712	31,556
Deluxe Coupe (5W) (770-B)	16,773	4	16,777
Standard Coupe (5W) Pickup (770-C)	382	64	446
Standard Sedan Delivery (780-A)	2,407	1,120	3,527
Deluxe Sedan Delivery (780-B)	22	6	28
Station Wagon (790)	6,681	4	6,685
Panel Delivery (81C-820)	6,032	–	6,032

The brake adjustment station at the end of the production line. The belt stripe and body color windshield frame identifies this car as an early 1938 model.

XI — Accessories

In general, "accessories" refers to those items installed on a vehicle which were not part of regular production and were usually at an added cost to the customer. At Ford, however, accessories referred only to those items which were installed by the dealer at extra cost. Items which were installed at the factory were referred to as "special equipment." In a few cases the same item could have been installed at the factory, which made it special equipment, or installed by the dealer as an accessory. In addition, accessories were further divided into two categories — Ford authorized accessories and dealer stock accessories. In the following we will list only those items which were listed as special equipment and/or Ford authorized accessories. In both these categories, the item could have been designed and produced by Ford or by an outside manufacturer but tooled to fit Ford products.

Some items may have started as regular production items and then changed to special equipment, or started as special equipment and later made a regular production item. Also, some items were installed as regular production on some body styles, but were special equipment on other body styles. Many items were both special equipment and dealer accessories, depending on when the buyer decided to have it installed.

ACCESSORY AND SPECIAL EQUIPMENT ITEMS FOR 1932

Name of Item	Usage	Availability
Cowl Lamps	Standard Models	Accessory or Special Equip.
Dust Hood	Std. Phaeton & Roadster	Special Equipment
Fabric Tire Cover	All	Accessory
Fender Well (RH & LH)	All	Accessory or Special Equip.
Governor	All	Accessory or Special Equip.
Luggage Rack	All Passenger	Accessory
Manifold Heater	All	Accessory
Metal Tire Cover	All	Accessory
Oil Bath Air Cleaner	All	Accessory or Special Equip.
Radio	All	Accessory
Rumble Seat	Standard Roadster	Accessory or Special Equip.
Rumble Seat	Standard Coupe (5W)	Accessory or Special Equip.
Rumble Seat	Deluxe Coupe (3W)	Accessory or Special Equip.
Seat Covers	All Cloth Trims	Accessory
Spare Tire	All	Accessory or Special Equip.
Spot Light	All	Accessory
Tail Lamp (Right Hand)	Standard Models	Accessory
Thermostat	All	Accessory
Tire Lock and Band	All	Accessory
Water Temperature Indicator	All	Accessory or Special Equip.
Wind Wings	Standard Phaeton	Accessory or Special Equip.
Wind Wings	Standard Roadster	Accessory or Special Equip.
Wind Wings	Closed Bodies	Accessory or Special Equip.
Winter Front	All	Accessory

ACCESSORY AND SPECIAL EQUIPMENT ITEMS FOR 1933

Name of Item	Usage	Availability
Ash Tray	Standard Models	Accessory
Cigar Lighter	Standard Models	Accessory
Cowl Lamps	Standard Models	Accessory or Special Equip.
Draft Deflectors*	Closed Bodies	Accessory or Special Equip.
Dust Hood	Std. Roadster & Phaeton	Accessory or Special Equip.
Dust Hood	Deluxe Roadster & Phaeton	Accessory or Special Equip.
Fabric Tire Cover	All	Accessory
Fender Well (RH & LH)	All	Accessory or Special Equip.
Governor	All	Accessory or Special Equip.
License Plate Frame	All	Accessory or Special Equip.
Luggage Rack	All Passenger	Accessory
Manifold Heater	All	Accessory
Metal Tire Cover	All	Accessory or Special Equip.
Oil Bath Air Cleaner	All	Accessory or Special Equip.
Radiator Ornament	All Passenger	Accessory
Radio	All	Accessory
Rumble Seat	Standard Roadster	Accessory or Special Equip.
Rumble Seat	Std. Coupe (3W) & (5W)	Accessory or Special Equip.
Rumble Seat	Deluxe Coupe (3W) & (5W)	Accessory or Special Equip.
Seat Covers	All Cloth Trims	Accessory
Spare Tire	All	Accessory or Special Equip.
Spot Light	All	Accessory
Tail Lamp (Right Hand)	Standard Models	Accessory
Tandem Windshield Wiper	All	Accessory
Thermostat	All	Accessory
Time Lock and Band	All	Accessory
Water Temp. & Fuel Gauge	All Passenger	Accessory or Special Equip.
Water Temp. Indicator	Commercial Units	Accessory or Special Equip.
Wind Wings	Standard Phaeton	Accessory or Special Equip.
Wind Wings	Standard Roadster	Accessory or Special Equip.
Winter Front	All	Accessory

*Adopted April 1933

ACCESSORY AND SPECIAL EQUIPMENT ITEMS FOR 1934

Name of Item	Usage	Availability
Ash Tray	Standard Models	Accessory
Bumper Bar Guards	All	Accessory
Clock, eight day	All	Accessory
Cowl Lamps	Standard Models	Accessory or Special Equip.
Draft Deflectors	Closed Bodies	Accessory or Special Equip.
Fender Well (RH & LH)	All	Accessory
Governor	All	Accessory or Special Equip.
Hot Air Heater	All	Special Equipment
License Plate Frame	All	Accessory or Special Equip.
Luggage Rack	All Passenger	Accessory or Special Equip.
Metal Tire Cover	All	Special Equipment
Oil Bath Air Cleaner	(Standard on Dual Carb.)	Special Equipment
Radiator Ornament	All Passenger	Accessory
Radio	All	Accessory or Special Equip.
Rumble Seat	Standard Coupe (5W)	Accessory or Special Equip.
Rumble Seat	Deluxe Coupe (3W) & (5W)	Accessory or Special Equip.
Seat Cover	All Cloth Trims	Accessory
Spot Light	All	Accessory or Special Equip.
Tail Lamp (Right Hand)	Standard Models	Accessory
Tandem Windshield Wiper	All	Accessory
Thermostat	All	Accessory
Trunk	All Passenger	Accessory or Special Equip.
Tire Lock and Band	All	Accessory or Special Equip.
Water Temp. and Fuel Gauge	All Passenger	Accessory or Special Equip.
Water Temp. Indicator	All Commercial Units	Accessory
Wheels, Chrome Plated	All	Accessory
Wind Wings	Standard Phaeton	Accessory or Special Equip.
Winter Front	All	Accessory

ACCESSORY AND SPECIAL EQUIPMENT ITEMS FOR 1935

Name of Item	Usage	Availability
Arm Rest (Right Hand Door)	All Passenger except Roadster & Phaeton	Special Equipment
Ash Tray	Standard Models	Accessory
Band Wheels	All	Accessory
Clock-Glove Compartment	All	Accessory or Special Equip.
Clock-Mirror	All	Accessory
Draft Deflectors	Closed Bodies	Accessory or Special Equip.
Fuel & Oil Pressure Gauge	Standard Models	Accessory or Special Equip.
Governor	All	Accessory or Special Equip.
Hot Air Heater	All	Special Equipment
License Plate Frame	All	Accessory or Special Equip.
Lock-Glove Compartment	All	Accessory or Special Equip.
Locking Gas Cap	All	Accessory
Luggage Rack	All Passenger	Accessory or Special Equip.
Metal Tire Cover	Commercial Units	Accessory or Special Equip.
Mirror-Visor	Bodies with Visor	Accessory
Oil Bath Air Cleaner	All	Accessory or Special Equip.
Outside Mirror	Closed Bodies	Accessory or Special Equip.

Radio	All	Accessory or Special Equip.
Rumble Seat (Deck Seat)	Coupe (3W) & (5W)	Accessory or Special Equip.
Seat Covers	All Cloth Trims	Accessory
Spot Light	All	Accessory or Special Equip.
Tail Lamp (Right Hand)	Standard Models	Accessory
Tandem Windshield Wiper	All	Accessory or Special Equip.
Thermostat	All	Accessory
Trunk	All Passenger	Accessory
Tire Lock and Band	All	Accessory or Special Equip.
Water Temp. & Ammeter	Standard Models	Accessory or Special Equip.
Visor (Right Hand)	Std. Tudor, Fordor, Coupe and Sedan Delivery	Special Equipment
Wheel Chrome Plated	All	Accessory
Winter Front	All	Accessory

ACCESSORY AND SPECIAL EQUIPMENT ITEMS FOR 1936

Name of Item	Usage	Availability
Arm Rest (Right Hand Door)	All Passenger except Roadster & Phaeton	Special Equipment
Ash Tray	Standard Models	Accessory or Special Equip.
Bands-Wheel	All	Accessory or Special Equip.
Clock-Glove Compartment	All	Accessory or Special Equip.
Clock-Mirror	All	Accessory or Special Equip.
Draft Deflectors	Closed Bodies	Accessory or Special Equip.
Electric Air Horn	All	Accessory
Fuel & Oil Pressure Gauge	Standard Models	Accessory or Special Equip.
Governor	All	Accessory or Special Equip.
Hot Air Heater	All	Accessory or Special Equip.
Hub Cap-Rustless Steel	All	Accessory or Special Equip.
Hub Cap-Spoke	All	Accessory or Special Equip.
License Plate Frame	All	Accessory or Special Equip.
Lock-Glove Compartment	All	Accessory or Special Equip.
Locking Gas Cap	All	Accessory or Special Equip.
Luggage Rack	All Passenger	Accessory or Special Equip.
Metal Tire Cover	All Commercial Units	Accessory or Special Equip.
Mirror-Visor	Bodies with Visor	Accessory or Special Equip.
Oil Bath Air Cleaner	All	Accessory or Special Equip.
Outside Mirror	Closed Bodies	Accessory or Special Equip.
Oil Filter	All	Accessory or Special Equip.
Radio	All	Accessory or Special Equip.
Rumble Seat (Deck Seat)	Coupe (3W) & (5W)	Accessory or Special Equip.
Seat Covers	All Cloth Trims	Accessory or Special Equip.
Spot Light	All	Accessory or Special Equip.
Steering Wheel Deluxe	Standard Models	Accessory or Special Equip.
Tail Lamp (Right Hand)	Standard Models	Accessory or Special Equip.
Tandem Windshield Wipers	All	Accessory or Special Equip.
Thermostat	All	Accessory or Special Equip.
Trunk	All Passenger	Accessory or Special Equip.
Tire Lock and Band	All	Accessory
Tires-White Sidewall	All	Accessory or Special Equip.
Visor (Right Hand)	Std. Tudor, Fordor, Coupe (5W), Sedan Deluxe	Special Equipment
Wheels 18"	All	Accessory or Special Equip.
Winter Front	All	Accessory or Special Equip.

ACCESSORY AND SPECIAL EQUIPMENT ITEMS FOR 1937

Name of Item	Usage	Availability
Ash Tray	Standard Models	Accessory
Bands-Wheel	Std. Models & Small Engine	Accessory or Special Equip.
Bumper Guard Center	All	Accessory
Clock-Glove Compartment	All	Accessory or Special Equip.
Clock-Mirror	All	Accessory
Directional Signals	All	Accessory or Special Equip.
Draft Deflectors	Closed Bodies	Accessory or Special Equip.
Fog Light (Road Lamp)	All	Accessory
Electric Air Horn	All	Accessory or Special Equip.
Governor	All	Accessory or Special Equip.
Hot Air Heater	All	Accessory or Special Equip.
Hub Cap Rustless Steel	All	Accessory or Special Equip.
License Plate Frame	All	Accessory
Lock-Glove Compartment	All	Accessory or Special Equip.
Locking Gas Cap	All	Accessory
Luggage Rack	All Passenger	Accessory
Metal Tire Cover	All Commercial Units	Accessory or Special Equip.
Mirror, Visor	Bodies with Visor	Accessory
Oil Bath Air Cleaner	All	Accessory or Special Equip.
Oil Filter	All	Accessory or Special Equip.
Outside Mirror	Closed Bodies	Accessory
Radiator Locking Ornament	All Passenger	Accessory
Radio	All	Accessory or Special Equip.

A 1937 accessory car with rear fender shields, rustless steel wheel covers, wheel bands, white sidewall tires, license plate frames and radio.

Rear Fender Shield	All Passenger	Accessory or Special Equip.
Rear Window Curtain	Std. Tudor, Fordor, Coupe (5W)	Special Equipment
Seat Covers	All Cloth Trims	Accessory
Spot Light	All	Accessory
Steering Wheel Deluxe	Standard Models	Accessory or Special Equip.
Tail Lamp (Right Hand)	All	Accessory or Special Equip.
Thermostat	All	Accessory or Special Equip.
Tires-White Sidewall	All	Accessory or Special Equip.
Trunk	All Passenger	Accessory
Winter Front	All	Accessory

ACCESSORY AND SPECIAL EQUIPMENT ITEMS FOR 1938

Name of Item	Usage	Availability
Arm Rest (Right Hand Door)	All Passenger except Phaeton	Special Equipment
Bands-Wheels	Std. Models & Small Engine	Accessory or Special Equip.
Bumper Guard Center	All	Accessory
Cigar Lighter Automatic	All	Accessory
Clock-Glove Compartment	All	Accessory or Special Equip.
Clock-Mirror	All	Accessory
Directional Signals	All	Accessory or Special Equip.
Draft Deflectors	Closed Bodies	Accessory or Special Equip.
Fog Light (Road Lamp)	All	Accessory
Electric Air Horn	All	Accessory or Special Equip.
Governor	All	Accessory or Special Equip.
Hot Air Heater	All	Accessory or Special Equip.
Hub Cap-Rustless Steel	All	Accessory or Special Equip.
Hub Cap-Spoke	All	Accessory or Special Equip.
License Plate Frame	All	Accessory
Lock-Glove Compartment	All	Accessory or Special Equip.
Locking Gas Cap	All	Accessory
Metal Tire Cover	All Commercial Units	Accessory or Special Equip.
Mirror, Visor	Bodies with Visor	Accessory
Oil Bath Air Cleaner	All	Accessory or Special Equip.
Oil Filter	All	Accessory or Special Equip.
Outside Mirror	Closed Bodies	Accessory
Radio	All	Accessory or Special Equip.
Rear Fender Shield	All Passenger	Accessory or Special Equip.
Seat Covers	All Cloth Trims	Accessory or Special Equip.
Spot Light	All	Accessory
Spring Covers	All	Accessory
Steering Wheel Deluxe	Standard Models	Accessory or Special Equip.
Thermostat	All	Accessory or Special Equip.
Thermostat-Manifold	All	Accessory or Special Equip.
Visor (Right Hand)	Std. Tudor, Fordor, Coupe (5W)	Special Equipment
Winter Front	All	Accessory
Wiper Right Hand	Standard Models	Accessory or Special Equip.

Wind Wings

All wind wings were produced by either Oaks Manufacturing Company or Dole Valve Company. In addition to those produced for open cars, wind wing sets were also available as special equipment on closed cars. However, three different sizes were required because of the window size differences between the various body styles. One size was common to the Fordor, Coupe (5W), Sport Coupe and Tudor, another to the Victoria and Convertible Sedan, and a third was for the Deluxe Coupe. The wind wing brackets were bright chrome plated.

Starting with 1933, the wind wings for closed cars were retitled "Draft Deflectors." Two sizes were produced for 1933 and 1934 — one for the Three Window Coupe and the other for all other closed cars. For 1935, and thereafter, only one size was released to fit the various closed body styles, but due to the styling changes of the body styles, a new draft deflector was released in 1936, 1937, and 1938.

Heaters

The first company special equipment heater was released in 1934. Produced by Sunday Products, it was a hot air type which utilized the engine fan as a blower and the exhaust manifold as a heat exchanger. A new Sunday design heater, mounted under the body and featuring a windshield defroster, was released for the 1935 models. This unit was rede-

A 1938 accessory car with rear fender shields, rustless steel wheel covers, wheel bands, white sidewall tires, draft deflectors, fog light, license plate frames, center bumper guard, spot light and radio.

signed for 1936 and included dash mounted controls which were painted to match the various dash colors.

An improved design was introduced with the 1937 cars, but this was in turn replaced in July 1937, with a new model containing an enclosed blower. These heaters were produced by both Novi Equipment and Sunday Products. Model number 1000-7F was used on vehicles with the 60 HP engine, number 3110 was used on cars with the 85 HP engine, and number 1000-8A on commercial vehicles.

In 1938, the heaters were available with or without the self contained blower. The Novi F-8-6000 and the Sunday 1000-20 were used with the 85 HP engine while Sunday 1000-21 was used with the 60 HP engine.

The hot water heater was available at dealers, but was not a Ford authorized heater until 1939.

Luggage Rack

Luggage racks were available as special equipment items 1932 through 1937. The 1932 rack was a carry over from Model A but with modified mounting brackets. These units were painted black with rustless steel slats. A unique mounting bracket was required on the Convertible Sedan while another design fitted all other body styles. The Model A style rack was also used on 1933 and 1934 cars, but with new mounting brackets to fit the new bodies.

Ford's 1934 hot air heater.

The 1936 luggage rack.

A new rack and mounting brackets were designed for 1935. Those installed at the factory were painted body color and those installed at the dealers were painted black. On both, the horizontal moldings were unpainted rustless steel. A V-8 emblem was mounted at the top center of the rack so it was in view with the rack in the up position. This rack was available for Tudor, Fordors, Convertible Fordor, and Phaeton, but could not be installed on Coupes or Touring Sedans because the rack interferred with the tire lock strap. The same rack was used on 1936 cars with the addition of a new mounting bracket to fit the Touring Sedan bodies.

For 1937, a new design with the rustless steel moldings running vertically was released. Similar to 1936, those installed at the factory were painted body color while those installed at the dealer were painted black. Two mounting supports were used, permitting installation on all body styles.

Outside Rear View Mirror

The outside door hinge mounted rear view mirror was introduced in June 1935. It was mounted with the center of the mirror 6½ inches out from the pillar and 7¾ inches above the top of the door hinge. Through 1935 the mounting arm was straight, but starting with the 1936 production it became the curved style.

Locking Gas Cap

A locking gas cap produced by Briggs-Stranton or Yale was introduced in April 1935. The Ford trademark appeared on its cover. In November 1936 the letters "U.S.A." were added under the Ford name.

The 1937 luggage rack.

Radiator Ornament

Only two radiator ornaments were released as special equipment by the company — the grayhound radiator cap for 1933 and 1934 production and a hood handle for 1937 which had three grooves instead of being smooth.

Spotlight

The Model A spotlight was a carry over item through the 1932 production. After that period three changes were made to the mounting handle. One style was used for 1933 and 1934, another for 1935 and the final for 1936, 1937, and 1938.

In April 1935 the lens diameter was changed from six inches to 5½ inches.

A 1937 fog light installation.

Index